Aho-Girl

\'ahô,gərl\ *Japanese, noun*.

A clueless girl.

8 | Hiroyuki

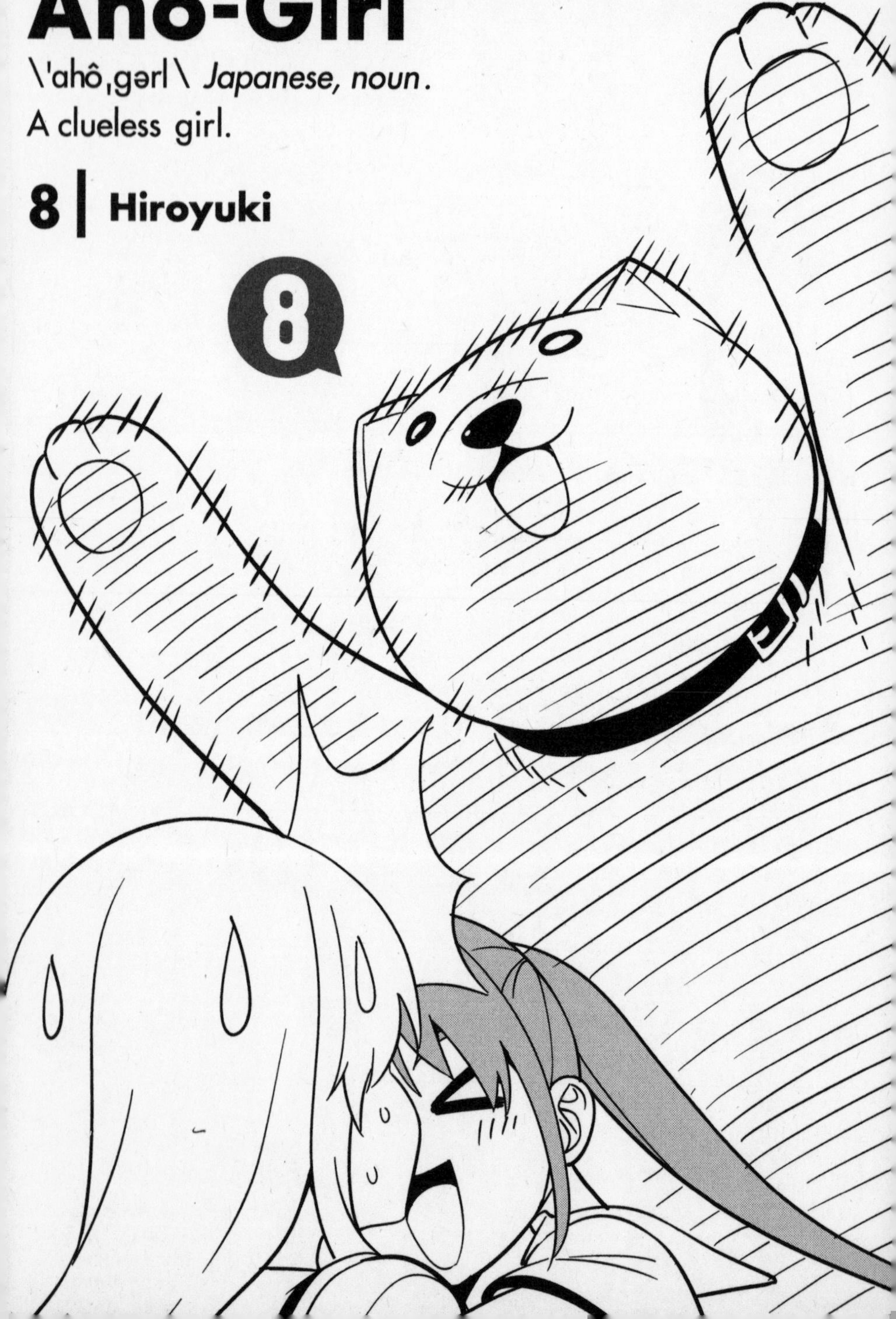

CHARACTER PROFILES

AHO-GIRL's Cast of Characters

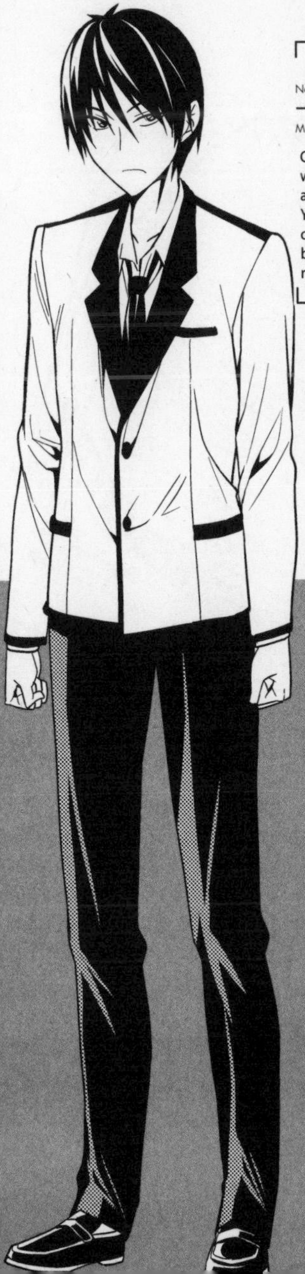

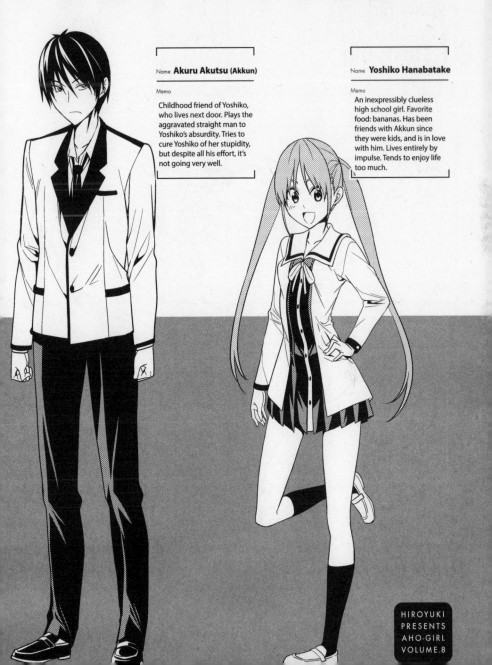

Name **Akuru Akutsu (Akkun)**

Memo

Childhood friend of Yoshiko, who lives next door. Plays the aggravated straight man to Yoshiko's absurdity. Tries to cure Yoshiko of her stupidity, but despite all his effort, it's not going very well.

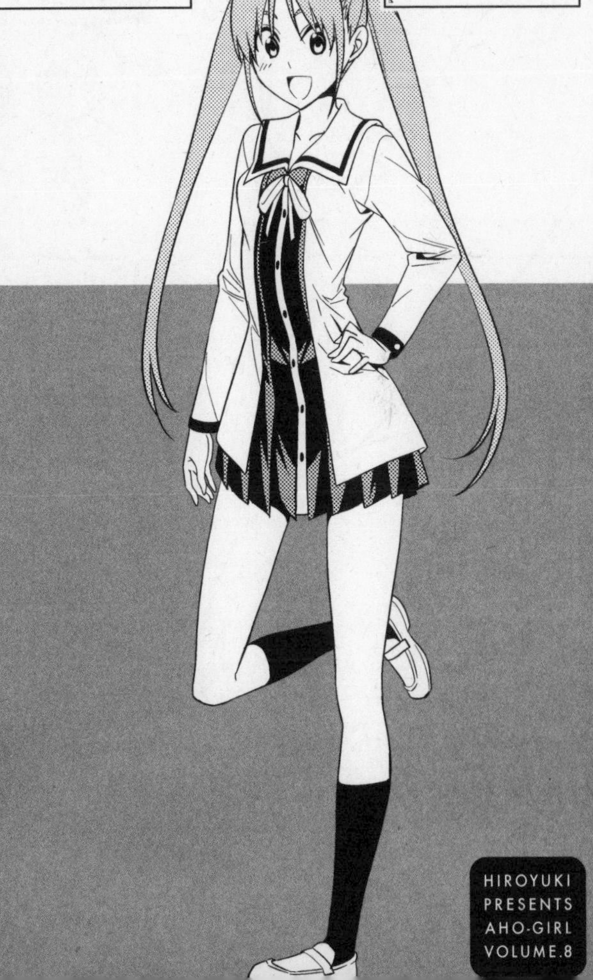

Name **Yoshiko Hanabatake**

Memo

An inexpressibly clueless high school girl. Favorite food: bananas. Has been friends with Akkun since they were kids, and is in love with him. Lives entirely by impulse. Tends to enjoy life too much.

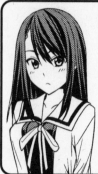

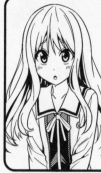

Name **Sayaka Sumino**

Memo

Yoshiko's friend. She's a very kind girl. She knows her kindness lands her in all sorts of trouble, yet she remains kind. Worries about being boring.

Name **Head Monitor**

Memo

An upperclassman at Yoshiko's school. Has fallen head over heels for Akkun and begun to stray from the moral path, but she doesn't realize it. G cup.

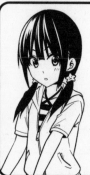

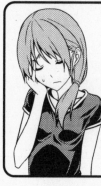

Name **Yoshie Hanabatake**

Memo

Yoshiko's mother. While she does worry about Yoshiko, she's far more worried about her own sunset years. Will use any means necessary to fix Yoshiko up with Akkun.

Name **Ruri Akutsu**

Memo

While her brother Akkun is an overachiever, Ruri's not quite so fortunate. She is constantly dismayed by her terrible grades. Perhaps the day will come when all her hard work pays off. Hates Yoshiko.

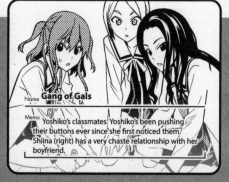

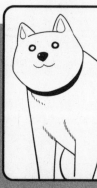

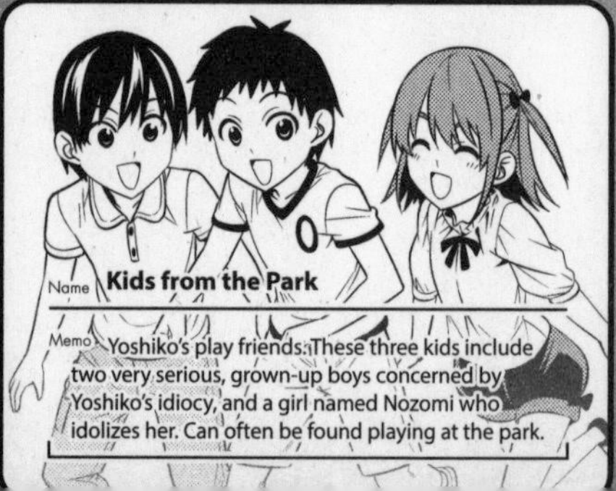

Name **Dog**

Memo

A ridiculously big dog Yoshiko found at the park. Started out vicious, but once vanquished by Yoshiko, has become docile. Is quite clever and tries to stop Yoshiko from her wilder impulses.

Name **Gang of Gals**

Memo Yoshiko's classmates. Yoshiko's been pushing their buttons ever since she first noticed them. Shiina (right) has a very chaste relationship with her boyfriend.

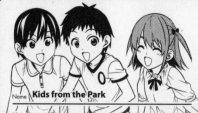

Name **Kids from the Park**

Memo Yoshiko's play friends. These three kids include two very serious, grown-up boys concerned by Yoshiko's idiocy, and a girl named Nozomi who idolizes her. Can often be found playing at the park.

AHO-GIRL

8

👤 + 🌻 + 🍌 = AHO-GIRL

CONTENTS

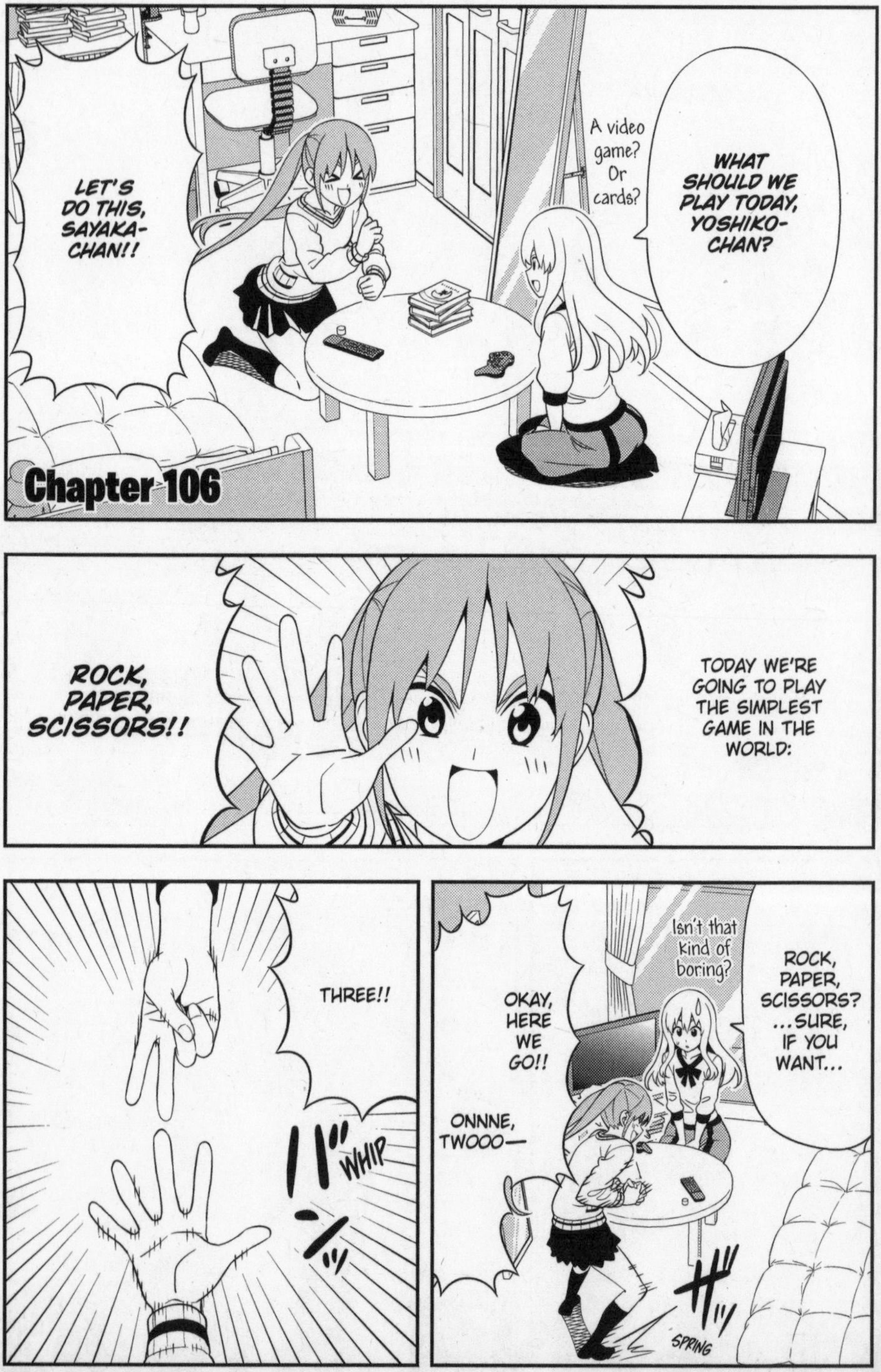
WHAT SHOULD WE PLAY TODAY, YOSHIKO-CHAN?
A video game? Or cards?
LET'S DO THIS, SAYAKA-CHAN!!
Chapter 106
TODAY WE'RE GOING TO PLAY THE SIMPLEST GAME IN THE WORLD:
ROCK, PAPER, SCISSORS!!
ROCK, PAPER, SCISSORS? ...SURE, IF YOU WANT...
Isn't that kind of boring?
OKAY, HERE WE GO!!
ONNNE, TWOOO—
SPRING
THREE!!
WHIP

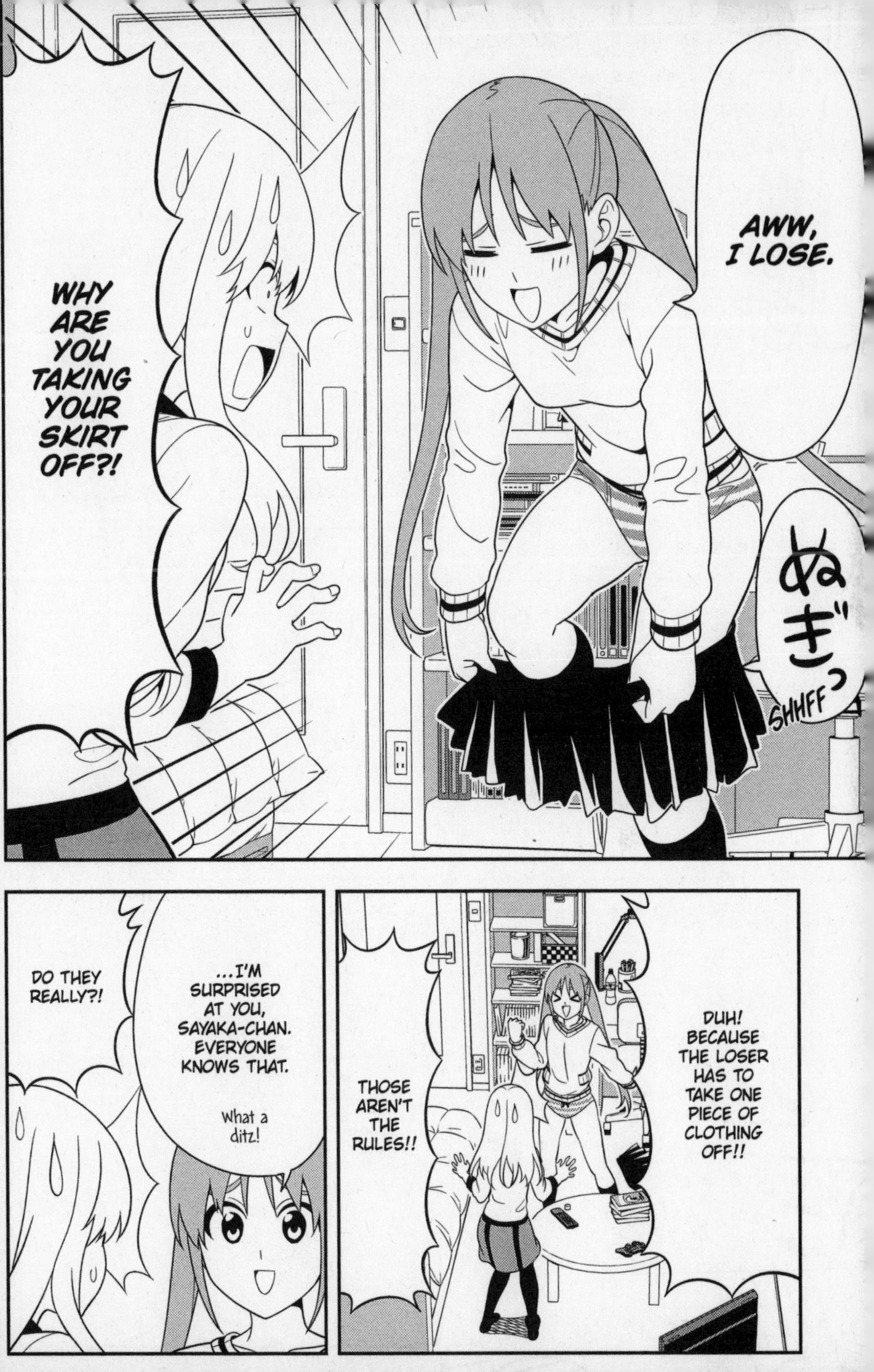
AWW, I LOSE.
ぬぎっ
SHHFF
WHY ARE YOU TAKING YOUR SKIRT OFF?!
DUH! BECAUSE THE LOSER HAS TO TAKE ONE PIECE OF CLOTHING OFF!!
THOSE AREN'T THE RULES!!
...I'M SURPRISED AT YOU, SAYAKA-CHAN. EVERYONE KNOWS THAT.
What a ditz!
DO THEY REALLY?!

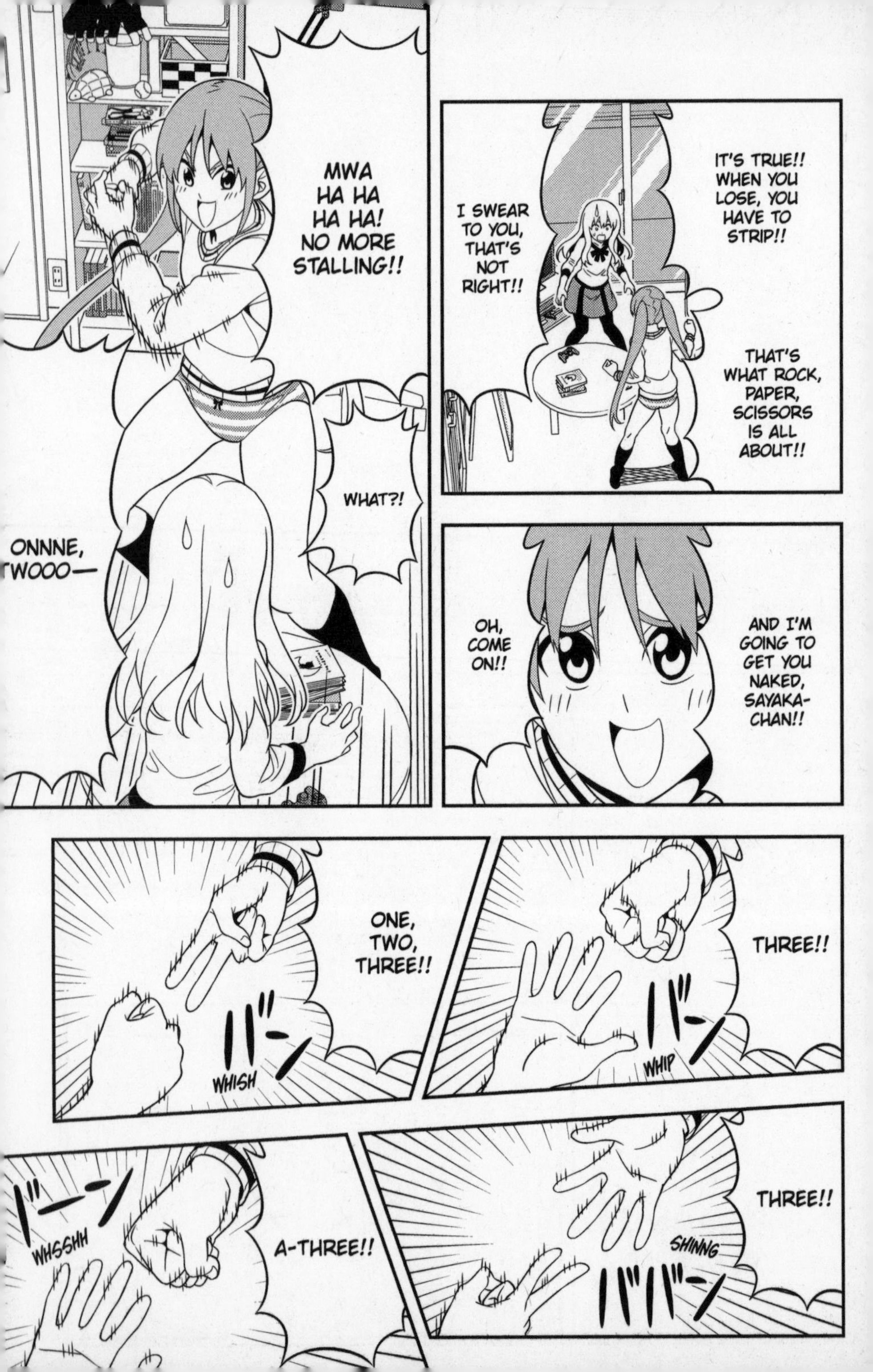
IT'S TRUE!! WHEN YOU LOSE, YOU HAVE TO STRIP!!
I SWEAR TO YOU, THAT'S NOT RIGHT!!
THAT'S WHAT ROCK, PAPER, SCISSORS IS ALL ABOUT!!
AND I'M GOING TO GET YOU NAKED, SAYAKA-CHAN!!
OH, COME ON!!
MWA HA HA HA HA! NO MORE STALLING!!
WHAT?!
ONNNE, TWOOO—
THREE!!
WHIP
ONE, TWO, THREE!!
WHISH
THREE!!
SHINNG
A-THREE!!
WHSSHH

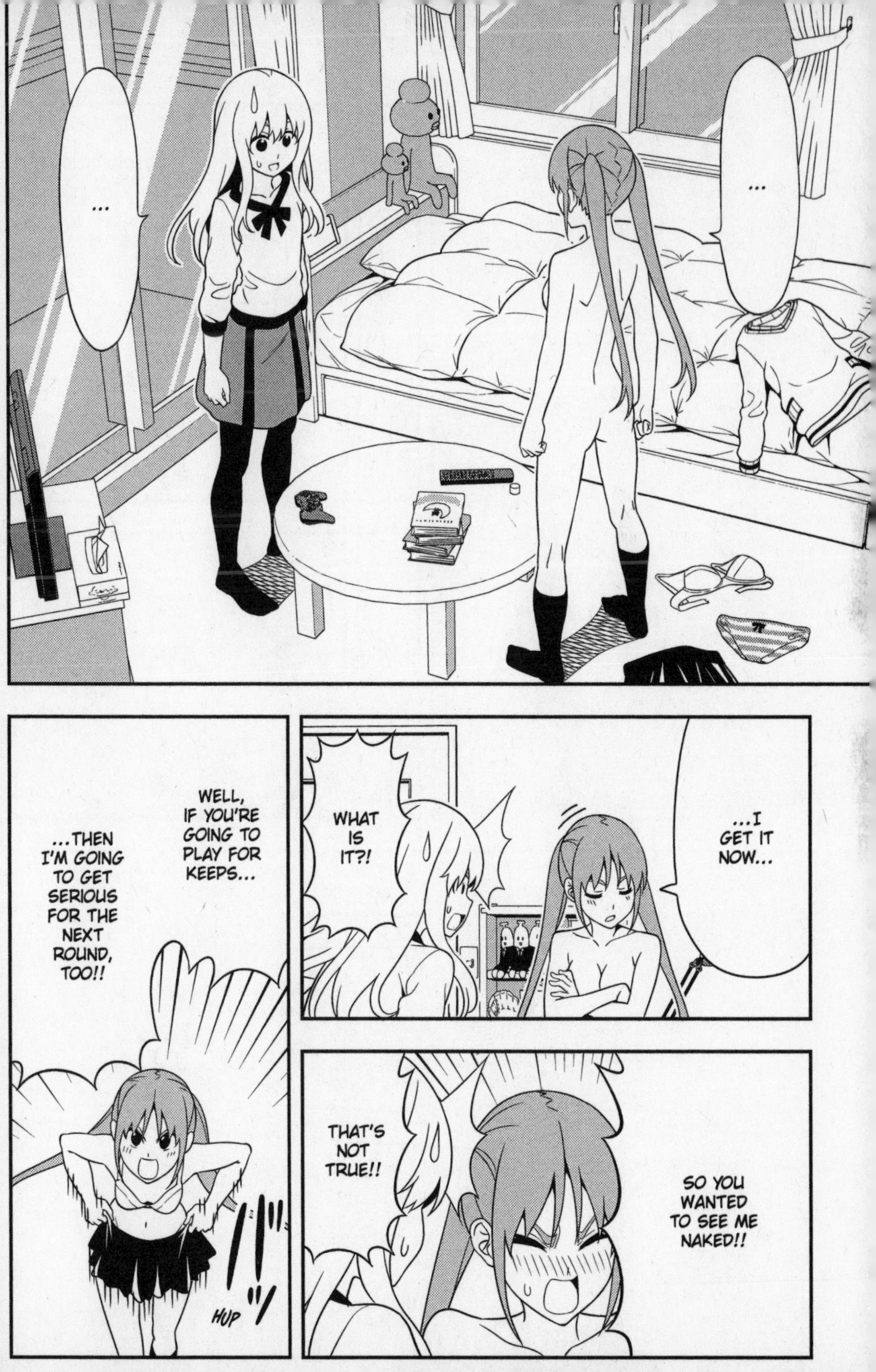
...
...
...I GET IT NOW...
WHAT IS IT?!
SO YOU WANTED TO SEE ME NAKED!!
THAT'S NOT TRUE!!
WELL, IF YOU'RE GOING TO PLAY FOR KEEPS...
...THEN I'M GOING TO GET SERIOUS FOR THE NEXT ROUND, TOO!!
HUP

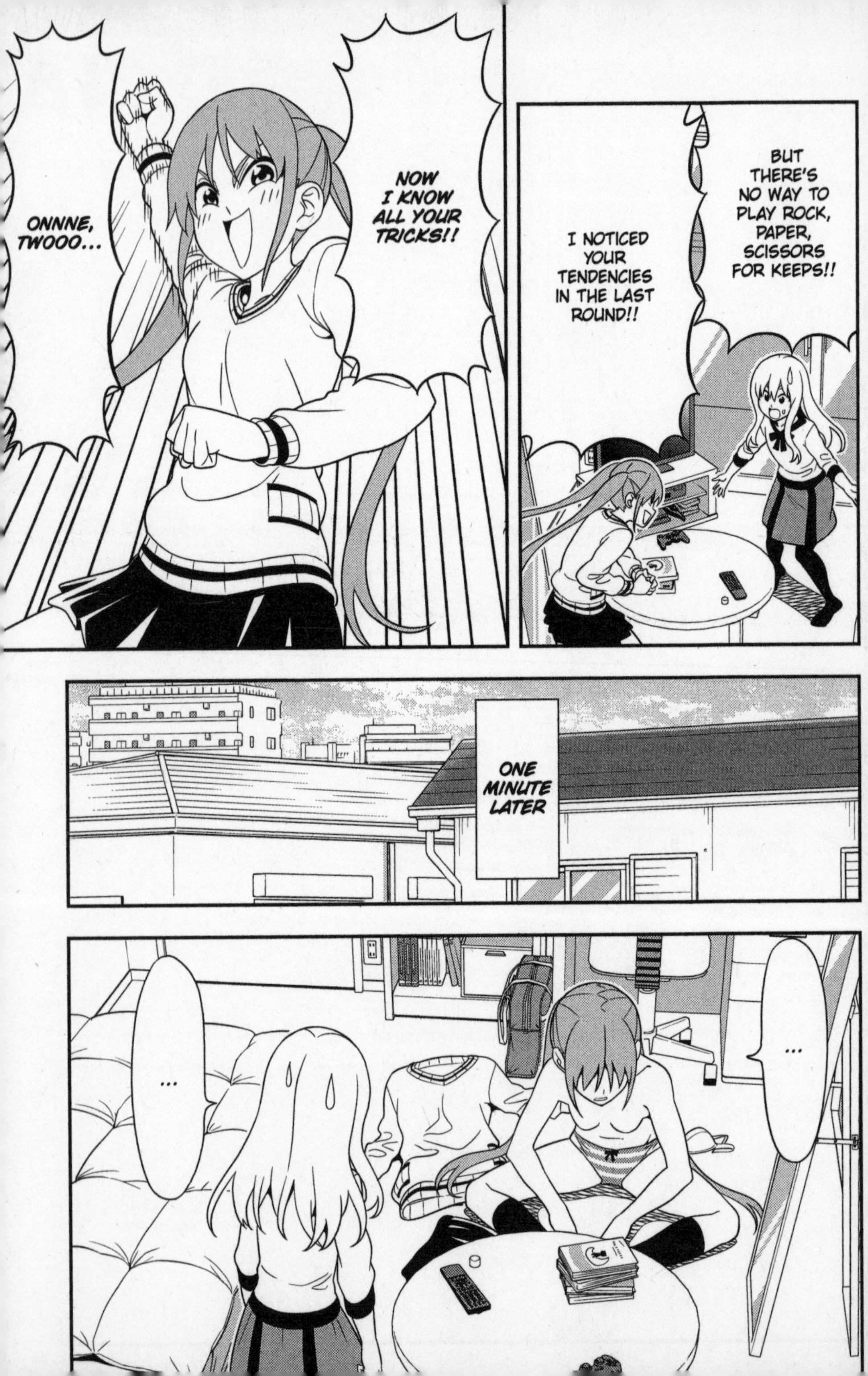
BUT THERE'S NO WAY TO PLAY ROCK, PAPER, SCISSORS FOR KEEPS!!
I NOTICED YOUR TENDENCIES IN THE LAST ROUND!!
NOW I KNOW ALL YOUR TRICKS!!
ONNNE, TWOOO...
ONE MINUTE LATER
...
...

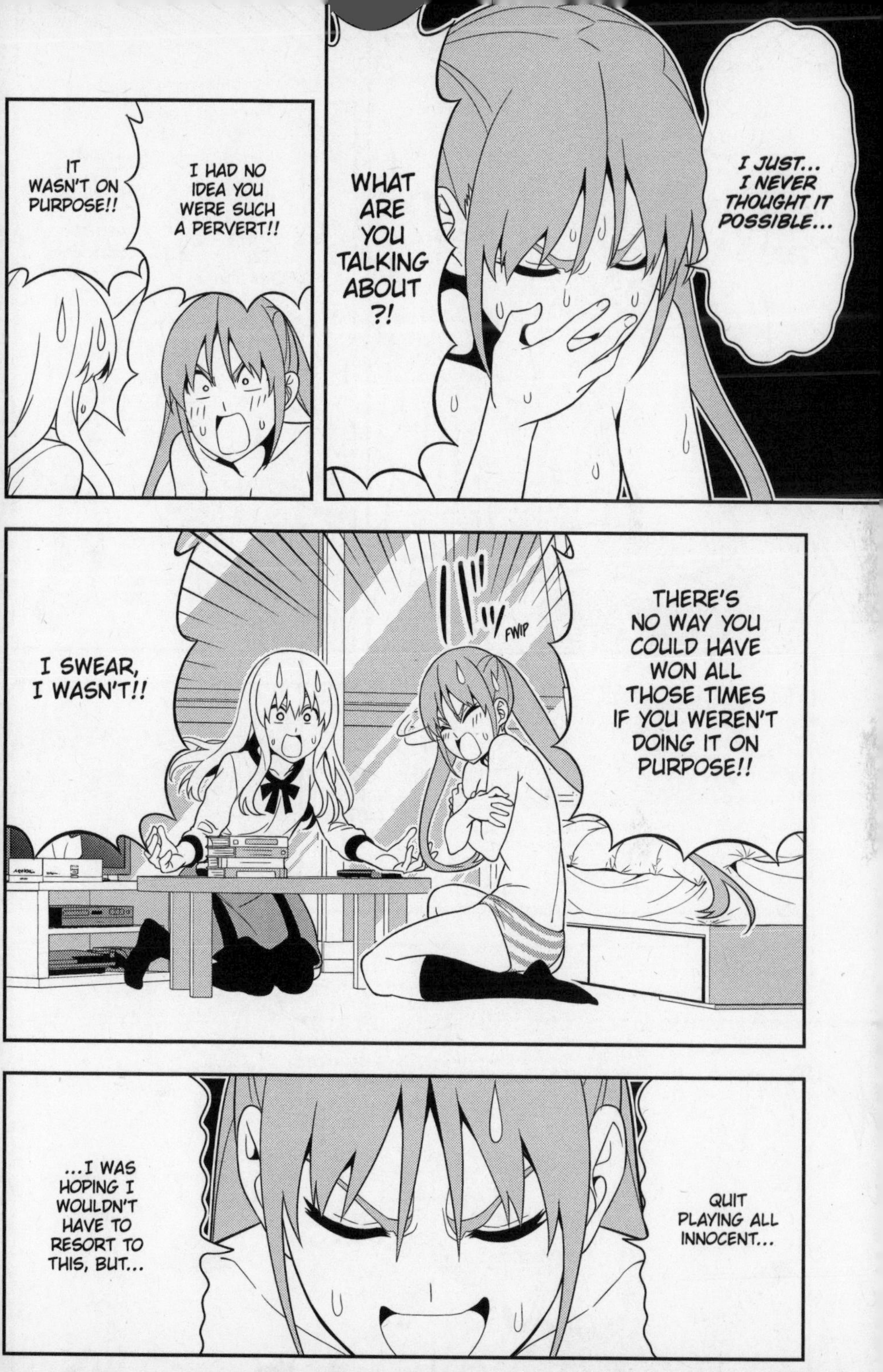
I JUST... I NEVER THOUGHT IT POSSIBLE...
WHAT ARE YOU TALKING ABOUT?!
I HAD NO IDEA YOU WERE SUCH A PERVERT!!
IT WASN'T ON PURPOSE!!
THERE'S NO WAY YOU COULD HAVE WON ALL THOSE TIMES IF YOU WEREN'T DOING IT ON PURPOSE!!
FWIP
I SWEAR, I WASN'T!!
QUIT PLAYING ALL INNOCENT...
...I WAS HOPING I WOULDN'T HAVE TO RESORT TO THIS, BUT...

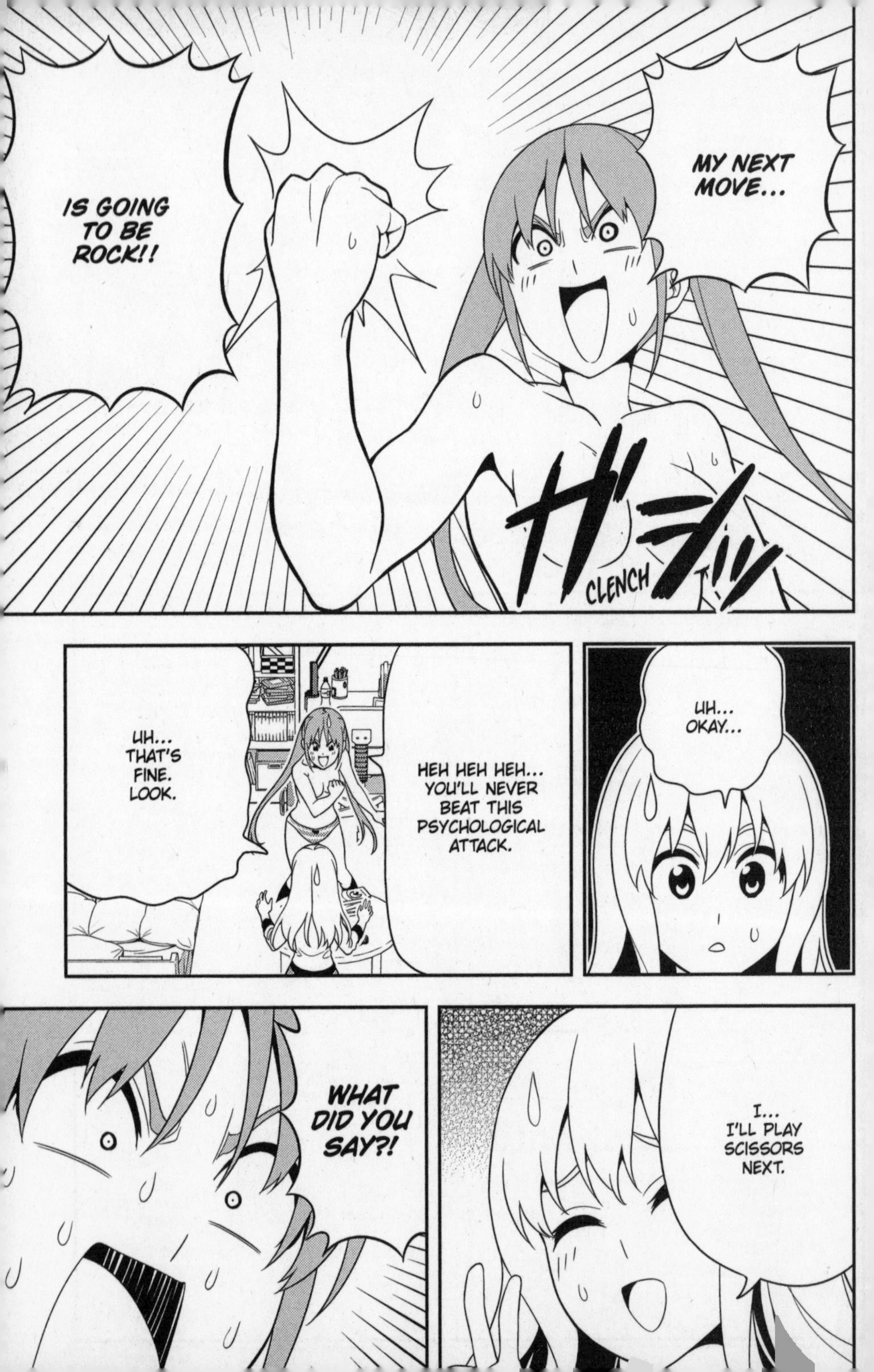
MY NEXT MOVE...
IS GOING TO BE ROCK!!
CLENCH
UH... OKAY...
HEH HEH HEH... YOU'LL NEVER BEAT THIS PSYCHOLOGICAL ATTACK.
UH... THAT'S FINE. LOOK.
I... I'LL PLAY SCISSORS NEXT.
WHAT DID YOU SAY?!

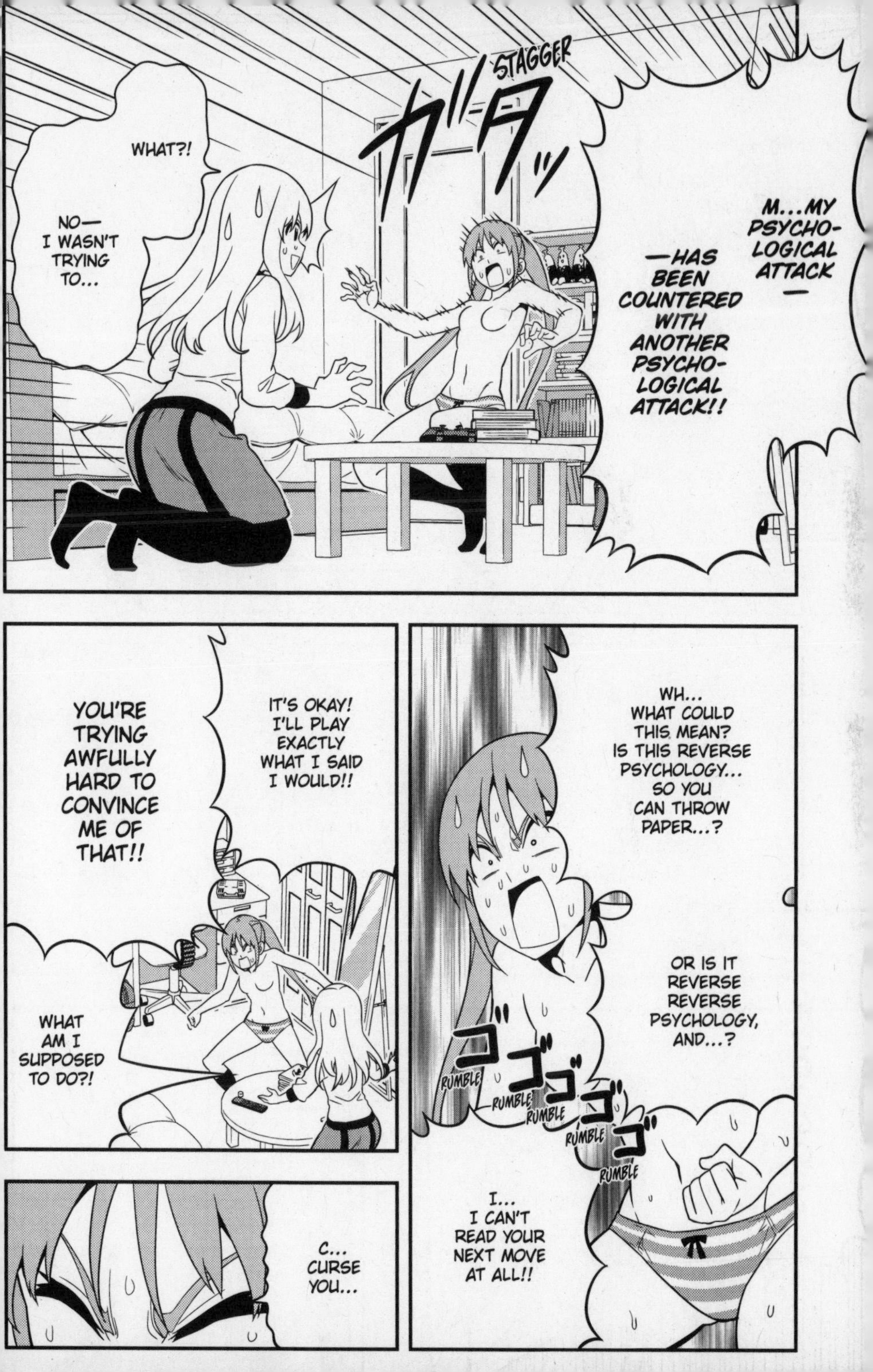
M...MY PSYCHOLOGICAL ATTACK—
—HAS BEEN COUNTERED WITH ANOTHER PSYCHOLOGICAL ATTACK!!
STAGGER
WHAT?!
NO— I WASN'T TRYING TO...
WH... WHAT COULD THIS MEAN? IS THIS REVERSE PSYCHOLOGY... SO YOU CAN THROW PAPER...?
OR IS IT REVERSE REVERSE PSYCHOLOGY, AND...?
RUMBLE RUMBLE RUMBLE RUMBLE RUMBLE
I... I CAN'T READ YOUR NEXT MOVE AT ALL!!
IT'S OKAY! I'LL PLAY EXACTLY WHAT I SAID I WOULD!!
YOU'RE TRYING AWFULLY HARD TO CONVINCE ME OF THAT!!
WHAT AM I SUPPOSED TO DO?!
C... CURSE YOU...

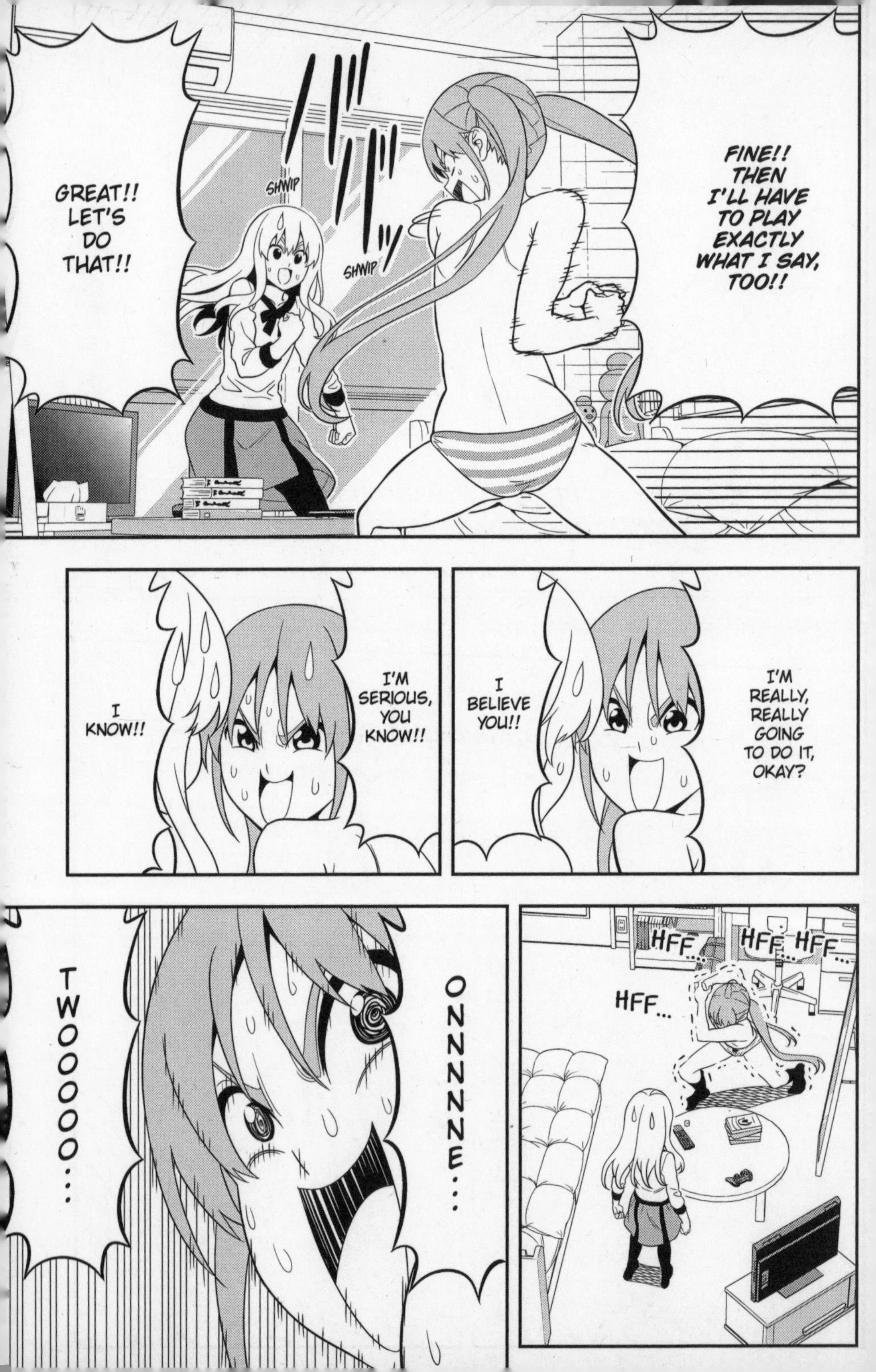
FINE!! THEN I'LL HAVE TO PLAY EXACTLY WHAT I SAY, TOO!!
SHWIP
SHWIP
GREAT!! LET'S DO THAT!!
I'M REALLY, REALLY GOING TO DO IT, OKAY?
I BELIEVE YOU!!
I'M SERIOUS, YOU KNOW!!
I KNOW!!
HFF... HFF... HFF...
HFF...
ONNNNNE...
TWOOOOOO...

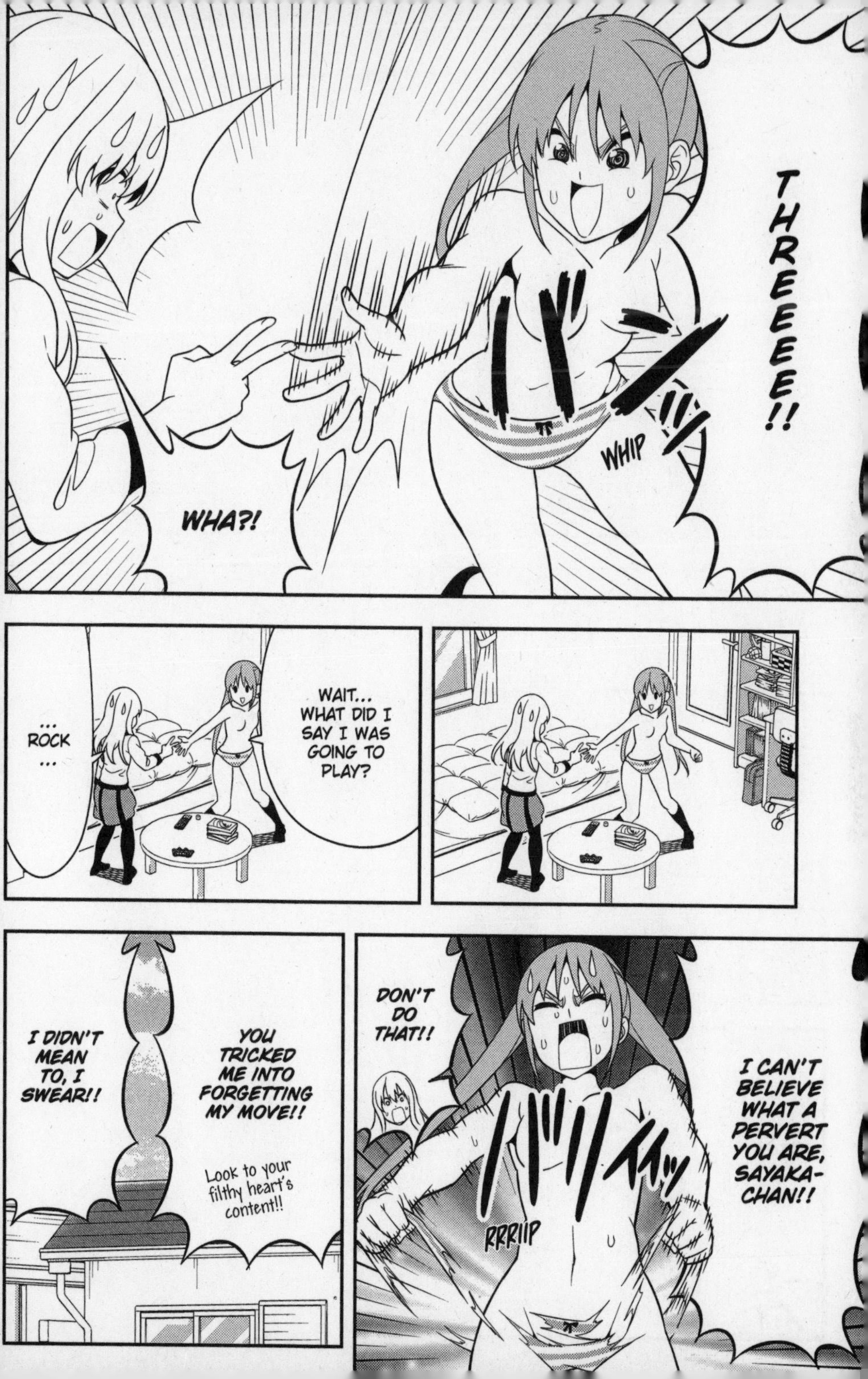
THREEEEE!!
WHIP
WHA?!
WAIT... WHAT DID I SAY I WAS GOING TO PLAY?
... ROCK ...
I CAN'T BELIEVE WHAT A PERVERT YOU ARE, SAYAKA-CHAN!!
DON'T DO THAT!!
RRRIIP
YOU TRICKED ME INTO FORGETTING MY MOVE!!
I DIDN'T MEAN TO, I SWEAR!!
Look to your filthy heart's content!!

Closer and Closer

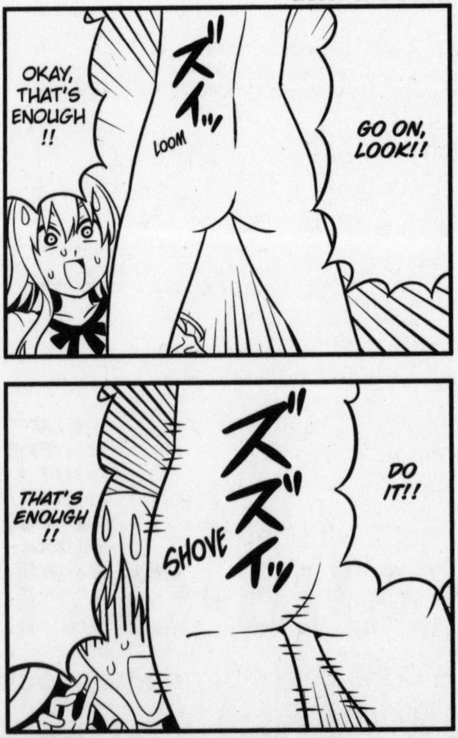
GO ON, LOOK!!
ズイッ
LOOM
OKAY, THAT'S ENOUGH !!
DO IT!!
ズズイッ
SHOVE
THAT'S ENOUGH !!

(You say you wanna live hard? Well)

Aho-Girl

\'ahô,gərl\ *Japanese, noun*.

A clueless girl.

Chapter 107

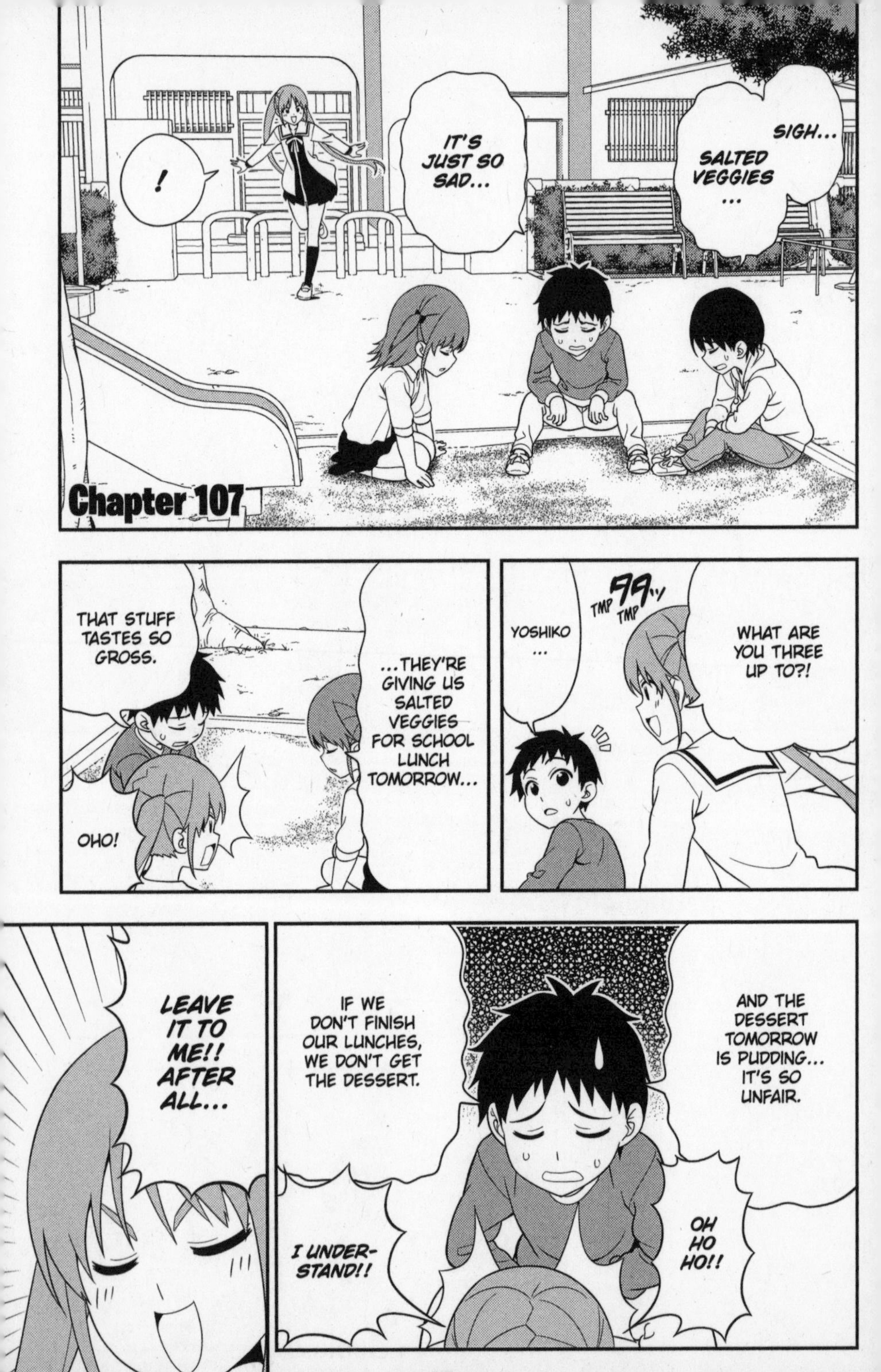
SIGH... SALTED VEGGIES ...
IT'S JUST SO SAD...
!
WHAT ARE YOU THREE UP TO?!
TMP TMP
YOSHIKO ...
...THEY'RE GIVING US SALTED VEGGIES FOR SCHOOL LUNCH TOMORROW...
THAT STUFF TASTES SO GROSS.
OHO!
AND THE DESSERT TOMORROW IS PUDDING... IT'S SO UNFAIR.
IF WE DON'T FINISH OUR LUNCHES, WE DON'T GET THE DESSERT.
OH HO HO!!
I UNDER-STAND!!
LEAVE IT TO ME!! AFTER ALL...

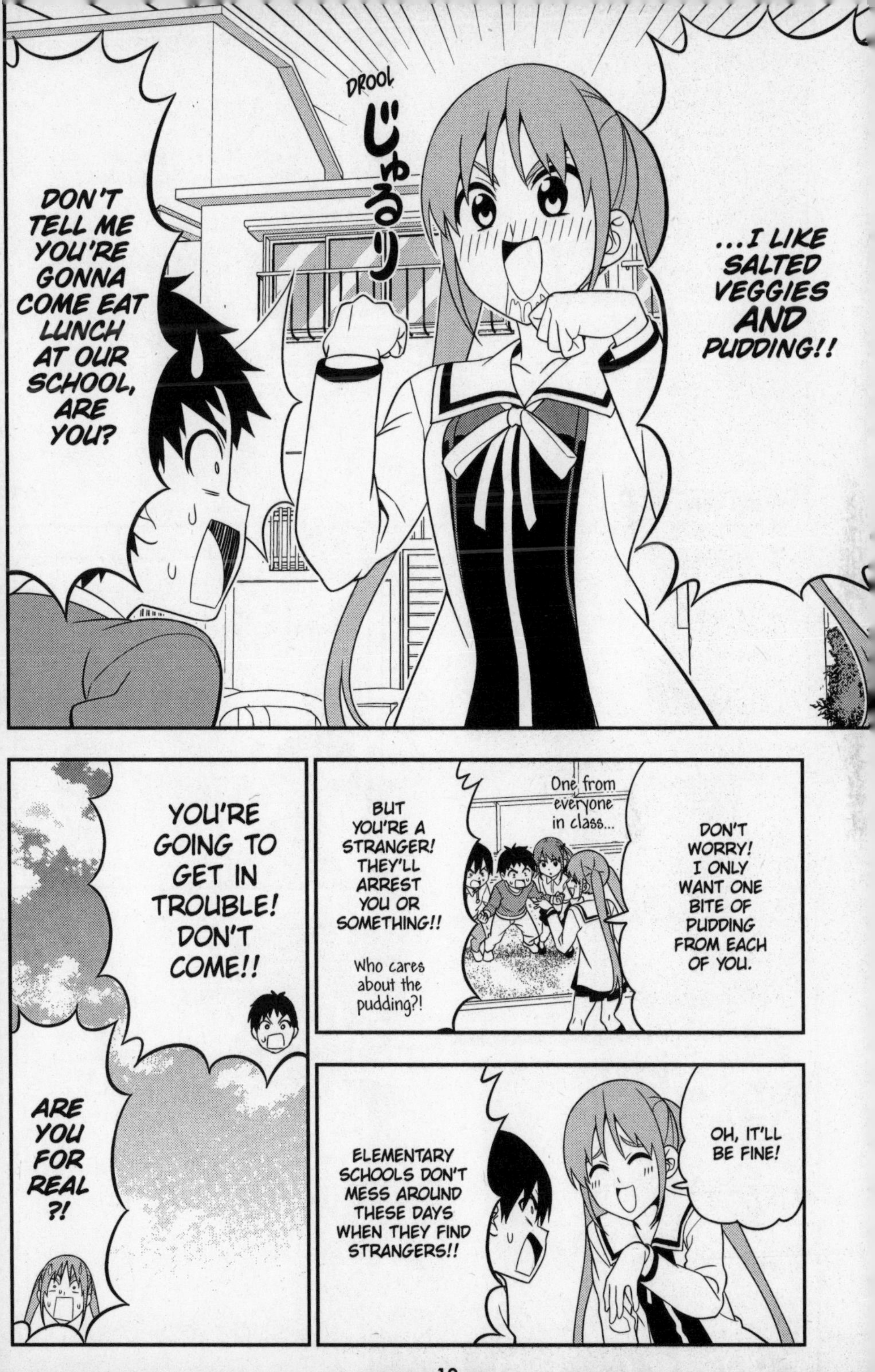
...I LIKE SALTED VEGGIES AND PUDDING!!
DROOL
じゅるり
DON'T TELL ME YOU'RE GONNA COME EAT LUNCH AT OUR SCHOOL, ARE YOU?
DON'T WORRY! I ONLY WANT ONE BITE OF PUDDING FROM EACH OF YOU.
One from everyone in class...
BUT YOU'RE A STRANGER! THEY'LL ARREST YOU OR SOMETHING!!
Who cares about the pudding?!
OH, IT'LL BE FINE!
ELEMENTARY SCHOOLS DON'T MESS AROUND THESE DAYS WHEN THEY FIND STRANGERS!!
YOU'RE GOING TO GET IN TROUBLE! DON'T COME!!
ARE YOU FOR REAL?!

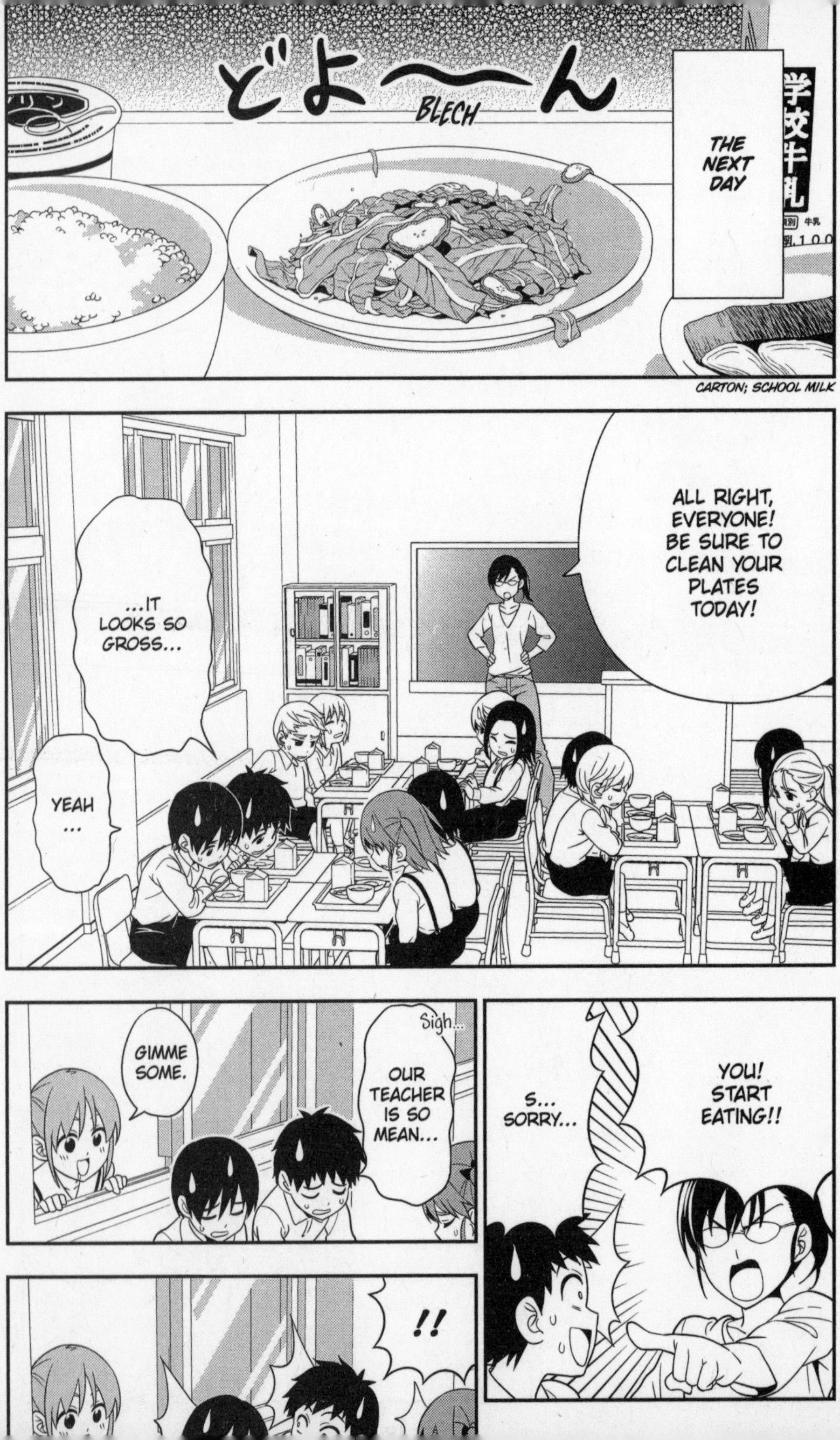

どよ〜〜ん
BLECH
THE NEXT DAY
学校牛乳
CARTON; SCHOOL MILK
ALL RIGHT, EVERYONE! BE SURE TO CLEAN YOUR PLATES TODAY!
...IT LOOKS SO GROSS...
YEAH ...
YOU! START EATING!!
S... SORRY...
Sigh...
OUR TEACHER IS SO MEAN...
GIMME SOME.
!!

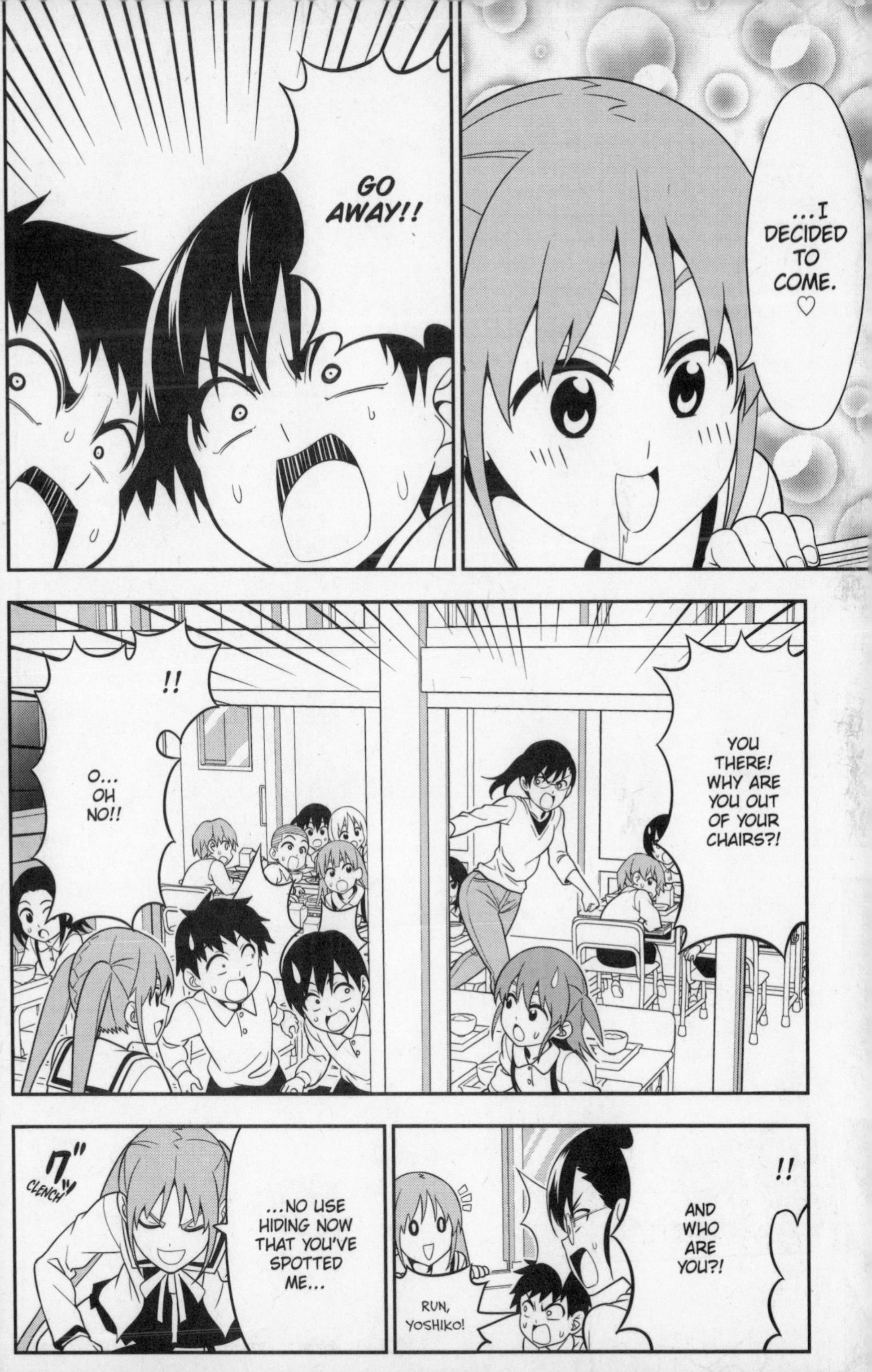
...I DECIDED TO COME. ♡
GO AWAY!!
YOU THERE! WHY ARE YOU OUT OF YOUR CHAIRS?!
!!
O... OH NO!!
!!
AND WHO ARE YOU?!
RUN, YOSHIKO!
...NO USE HIDING NOW THAT YOU'VE SPOTTED ME...
グッ
CLENCH

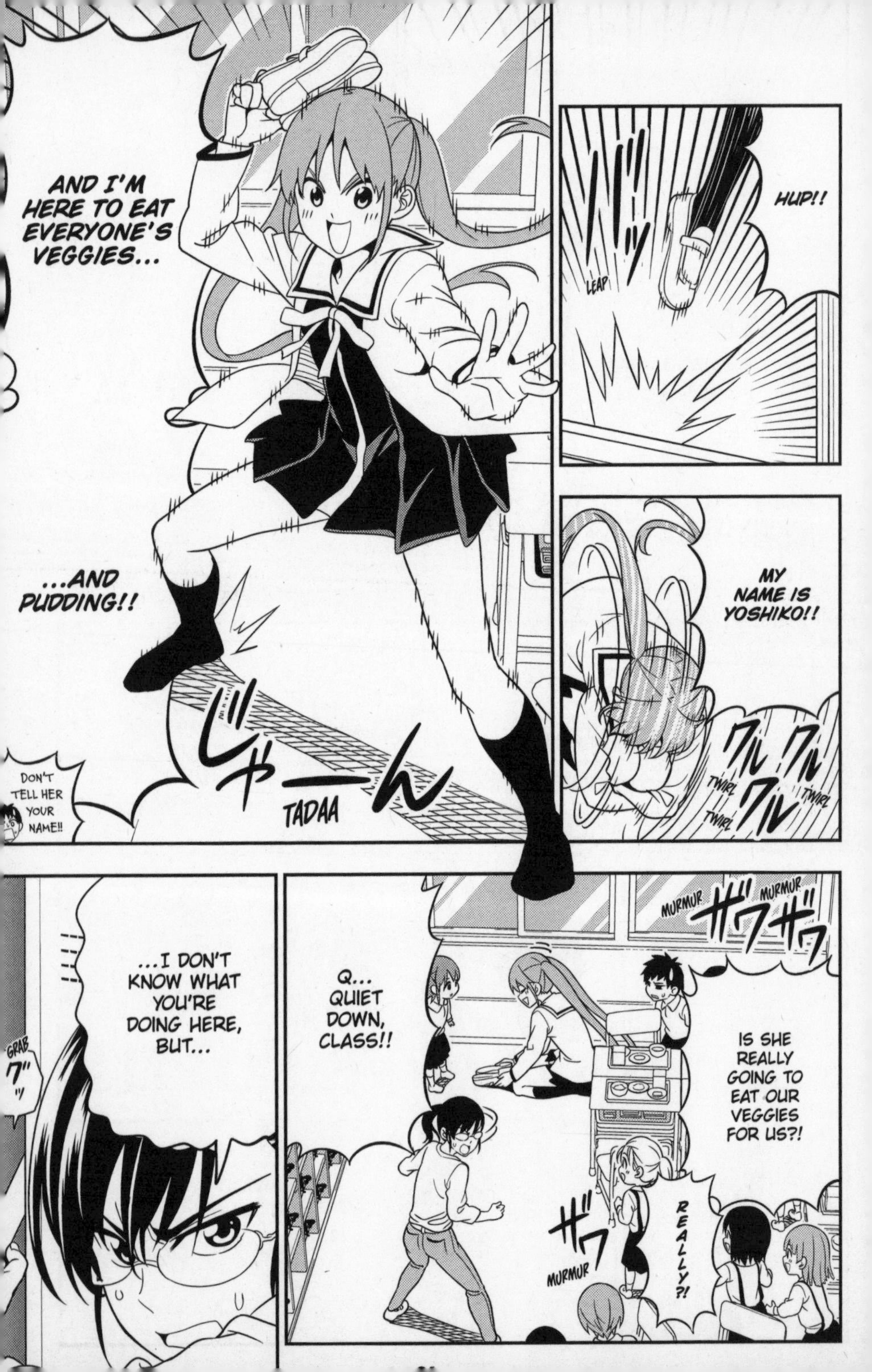
HUP!!
LEAP
MY NAME IS YOSHIKO!!
TWIRL
TWIRL
TWIRL
AND I'M HERE TO EAT EVERYONE'S VEGGIES...
...AND PUDDING!!
TADAA
DON'T TELL HER YOUR NAME!!
MURMUR
MURMUR
IS SHE REALLY GOING TO EAT OUR VEGGIES FOR US?!
Q... QUIET DOWN, CLASS!!
REALLY?!
MURMUR
GRAB
...I DON'T KNOW WHAT YOU'RE DOING HERE, BUT...

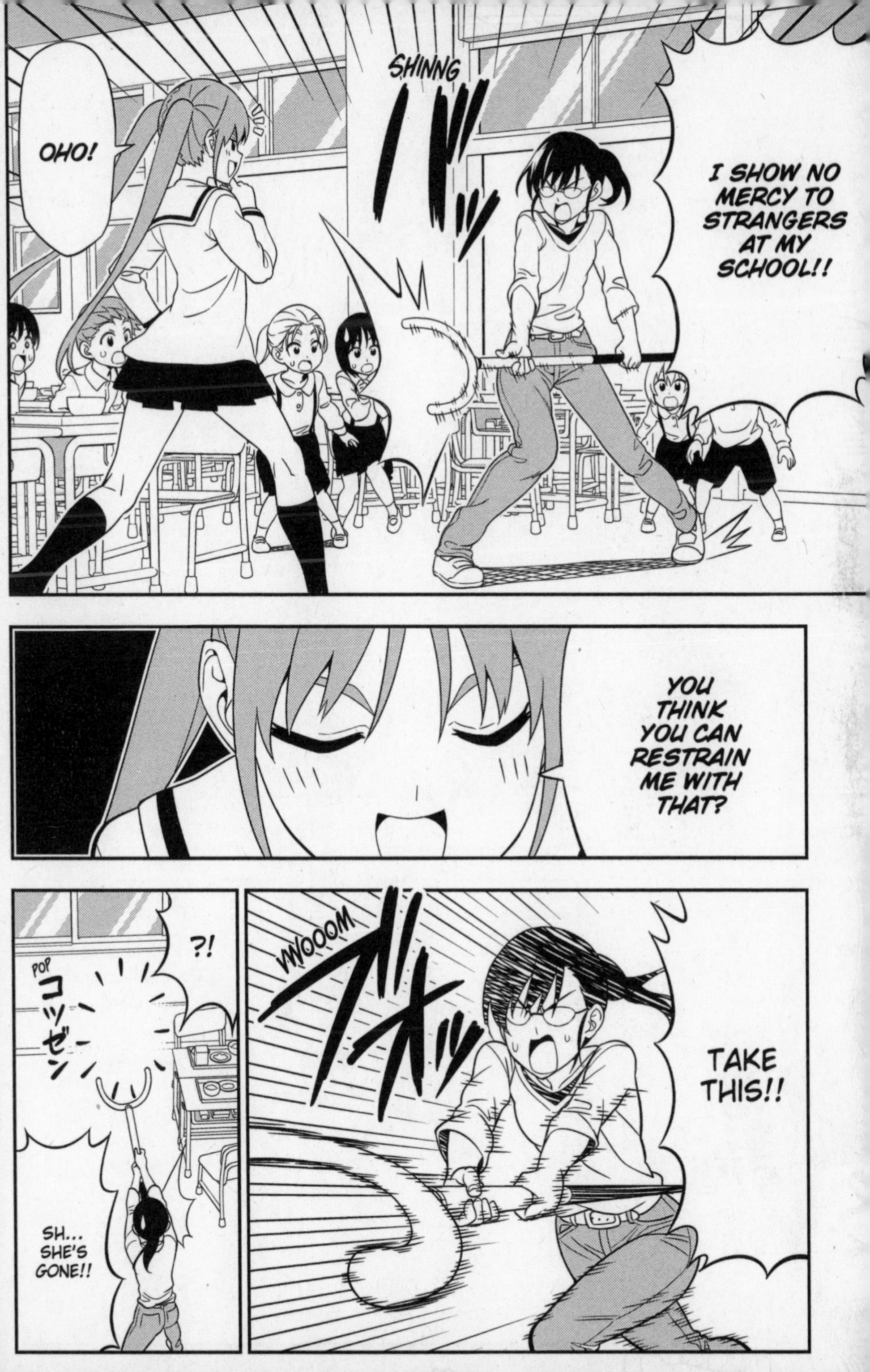
I SHOW NO MERCY TO STRANGERS AT MY SCHOOL!!
SHINNG
OHO!
YOU THINK YOU CAN RESTRAIN ME WITH THAT?
VWOOOM
TAKE THIS!!
?!
POP
コツゼン
SH... SHE'S GONE!!

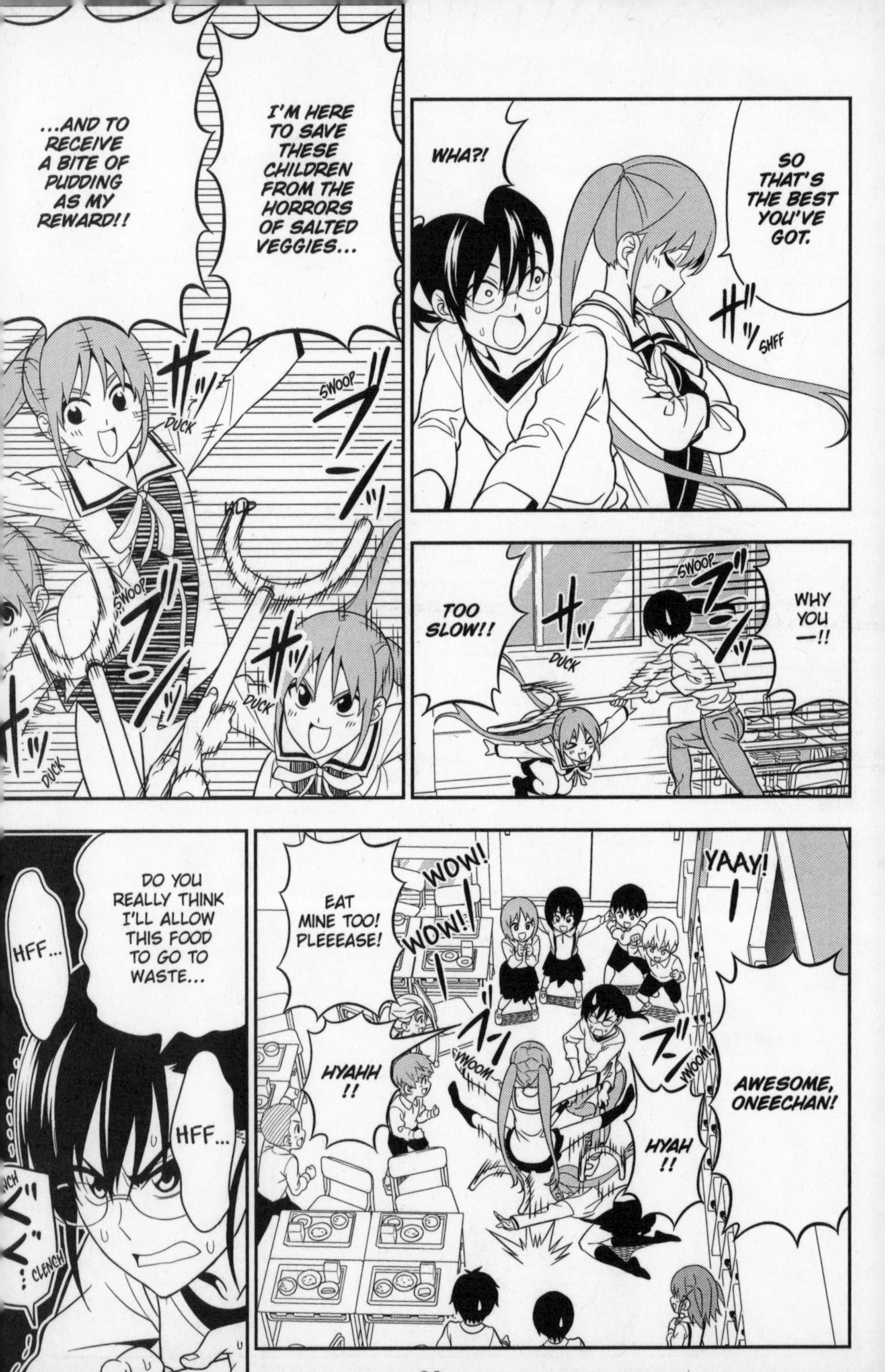
SO THAT'S THE BEST YOU'VE GOT.
WHA?!
SHFF
WHY YOU—!!
SWOOP
TOO SLOW!!
DUCK
I'M HERE TO SAVE THESE CHILDREN FROM THE HORRORS OF SALTED VEGGIES...
...AND TO RECEIVE A BITE OF PUDDING AS MY REWARD!!
SWOOP
DUCK
SWOOP
DUCK
DUCK
YAAY!
WOW!
WOW!
EAT MINE TOO! PLEEEASE!
AWESOME, ONEECHAN!
VWOOM
VWOOM
HYAHH!!
HYAH!!
DO YOU REALLY THINK I'LL ALLOW THIS FOOD TO GO TO WASTE...
HFF...
HFF...
CLENCH

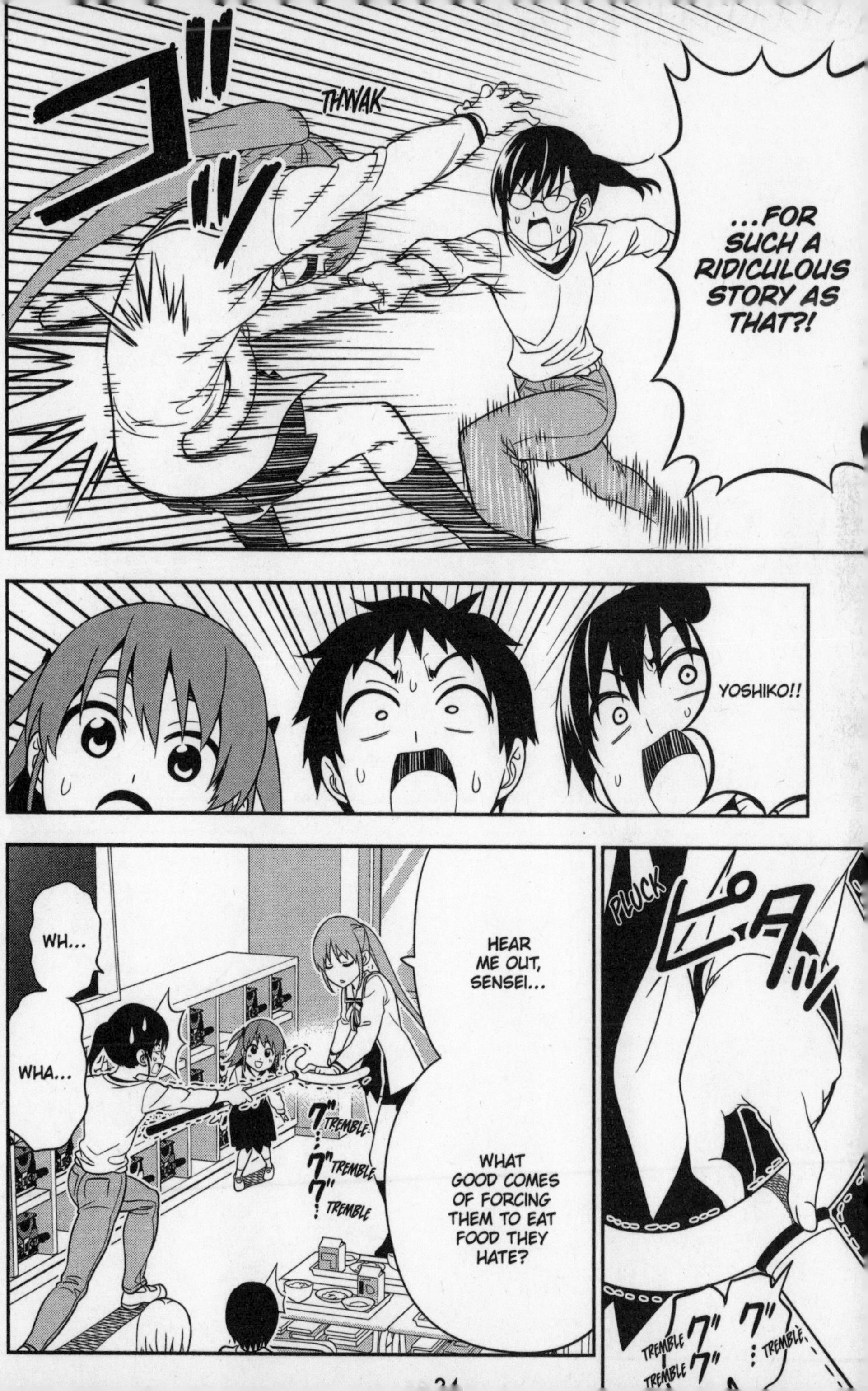
...FOR SUCH A RIDICULOUS STORY AS THAT?!
THWAK
YOSHIKO!!
PLUCK
TREMBLE
TREMBLE
TREMBLE
HEAR ME OUT, SENSEI...
WHAT GOOD COMES OF FORCING THEM TO EAT FOOD THEY HATE?
WH...
WHA...
TREMBLE
TREMBLE
TREMBLE

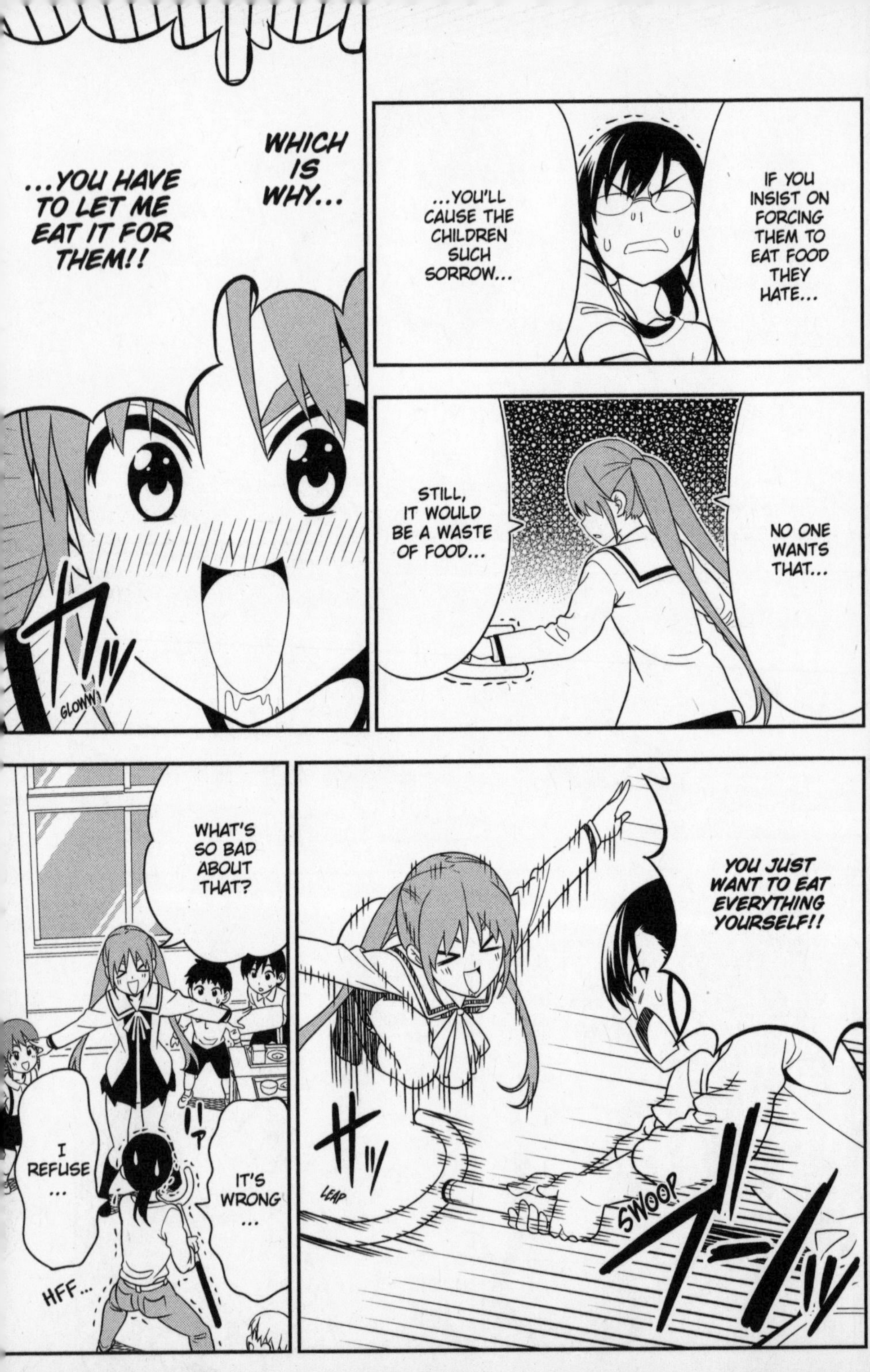
IF YOU INSIST ON FORCING THEM TO EAT FOOD THEY HATE...
...YOU'LL CAUSE THE CHILDREN SUCH SORROW...
NO ONE WANTS THAT...
STILL, IT WOULD BE A WASTE OF FOOD...
WHICH IS WHY...
...YOU HAVE TO LET ME EAT IT FOR THEM!!
GLOWW
YOU JUST WANT TO EAT EVERYTHING YOURSELF!!
SWOOP
LEAP
WHAT'S SO BAD ABOUT THAT?
IT'S WRONG...
I REFUSE...
HFF...

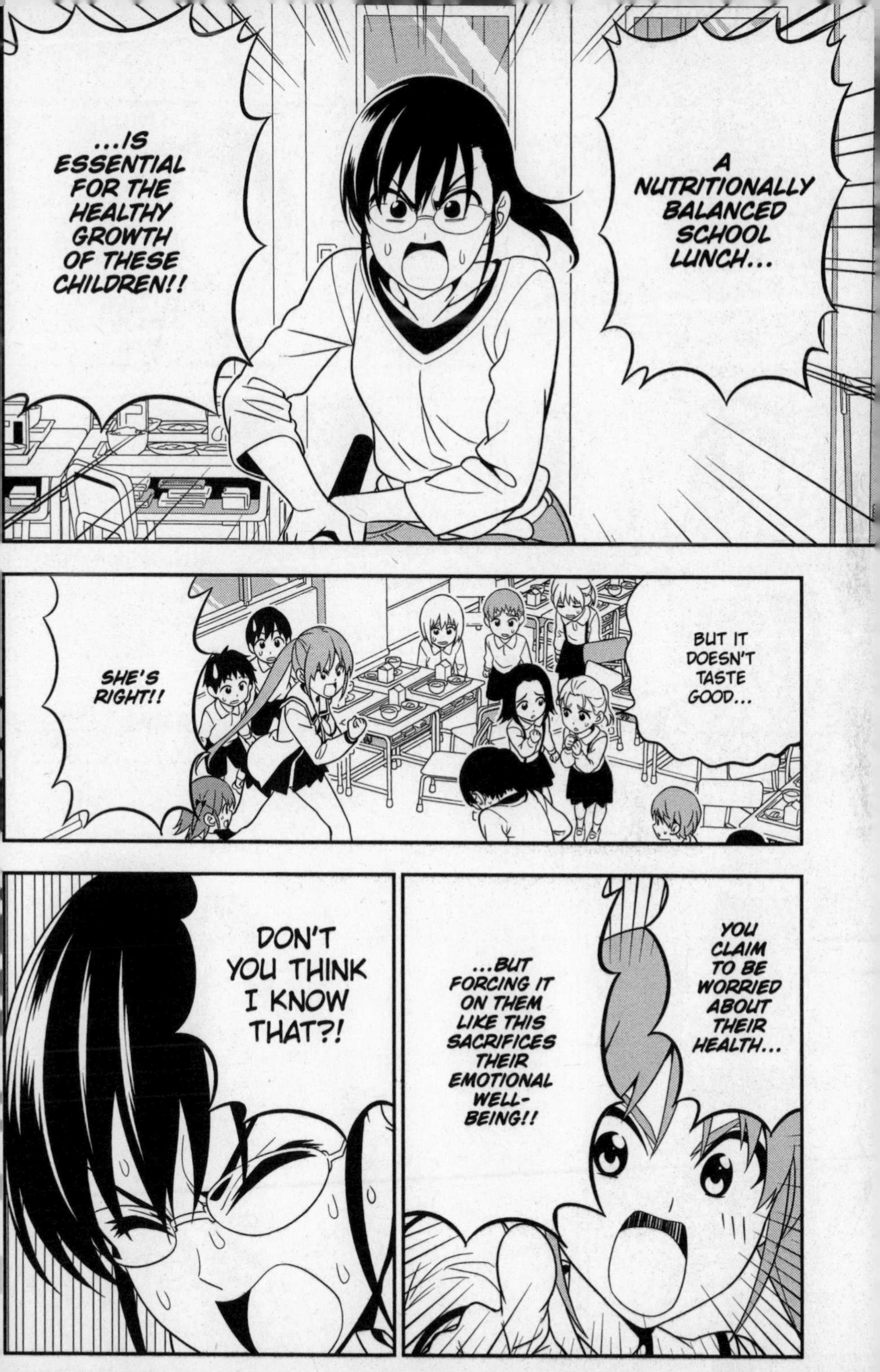
A NUTRITIONALLY BALANCED SCHOOL LUNCH...
...IS ESSENTIAL FOR THE HEALTHY GROWTH OF THESE CHILDREN!!
BUT IT DOESN'T TASTE GOOD...
SHE'S RIGHT!!
YOU CLAIM TO BE WORRIED ABOUT THEIR HEALTH...
...BUT FORCING IT ON THEM LIKE THIS SACRIFICES THEIR EMOTIONAL WELL-BEING!!
DON'T YOU THINK I KNOW THAT?!

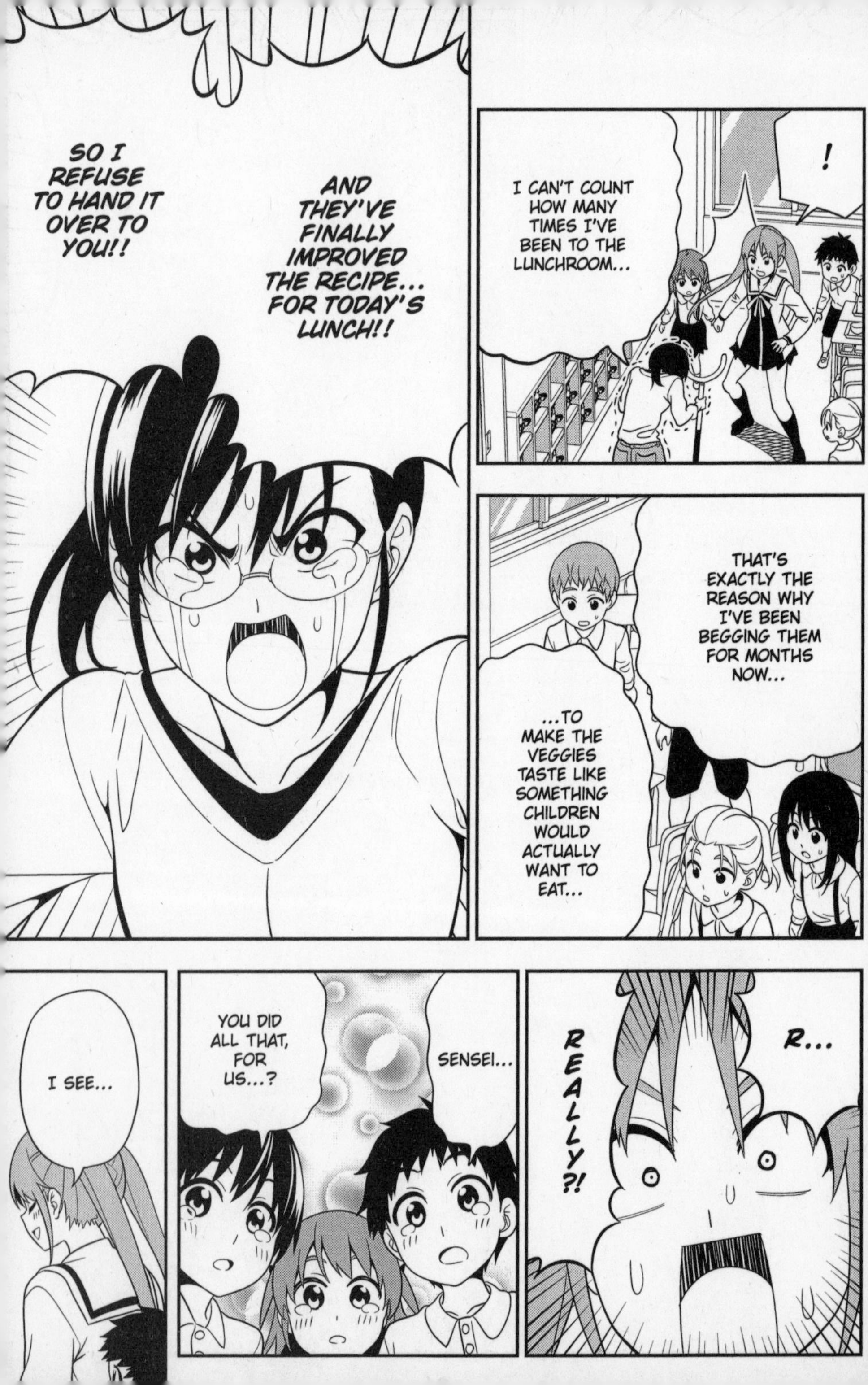
!
I CAN'T COUNT HOW MANY TIMES I'VE BEEN TO THE LUNCHROOM...
THAT'S EXACTLY THE REASON WHY I'VE BEEN BEGGING THEM FOR MONTHS NOW...
...TO MAKE THE VEGGIES TASTE LIKE SOMETHING CHILDREN WOULD ACTUALLY WANT TO EAT...
AND THEY'VE FINALLY IMPROVED THE RECIPE... FOR TODAY'S LUNCH!!
SO I REFUSE TO HAND IT OVER TO YOU!!
R...
REALLY?!
SENSEI...
YOU DID ALL THAT, FOR US...?
I SEE...

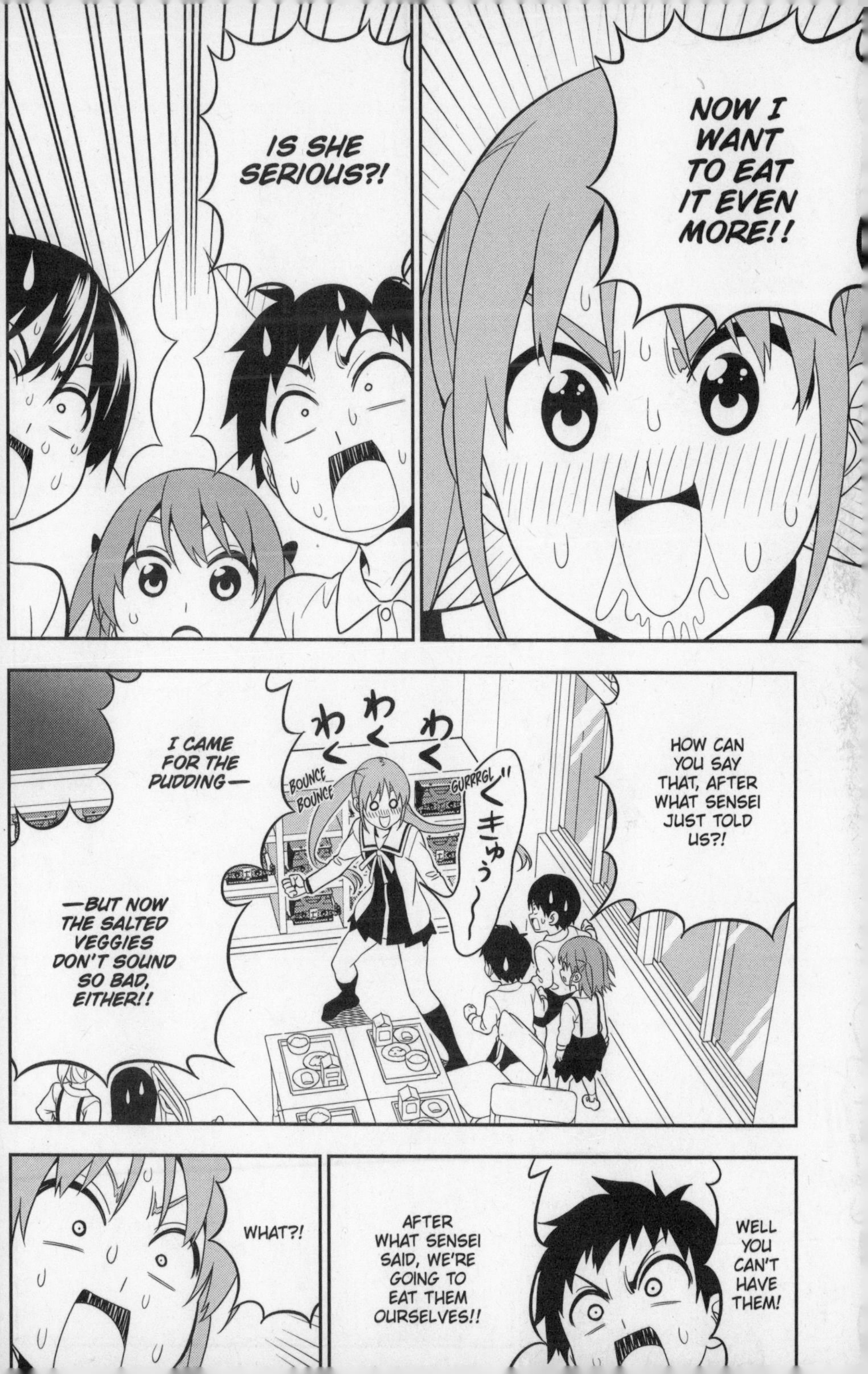
NOW I WANT TO EAT IT EVEN MORE!!
IS SHE SERIOUS?!
HOW CAN YOU SAY THAT, AFTER WHAT SENSEI JUST TOLD US?!
わくわく
ぐきゅう
GURRRGL
BOUNCE BOUNCE
I CAME FOR THE PUDDING—
—BUT NOW THE SALTED VEGGIES DON'T SOUND SO BAD, EITHER!!
WELL YOU CAN'T HAVE THEM!
AFTER WHAT SENSEI SAID, WE'RE GOING TO EAT THEM OURSELVES!!
WHAT?!

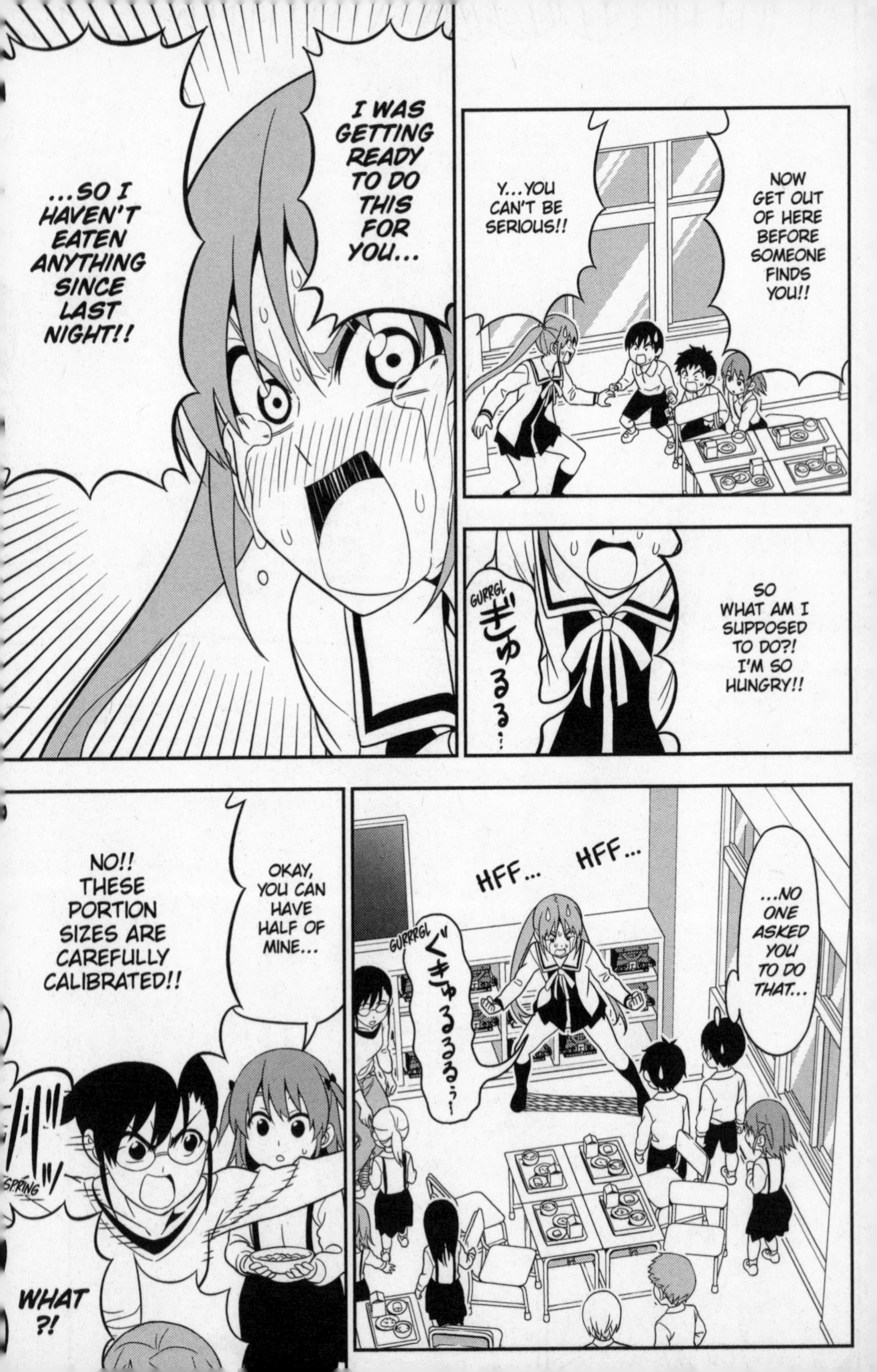
NOW GET OUT OF HERE BEFORE SOMEONE FINDS YOU!!
Y...YOU CAN'T BE SERIOUS!!
SO WHAT AM I SUPPOSED TO DO?! I'M SO HUNGRY!!
GURRGL
ぎゅるる...
I WAS GETTING READY TO DO THIS FOR YOU...
...SO I HAVEN'T EATEN ANYTHING SINCE LAST NIGHT!!
...NO ONE ASKED YOU TO DO THAT...
HFF... HFF...
GURRRGL
ぐきゅるるるる...
OKAY, YOU CAN HAVE HALF OF MINE...
NO!! THESE PORTION SIZES ARE CAREFULLY CALIBRATED!!
SPRING
WHAT?!

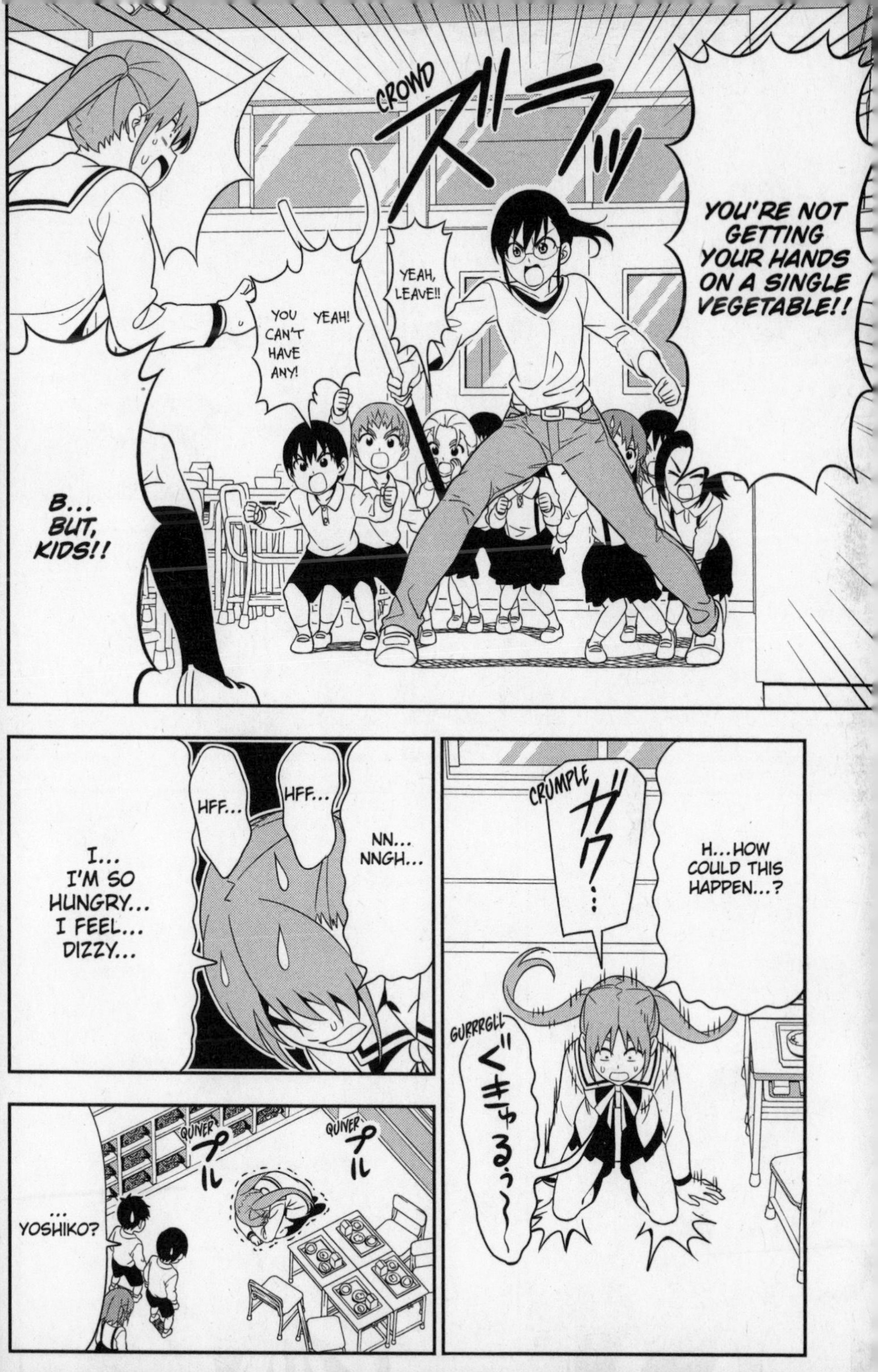
YOU'RE NOT GETTING YOUR HANDS ON A SINGLE VEGETABLE!!
CROWD
ズラッ
YEAH, LEAVE!!
YEAH!
YOU CAN'T HAVE ANY!
B... BUT, KIDS!!
CRUMPLE
ガク…
H...HOW COULD THIS HAPPEN...?
GURRRGLL
ぎゅるぅ~
NN... NNGH...
HFF...
HFF...
I... I'M SO HUNGRY... I FEEL... DIZZY...
QUIVER
プル
QUIVER
プル
... YOSHIKO?

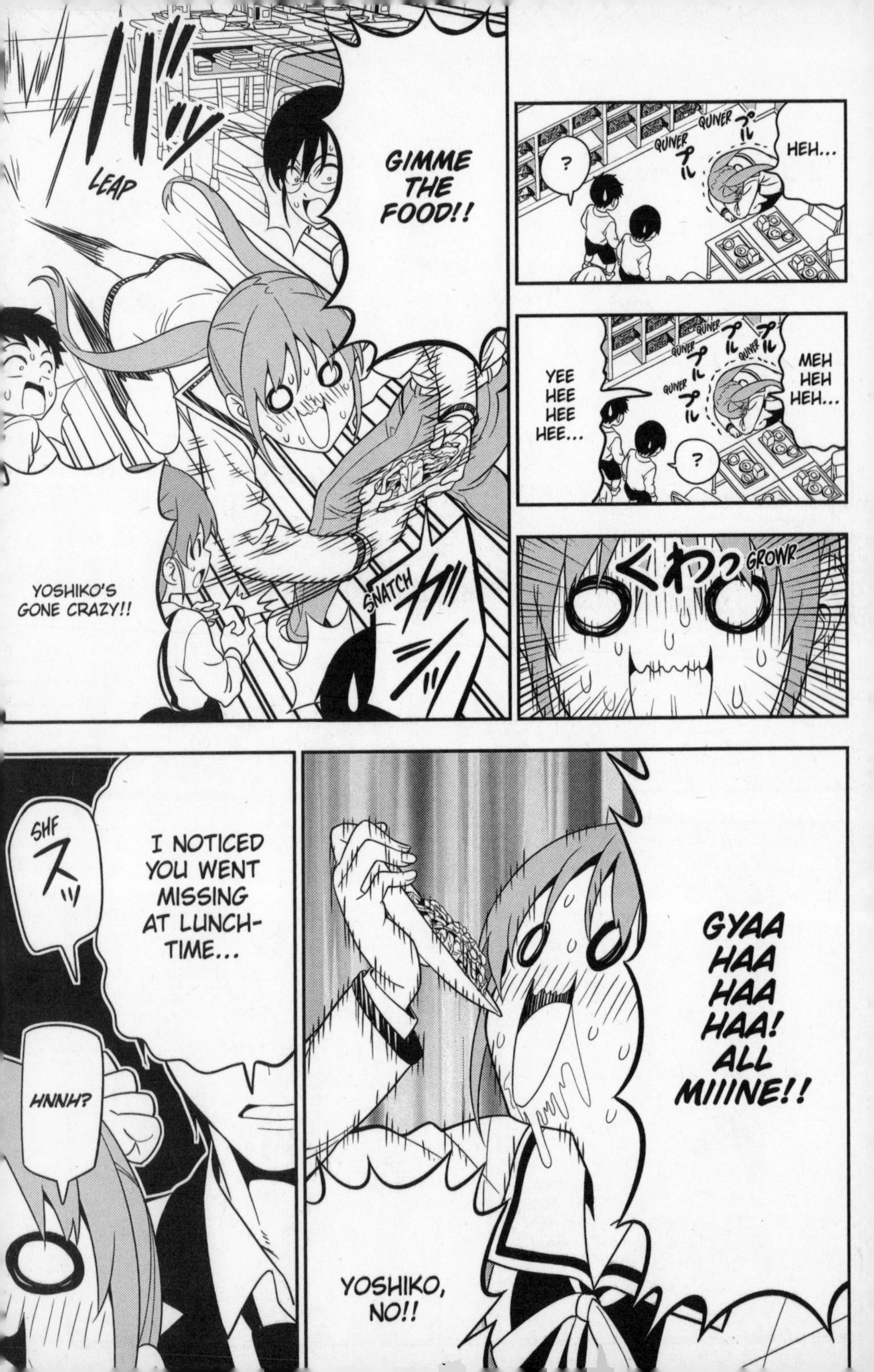
HEH...
QUIVER プル
QUIVER プル
?
MEH HEH HEH...
QUIVER プル
QUIVER プル
YEE HEE HEE HEE...
?
くわっ GROWR
GIMME THE FOOD!!
LEAP
SNATCH
YOSHIKO'S GONE CRAZY!!
GYAA HAA HAA HAA! ALL MIIINE!!
YOSHIKO, NO!!
SHF スッ
I NOTICED YOU WENT MISSING AT LUNCH-TIME...
HNNH?

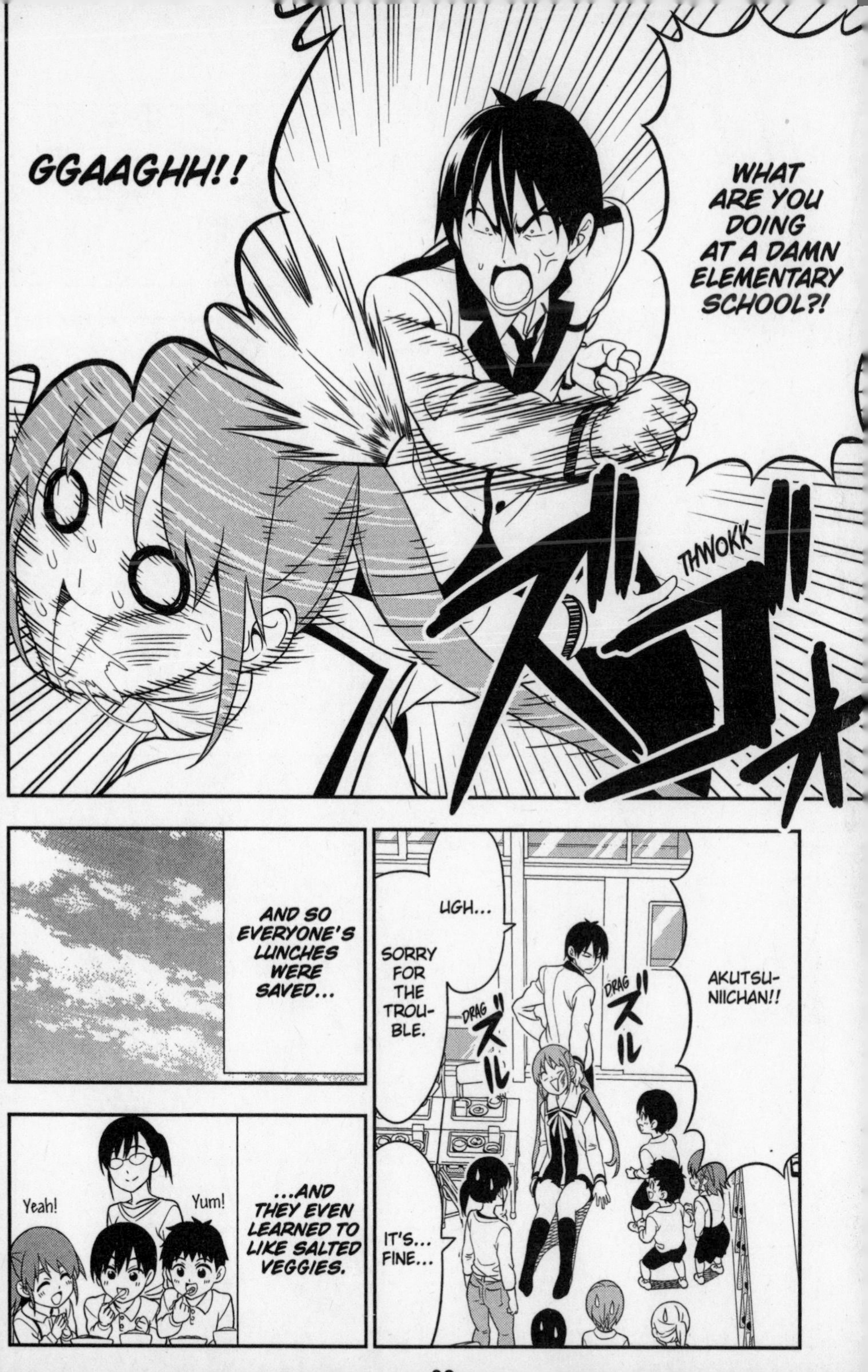
WHAT ARE YOU DOING AT A DAMN ELEMENTARY SCHOOL?!
GGAAGHH!!
THWOKK
AKUTSU-NIICHAN!!
DRAG
DRAG
UGH...
SORRY FOR THE TROU-BLE.
IT'S... FINE...
AND SO EVERYONE'S LUNCHES WERE SAVED...
...AND THEY EVEN LEARNED TO LIKE SALTED VEGGIES.
Yum!
Yeah!

Resolution

DAMMIT!! I WANTED THOSE SALTED VEGGIES!!
SHUT UP AND EAT A BANANA!!
ドサッ
THWAP
SOOO GOOD...

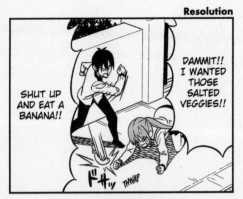

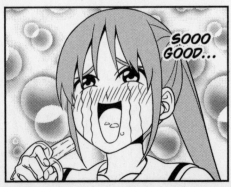

(If you really push yourself to your limits, you'll be surprised to find)

Aho-Girl

\\'ahô͵gərl\\ *Japanese, noun*.
A clueless girl.

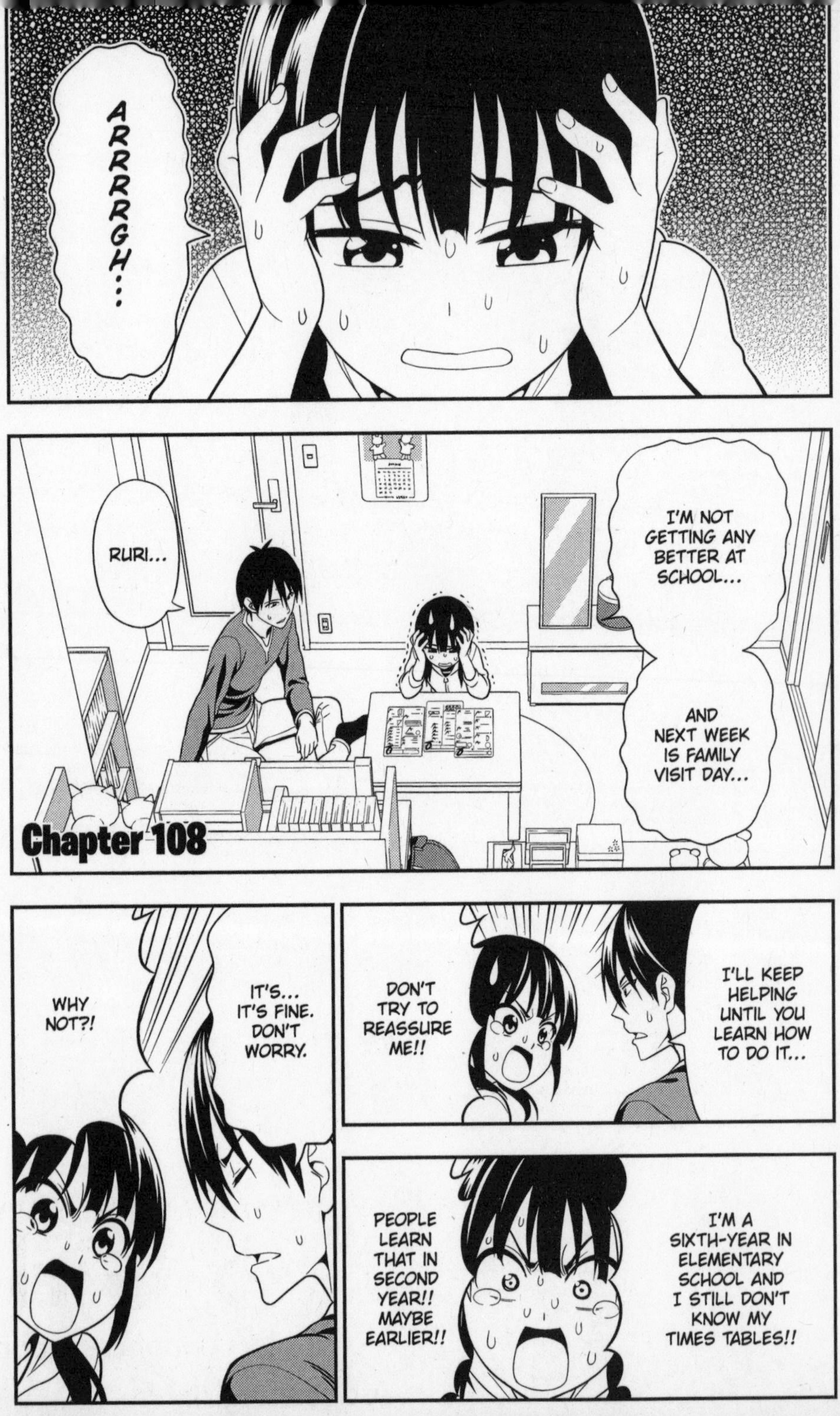
ARRRRGH...
I'M NOT GETTING ANY BETTER AT SCHOOL...
AND NEXT WEEK IS FAMILY VISIT DAY...
RURI...
Chapter 108
I'LL KEEP HELPING UNTIL YOU LEARN HOW TO DO IT...
DON'T TRY TO REASSURE ME!!
I'M A SIXTH-YEAR IN ELEMENTARY SCHOOL AND I STILL DON'T KNOW MY TIMES TABLES!!
PEOPLE LEARN THAT IN SECOND YEAR!! MAYBE EARLIER!!
IT'S... IT'S FINE. DON'T WORRY.
WHY NOT?!

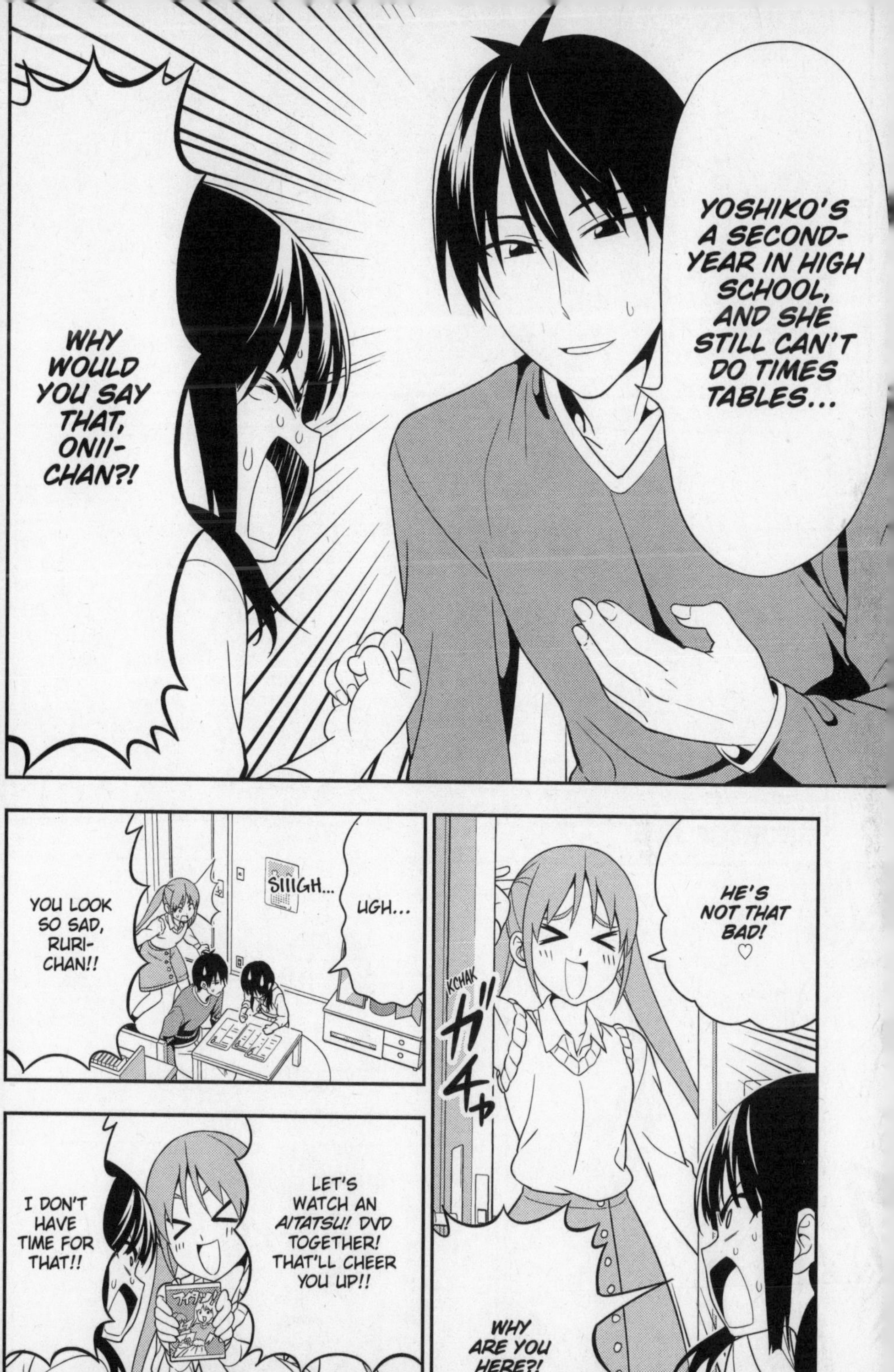
YOSHIKO'S A SECOND-YEAR IN HIGH SCHOOL, AND SHE STILL CAN'T DO TIMES TABLES...
WHY WOULD YOU SAY THAT, ONII-CHAN?!
HE'S NOT THAT BAD! ♡
KCHAK
WHY ARE YOU HERE?!
UGH...
SIIIGH...
YOU LOOK SO SAD, RURI-CHAN!!
LET'S WATCH AN *AITATSU!* DVD TOGETHER! THAT'LL CHEER YOU UP!!
I DON'T HAVE TIME FOR THAT!!

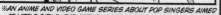

※AN ANIME AND VIDEO GAME SERIES ABOUT POP SINGERS AIMED

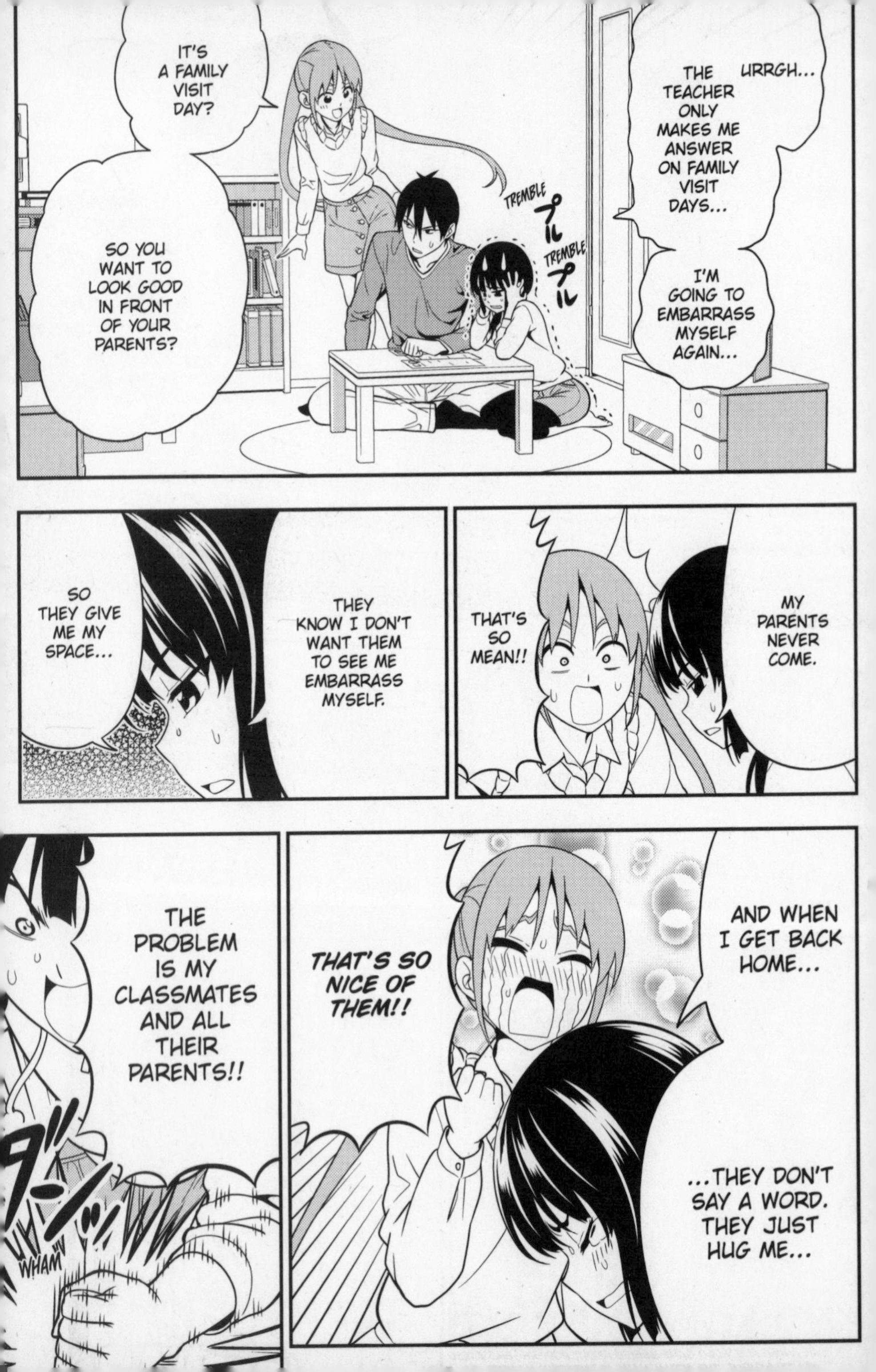
URRGH...
THE TEACHER ONLY MAKES ME ANSWER ON FAMILY VISIT DAYS...
I'M GOING TO EMBARRASS MYSELF AGAIN...
TREMBLE
プル
TREMBLE
プル
IT'S A FAMILY VISIT DAY?
SO YOU WANT TO LOOK GOOD IN FRONT OF YOUR PARENTS?
MY PARENTS NEVER COME.
THAT'S SO MEAN!!
THEY KNOW I DON'T WANT THEM TO SEE ME EMBARRASS MYSELF.
SO THEY GIVE ME MY SPACE...
AND WHEN I GET BACK HOME...
...THEY DON'T SAY A WORD. THEY JUST HUG ME...
THAT'S SO NICE OF THEM!!
THE PROBLEM IS MY CLASSMATES AND ALL THEIR PARENTS!!
WHAM

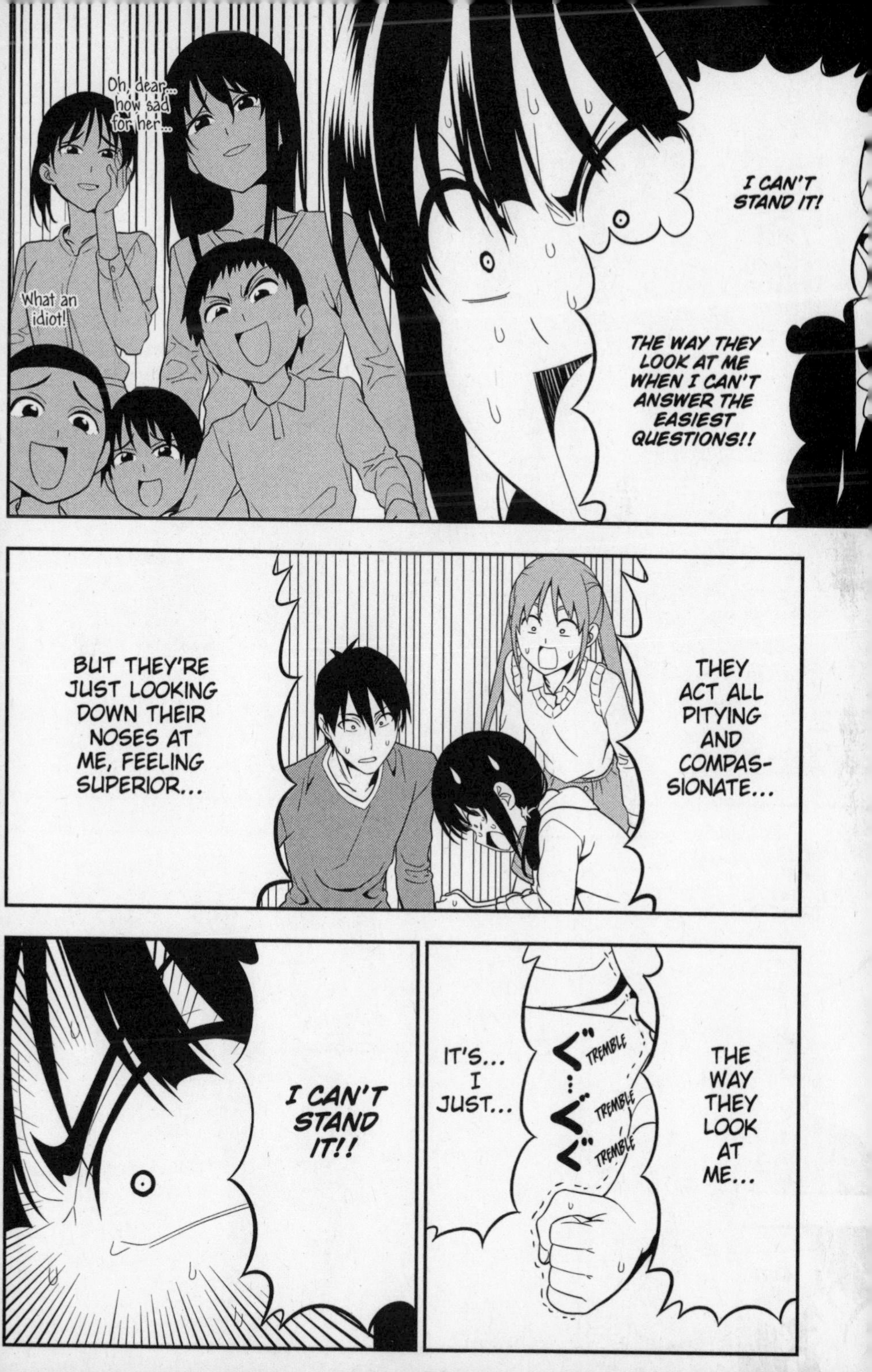
I CAN'T STAND IT!
THE WAY THEY LOOK AT ME WHEN I CAN'T ANSWER THE EASIEST QUESTIONS!!
Oh, dear... how sad for her...
What an idiot!
THEY ACT ALL PITYING AND COMPASSIONATE...
BUT THEY'RE JUST LOOKING DOWN THEIR NOSES AT ME, FEELING SUPERIOR...
THE WAY THEY LOOK AT ME...
TREMBLE
TREMBLE
TREMBLE
IT'S... I JUST...
I CAN'T STAND IT!!

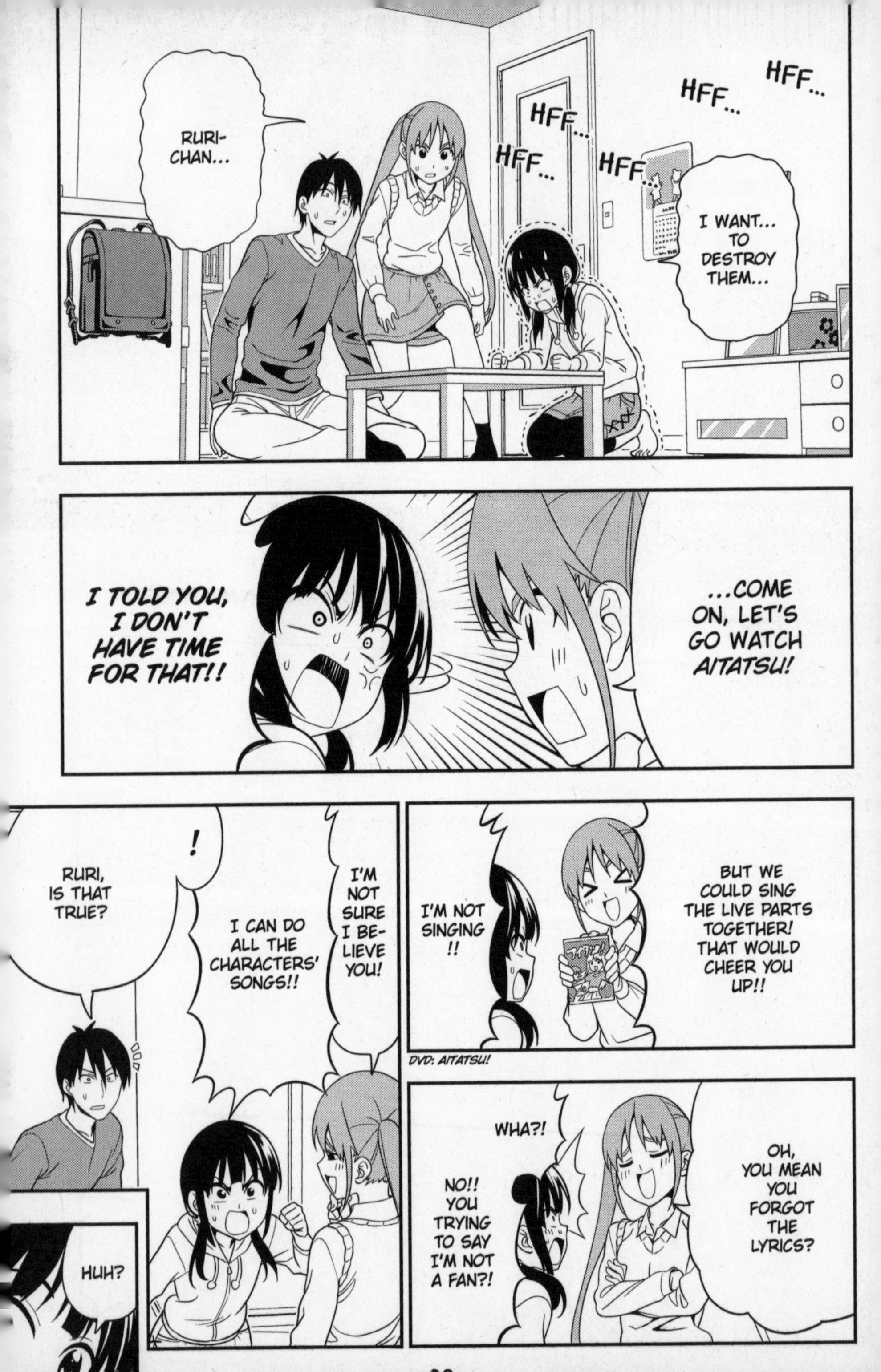
HFF...
HFF...
HFF...
HFF...
HFF...
I WANT... TO DESTROY THEM...
RURI-CHAN...
...COME ON, LET'S GO WATCH AITATSU!
I TOLD YOU, I DON'T HAVE TIME FOR THAT!!
BUT WE COULD SING THE LIVE PARTS TOGETHER! THAT WOULD CHEER YOU UP!!
I'M NOT SINGING!!
DVD: AITATSU!
OH, YOU MEAN YOU FORGOT THE LYRICS?
WHA?!
NO!! YOU TRYING TO SAY I'M NOT A FAN?!
I'M NOT SURE I BELIEVE YOU!
!
I CAN DO ALL THE CHARACTERS' SONGS!!
RURI, IS THAT TRUE?
HUH?

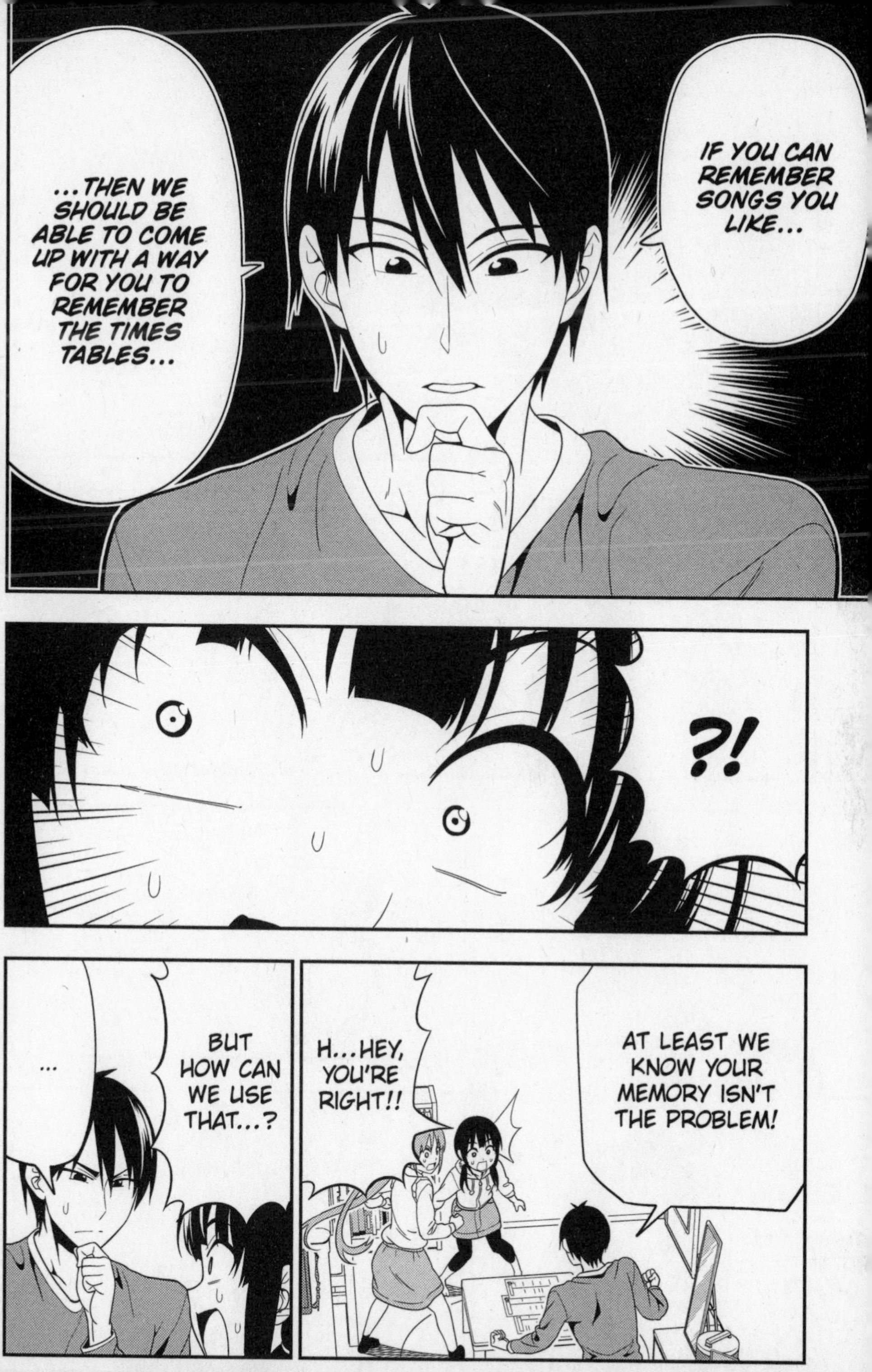
IF YOU CAN REMEMBER SONGS YOU LIKE...
...THEN WE SHOULD BE ABLE TO COME UP WITH A WAY FOR YOU TO REMEMBER THE TIMES TABLES...
?!
AT LEAST WE KNOW YOUR MEMORY ISN'T THE PROBLEM!
H...HEY, YOU'RE RIGHT!!
BUT HOW CAN WE USE THAT...?
...

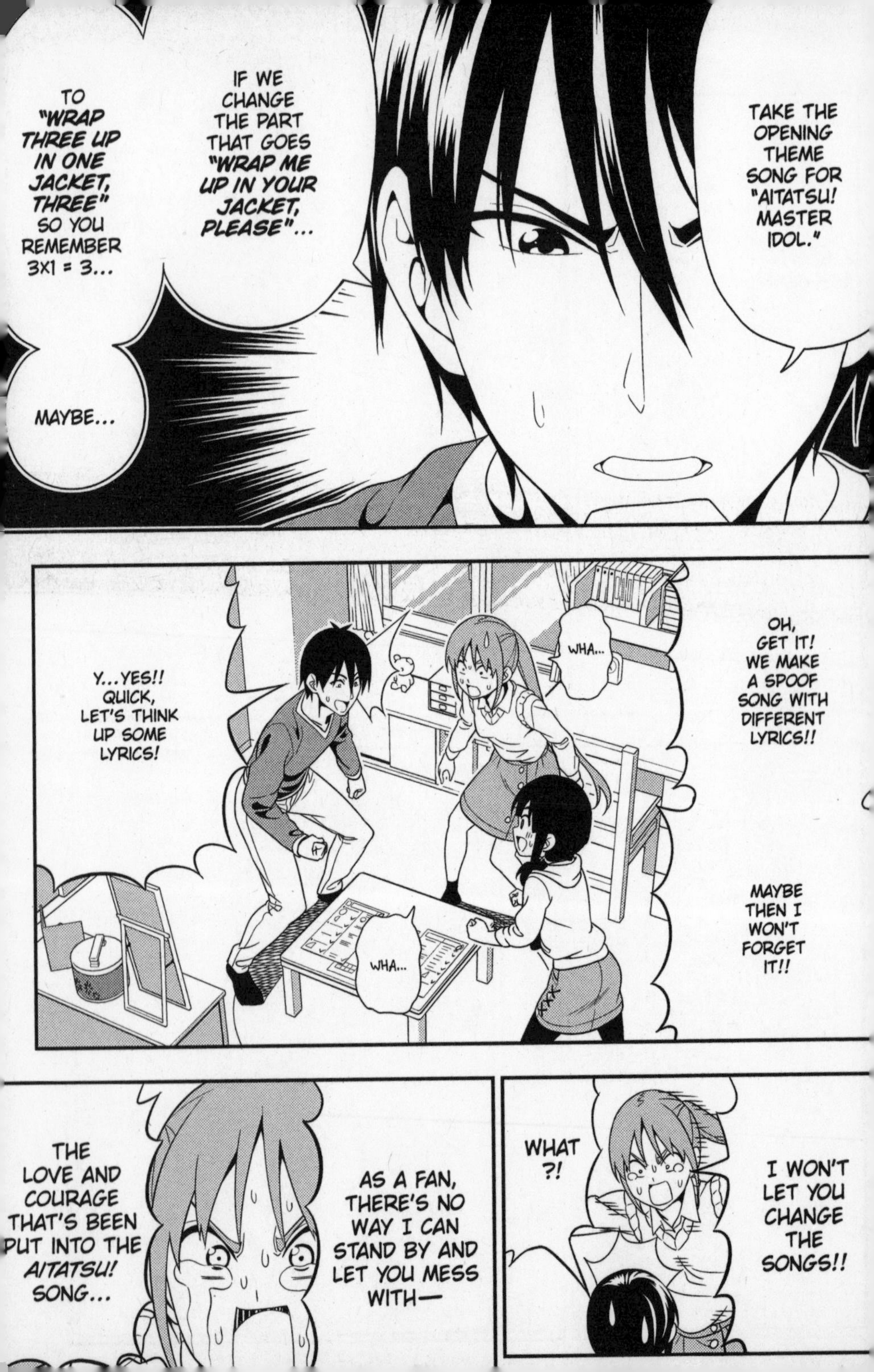
TAKE THE OPENING THEME SONG FOR "AITATSU! MASTER IDOL."
IF WE CHANGE THE PART THAT GOES *"WRAP ME UP IN YOUR JACKET, PLEASE"*...
TO *"WRAP THREE UP IN ONE JACKET, THREE"* SO YOU REMEMBER 3X1 = 3...
MAYBE...
OH, GET IT! WE MAKE A SPOOF SONG WITH DIFFERENT LYRICS!!
WHA...
MAYBE THEN I WON'T FORGET IT!!
Y...YES!! QUICK, LET'S THINK UP SOME LYRICS!
WHA...
I WON'T LET YOU CHANGE THE SONGS!!
WHAT?!
AS A FAN, THERE'S NO WAY I CAN STAND BY AND LET YOU MESS WITH—
THE LOVE AND COURAGE THAT'S BEEN PUT INTO THE *AITATSU!* SONG...

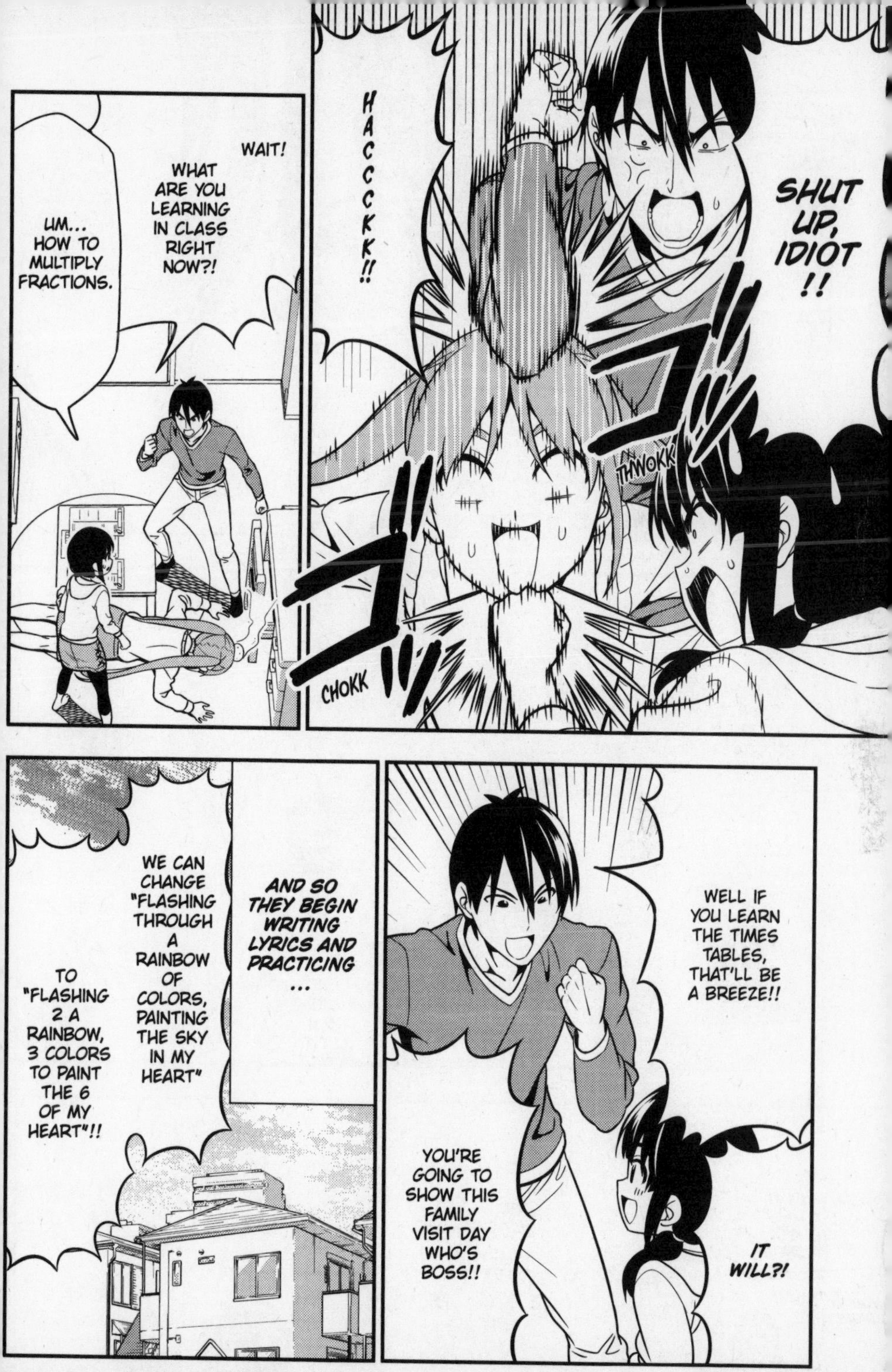
SHUT UP, IDIOT!!
HACCCKK!!
THWOKK
CHOKK
WAIT! WHAT ARE YOU LEARNING IN CLASS RIGHT NOW?!
UM... HOW TO MULTIPLY FRACTIONS.
WELL IF YOU LEARN THE TIMES TABLES, THAT'LL BE A BREEZE!!
IT WILL?!
YOU'RE GOING TO SHOW THIS FAMILY VISIT DAY WHO'S BOSS!!
AND SO THEY BEGIN WRITING LYRICS AND PRACTICING ...
WE CAN CHANGE "FLASHING THROUGH A RAINBOW OF COLORS, PAINTING THE SKY IN MY HEART"
TO "FLASHING 2 A RAINBOW, 3 COLORS TO PAINT THE 6 OF MY HEART"!!

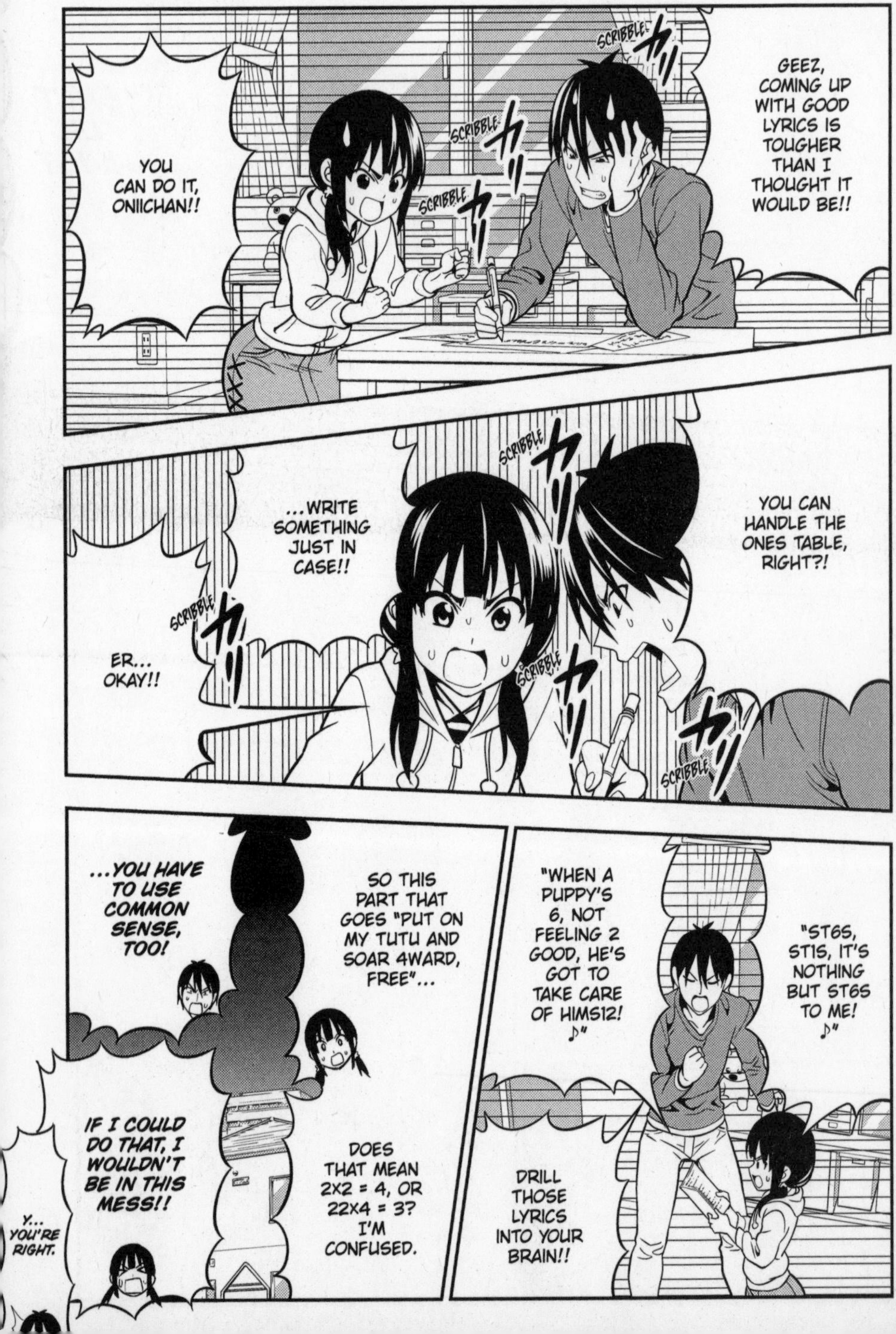
GEEZ, COMING UP WITH GOOD LYRICS IS TOUGHER THAN I THOUGHT IT WOULD BE!!
SCRIBBLE
SCRIBBLE
SCRIBBLE
YOU CAN DO IT, ONIICHAN!!
SCRIBBLE
YOU CAN HANDLE THE ONES TABLE, RIGHT?!
...WRITE SOMETHING JUST IN CASE!!
SCRIBBLE
SCRIBBLE
SCRIBBLE
ER... OKAY!!
"ST6S, ST1S, IT'S NOTHING BUT ST6S TO ME! ♪"
"WHEN A PUPPY'S 6, NOT FEELING 2 GOOD, HE'S GOT TO TAKE CARE OF HIMS12! ♪"
DRILL THOSE LYRICS INTO YOUR BRAIN!!
SO THIS PART THAT GOES "PUT ON MY TUTU AND SOAR 4WARD, FREE"...
DOES THAT MEAN 2X2 = 4, OR 22X4 = 3? I'M CONFUSED.
...YOU HAVE TO USE COMMON SENSE, TOO!
IF I COULD DO THAT, I WOULDN'T BE IN THIS MESS!!
Y... YOU'RE RIGHT.

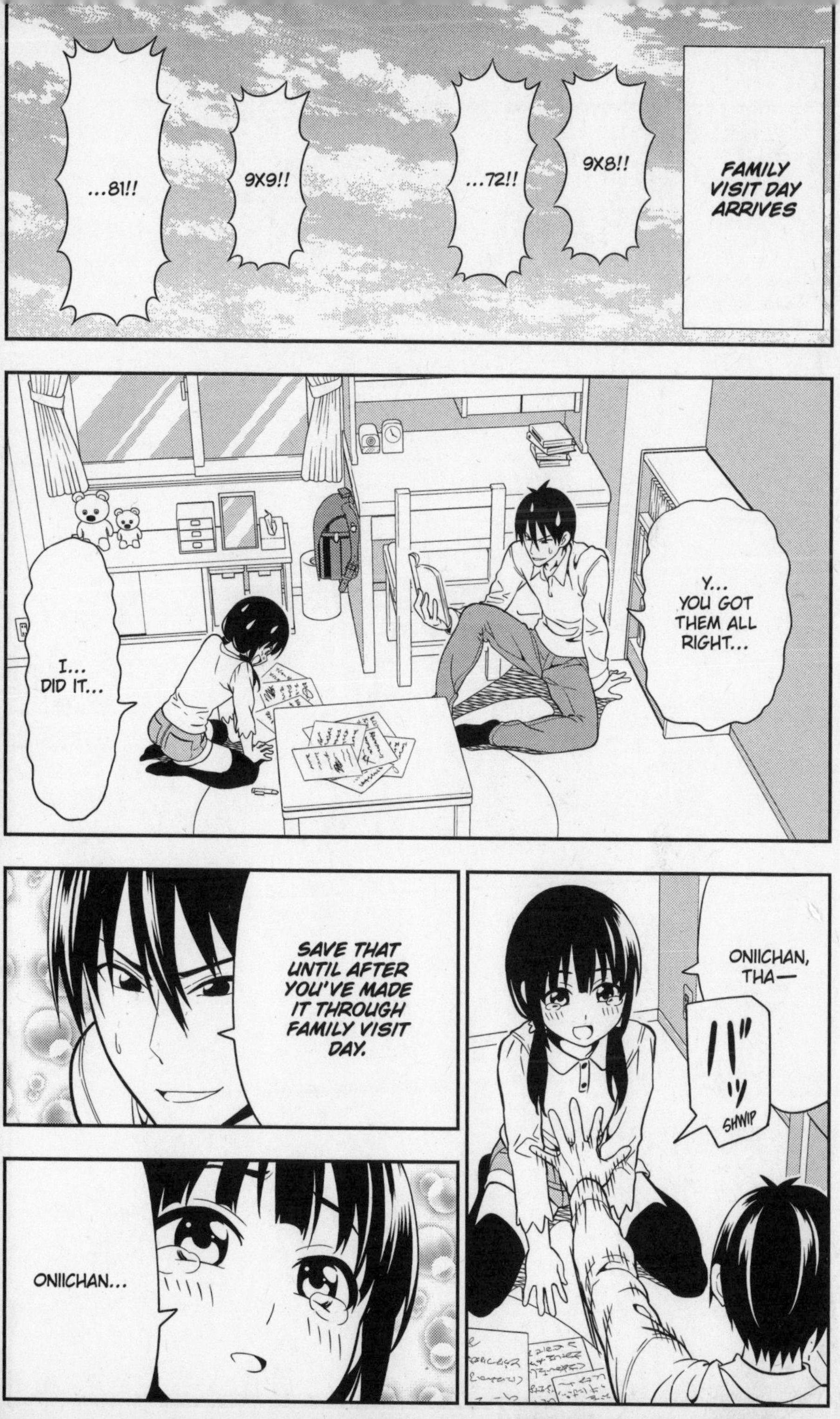
FAMILY VISIT DAY ARRIVES
9X8!!
...72!!
9X9!!
...81!!
Y... YOU GOT THEM ALL RIGHT...
I... DID IT...
ONIICHAN, THA—
バッ
SHWIP
SAVE THAT UNTIL AFTER YOU'VE MADE IT THROUGH FAMILY VISIT DAY.
ONIICHAN...

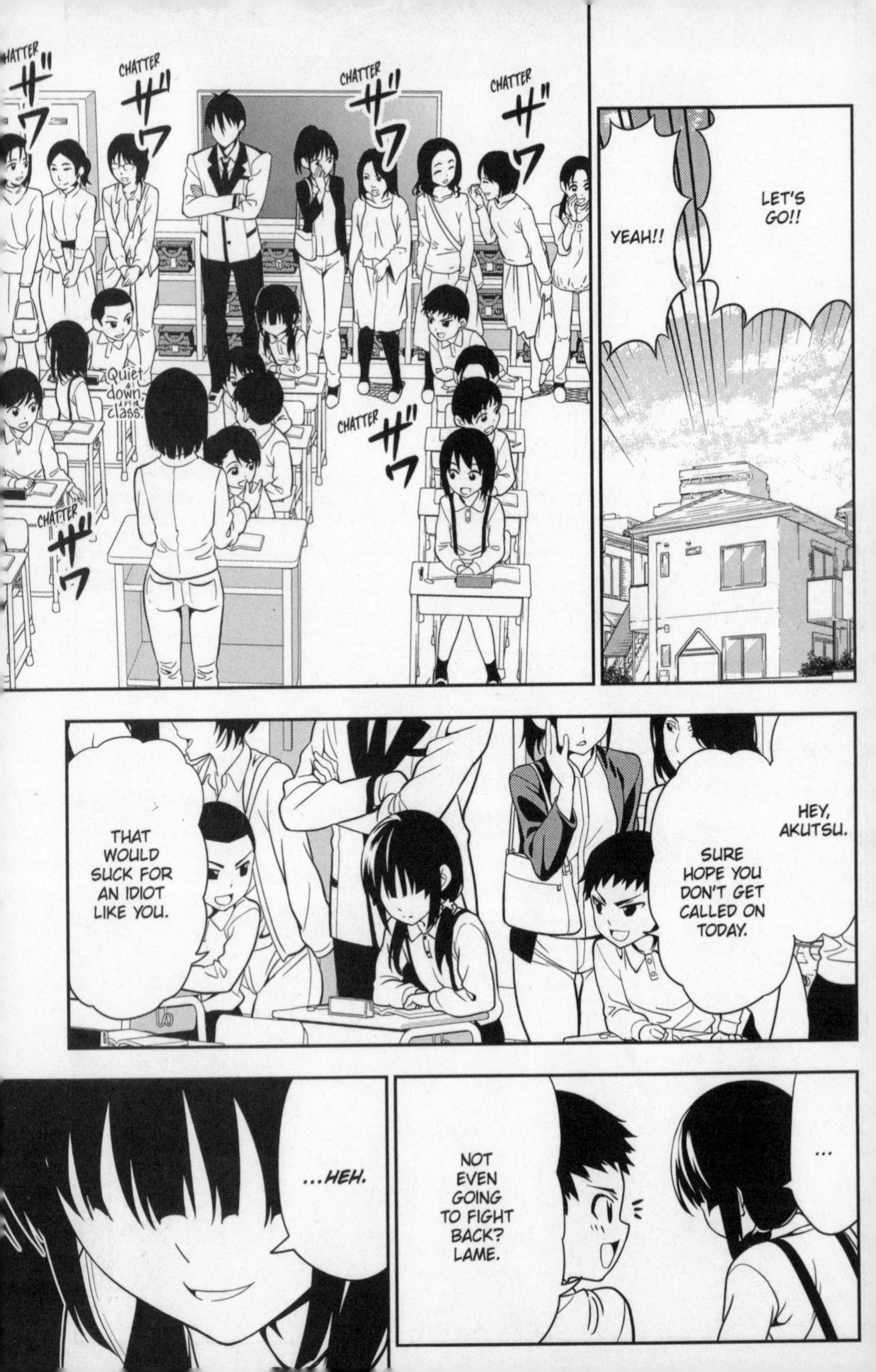
LET'S GO!!
YEAH!!
CHATTER
ザワ
CHATTER
ザワ
CHATTER
ザワ
HATTER
ザワ
Quiet down, class.
CHATTER
ザワ
CHAT-TER
ザワ
HEY, AKUTSU.
SURE HOPE YOU DON'T GET CALLED ON TODAY.
THAT WOULD SUCK FOR AN IDIOT LIKE YOU.
...
NOT EVEN GOING TO FIGHT BACK? LAME.
...HEH.

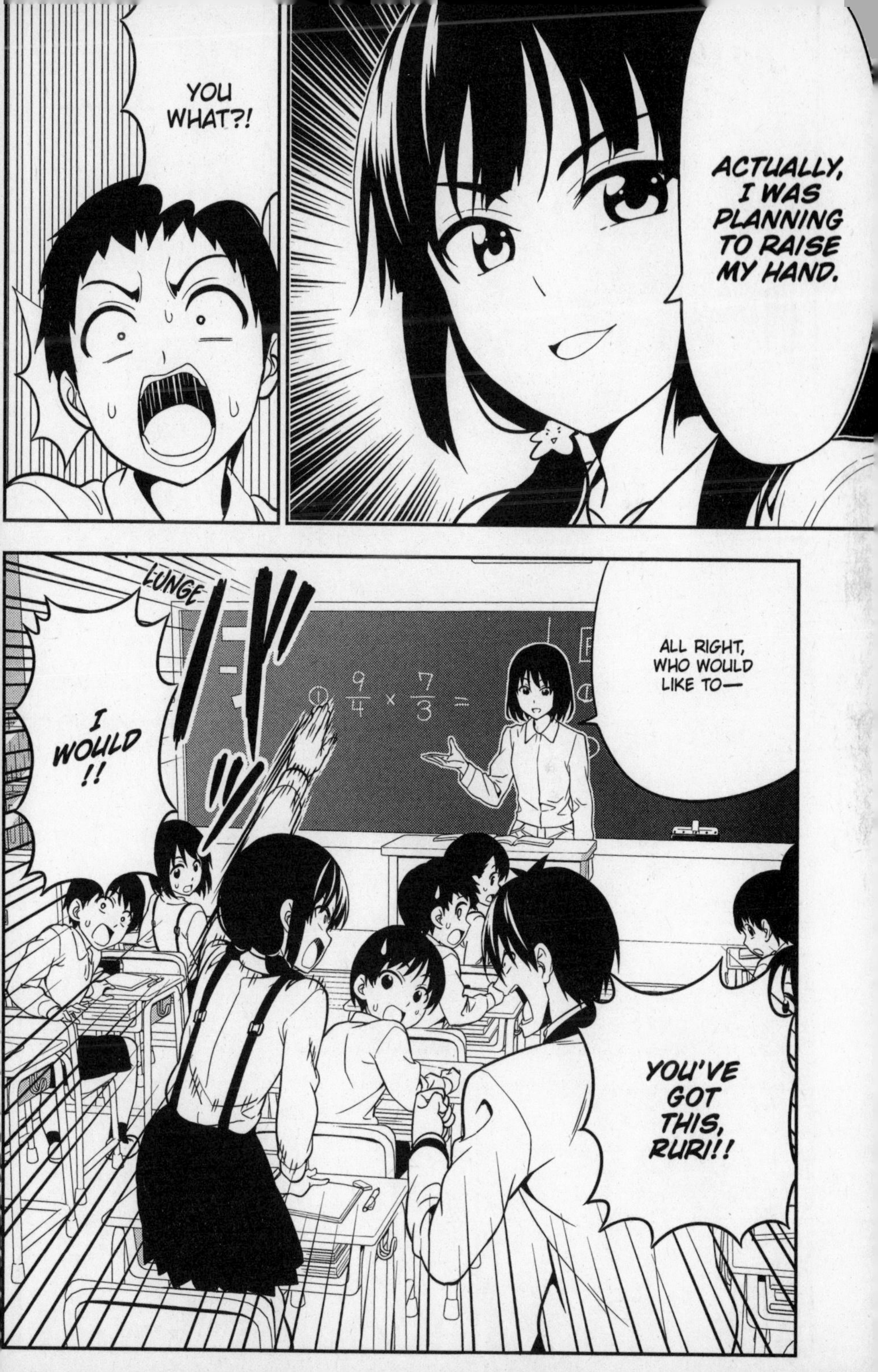
ACTUALLY, I WAS PLANNING TO RAISE MY HAND.
YOU WHAT?!
ALL RIGHT, WHO WOULD LIKE TO—
LUNGE
I WOULD!!
YOU'VE GOT THIS, RURI!!

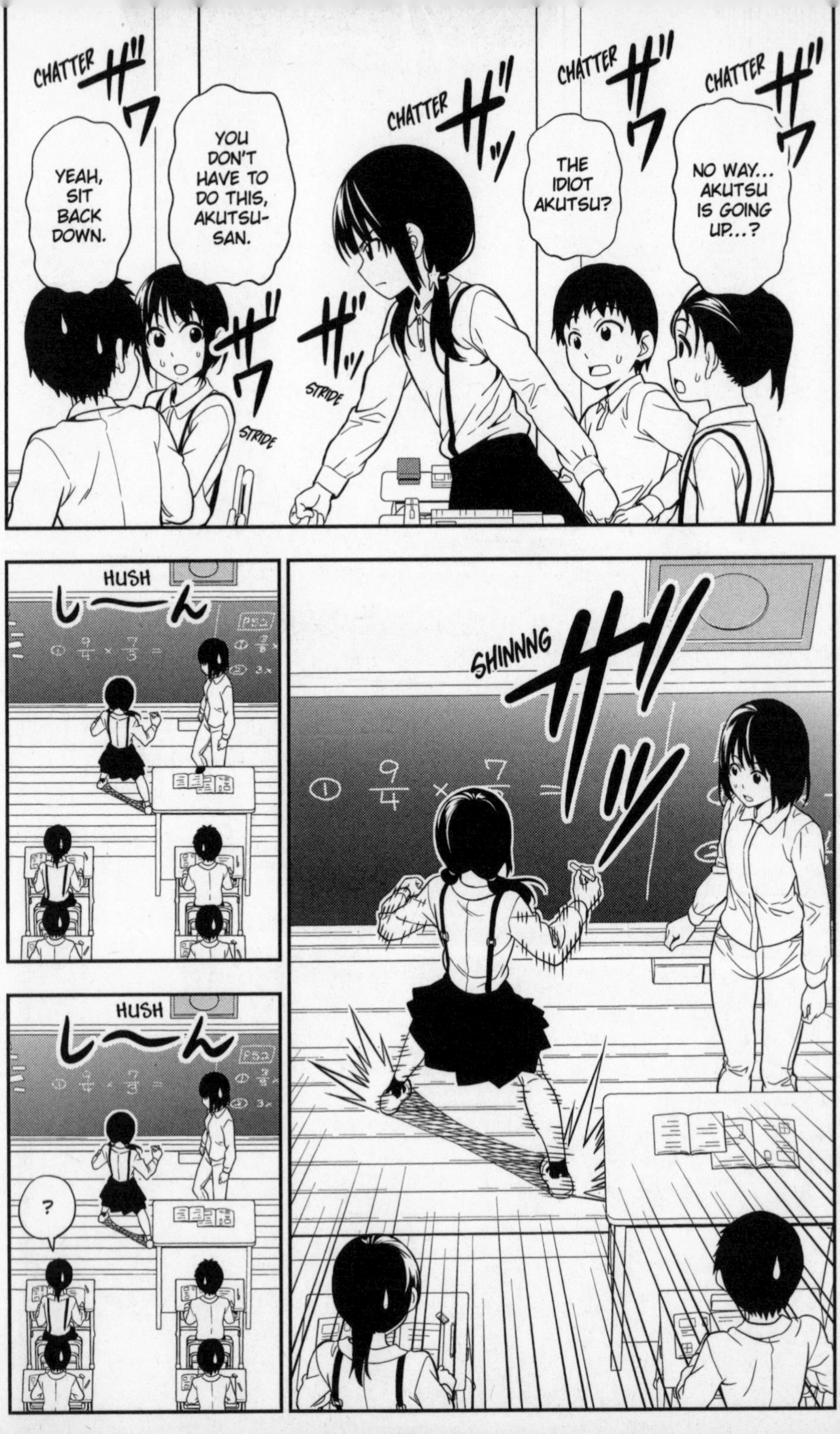
CHATTER
NO WAY... AKUTSU IS GOING UP...?
CHATTER
THE IDIOT AKUTSU?
CHATTER
CHATTER
YOU DON'T HAVE TO DO THIS, AKUTSU-SAN.
YEAH, SIT BACK DOWN.
STRIDE
STRIDE
SHINNNG
HUSH
HUSH
?

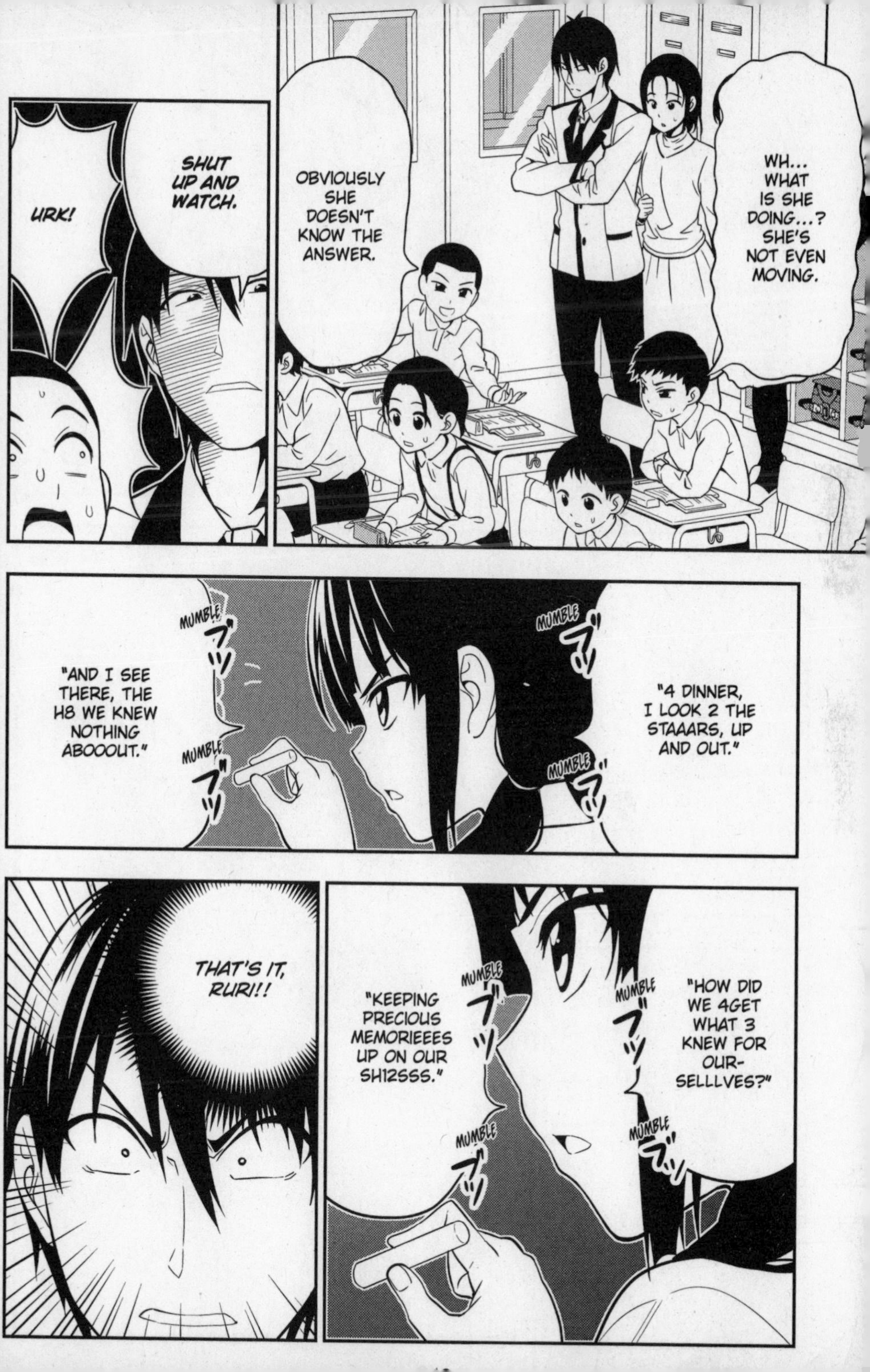
WH... WHAT IS SHE DOING...? SHE'S NOT EVEN MOVING.
OBVIOUSLY SHE DOESN'T KNOW THE ANSWER.
SHUT UP AND WATCH.
URK!
MUMBLE
MUMBLE
"4 DINNER, I LOOK 2 THE STAAARS, UP AND OUT."
MUMBLE
MUMBLE
"AND I SEE THERE, THE H8 WE KNEW NOTHING ABOOOUT."
MUMBLE
MUMBLE
"HOW DID WE 4GET WHAT 3 KNEW FOR OUR-SELLLVES?"
MUMBLE
MUMBLE
"KEEPING PRECIOUS MEMORIEEES UP ON OUR SH12SSS."
THAT'S IT, RURI!!

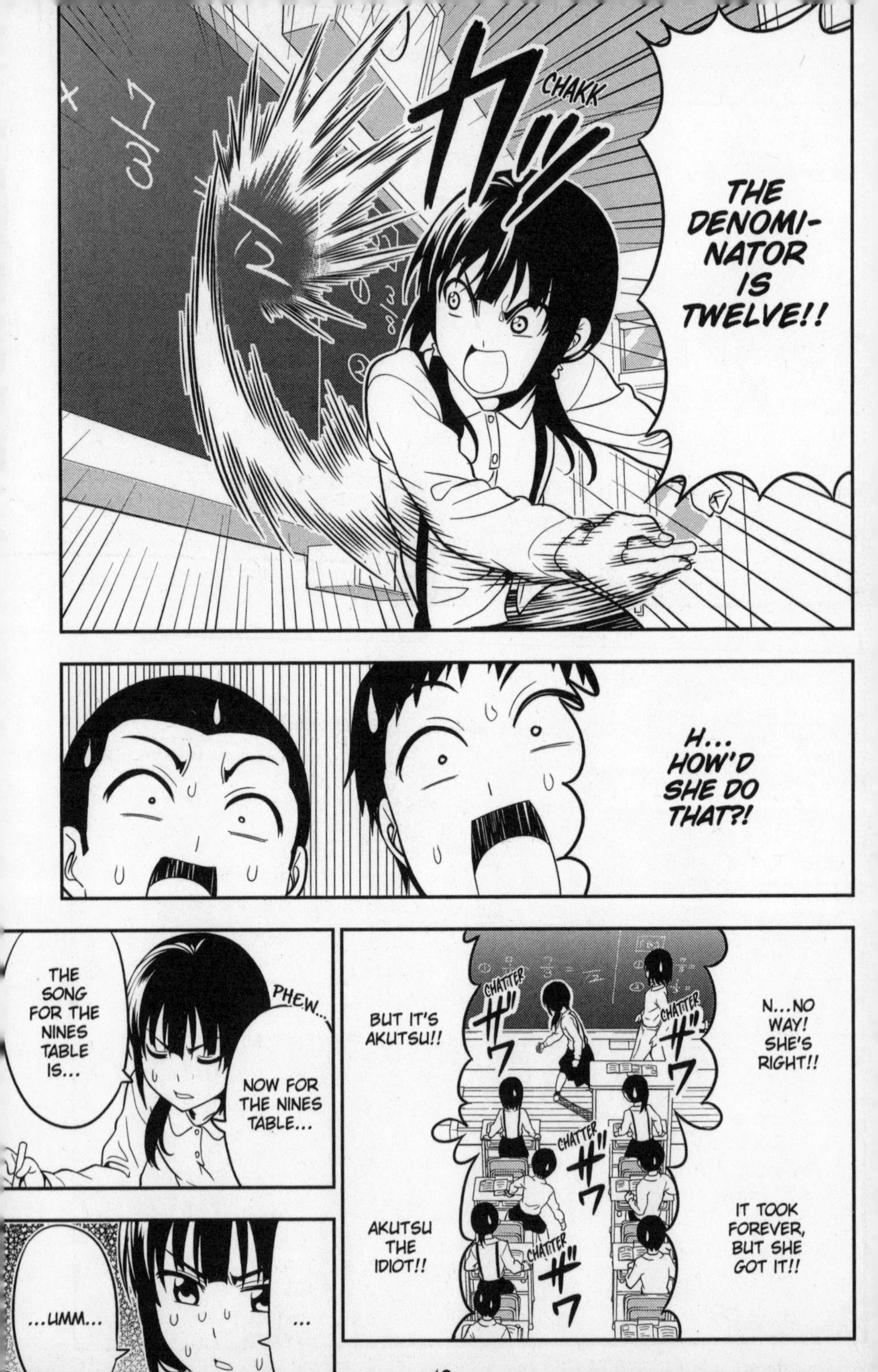
CHAKK
THE DENOMI-NATOR IS TWELVE!!
H... HOW'D SHE DO THAT?!
N...NO WAY! SHE'S RIGHT!!
CHATTER
BUT IT'S AKUTSU!!
CHATTER
CHATTER
IT TOOK FOREVER, BUT SHE GOT IT!!
AKUTSU THE IDIOT!!
CHATTER
PHEW...
NOW FOR THE NINES TABLE...
THE SONG FOR THE NINES TABLE IS...
...
...UMM...

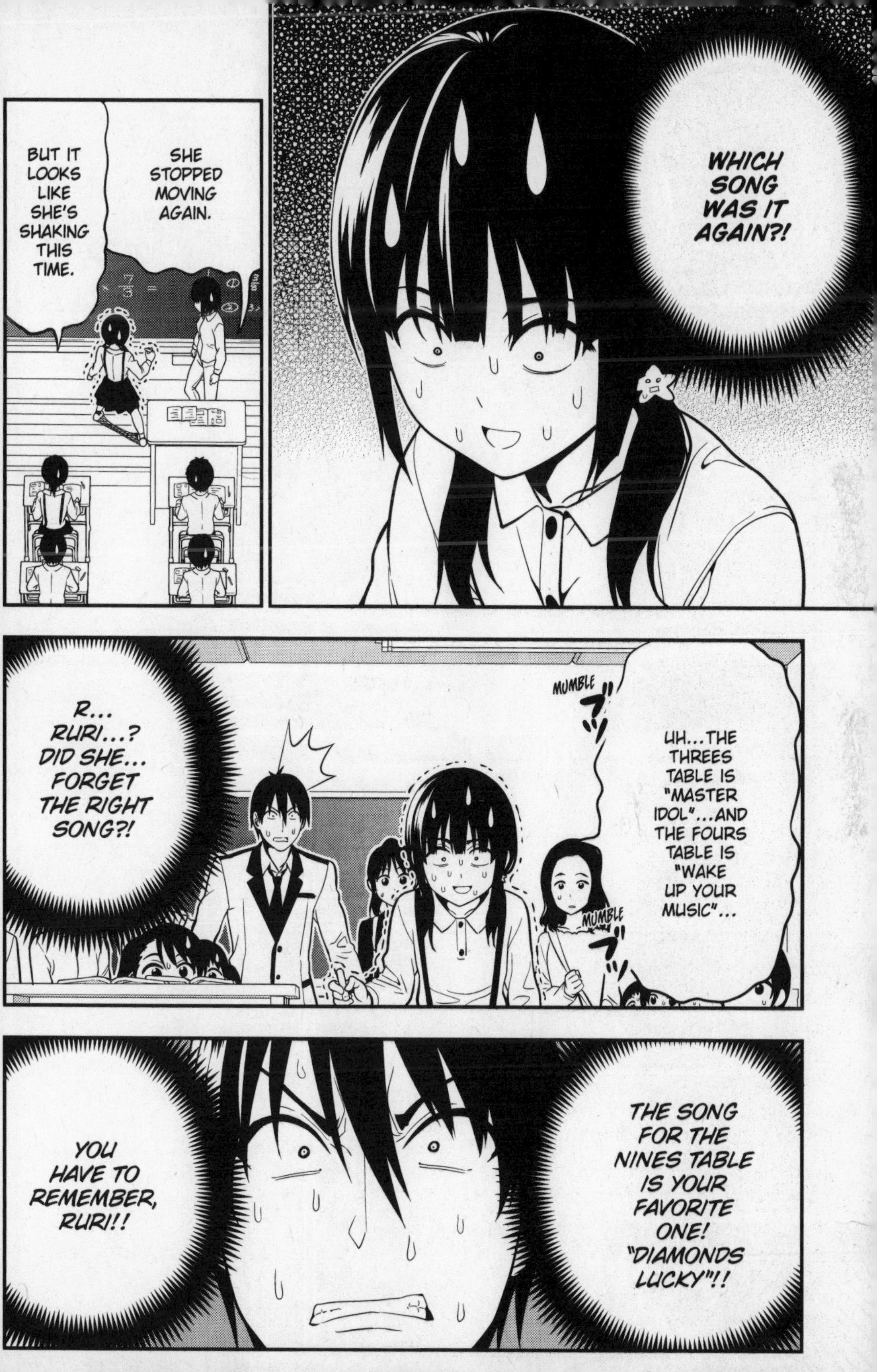
WHICH SONG WAS IT AGAIN?!
SHE STOPPED MOVING AGAIN.
BUT IT LOOKS LIKE SHE'S SHAKING THIS TIME.
MUMBLE
UH...THE THREES TABLE IS "MASTER IDOL"...AND THE FOURS TABLE IS "WAKE UP YOUR MUSIC"...
MUMBLE
R... RURI...? DID SHE... FORGET THE RIGHT SONG?!
THE SONG FOR THE NINES TABLE IS YOUR FAVORITE ONE! "DIAMONDS LUCKY"!!
YOU HAVE TO REMEMBER, RURI!!

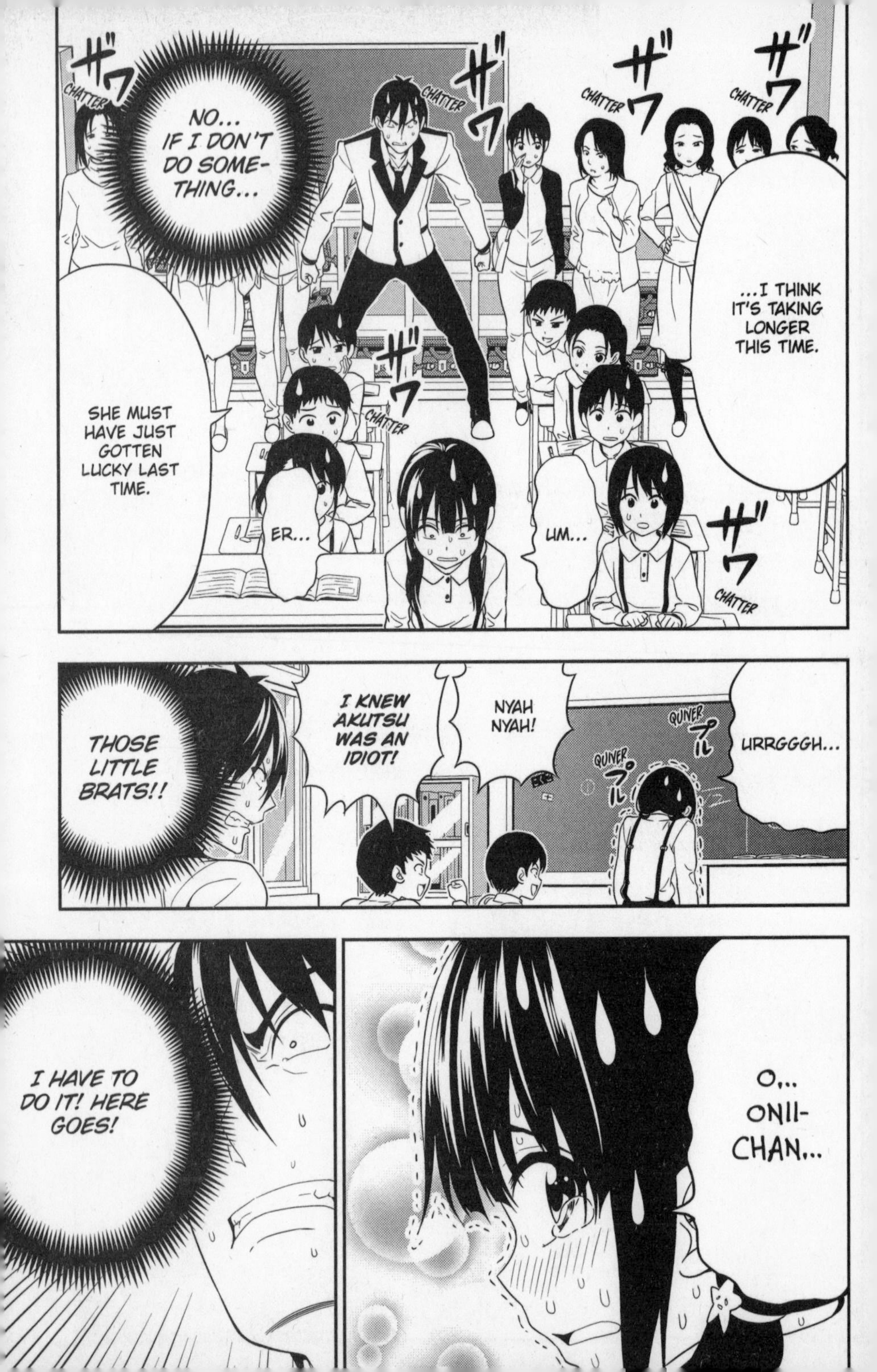
ザワ
CHATTER
ザワ
CHATTER
...I THINK IT'S TAKING LONGER THIS TIME.
ザワ
CHATTER
ザワ
CHATTER
NO... IF I DON'T DO SOME-THING...
ザワ
CHATTER
ザワ
CHATTER
ザワ
CHATTER
UM...
ER...
SHE MUST HAVE JUST GOTTEN LUCKY LAST TIME.
URRGGGH...
QUIVER
プル
QUIVER
プル
NYAH NYAH!
I KNEW AKUTSU WAS AN IDIOT!
THOSE LITTLE BRATS!!
O... ONII-CHAN...
I HAVE TO DO IT! HERE GOES!

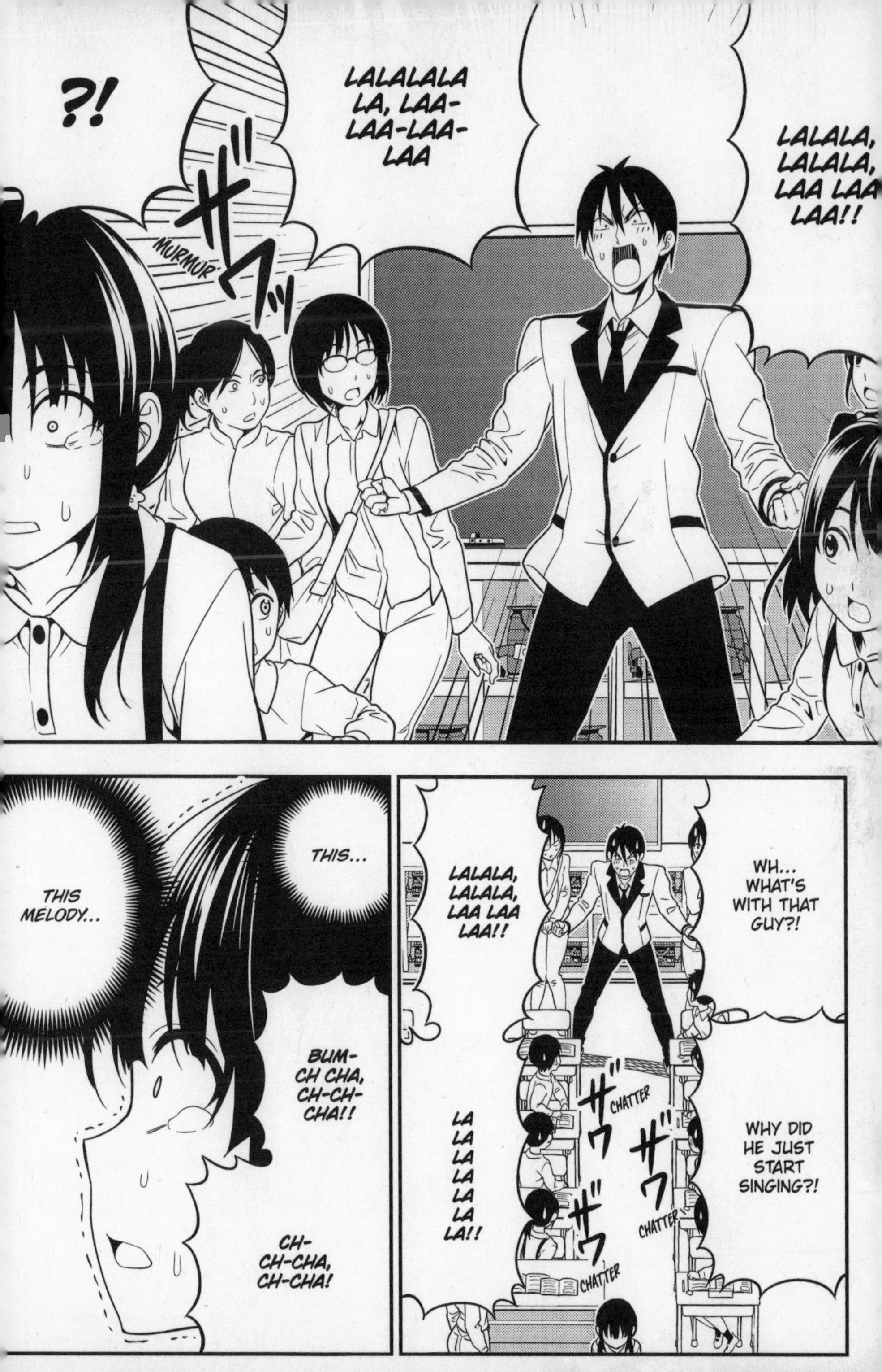
LALALA, LALALA, LAA LAA LAA!!
LALALALA LA, LAA-LAA-LAA-LAA
?!
MURMUR
WH... WHAT'S WITH THAT GUY?!
LALALA, LALALA, LAA LAA LAA!!
WHY DID HE JUST START SINGING?!
CHATTER
CHATTER
CHATTER
LA LA LA LA LA LA LA!!
THIS...
THIS MELODY...
BUM-CH CHA, CH-CH-CHA!!
CH-CH-CHA, CH-CHA!

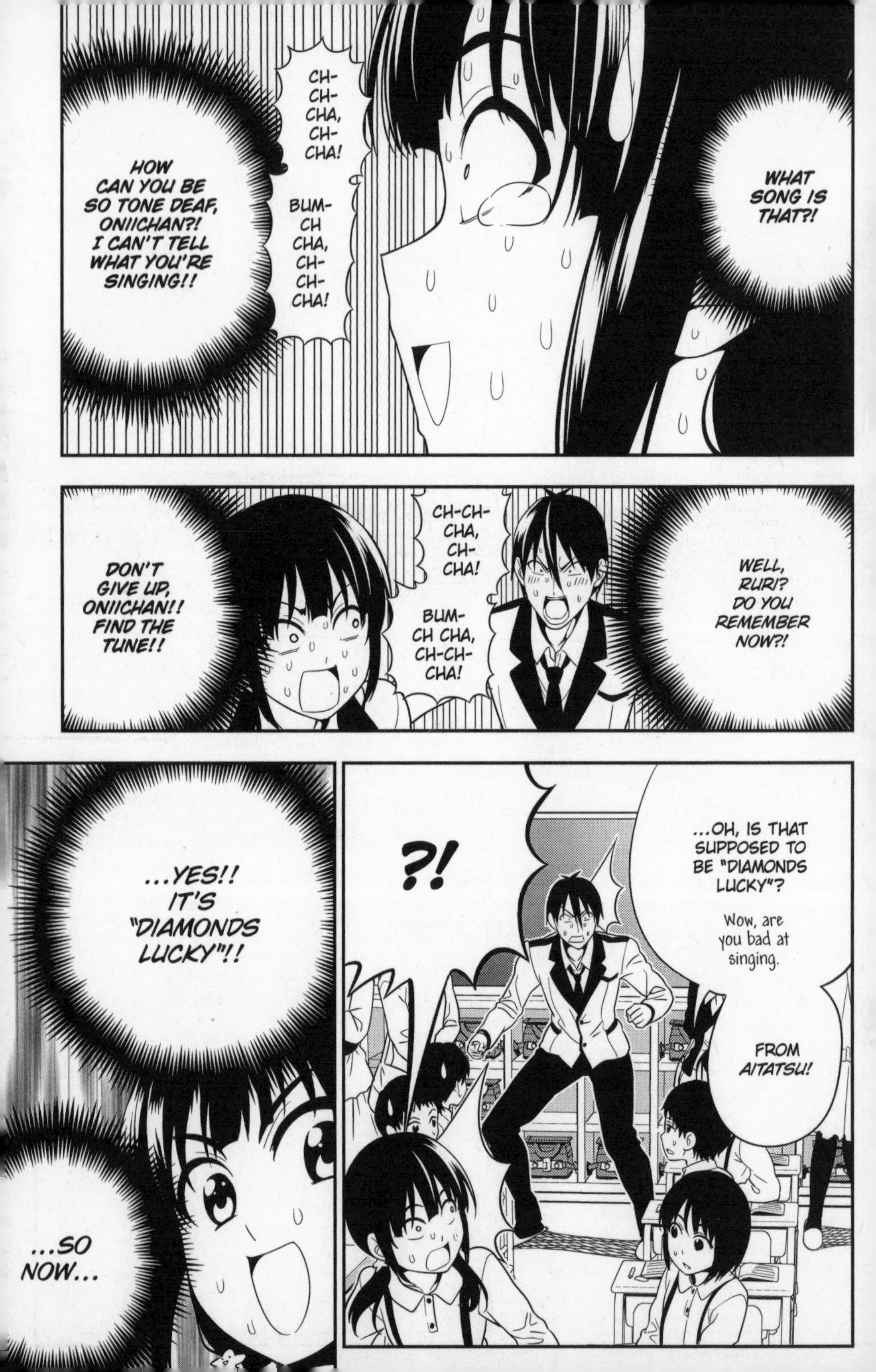
WHAT SONG IS THAT?!
CH-CH-CHA, CH-CHA!
BUM-CH CHA, CH-CH-CHA!
HOW CAN YOU BE SO TONE DEAF, ONIICHAN?! I CAN'T TELL WHAT YOU'RE SINGING!!
WELL, RURI? DO YOU REMEMBER NOW?!
CH-CH-CHA, CH-CHA!
BUM-CH CHA, CH-CH-CHA!
DON'T GIVE UP, ONIICHAN!! FIND THE TUNE!!
...OH, IS THAT SUPPOSED TO BE "DIAMONDS LUCKY"?
Wow, are you bad at singing.
FROM AITATSU!
?!
...YES!! IT'S "DIAMONDS LUCKY"!!
...SO NOW...

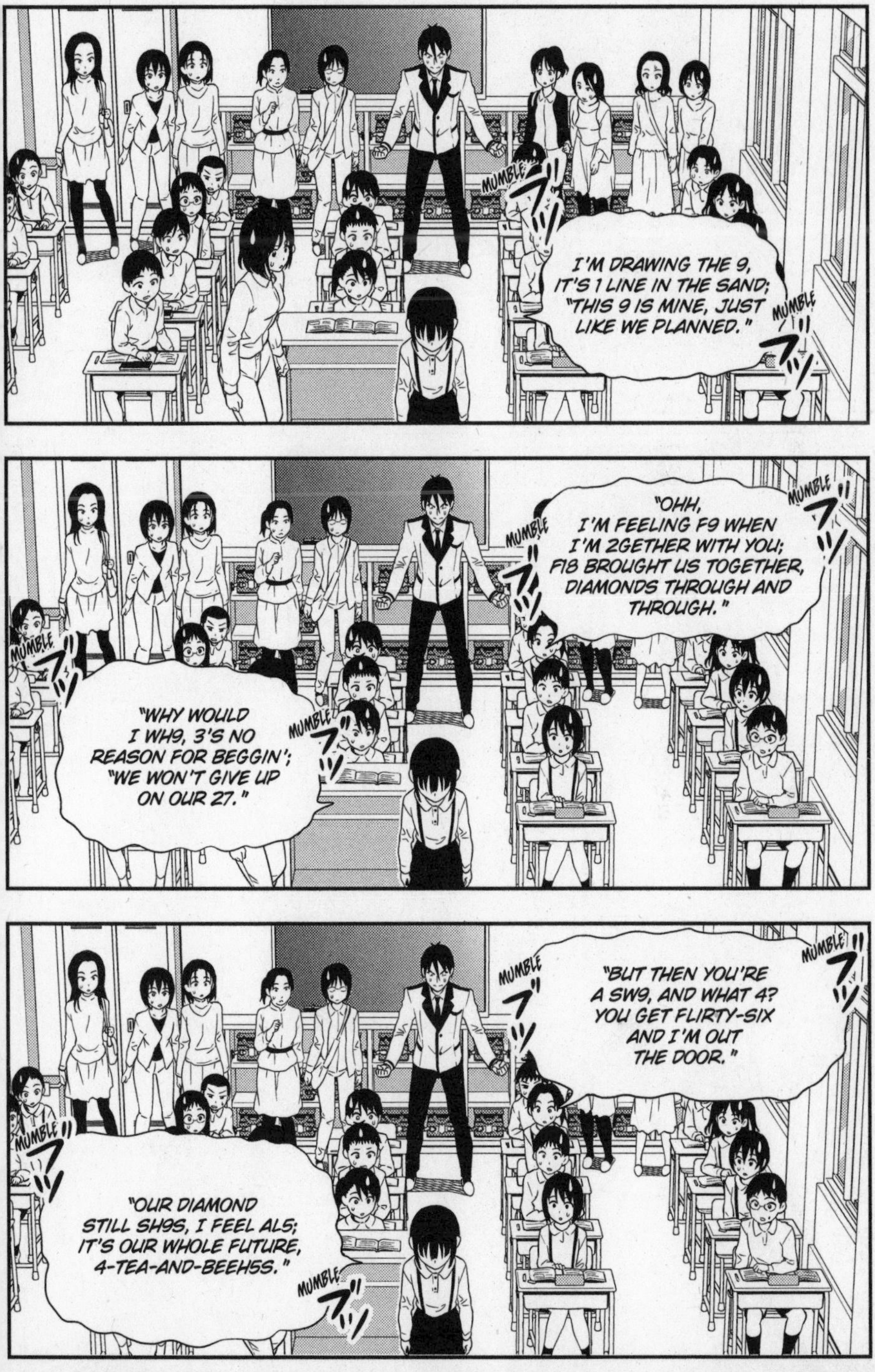
MUMBLE
I'M DRAWING THE 9, IT'S 1 LINE IN THE SAND; "THIS 9 IS MINE, JUST LIKE WE PLANNED."
MUMBLE
MUMBLE
"OHH, I'M FEELING F9 WHEN I'M 2GETHER WITH YOU; F18 BROUGHT US TOGETHER, DIAMONDS THROUGH AND THROUGH."
MUMBLE
MUMBLE
MUMBLE
"WHY WOULD I WH9, 3'S NO REASON FOR BEGGIN'; "WE WON'T GIVE UP ON OUR 27."
MUMBLE
MUMBLE
"BUT THEN YOU'RE A SW9, AND WHAT 4? YOU GET FLIRTY-SIX AND I'M OUT THE DOOR."
MUMBLE
"OUR DIAMOND STILL SH9S, I FEEL AL5; IT'S OUR WHOLE FUTURE, 4-TEA-AND-BEEHSS."
MUMBLE

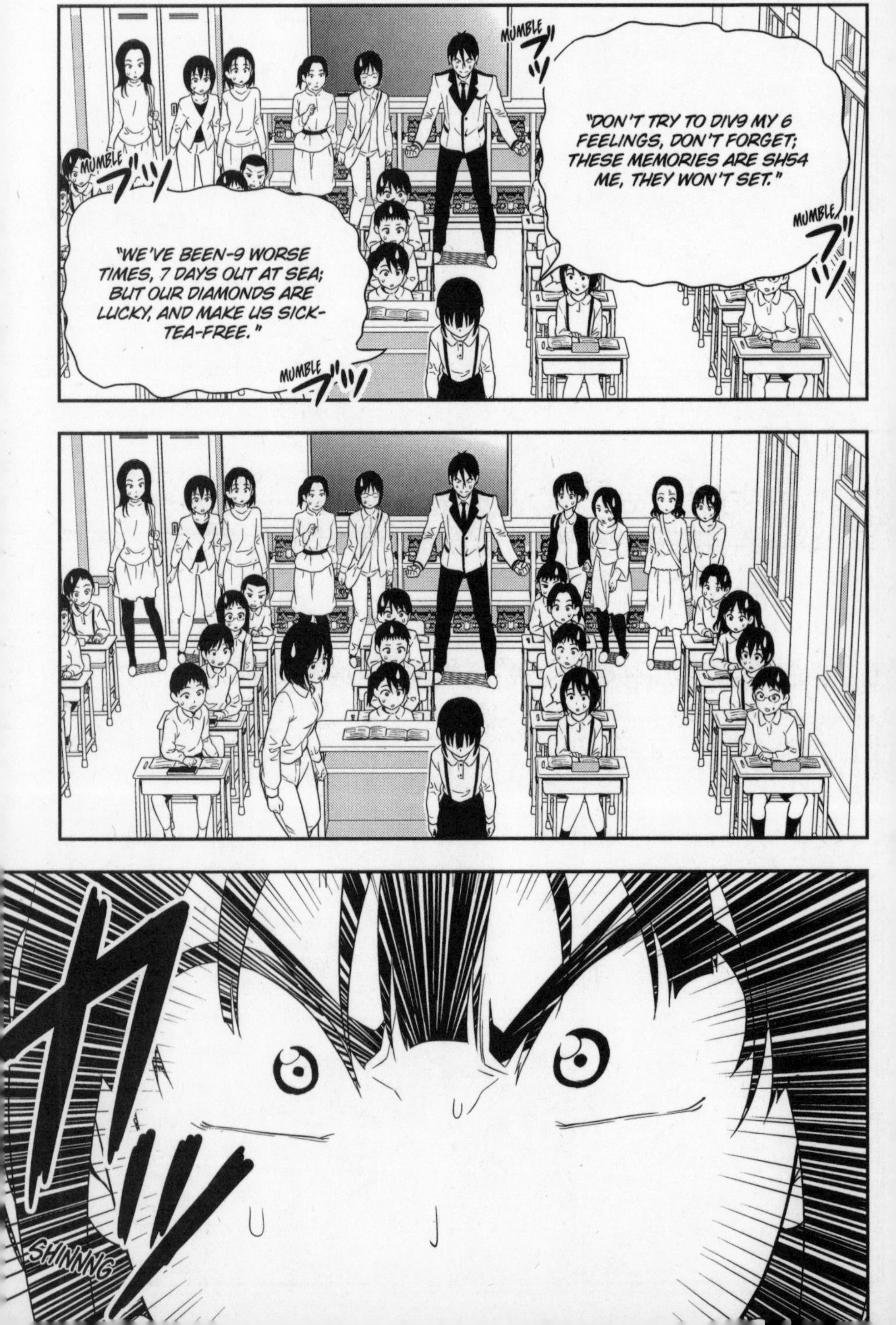
MUMBLE
"DON'T TRY TO DIV9 MY 6 FEELINGS, DON'T FORGET; THESE MEMORIES ARE SH54 ME, THEY WON'T SET."
MUMBLE
MUMBLE
"WE'VE BEEN-9 WORSE TIMES, 7 DAYS OUT AT SEA; BUT OUR DIAMONDS ARE LUCKY, AND MAKE US SICK-TEA-FREE."
MUMBLE
SHINNNG

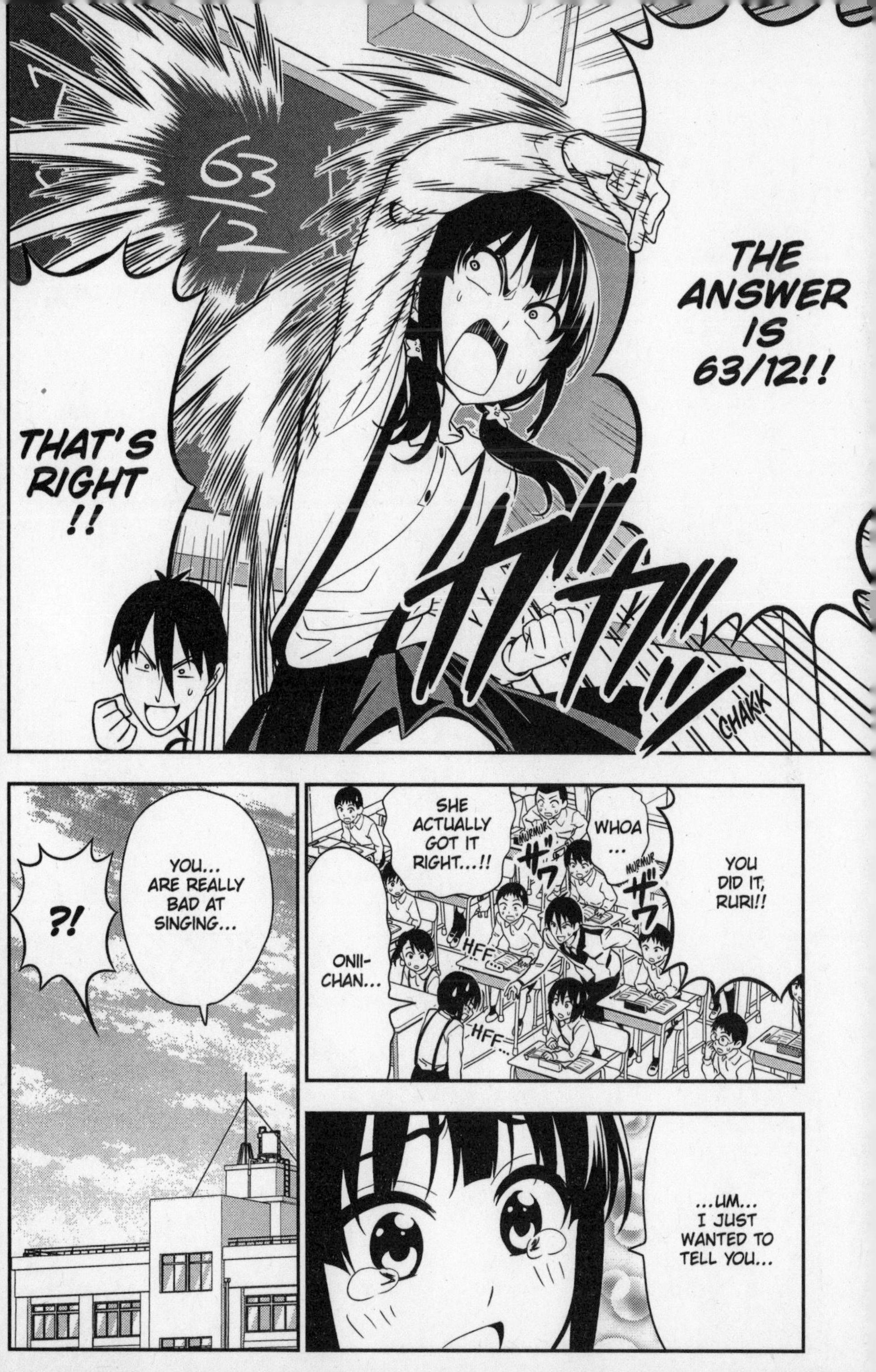
63/12
THE ANSWER IS 63/12!!
CHAKK
THAT'S RIGHT !!
YOU DID IT, RURI!!
WHOA...
MURMUR
MURMUR
SHE ACTUALLY GOT IT RIGHT...!!
ONII-CHAN...
HFF
HFF...
...UM... I JUST WANTED TO TELL YOU...
YOU... ARE REALLY BAD AT SINGING...
?!

Higher Ground

BUT... THIS ISN'T SIMPLIFIED, SO...
OH NO!!
ONII-CHAN, WHAT'S SHE TALKING ABOUT?!
IN ORDER TO SIMPLIFY... YOU HAVE TO KNOW HOW TO DIVIDE...
D... DIVISION TOO?!
A LONG ROAD AHEAD.

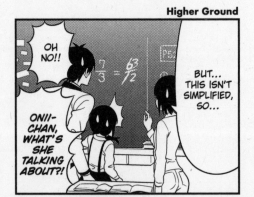

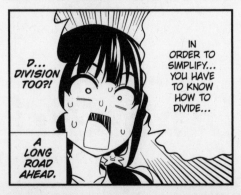

(If something looks off, take it back to)

Aho-Girl

\'ahô,gərl\ *Japanese, noun*.

A clueless girl.

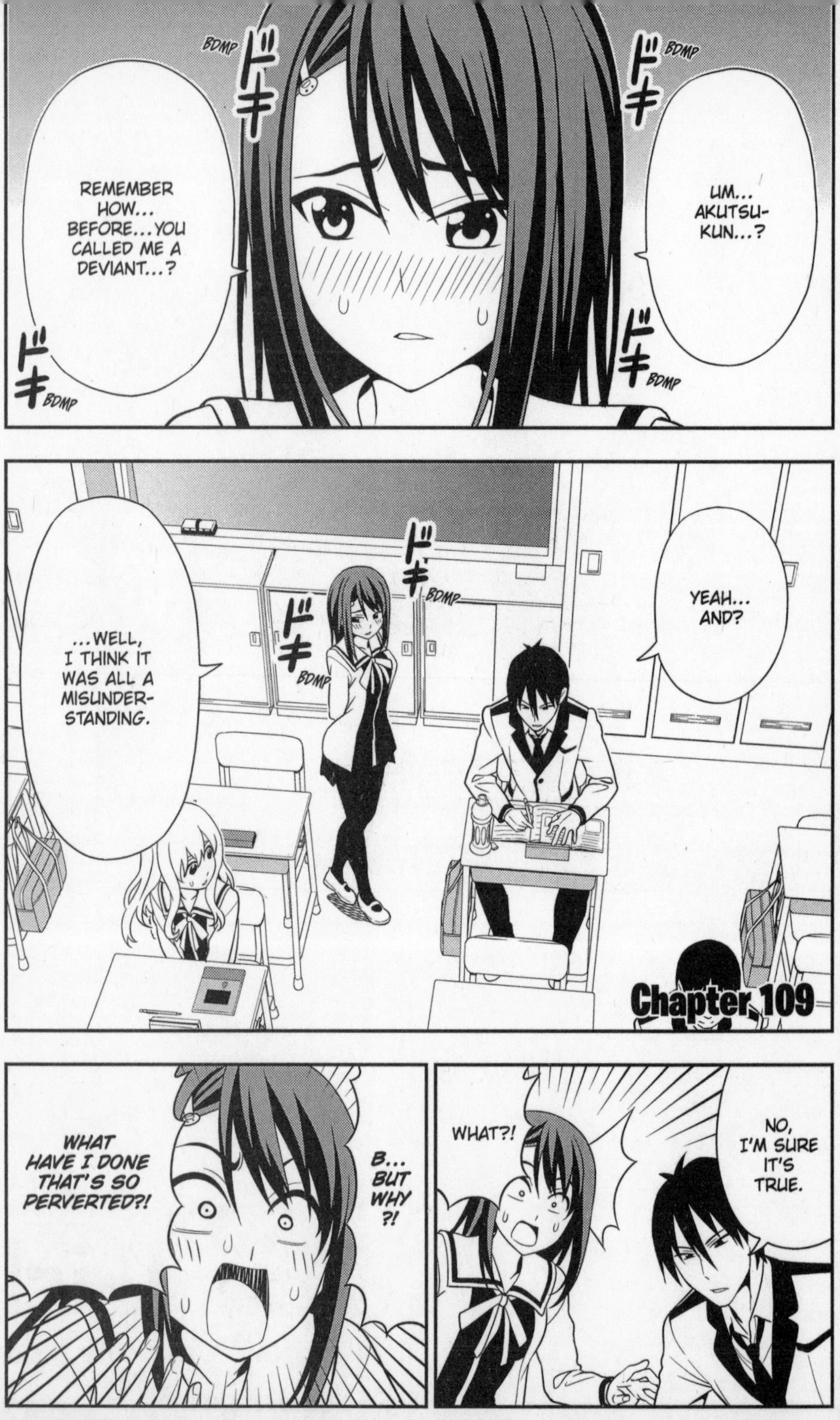
ドキ BDMP
ドキ BDMP
UM... AKUTSU-KUN...?
REMEMBER HOW... BEFORE...YOU CALLED ME A DEVIANT...?
ドキ BDMP
ドキ BDMP
YEAH... AND?
ドキ BDMP
ドキ BDMP
...WELL, I THINK IT WAS ALL A MISUNDERSTANDING.
Chapter 109
NO, I'M SURE IT'S TRUE.
WHAT?!
B... BUT WHY?!
WHAT HAVE I DONE THAT'S SO PERVERTED?!

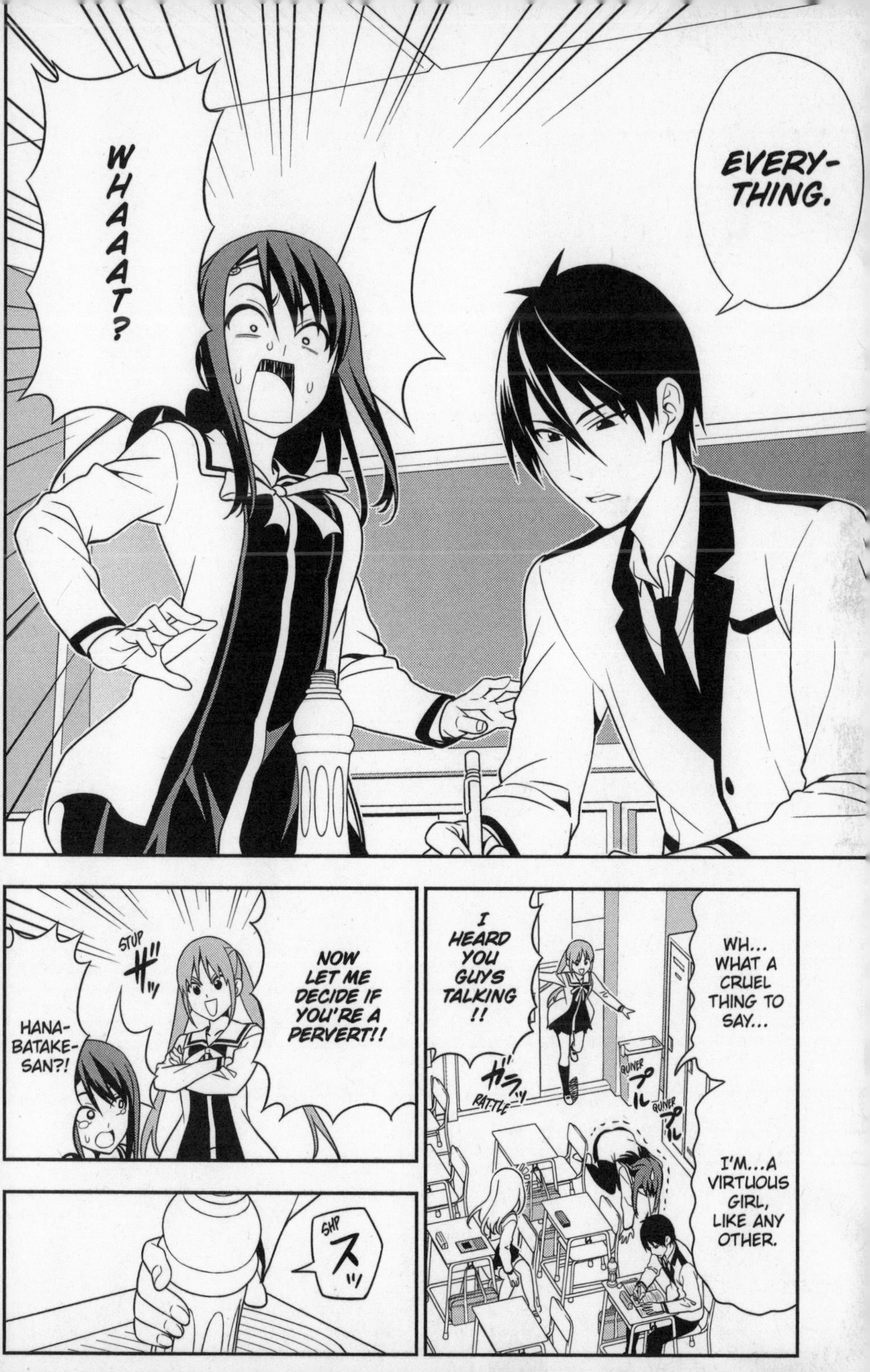
EVERY-THING.
WHAAAT?
WH... WHAT A CRUEL THING TO SAY...
QUIVER プル
QUIVER プル
I'M...A VIRTUOUS GIRL, LIKE ANY OTHER.
I HEARD YOU GUYS TALKING!!
RATTLE ガラッ
NOW LET ME DECIDE IF YOU'RE A PERVERT!!
STUP ザッ
HANA-BATAKE-SAN?!
SHP スッ

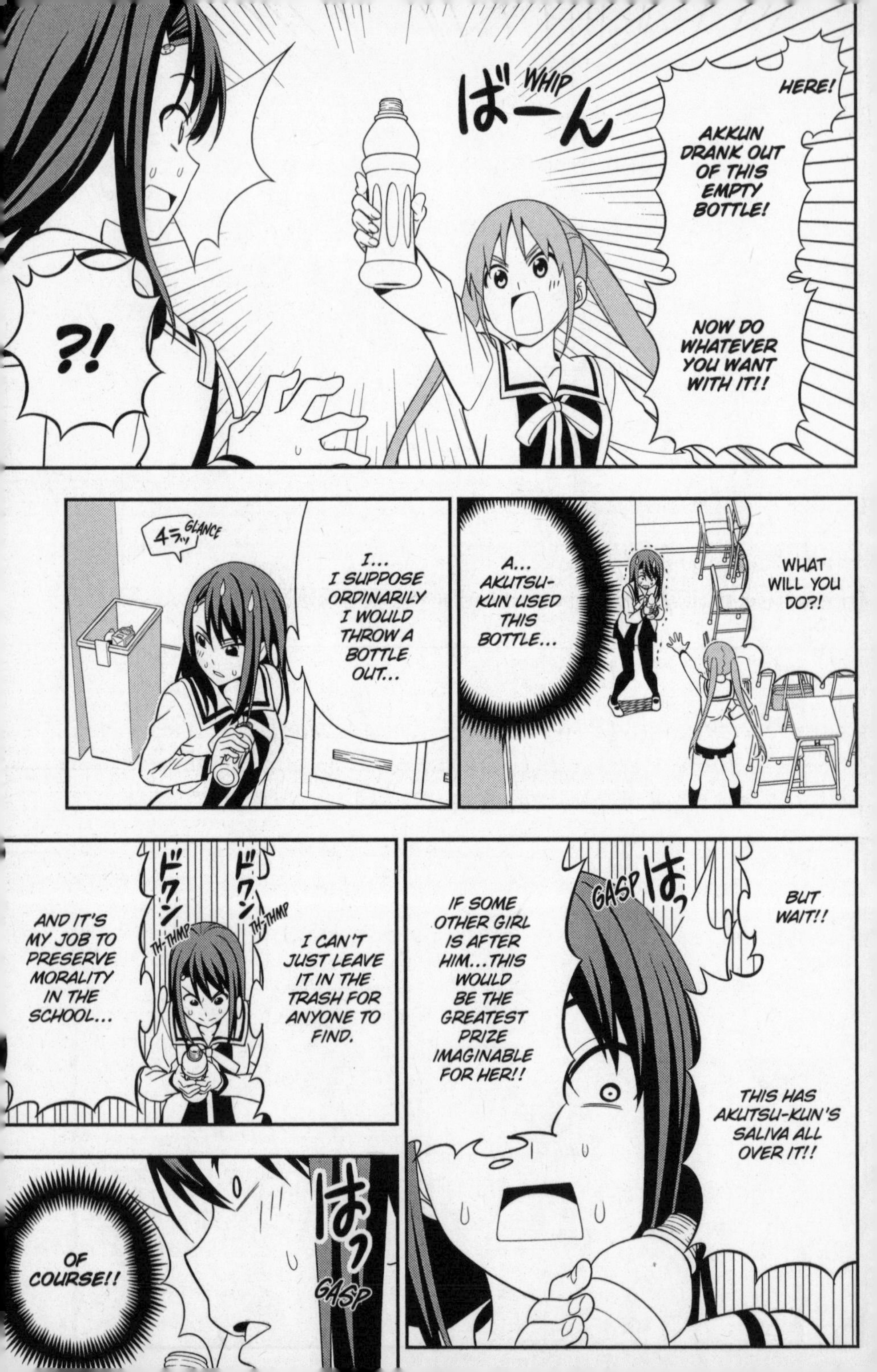
ばーん WHIP
HERE!
AKKUN DRANK OUT OF THIS EMPTY BOTTLE!
NOW DO WHATEVER YOU WANT WITH IT!!
?!
WHAT WILL YOU DO?!
A... AKUTSU-KUN USED THIS BOTTLE...
I... I SUPPOSE ORDINARILY I WOULD THROW A BOTTLE OUT...
チラッ GLANCE
BUT WAIT!!
はっ GASP
IF SOME OTHER GIRL IS AFTER HIM...THIS WOULD BE THE GREATEST PRIZE IMAGINABLE FOR HER!!
THIS HAS AKUTSU-KUN'S SALIVA ALL OVER IT!!
I CAN'T JUST LEAVE IT IN THE TRASH FOR ANYONE TO FIND.
ドクン TH-THMP
ドクン TH-THMP
AND IT'S MY JOB TO PRESERVE MORALITY IN THE SCHOOL...
はっ GASP
OF COURSE!!

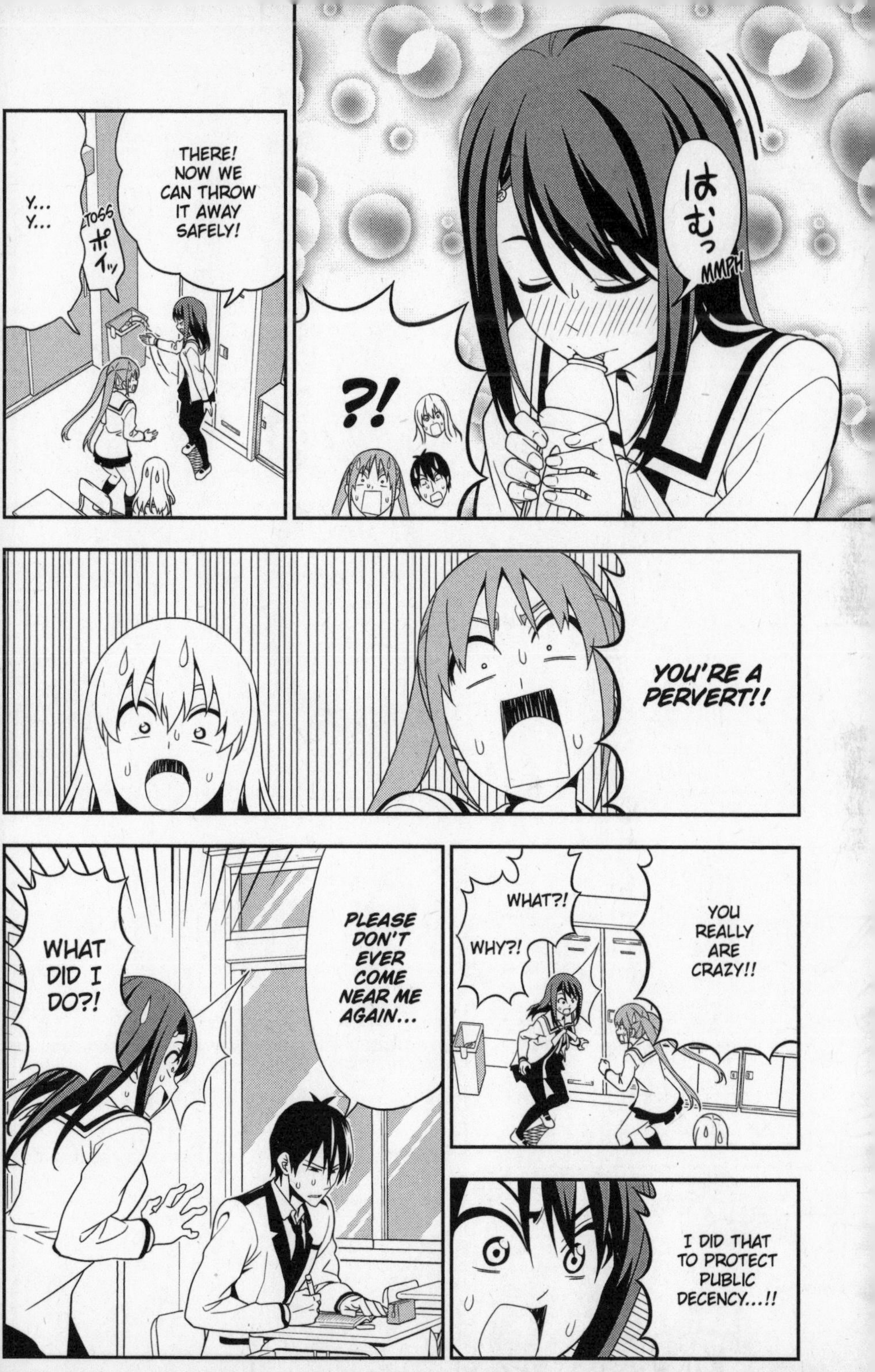
はむっ
MMPH
?!
THERE! NOW WE CAN THROW IT AWAY SAFELY!
TOSS
ポイッ
Y... Y...
YOU'RE A PERVERT!!
YOU REALLY ARE CRAZY!!
WHAT?!
WHY?!
I DID THAT TO PROTECT PUBLIC DECENCY...!!
PLEASE DON'T EVER COME NEAR ME AGAIN...
WHAT DID I DO?!

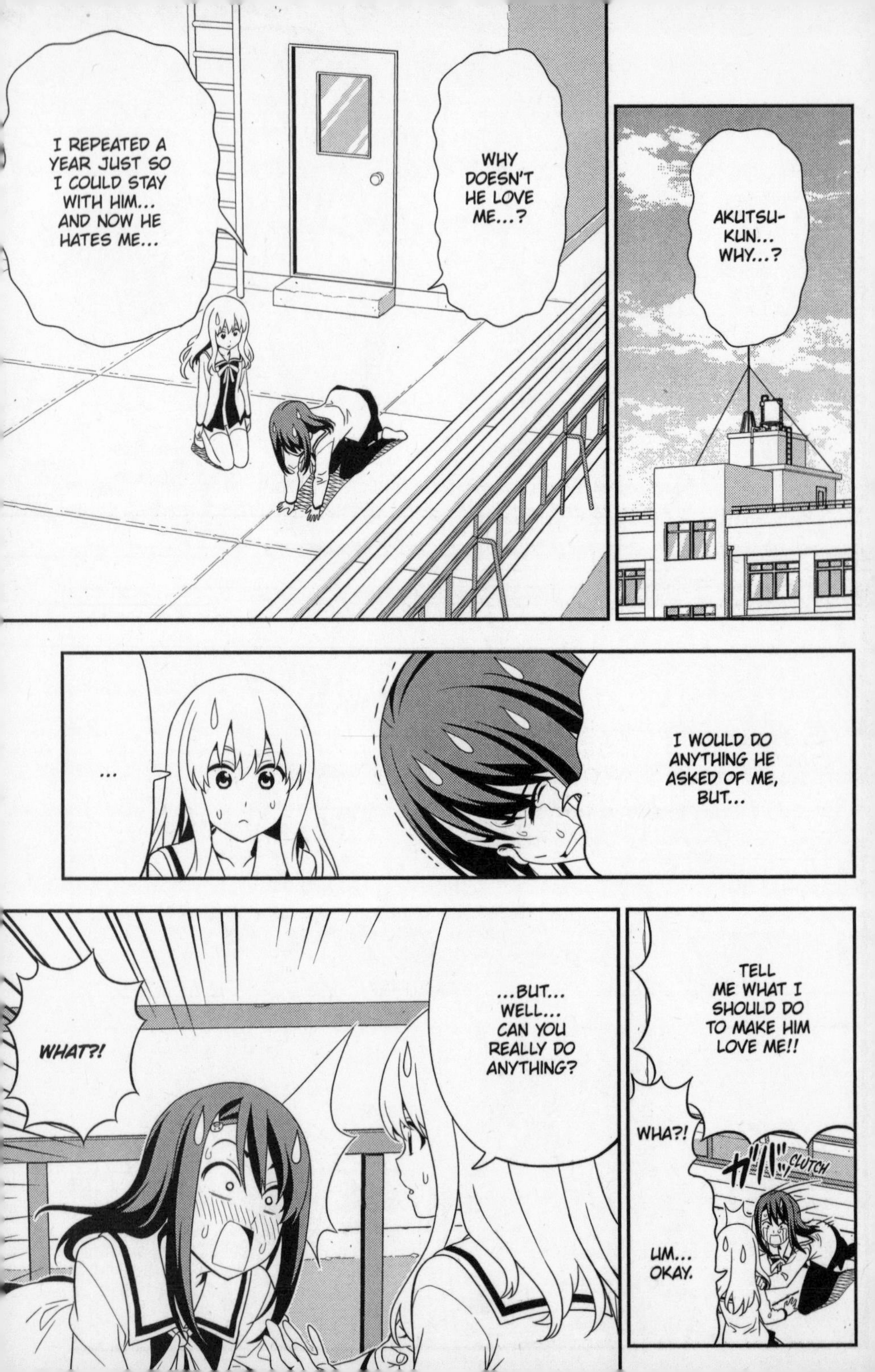
AKUTSU-KUN... WHY...?
WHY DOESN'T HE LOVE ME...?
I REPEATED A YEAR JUST SO I COULD STAY WITH HIM... AND NOW HE HATES ME...
I WOULD DO ANYTHING HE ASKED OF ME, BUT...
...
TELL ME WHAT I SHOULD DO TO MAKE HIM LOVE ME!!
WHA?!
CLUTCH
UM... OKAY.
...BUT... WELL... CAN YOU REALLY DO ANYTHING?
WHAT?!

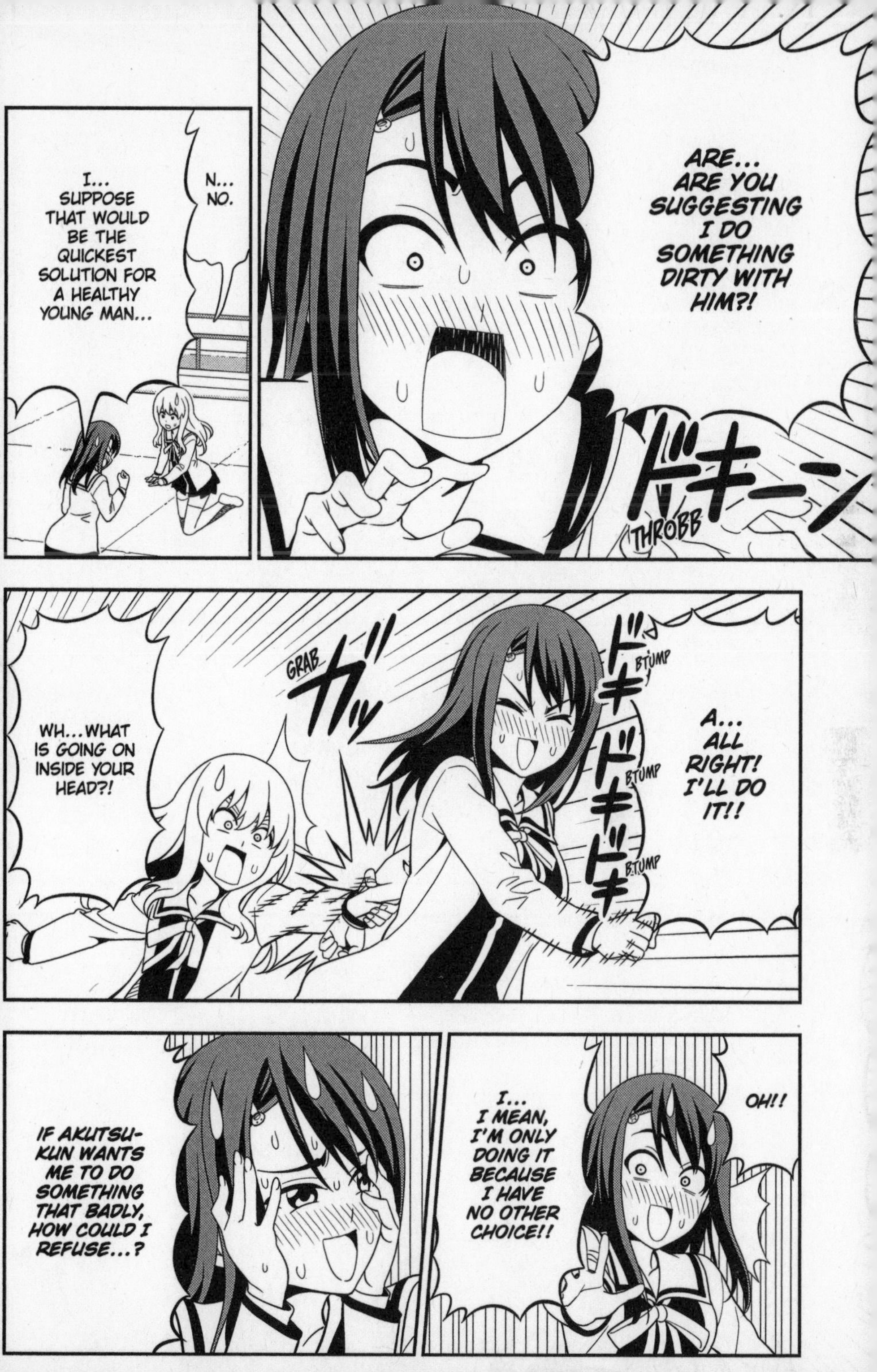
ARE... ARE YOU SUGGESTING I DO SOMETHING DIRTY WITH HIM?!
ドキーン
THROBB
N... NO.
I... SUPPOSE THAT WOULD BE THE QUICKEST SOLUTION FOR A HEALTHY YOUNG MAN...
A... ALL RIGHT! I'LL DO IT!!
ドキドキドキ
BTUMP
BTUMP
BTUMP
ガッ
GRAB
WH...WHAT IS GOING ON INSIDE YOUR HEAD?!
OH!!
I... I MEAN, I'M ONLY DOING IT BECAUSE I HAVE NO OTHER CHOICE!!
IF AKUTSU-KUN WANTS ME TO DO SOMETHING THAT BADLY, HOW COULD I REFUSE...?

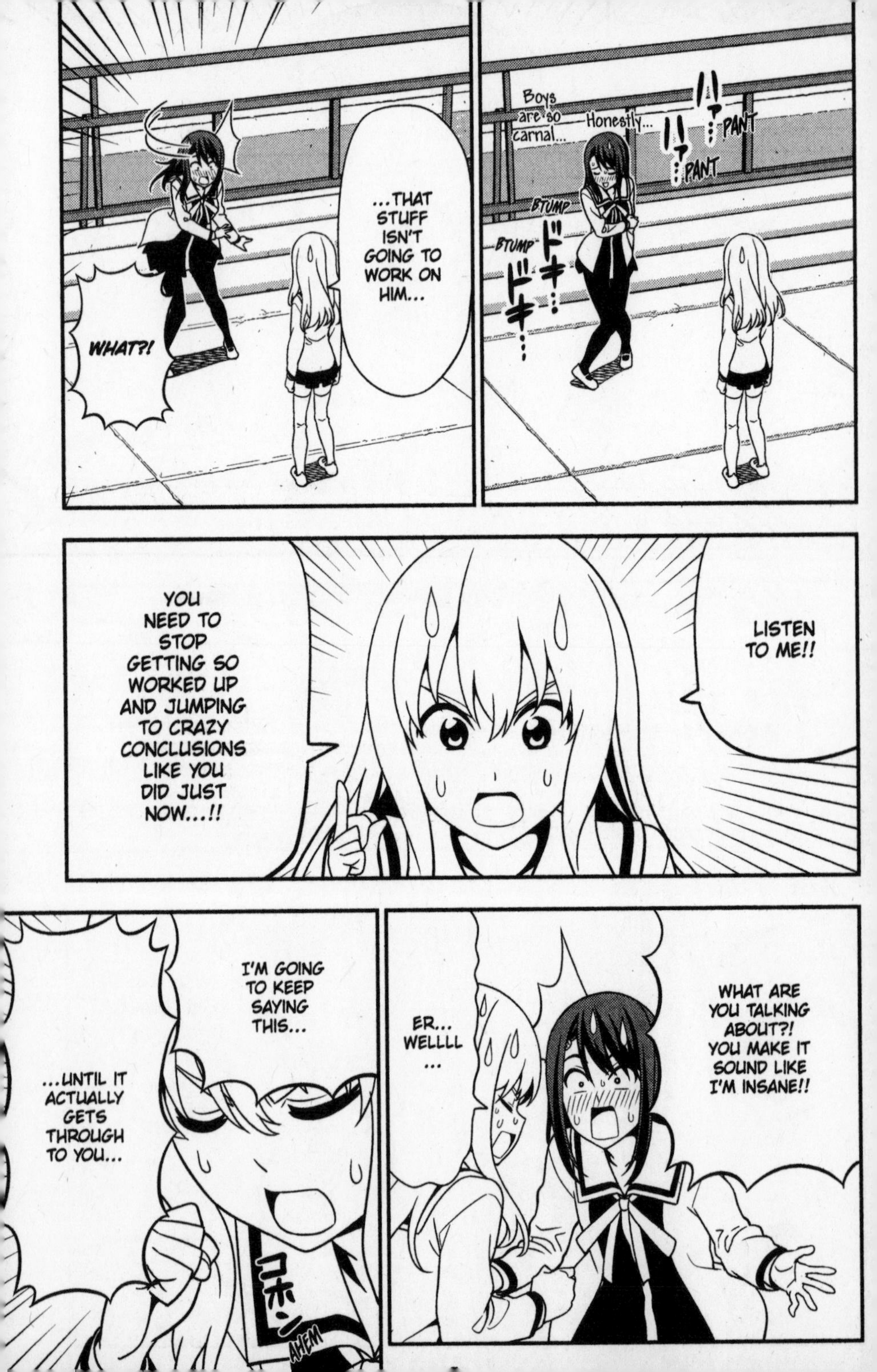
ハァ…ハァ…
PANT PANT
Honestly...
Boys are so carnal...
ドキ…ドキ…
BTUMP BTUMP
...THAT STUFF ISN'T GOING TO WORK ON HIM...
WHAT?!
LISTEN TO ME!!
YOU NEED TO STOP GETTING SO WORKED UP AND JUMPING TO CRAZY CONCLUSIONS LIKE YOU DID JUST NOW...!!
WHAT ARE YOU TALKING ABOUT?! YOU MAKE IT SOUND LIKE I'M INSANE!!
ER... WELLLL...
I'M GOING TO KEEP SAYING THIS...
...UNTIL IT ACTUALLY GETS THROUGH TO YOU...
コホン
AHEM

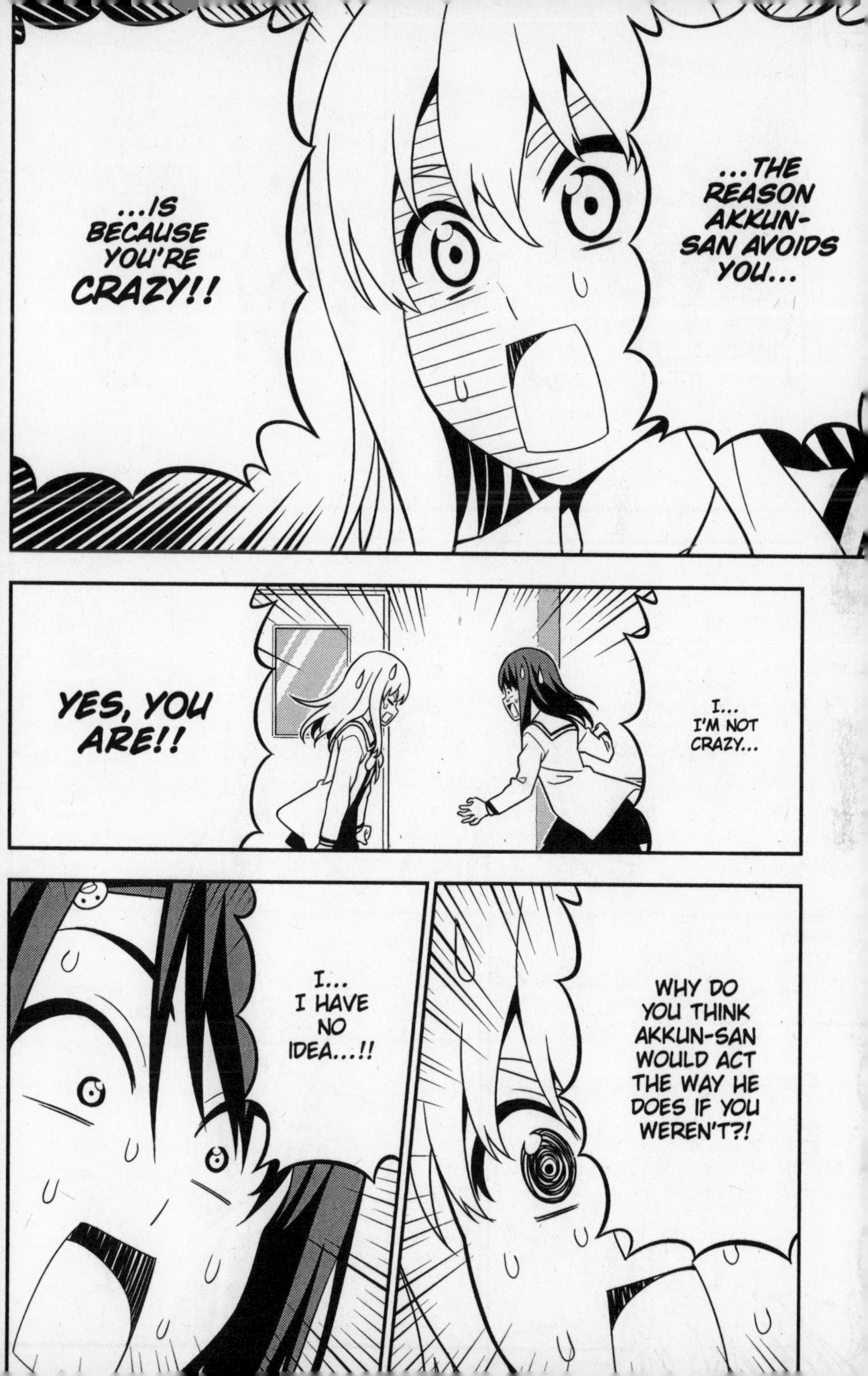
...THE REASON AKKUN-SAN AVOIDS YOU...
...IS BECAUSE YOU'RE CRAZY!!
I... I'M NOT CRAZY...
YES, YOU ARE!!
WHY DO YOU THINK AKKUN-SAN WOULD ACT THE WAY HE DOES IF YOU WEREN'T?!
I... I HAVE NO IDEA...!!

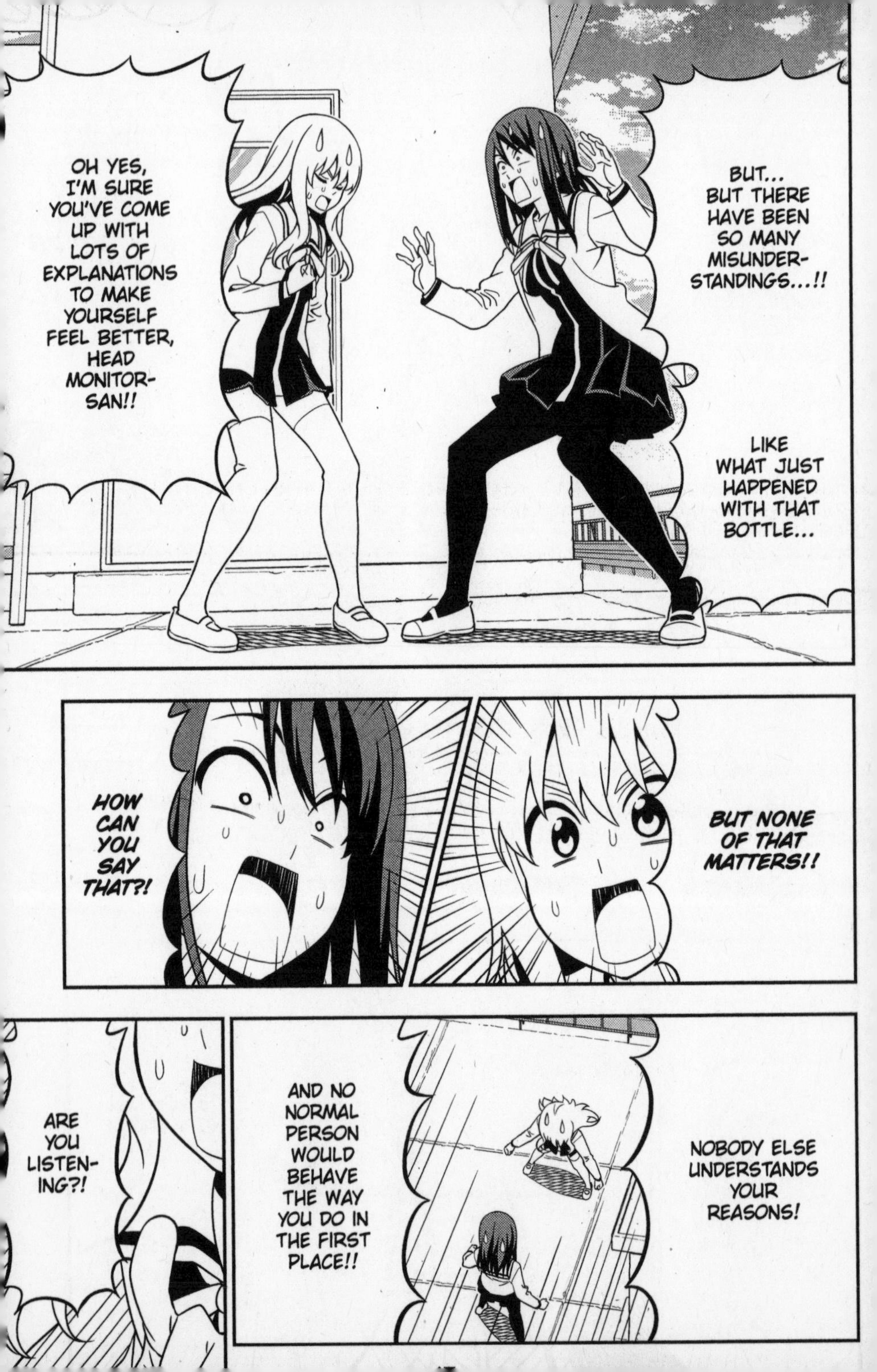
BUT... BUT THERE HAVE BEEN SO MANY MISUNDER-STANDINGS...!!
LIKE WHAT JUST HAPPENED WITH THAT BOTTLE...
OH YES, I'M SURE YOU'VE COME UP WITH LOTS OF EXPLANATIONS TO MAKE YOURSELF FEEL BETTER, HEAD MONITOR-SAN!!
BUT NONE OF THAT MATTERS!!
HOW CAN YOU SAY THAT?!
NOBODY ELSE UNDERSTANDS YOUR REASONS!
AND NO NORMAL PERSON WOULD BEHAVE THE WAY YOU DO IN THE FIRST PLACE!!
ARE YOU LISTEN-ING?!

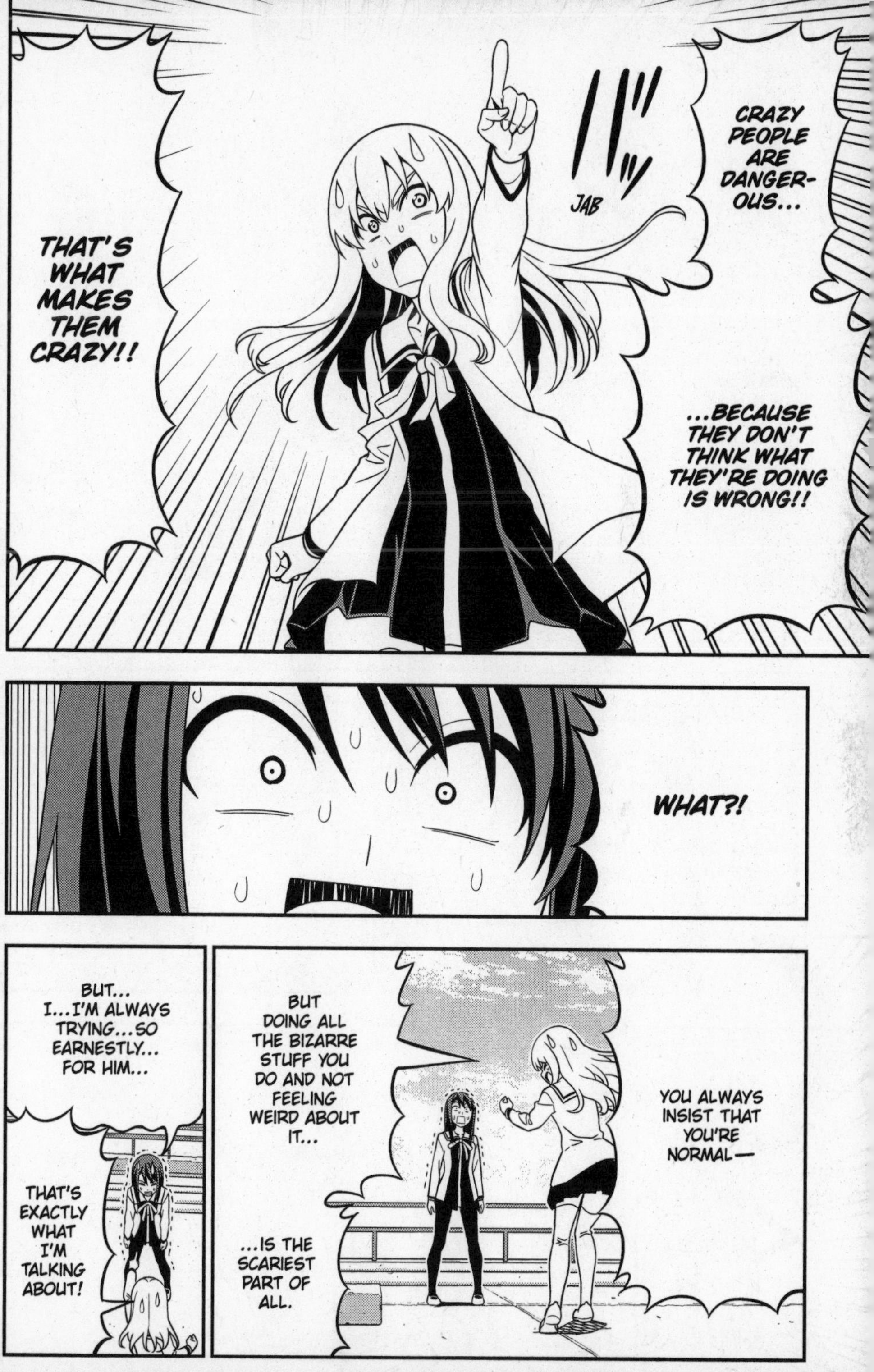
CRAZY PEOPLE ARE DANGER-OUS...
JAB
...BECAUSE THEY DON'T THINK WHAT THEY'RE DOING IS WRONG!!
THAT'S WHAT MAKES THEM CRAZY!!
WHAT?!
YOU ALWAYS INSIST THAT YOU'RE NORMAL—
BUT DOING ALL THE BIZARRE STUFF YOU DO AND NOT FEELING WEIRD ABOUT IT...
...IS THE SCARIEST PART OF ALL.
BUT... I...I'M ALWAYS TRYING...SO EARNESTLY... FOR HIM...
THAT'S EXACTLY WHAT I'M TALKING ABOUT!

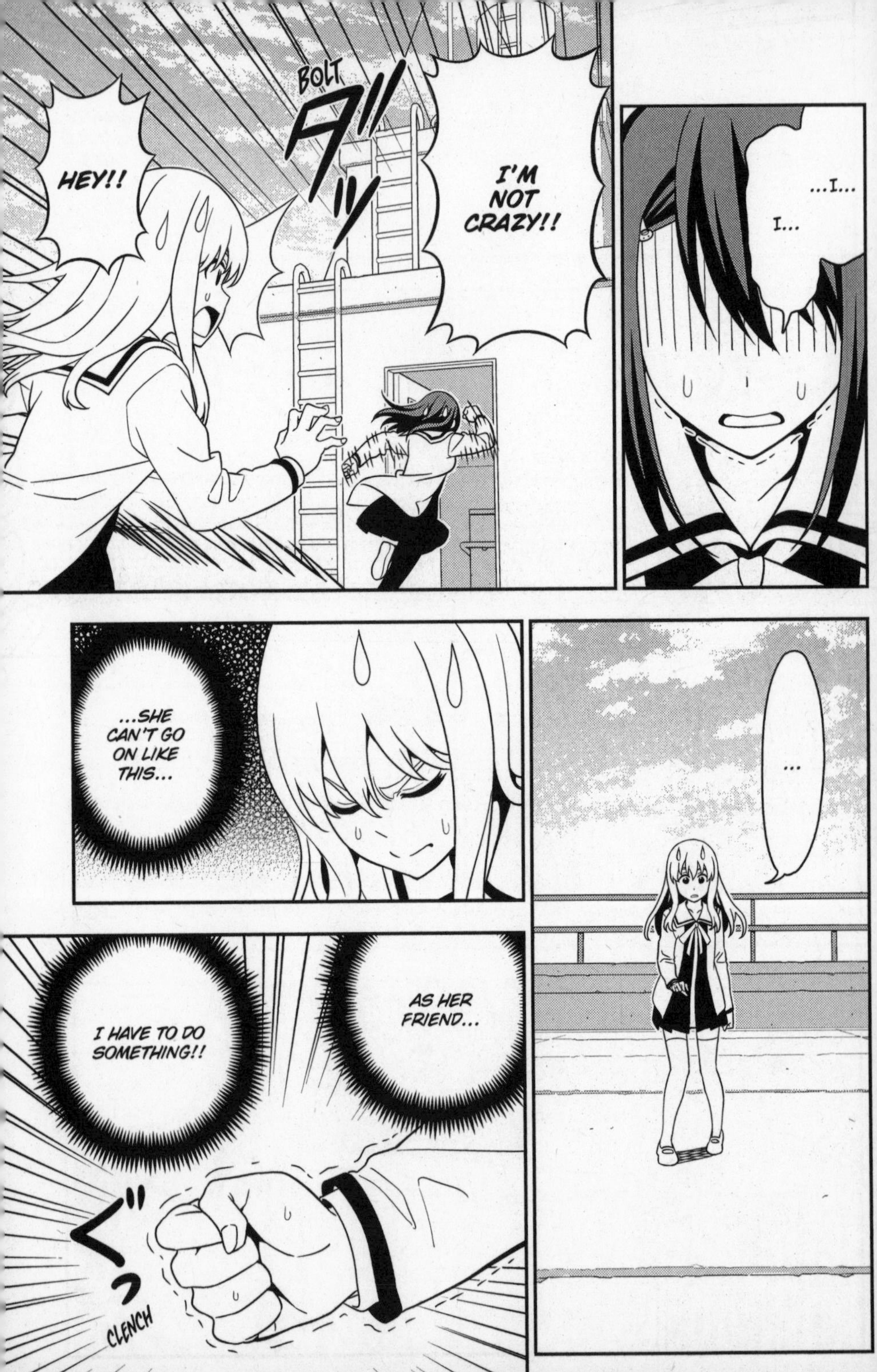
...I...
I...
I'M NOT CRAZY!!
BOLT
ダッ
HEY!!
...
...SHE CAN'T GO ON LIKE THIS...
AS HER FRIEND...
I HAVE TO DO SOMETHING!!
ぐっ
CLENCH

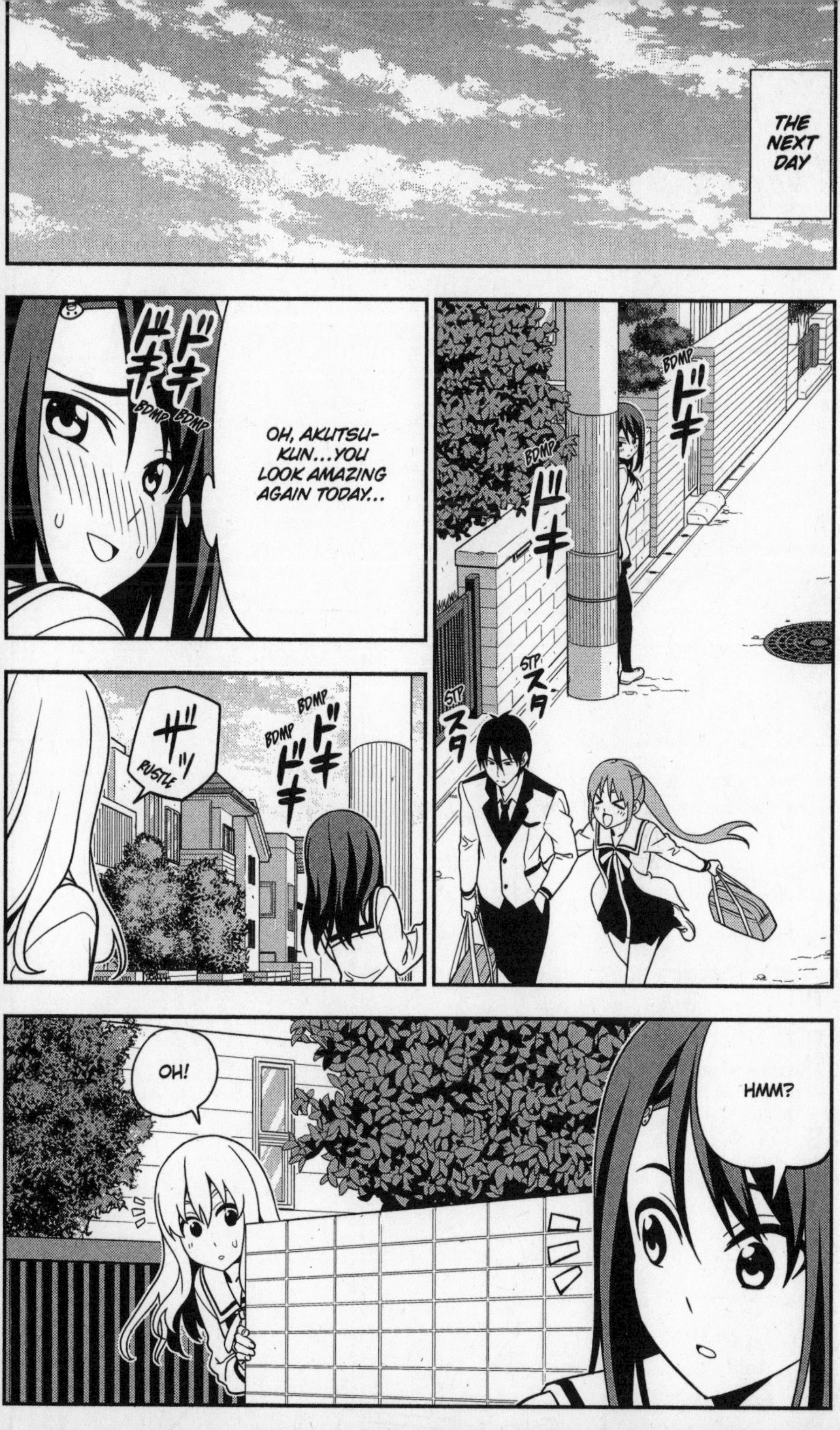
THE NEXT DAY
BDMP
ドキ
BDMP
ドキ
STP
スタ
STP
スタ
ドキドキ
BDMP BDMP
OH, AKUTSU-KUN...YOU LOOK AMAZING AGAIN TODAY...
ザッ
RUSTLE
BDMP
ドキ
BDMP
ドキ
HMM?
OH!

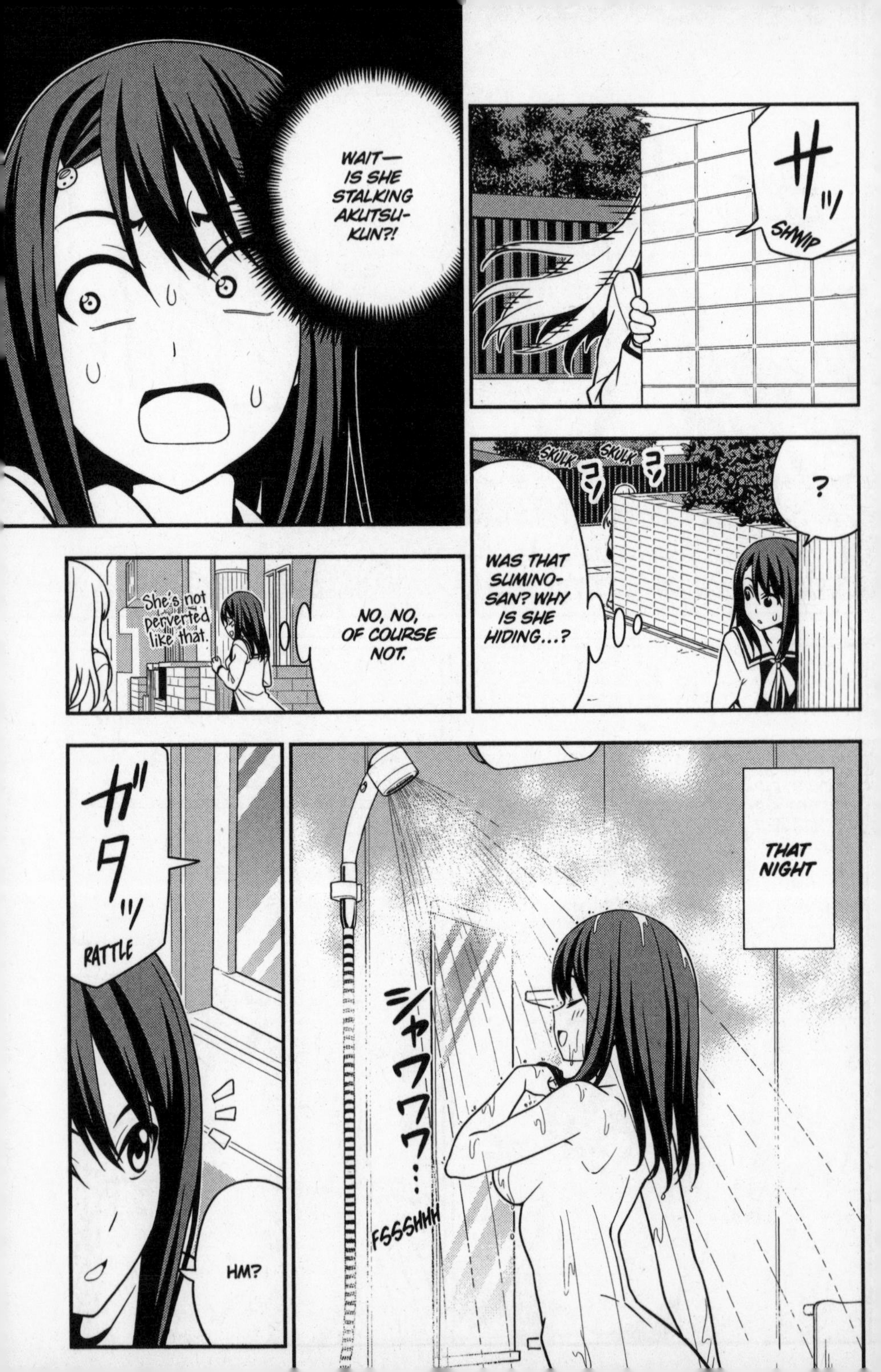

SHWIP
?
WAS THAT SUMINO-SAN? WHY IS SHE HIDING...?
SKULK SKULK
WAIT— IS SHE STALKING AKUTSU-KUN?!
NO, NO, OF COURSE NOT.
She's not perverted like that.
THAT NIGHT
FSSSHHH
RATTLE
HM?

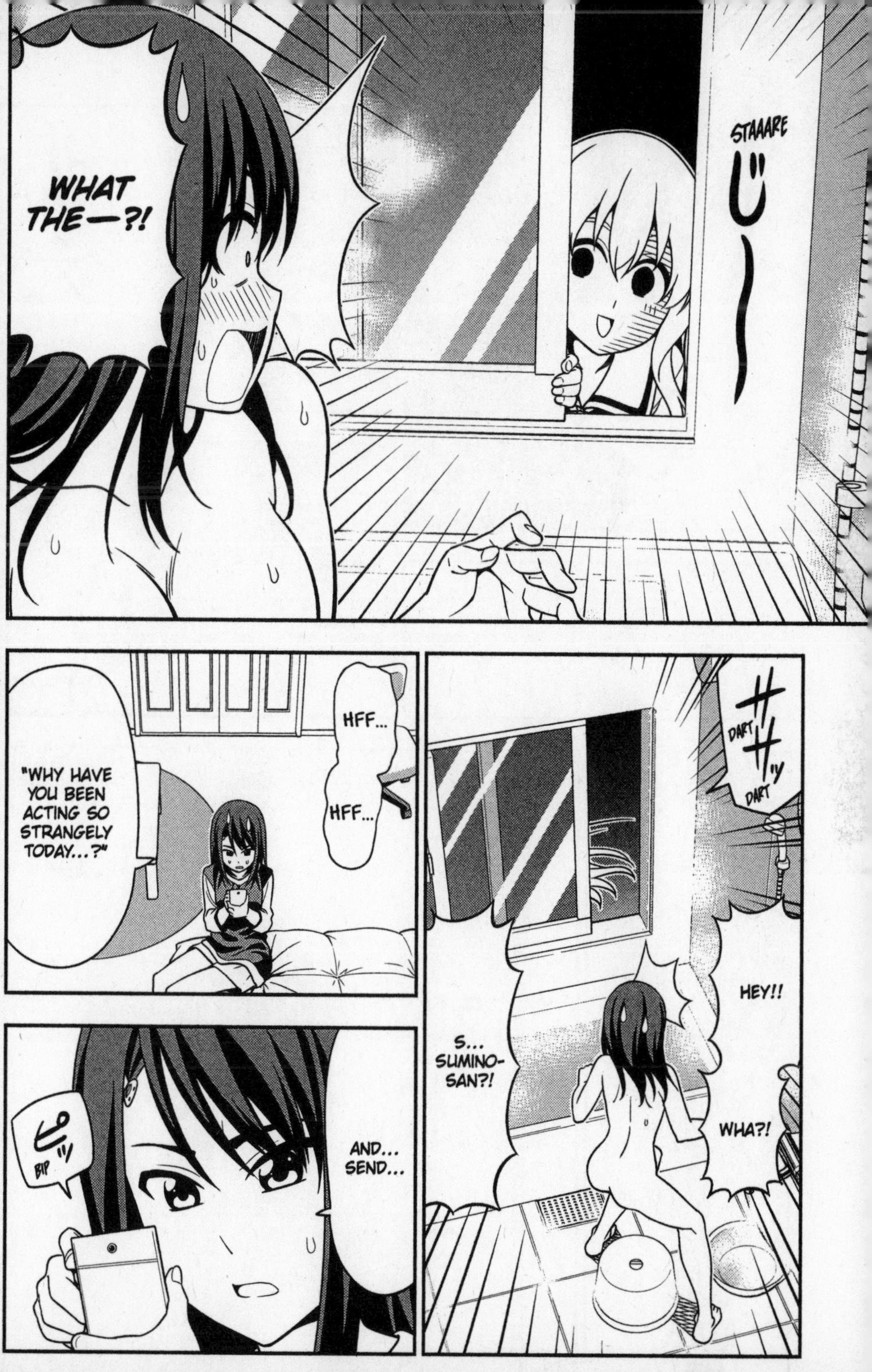
STAAARE
じー
WHAT THE—?!
ザッ
DART
ザッ
DART
HEY!!
S... SUMINO-SAN?!
WHA?!
HFF...
HFF...
"WHY HAVE YOU BEEN ACTING SO STRANGELY TODAY...?"
AND... SEND...
ピッ
BIP

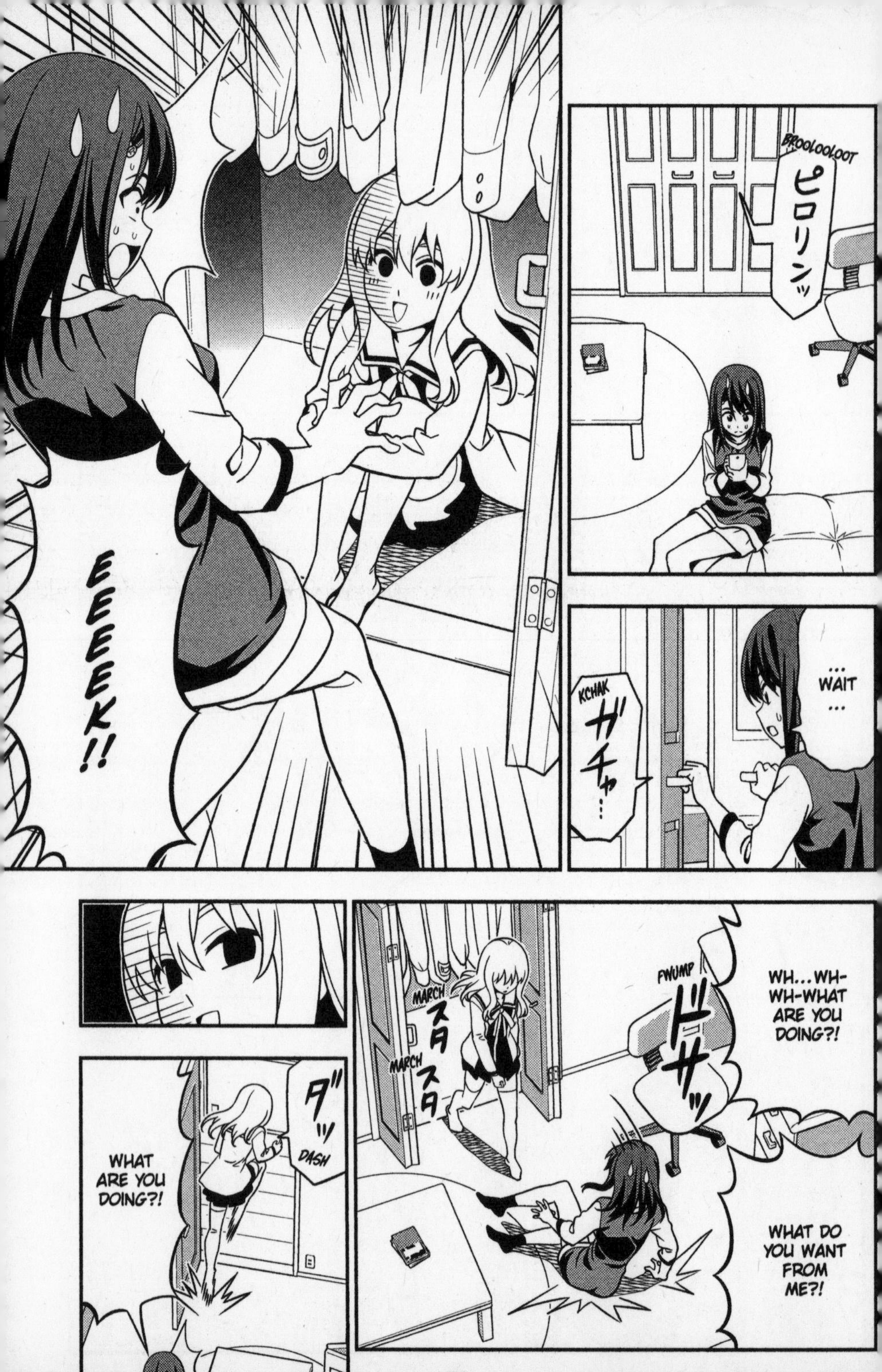
BROOLOOLOOT
ピロリンッ
...WAIT...
KCHAK
ガチャ...
EEEEEK!!
WH...WH-WH-WHAT ARE YOU DOING?!
FWUMP
ドサッ
MARCH
スタ
MARCH
スタ
WHAT DO YOU WANT FROM ME?!
ダッ
DASH
WHAT ARE YOU DOING?!

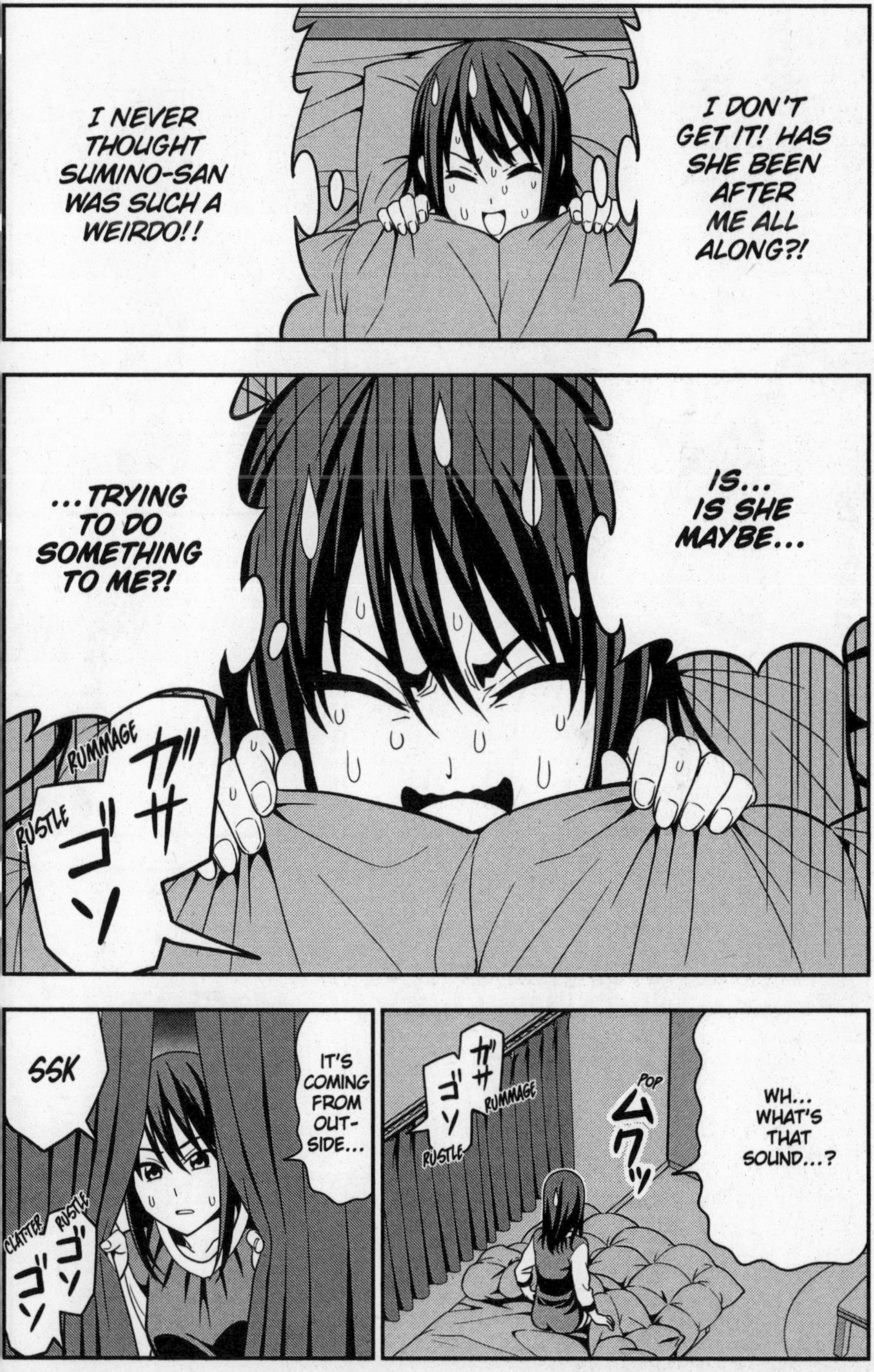
I DON'T GET IT! HAS SHE BEEN AFTER ME ALL ALONG?!
I NEVER THOUGHT SUMINO-SAN WAS SUCH A WEIRDO!!
IS... IS SHE MAYBE...
...TRYING TO DO SOMETHING TO ME?!
ガサ
RUMMAGE
ゴソ
RUSTLE
WH... WHAT'S THAT SOUND...?
ムクッ
POP
ガサ
RUMMAGE
ゴソ
RUSTLE
IT'S COMING FROM OUT-SIDE...
SSK
ゴソ
RUSTLE
ゴソ
CLATTER

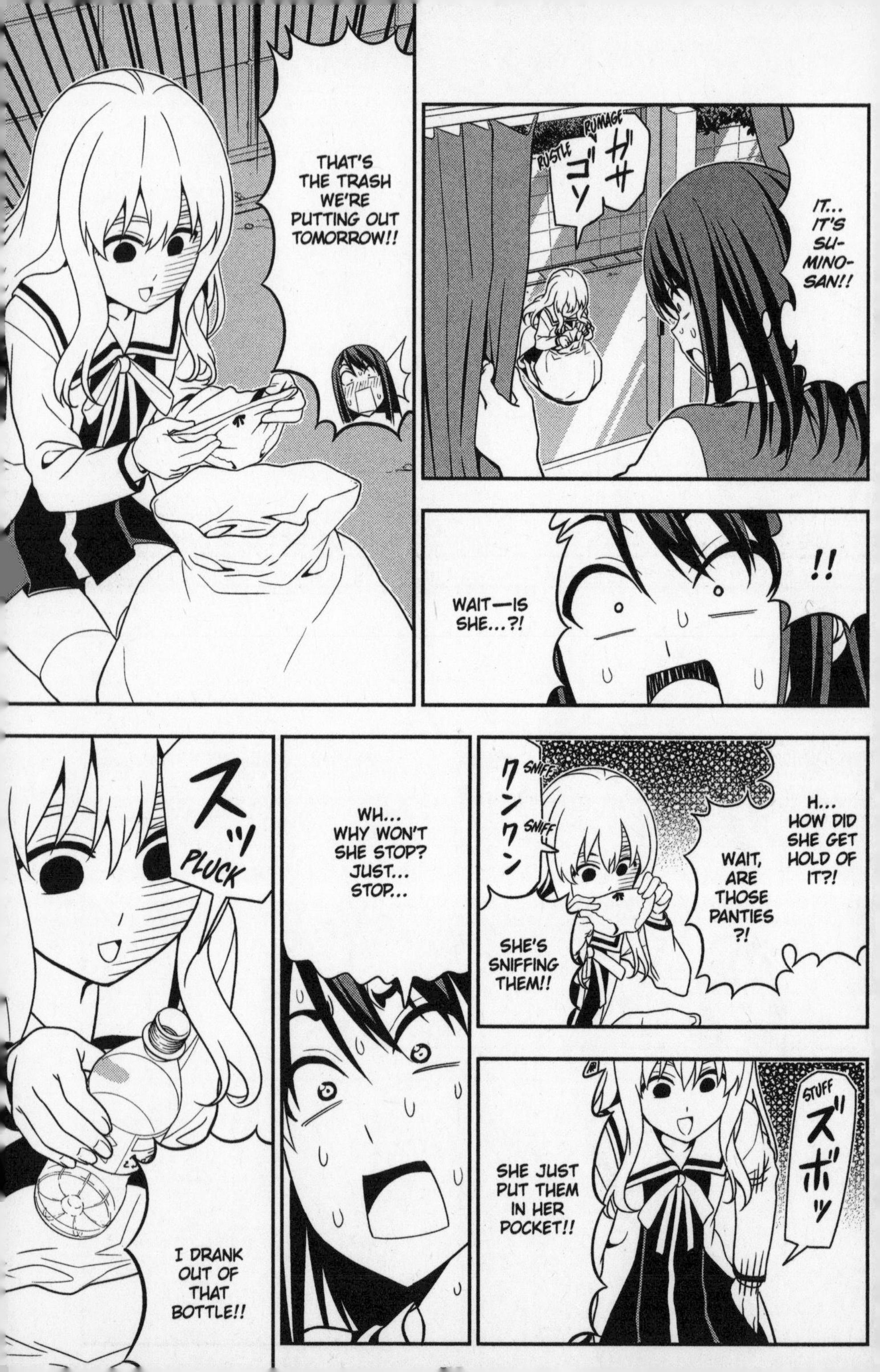
RUMAGE
RUSTLE
ガサゴソ
IT... IT'S SU-MINO-SAN!!
!!
WAIT—IS SHE...?!
THAT'S THE TRASH WE'RE PUTTING OUT TOMORROW!!
H... HOW DID SHE GET HOLD OF IT?!
WAIT, ARE THOSE PANTIES ?!
SNIFF
SNIFF
クンクン
SHE'S SNIFFING THEM!!
STUFF
ズボッ
SHE JUST PUT THEM IN HER POCKET!!
WH... WHY WON'T SHE STOP? JUST... STOP...
スッ
PLUCK
I DRANK OUT OF THAT BOTTLE!!

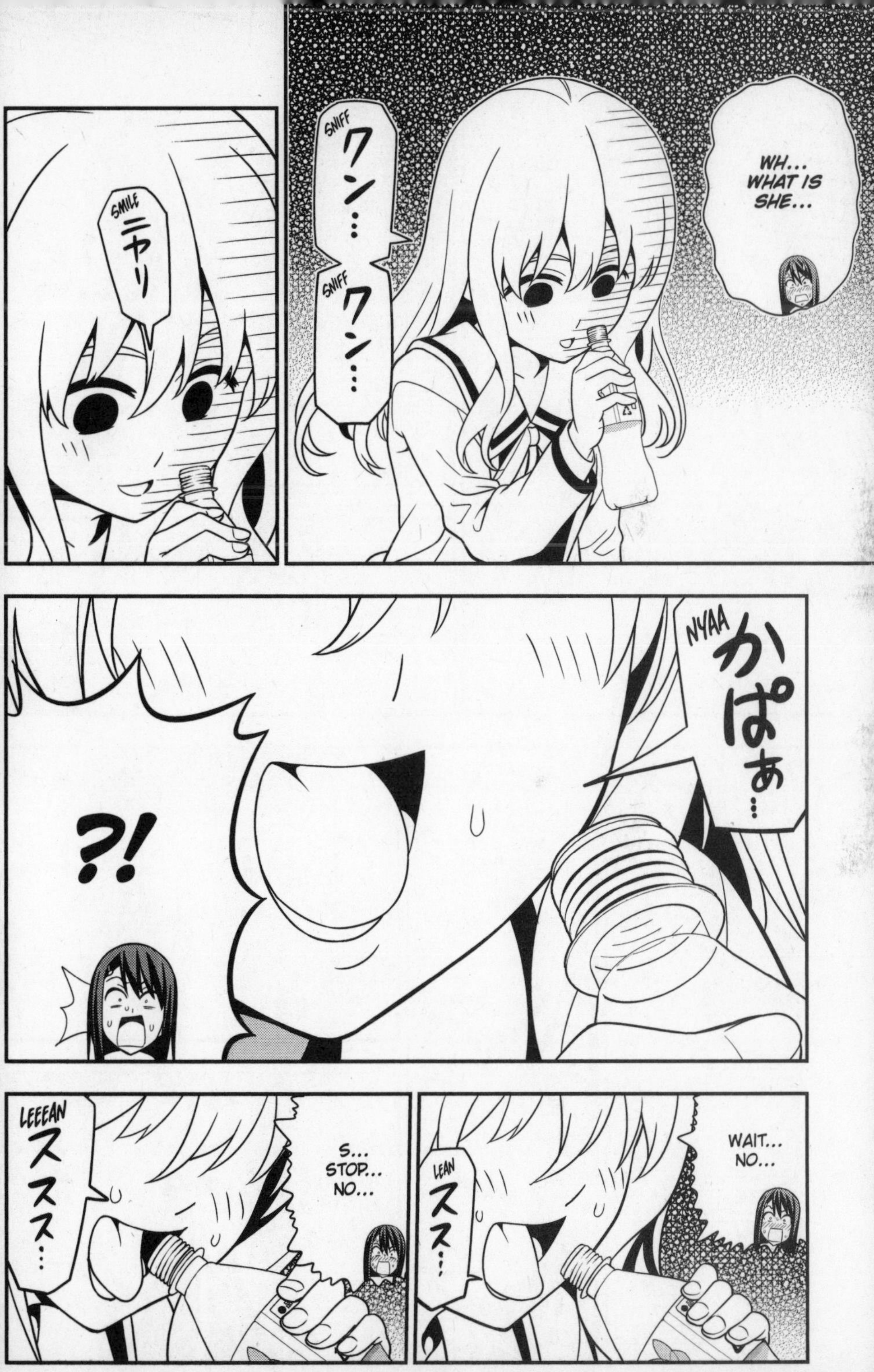
WH... WHAT IS SHE...
SNIFF
クン...
SNIFF
クン...
SMILE
ニヤリ
NYAA
かぱぁ...
?!
WAIT... NO...
LEAN
スス...
S... STOP... NO...
LEEEAN
ススス...

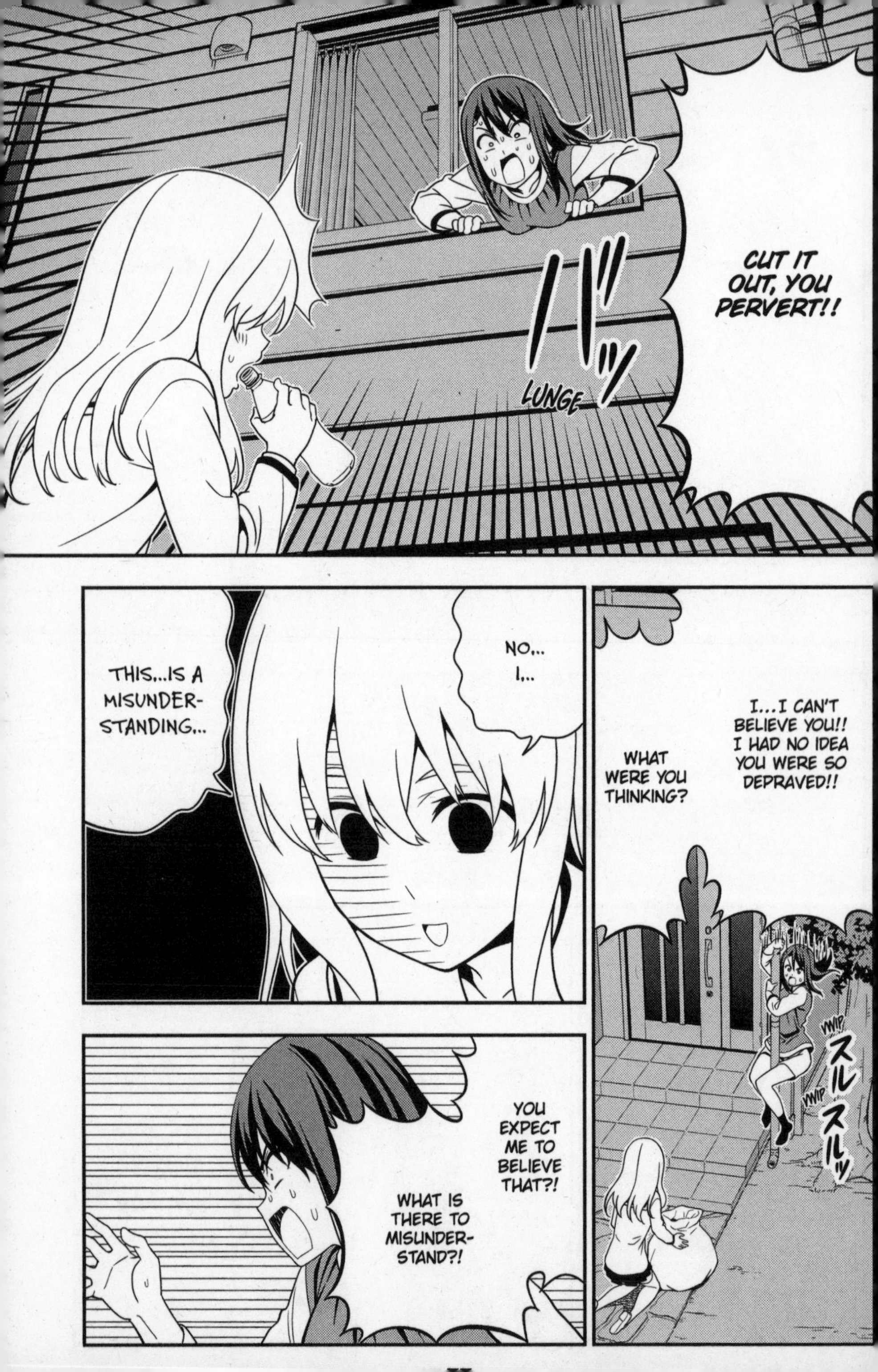
CUT IT OUT, YOU PERVERT!!
バッ
LUNGE
I…I CAN'T BELIEVE YOU!! I HAD NO IDEA YOU WERE SO DEPRAVED!!
WHAT WERE YOU THINKING?
VWIP
スルスルッ
VWIP
NO… I…
THIS…IS A MISUNDERSTANDING…
YOU EXPECT ME TO BELIEVE THAT?!
WHAT IS THERE TO MISUNDERSTAND?!

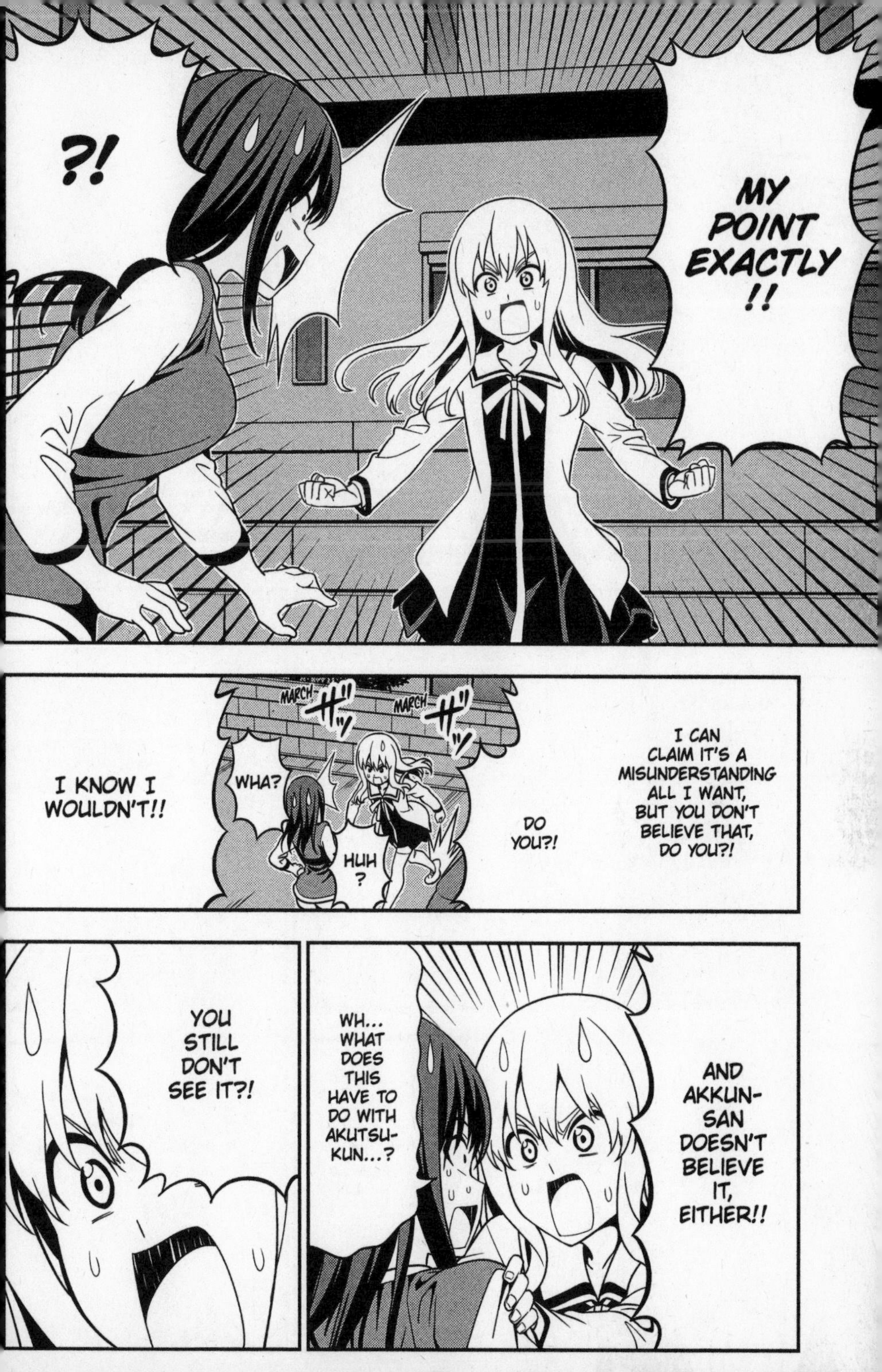
MY POINT EXACTLY !!
?!
I CAN CLAIM IT'S A MISUNDERSTANDING ALL I WANT, BUT YOU DON'T BELIEVE THAT, DO YOU?!
DO YOU?!
MARCH
MARCH
HUH ?
WHA?
I KNOW I WOULDN'T!!
AND AKKUN-SAN DOESN'T BELIEVE IT, EITHER!!
WH... WHAT DOES THIS HAVE TO DO WITH AKUTSU-KUN...?
YOU STILL DON'T SEE IT?!

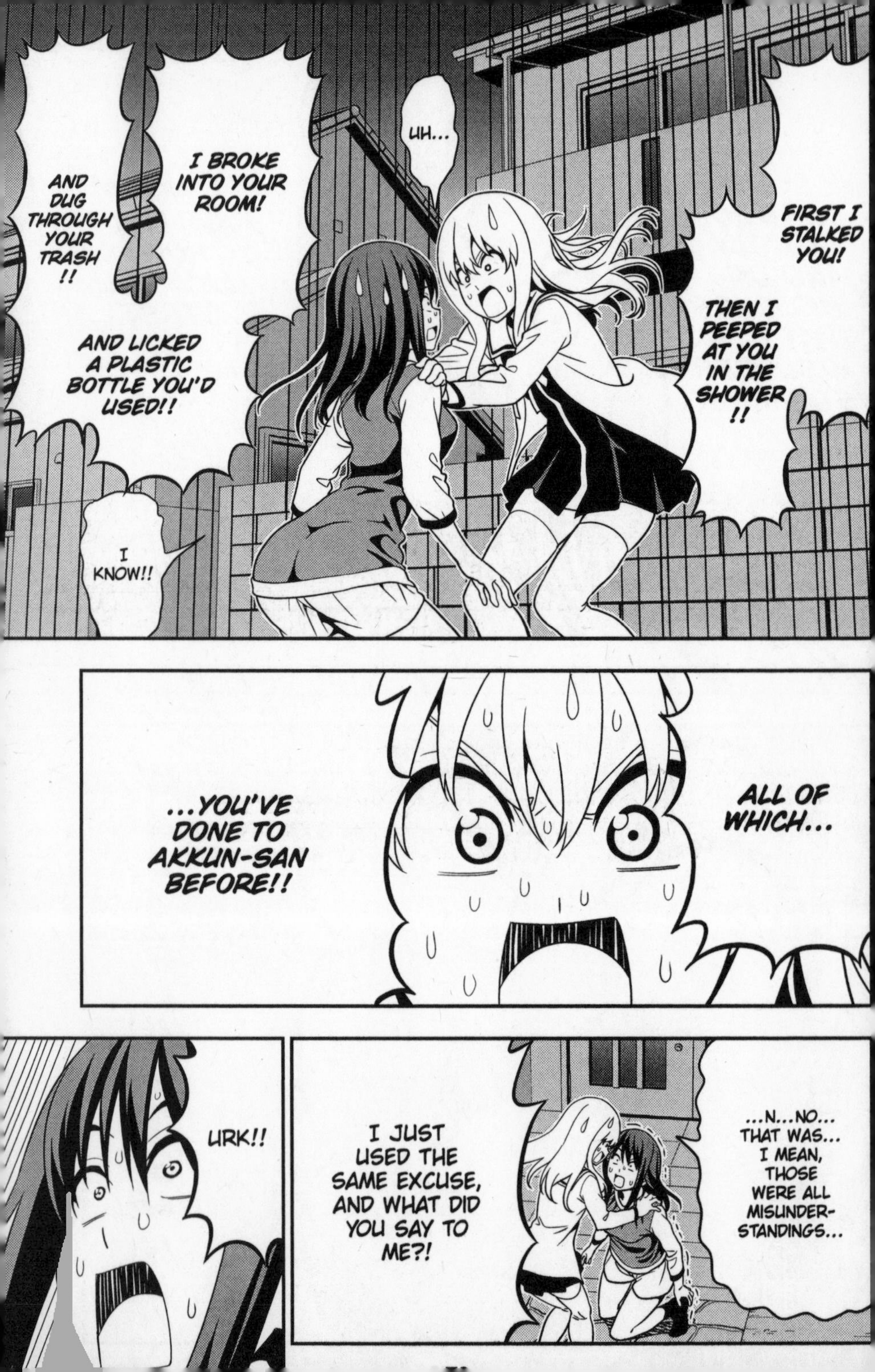
FIRST I STALKED YOU!
THEN I PEEPED AT YOU IN THE SHOWER!!
UH...
I BROKE INTO YOUR ROOM!
AND DUG THROUGH YOUR TRASH!!
AND LICKED A PLASTIC BOTTLE YOU'D USED!!
I KNOW!!
ALL OF WHICH...
...YOU'VE DONE TO AKKUN-SAN BEFORE!!
...N...NO... THAT WAS... I MEAN, THOSE WERE ALL MISUNDER-STANDINGS...
I JUST USED THE SAME EXCUSE, AND WHAT DID YOU SAY TO ME?!
URK!!

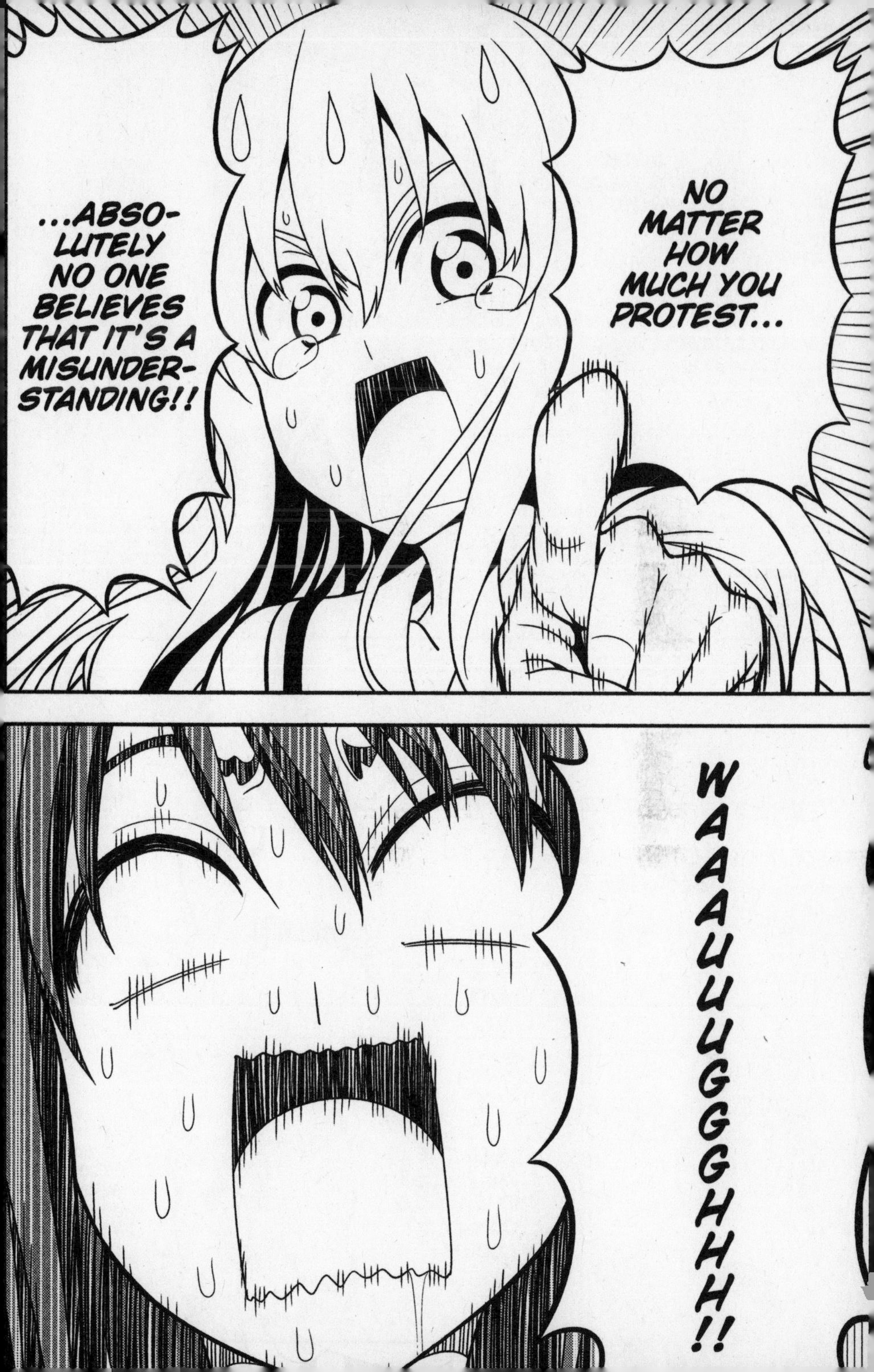
NO MATTER HOW MUCH YOU PROTEST...
...ABSO-LUTELY NO ONE BELIEVES THAT IT'S A MISUNDER-STANDING!!
WAAAUUUGGGHHH!!

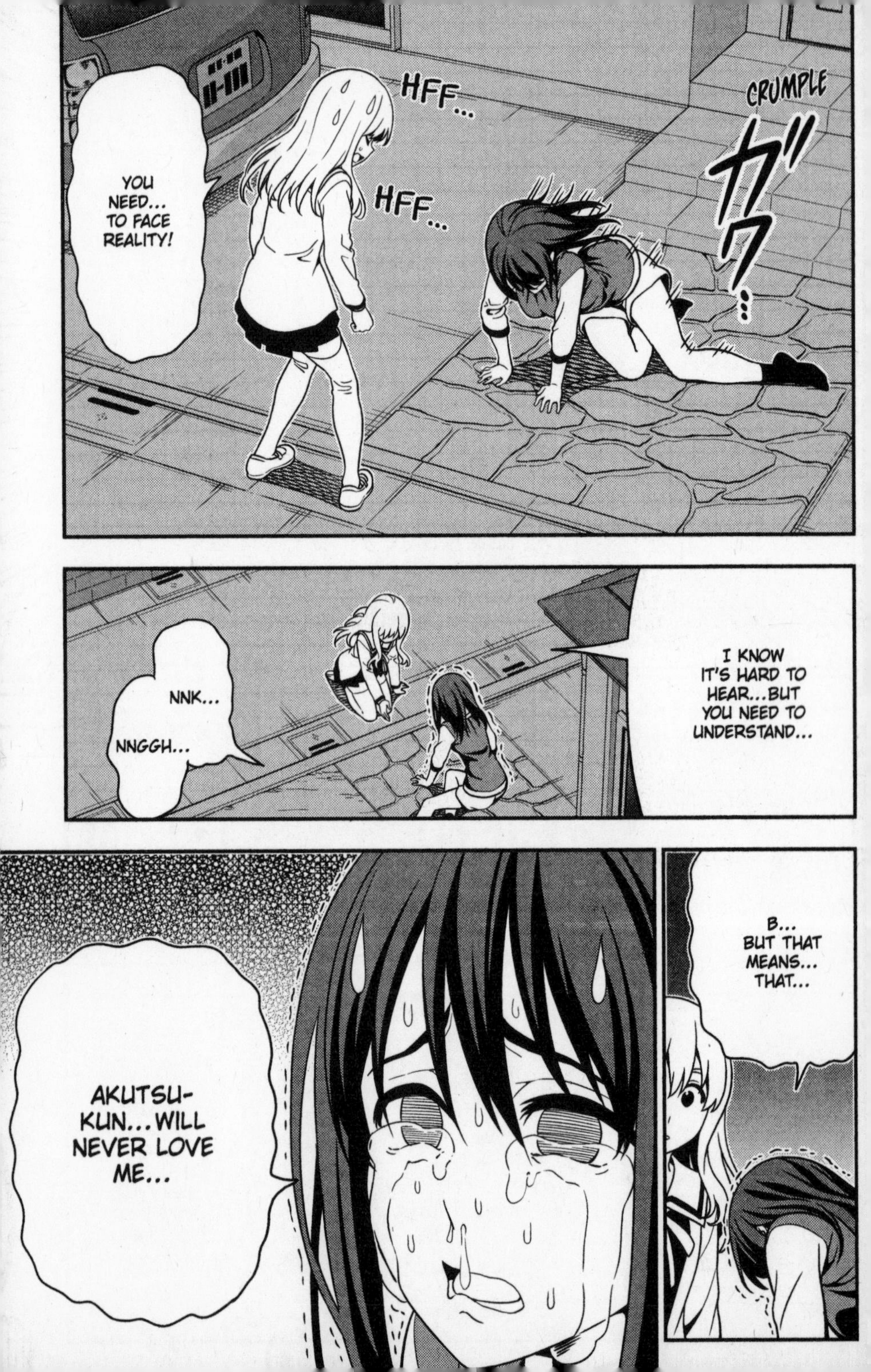
CRUMPLE
ガク…
HFF...
HFF...
YOU NEED... TO FACE REALITY!
I KNOW IT'S HARD TO HEAR...BUT YOU NEED TO UNDERSTAND...
NNK...
NNGH...
B... BUT THAT MEANS... THAT...
AKUTSU-KUN...WILL NEVER LOVE ME...

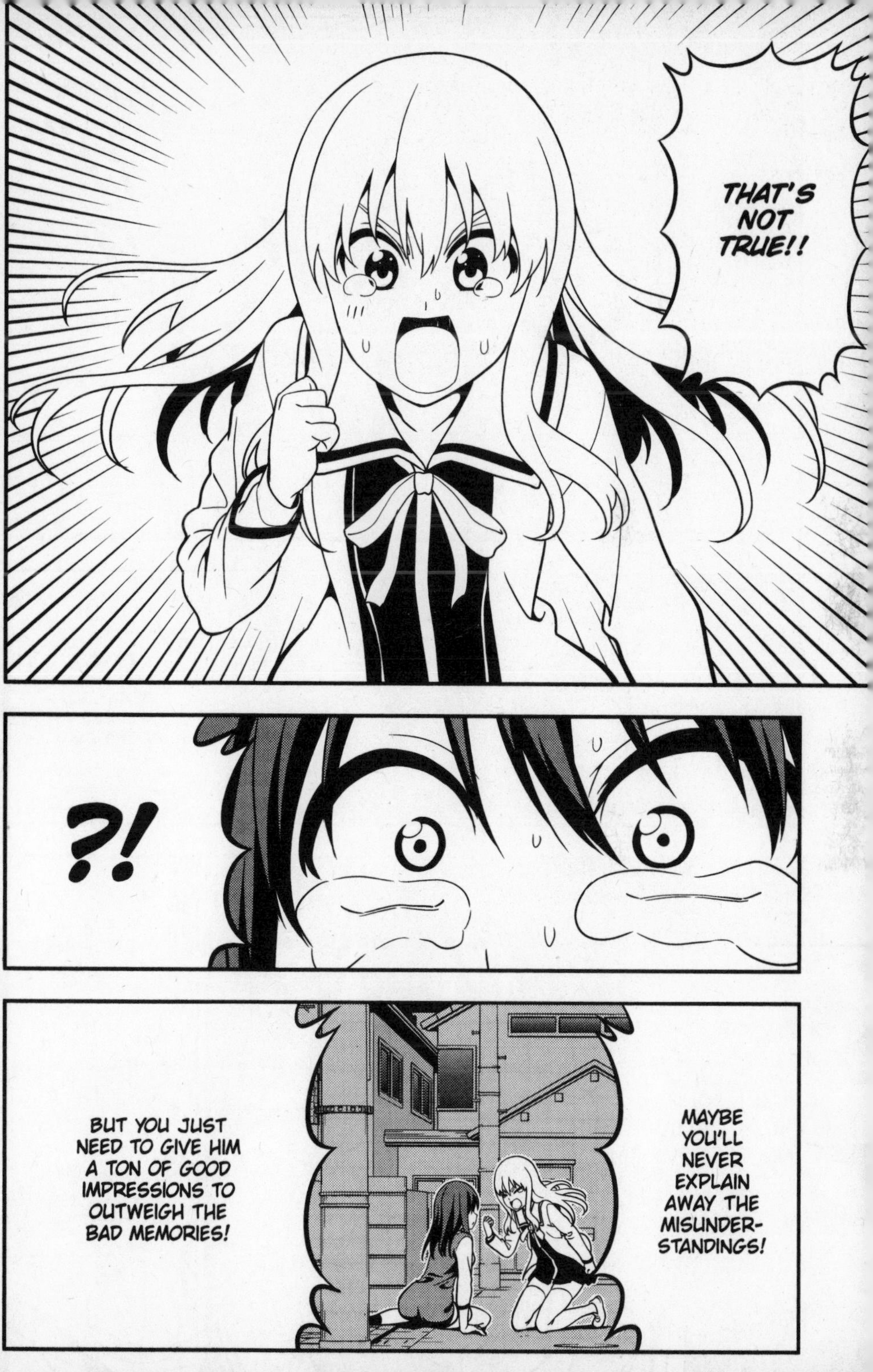
THAT'S NOT TRUE!!
?!
MAYBE YOU'LL NEVER EXPLAIN AWAY THE MISUNDER-STANDINGS!
BUT YOU JUST NEED TO GIVE HIM A TON OF GOOD IMPRESSIONS TO OUTWEIGH THE BAD MEMORIES!

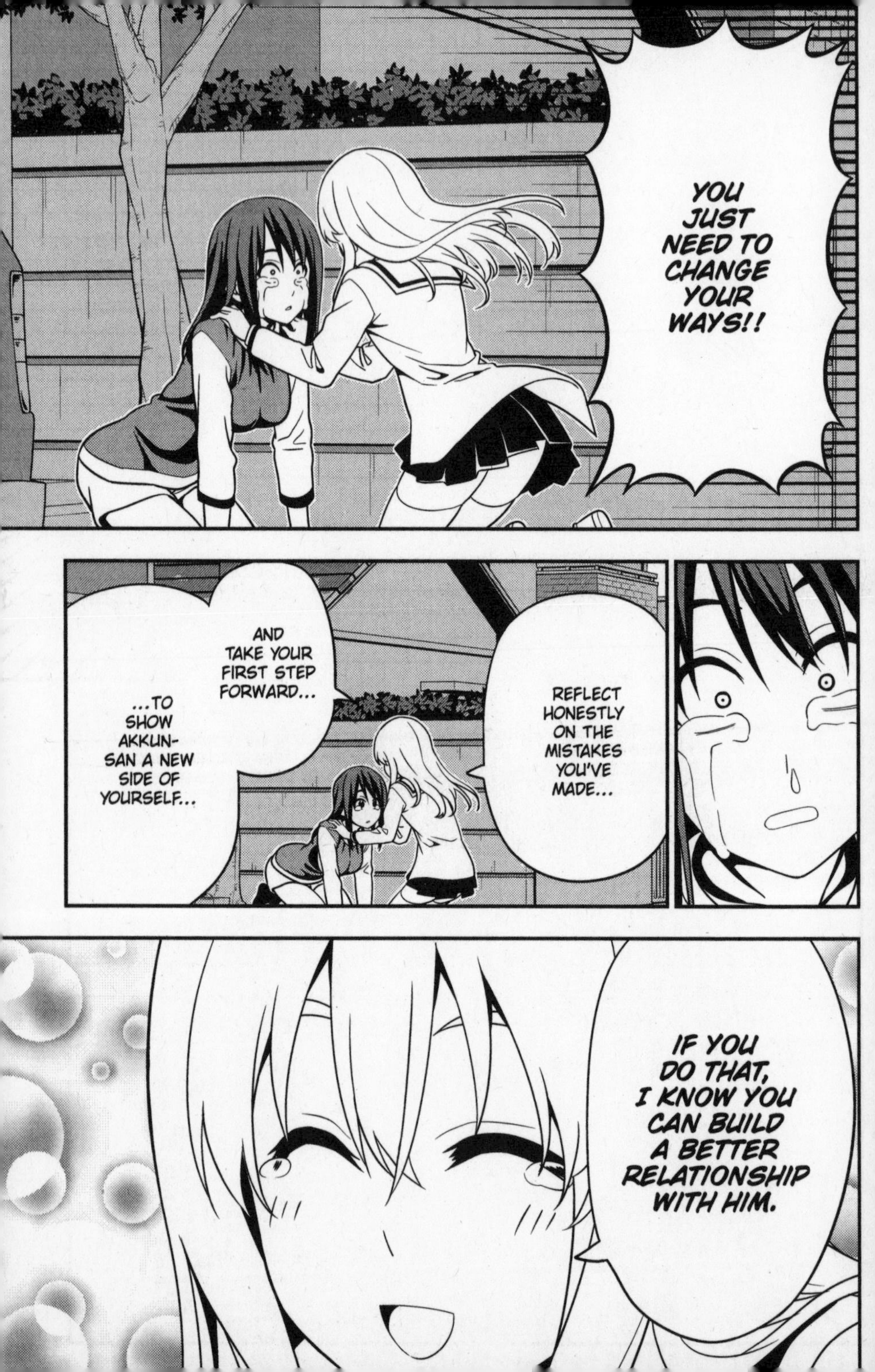
YOU JUST NEED TO CHANGE YOUR WAYS!!
REFLECT HONESTLY ON THE MISTAKES YOU'VE MADE...
AND TAKE YOUR FIRST STEP FORWARD...
...TO SHOW AKKUN-SAN A NEW SIDE OF YOURSELF...
IF YOU DO THAT, I KNOW YOU CAN BUILD A BETTER RELATIONSHIP WITH HIM.

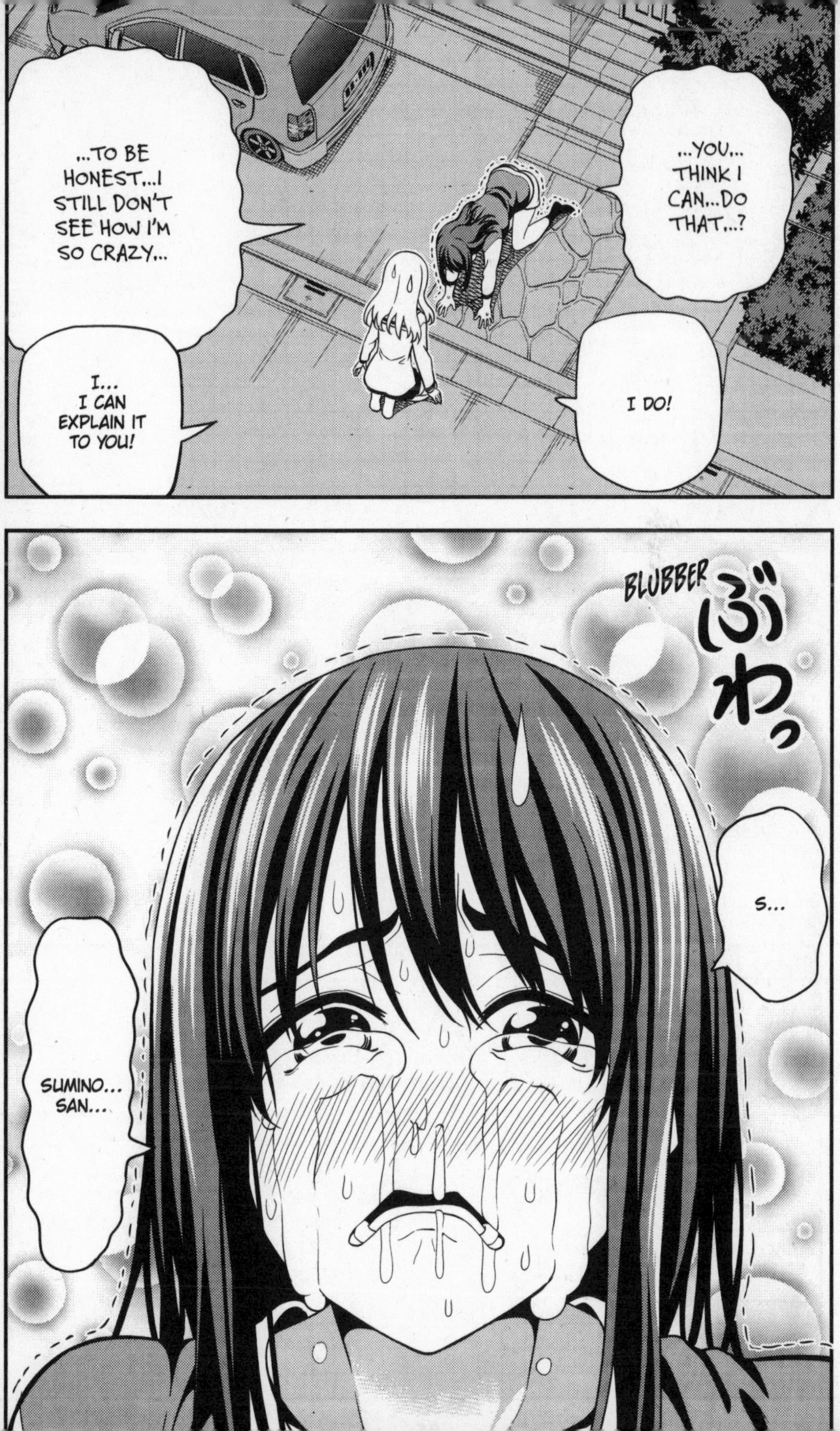
...YOU... THINK I CAN...DO THAT...?
...TO BE HONEST...I STILL DON'T SEE HOW I'M SO CRAZY...
I DO!
I... I CAN EXPLAIN IT TO YOU!
BLUBBER
ぶわっ
S...
SUMINO... SAN...

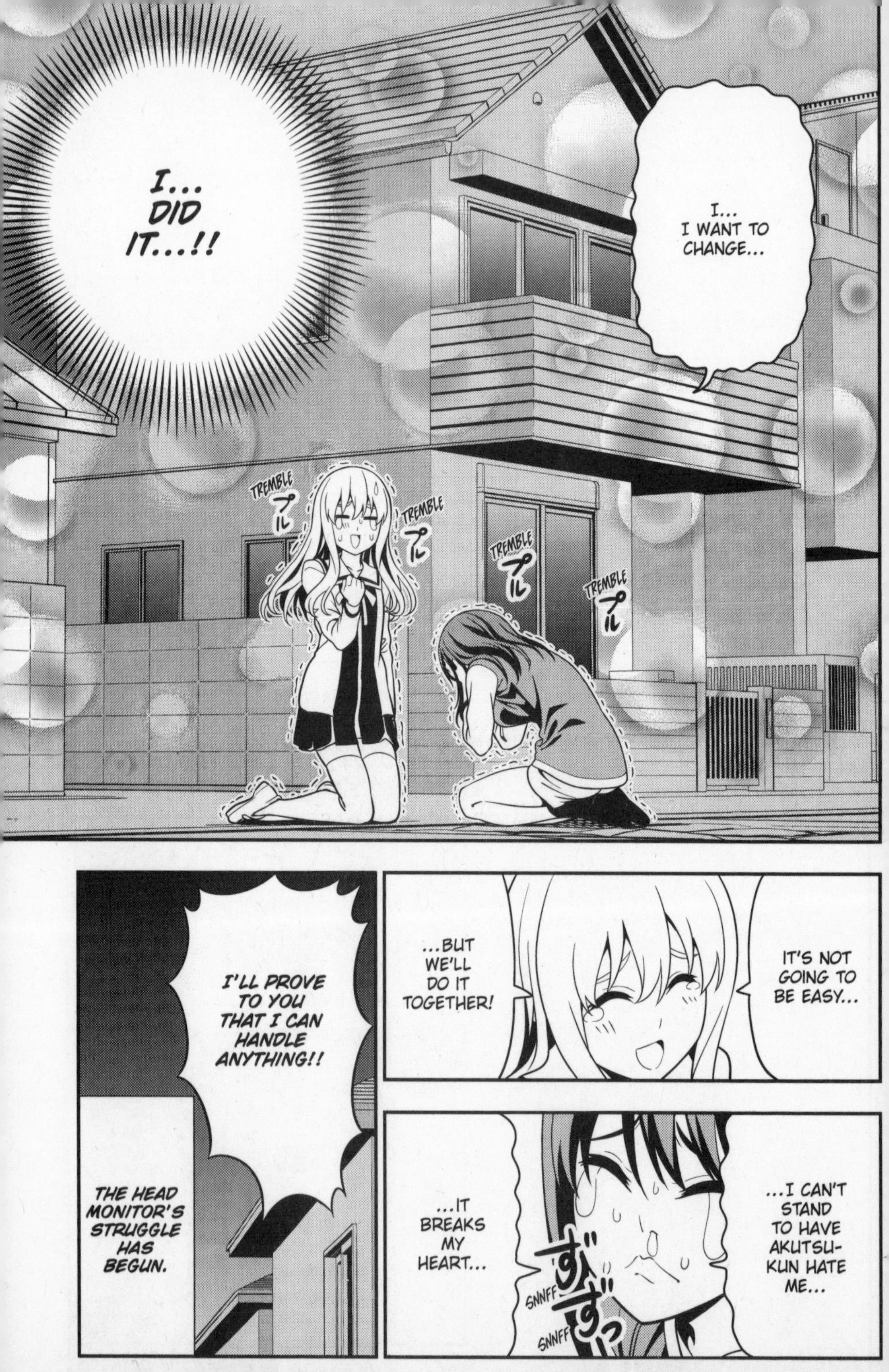
I... I WANT TO CHANGE...
I... DID IT...!!
TREMBLE
プル
TREMBLE
プル
TREMBLE
プル
TREMBLE
プル
IT'S NOT GOING TO BE EASY...
...BUT WE'LL DO IT TOGETHER!
...I CAN'T STAND TO HAVE AKUTSU-KUN HATE ME...
...IT BREAKS MY HEART...
ずずっ
SNNFF
SNNFF
I'LL PROVE TO YOU THAT I CAN HANDLE ANYTHING!!
THE HEAD MONITOR'S STRUGGLE HAS BEGUN.

Sayaka-chan! So Honest

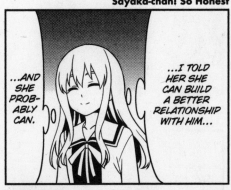

...I TOLD HER SHE CAN BUILD A BETTER RELATIONSHIP WITH HIM...
...AND SHE PROBABLY CAN.
BUT I NEVER SAID HE'D GO OUT WITH HER!!
WE CALL THAT "HEDG-ING."

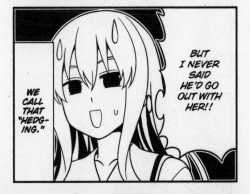

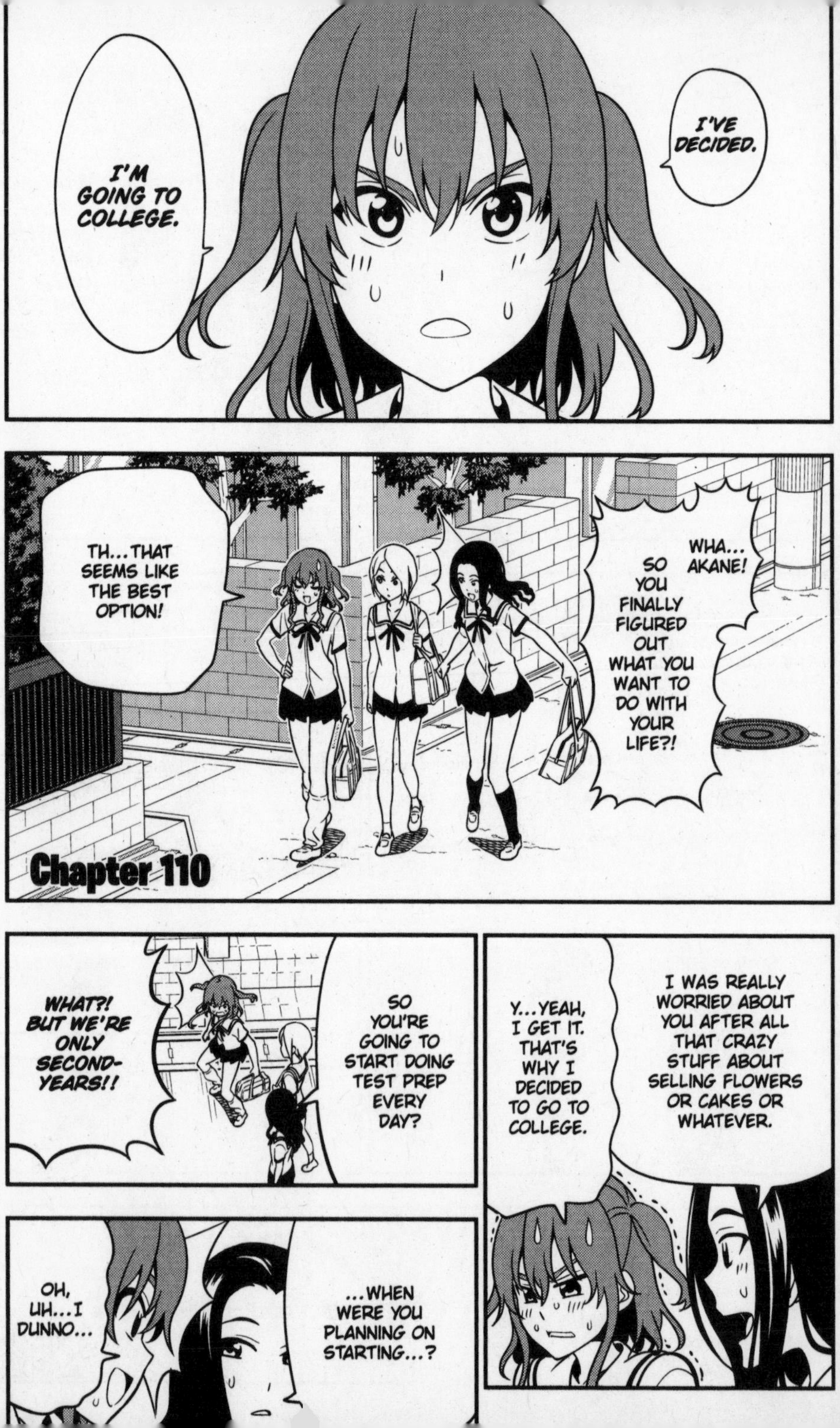
I'VE DECIDED.
I'M GOING TO COLLEGE.
WHA... AKANE! SO YOU FINALLY FIGURED OUT WHAT YOU WANT TO DO WITH YOUR LIFE?!
TH...THAT SEEMS LIKE THE BEST OPTION!
Chapter 110
I WAS REALLY WORRIED ABOUT YOU AFTER ALL THAT CRAZY STUFF ABOUT SELLING FLOWERS OR CAKES OR WHATEVER.
Y...YEAH, I GET IT. THAT'S WHY I DECIDED TO GO TO COLLEGE.
SO YOU'RE GOING TO START DOING TEST PREP EVERY DAY?
WHAT?! BUT WE'RE ONLY SECOND-YEARS!!
...WHEN WERE YOU PLANNING ON STARTING...?
OH, UH...I DUNNO...

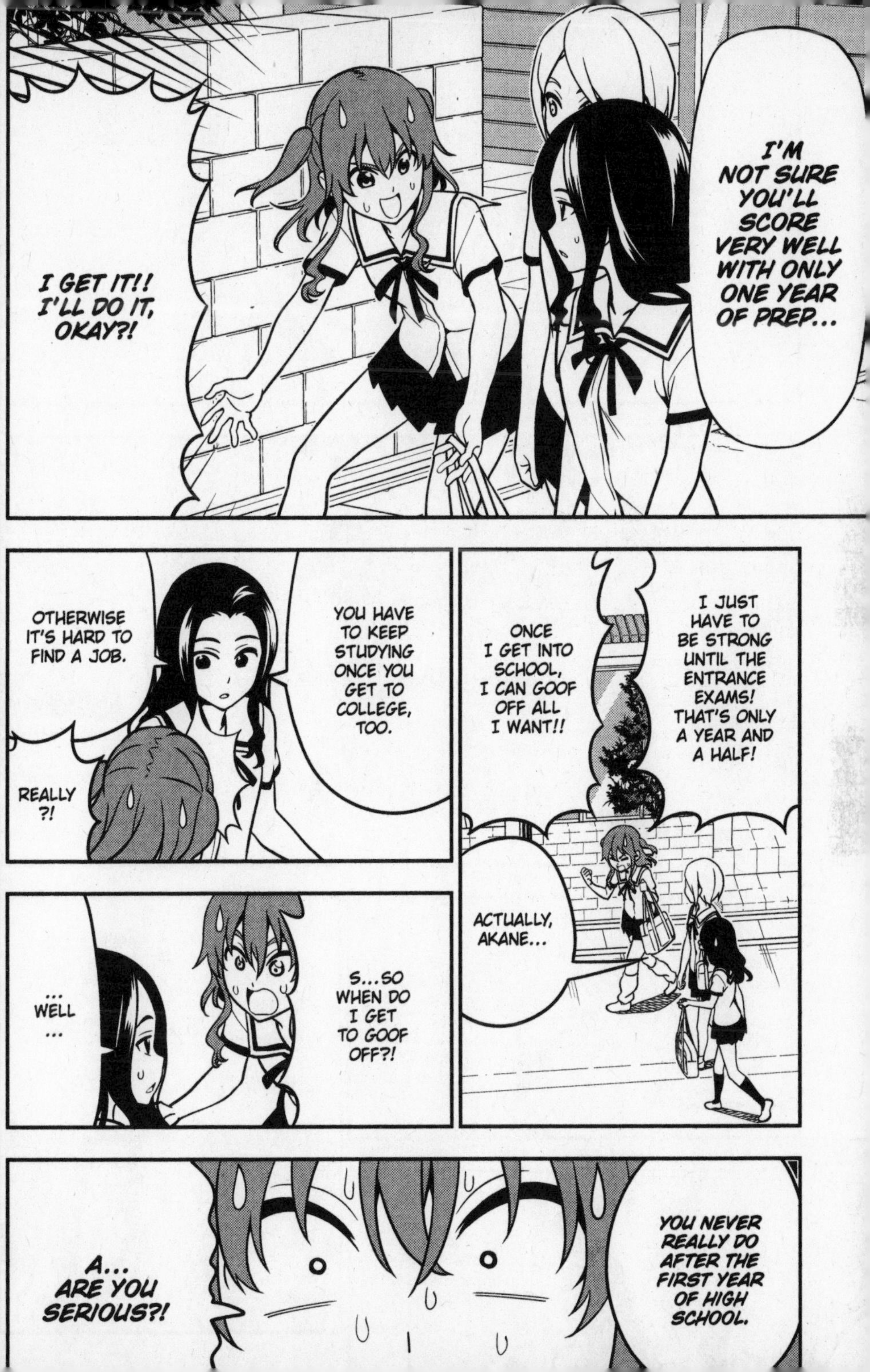
I'M NOT SURE YOU'LL SCORE VERY WELL WITH ONLY ONE YEAR OF PREP...
I GET IT!! I'LL DO IT, OKAY?!
I JUST HAVE TO BE STRONG UNTIL THE ENTRANCE EXAMS! THAT'S ONLY A YEAR AND A HALF!
ONCE I GET INTO SCHOOL, I CAN GOOF OFF ALL I WANT!!
ACTUALLY, AKANE...
YOU HAVE TO KEEP STUDYING ONCE YOU GET TO COLLEGE, TOO.
OTHERWISE IT'S HARD TO FIND A JOB.
REALLY ?!
S...SO WHEN DO I GET TO GOOF OFF?!
... WELL ...
YOU NEVER REALLY DO AFTER THE FIRST YEAR OF HIGH SCHOOL.
A... ARE YOU SERIOUS?!

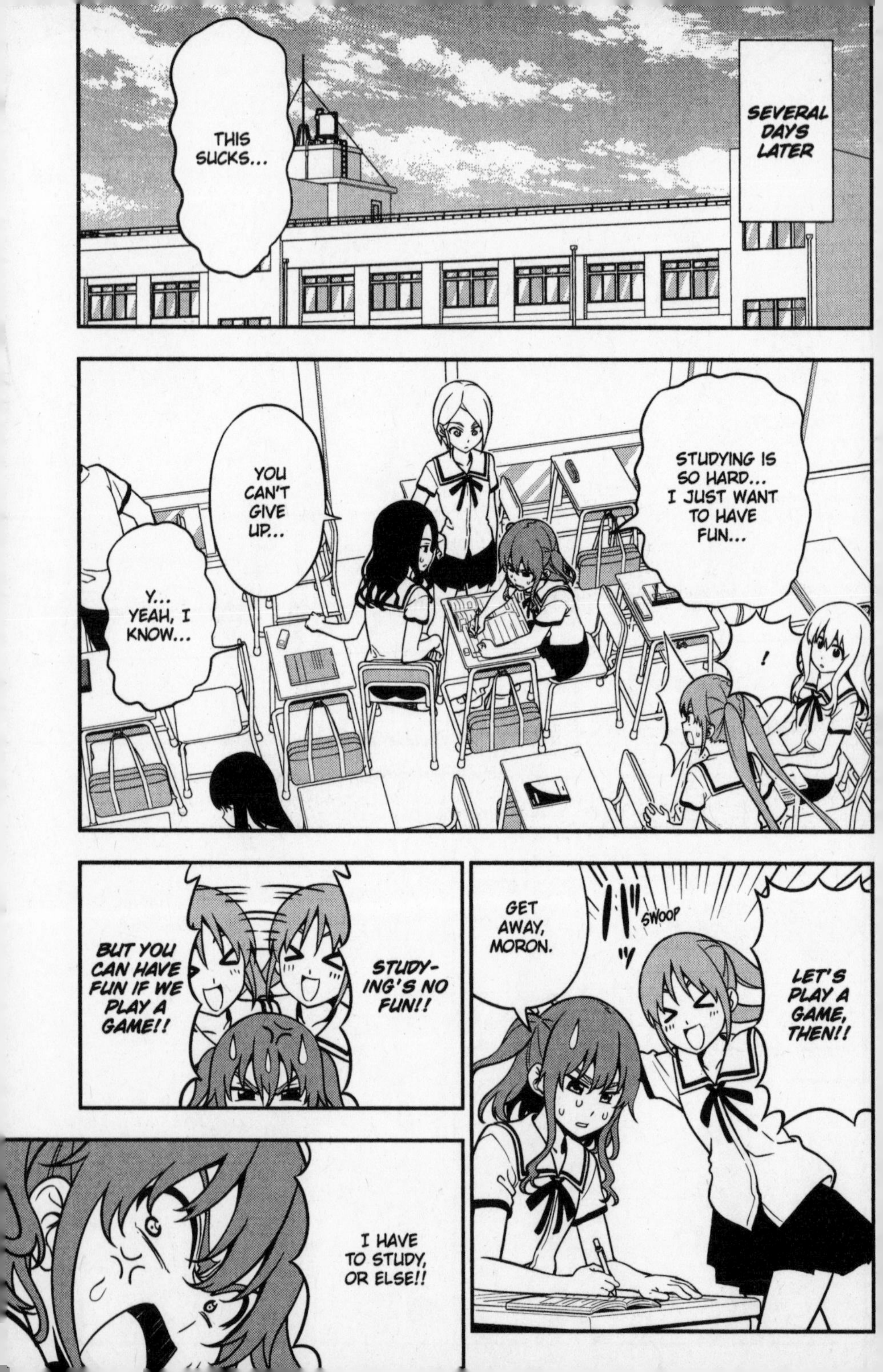
SEVERAL DAYS LATER
THIS SUCKS...
STUDYING IS SO HARD... I JUST WANT TO HAVE FUN...
!
YOU CAN'T GIVE UP...
Y... YEAH, I KNOW...
LET'S PLAY A GAME, THEN!!
SWOOP
GET AWAY, MORON.
STUDY-ING'S NO FUN!!
BUT YOU CAN HAVE FUN IF WE PLAY A GAME!!
I HAVE TO STUDY, OR ELSE!!

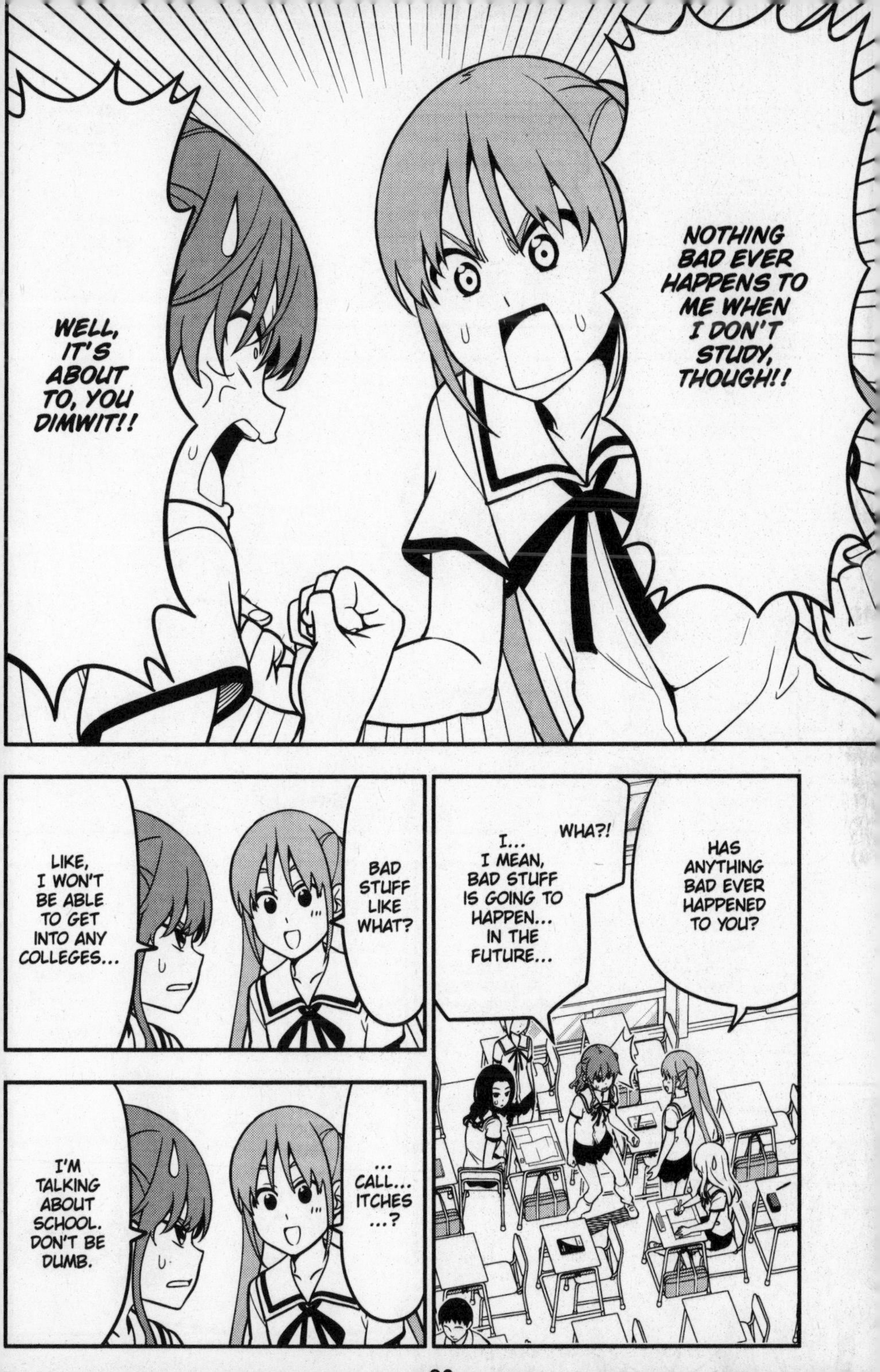
NOTHING BAD EVER HAPPENS TO ME WHEN I DON'T STUDY, THOUGH!!
WELL, IT'S ABOUT TO, YOU DIMWIT!!
HAS ANYTHING BAD EVER HAPPENED TO YOU?
WHA?!
I... I MEAN, BAD STUFF IS GOING TO HAPPEN... IN THE FUTURE...
BAD STUFF LIKE WHAT?
LIKE, I WON'T BE ABLE TO GET INTO ANY COLLEGES...
...CALL... ITCHES ...?
I'M TALKING ABOUT SCHOOL. DON'T BE DUMB.

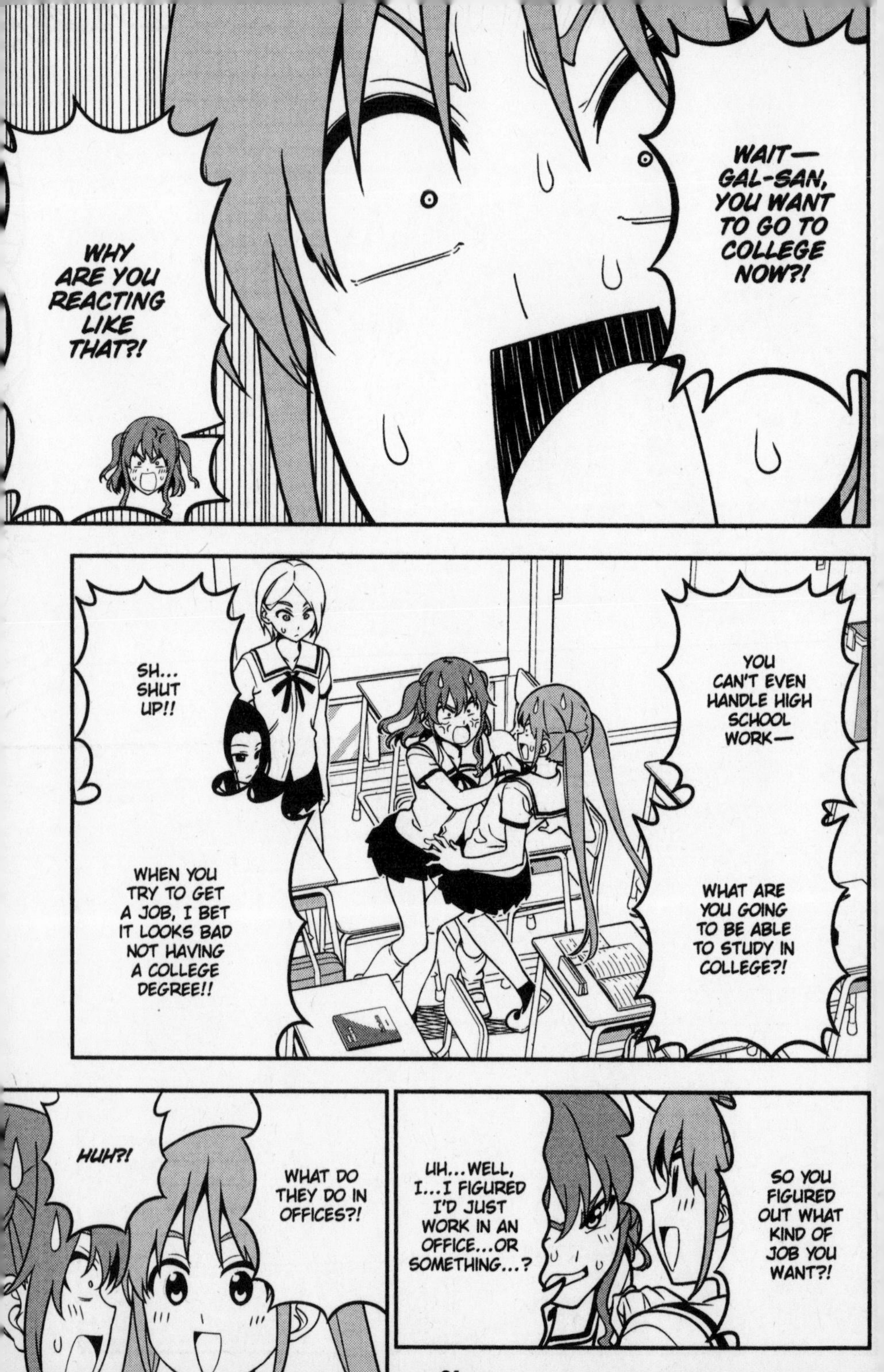
WAIT— GAL-SAN, YOU WANT TO GO TO COLLEGE NOW?!
WHY ARE YOU REACTING LIKE THAT?!
YOU CAN'T EVEN HANDLE HIGH SCHOOL WORK—
WHAT ARE YOU GOING TO BE ABLE TO STUDY IN COLLEGE?!
SH... SHUT UP!!
WHEN YOU TRY TO GET A JOB, I BET IT LOOKS BAD NOT HAVING A COLLEGE DEGREE!!
SO YOU FIGURED OUT WHAT KIND OF JOB YOU WANT?!
UH...WELL, I...I FIGURED I'D JUST WORK IN AN OFFICE...OR SOMETHING...?
WHAT DO THEY DO IN OFFICES?!
HUH?!

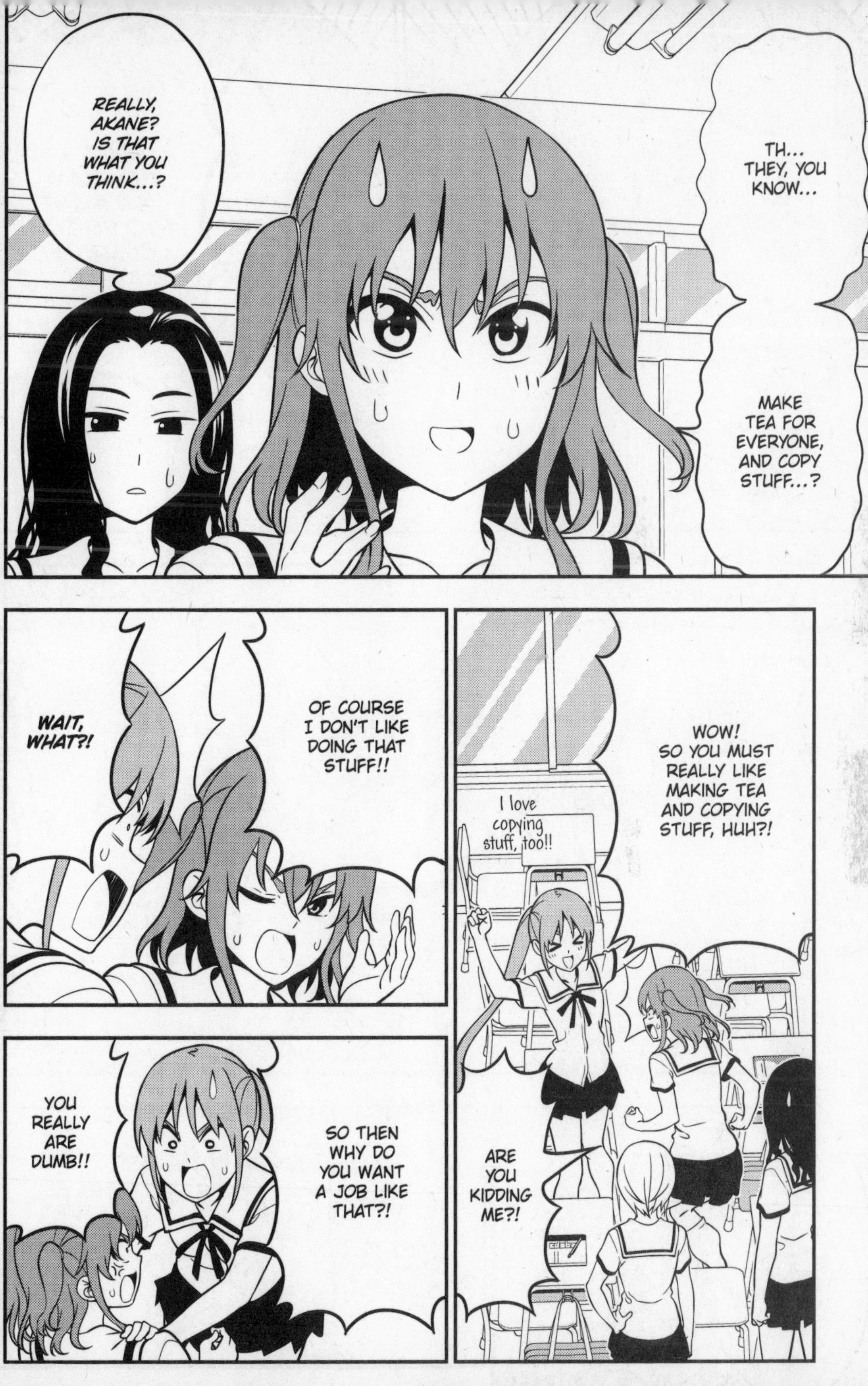
TH... THEY, YOU KNOW...
MAKE TEA FOR EVERYONE, AND COPY STUFF...?
REALLY, AKANE? IS THAT WHAT YOU THINK...?
WOW! SO YOU MUST REALLY LIKE MAKING TEA AND COPYING STUFF, HUH?!
I love copying stuff, too!!
ARE YOU KIDDING ME?!
OF COURSE I DON'T LIKE DOING THAT STUFF!!
WAIT, WHAT?!
SO THEN WHY DO YOU WANT A JOB LIKE THAT?!
YOU REALLY ARE DUMB!!

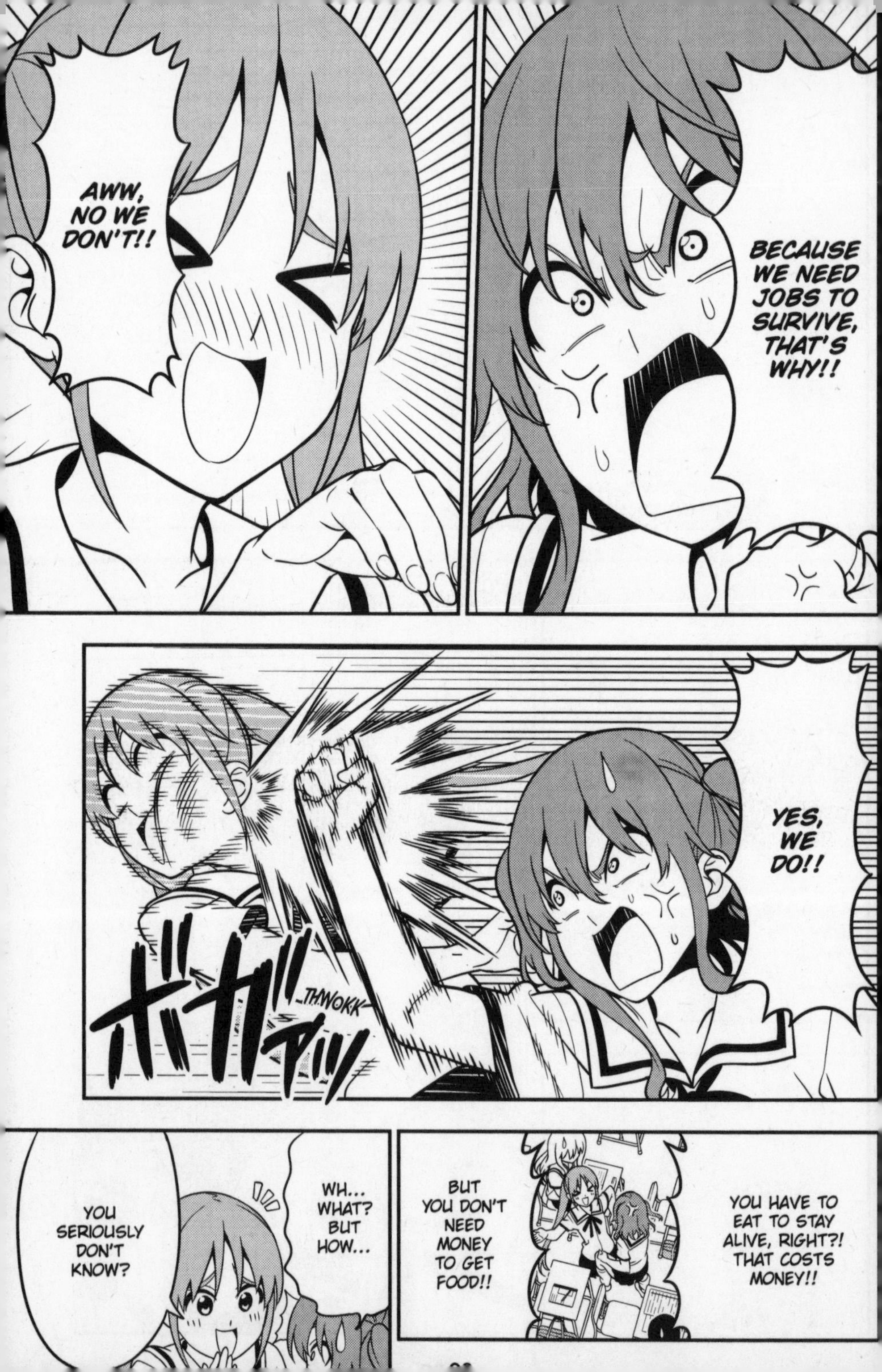
BECAUSE WE NEED JOBS TO SURVIVE, THAT'S WHY!!
AWW, NO WE DON'T!!
YES, WE DO!!
THWOKK
YOU HAVE TO EAT TO STAY ALIVE, RIGHT?! THAT COSTS MONEY!!
BUT YOU DON'T NEED MONEY TO GET FOOD!!
WH... WHAT? BUT HOW...
YOU SERIOUSLY DON'T KNOW?

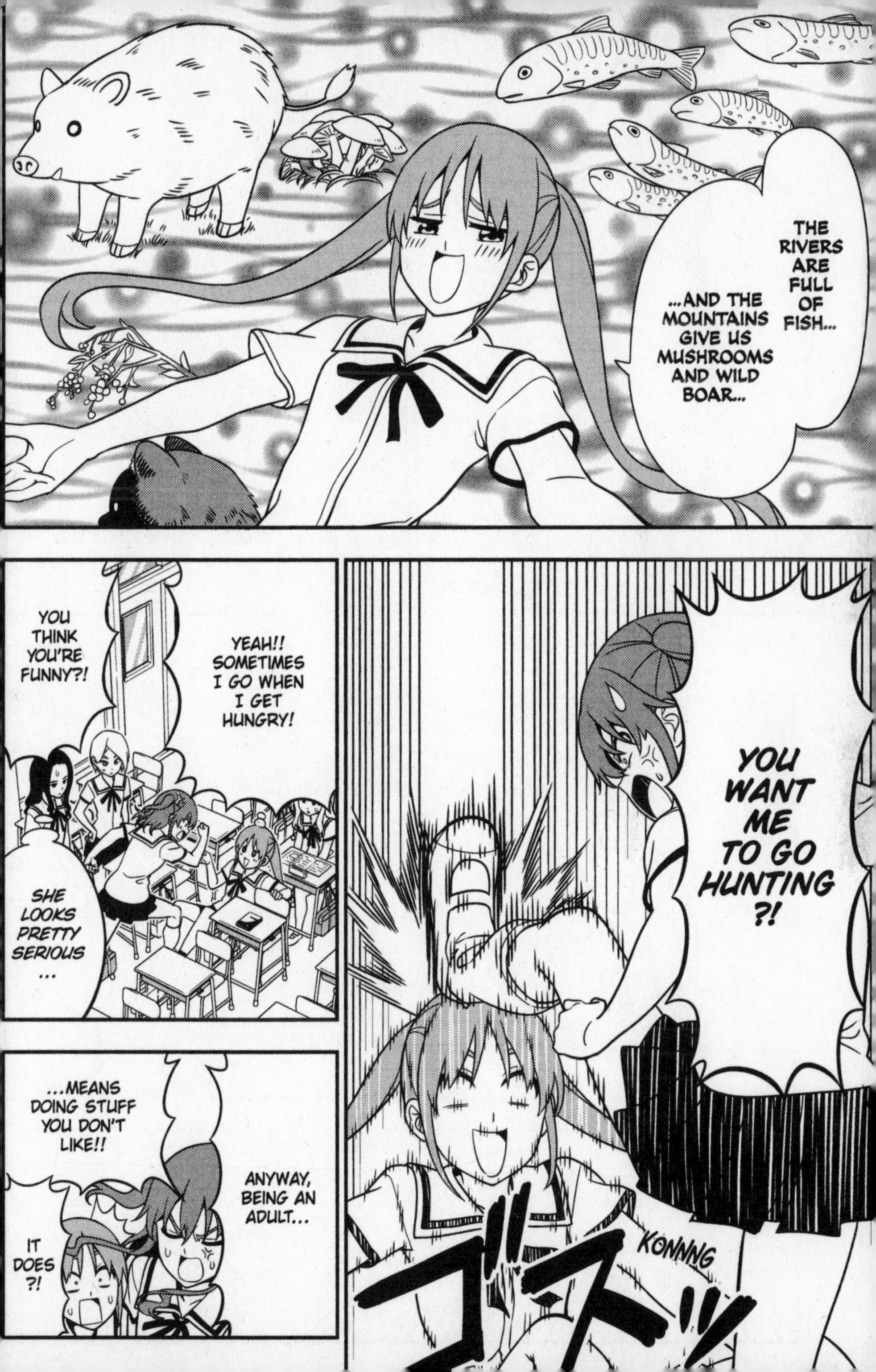
THE RIVERS ARE FULL OF FISH...
...AND THE MOUNTAINS GIVE US MUSHROOMS AND WILD BOAR...
YOU WANT ME TO GO HUNTING?!
KONNNG
YEAH!! SOMETIMES I GO WHEN I GET HUNGRY!
YOU THINK YOU'RE FUNNY?!
SHE LOOKS PRETTY SERIOUS ...
ANYWAY, BEING AN ADULT...
...MEANS DOING STUFF YOU DON'T LIKE!!
IT DOES?!

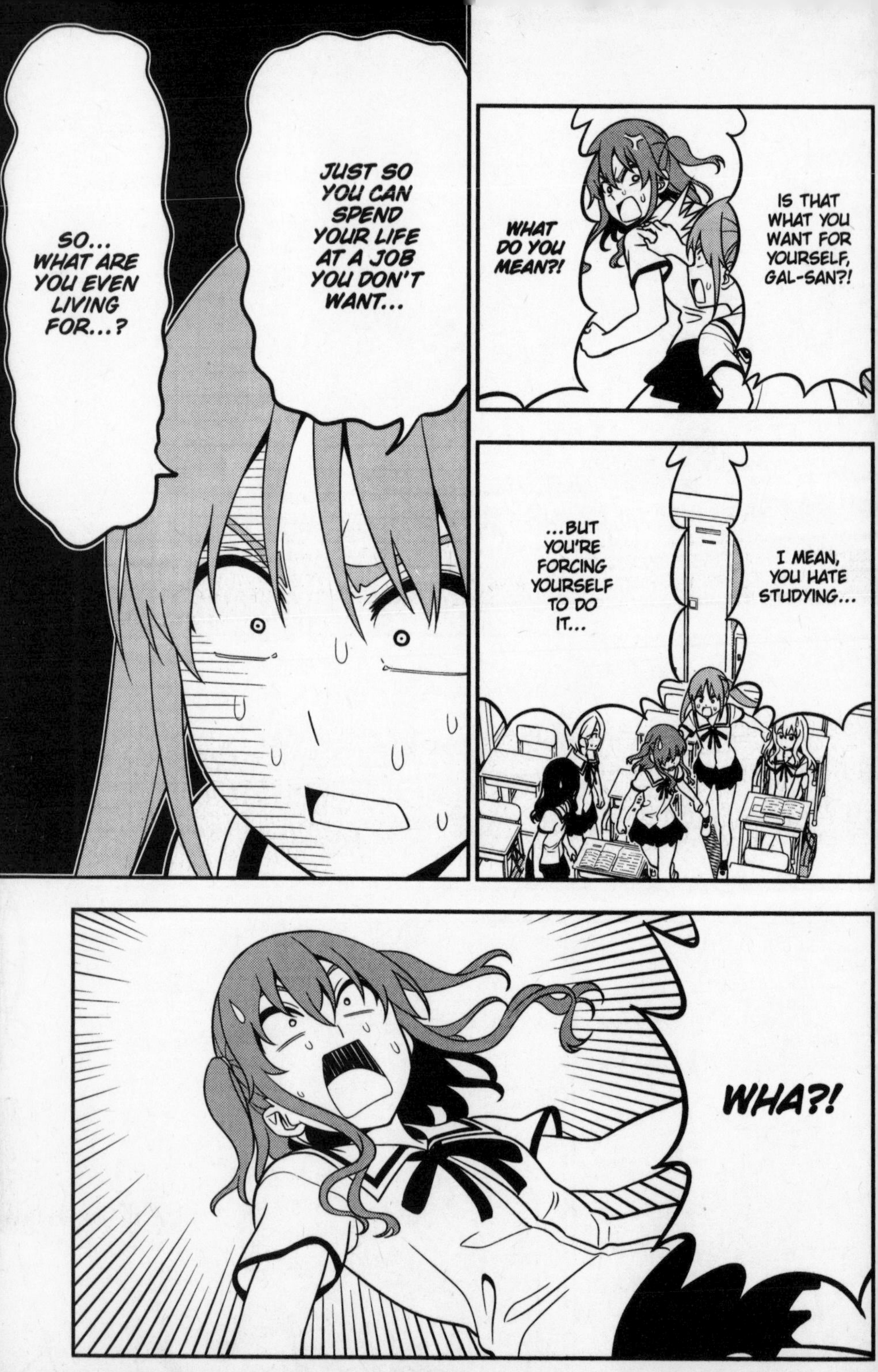
IS THAT WHAT YOU WANT FOR YOURSELF, GAL-SAN?!
WHAT DO YOU MEAN?!
I MEAN, YOU HATE STUDYING...
...BUT YOU'RE FORCING YOURSELF TO DO IT...
JUST SO YOU CAN SPEND YOUR LIFE AT A JOB YOU DON'T WANT...
SO... WHAT ARE YOU EVEN LIVING FOR...?
WHA?!

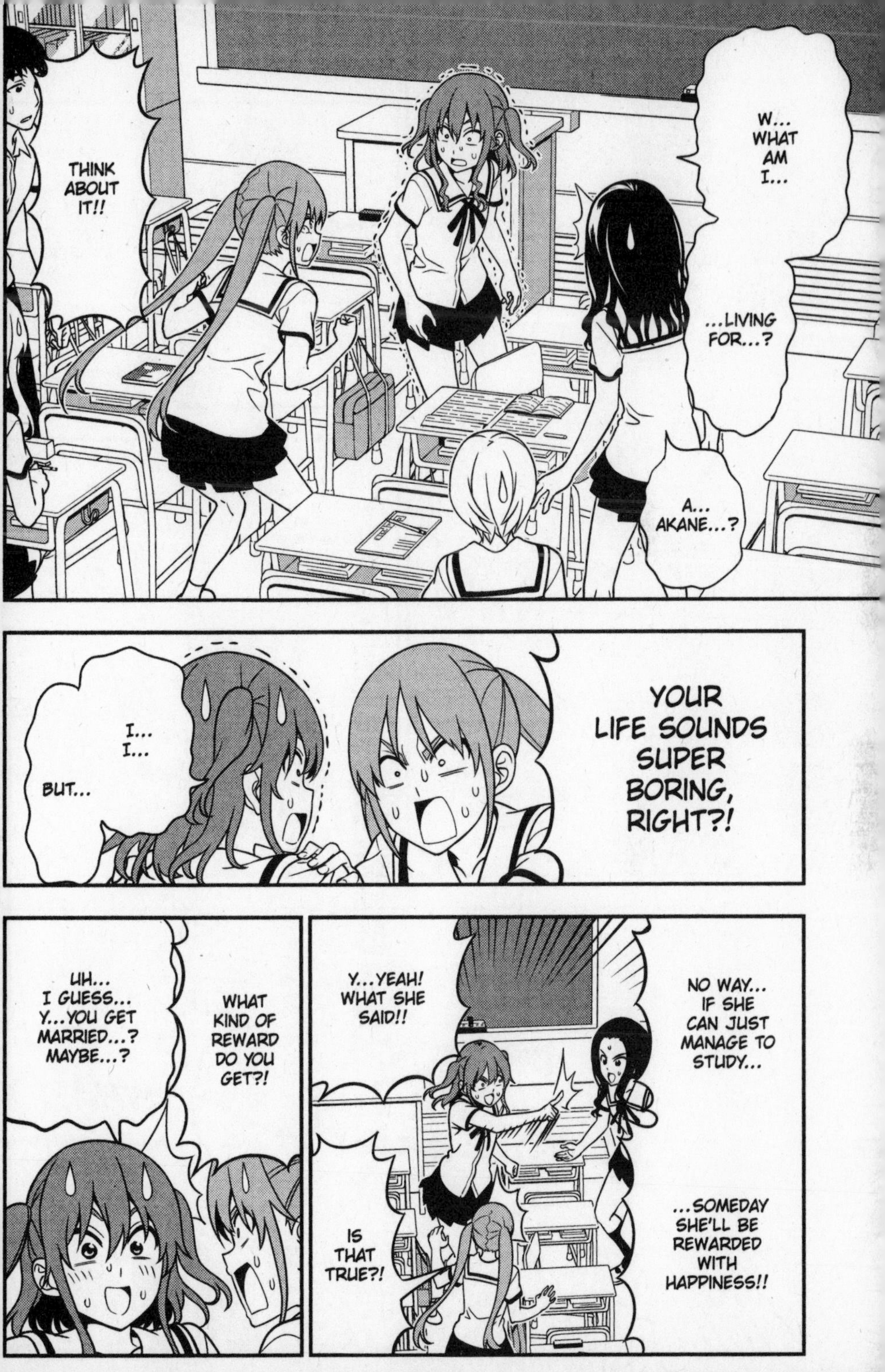
W... WHAT AM I...
...LIVING FOR...?
A... AKANE...?
THINK ABOUT IT!!
YOUR LIFE SOUNDS SUPER BORING, RIGHT?!
I... I...
BUT...
NO WAY... IF SHE CAN JUST MANAGE TO STUDY...
...SOMEDAY SHE'LL BE REWARDED WITH HAPPINESS!!
Y...YEAH! WHAT SHE SAID!!
IS THAT TRUE?!
WHAT KIND OF REWARD DO YOU GET?!
UH... I GUESS... Y...YOU GET MARRIED...? MAYBE...?

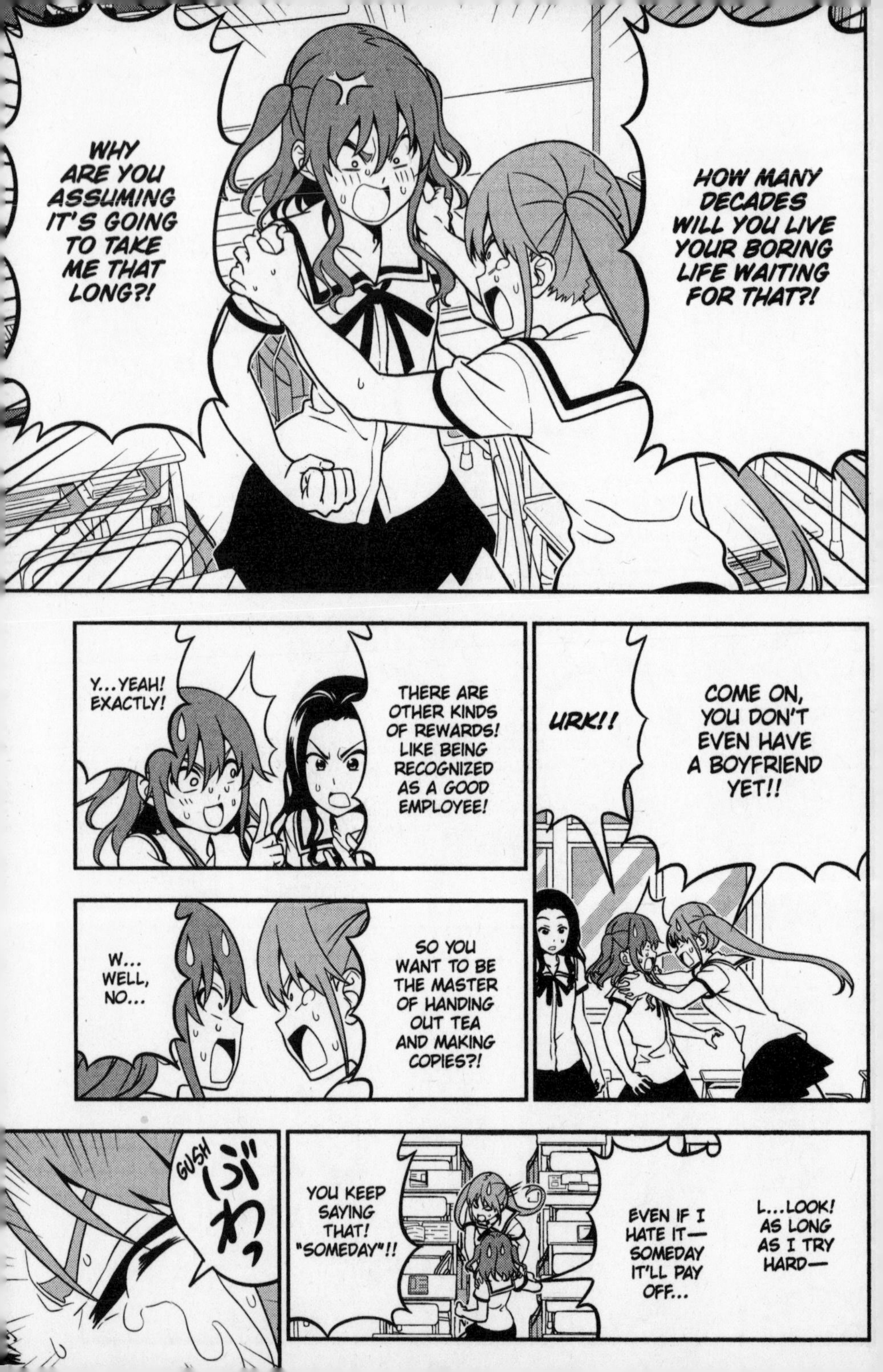
HOW MANY DECADES WILL YOU LIVE YOUR BORING LIFE WAITING FOR THAT?!
WHY ARE YOU ASSUMING IT'S GOING TO TAKE ME THAT LONG?!
COME ON, YOU DON'T EVEN HAVE A BOYFRIEND YET!!
URK!!
THERE ARE OTHER KINDS OF REWARDS! LIKE BEING RECOGNIZED AS A GOOD EMPLOYEE!
Y...YEAH! EXACTLY!
SO YOU WANT TO BE THE MASTER OF HANDING OUT TEA AND MAKING COPIES?!
W... WELL, NO...
L...LOOK! AS LONG AS I TRY HARD—
EVEN IF I HATE IT— SOMEDAY IT'LL PAY OFF...
YOU KEEP SAYING THAT! "SOMEDAY"!!
GUSH
ぶわっ

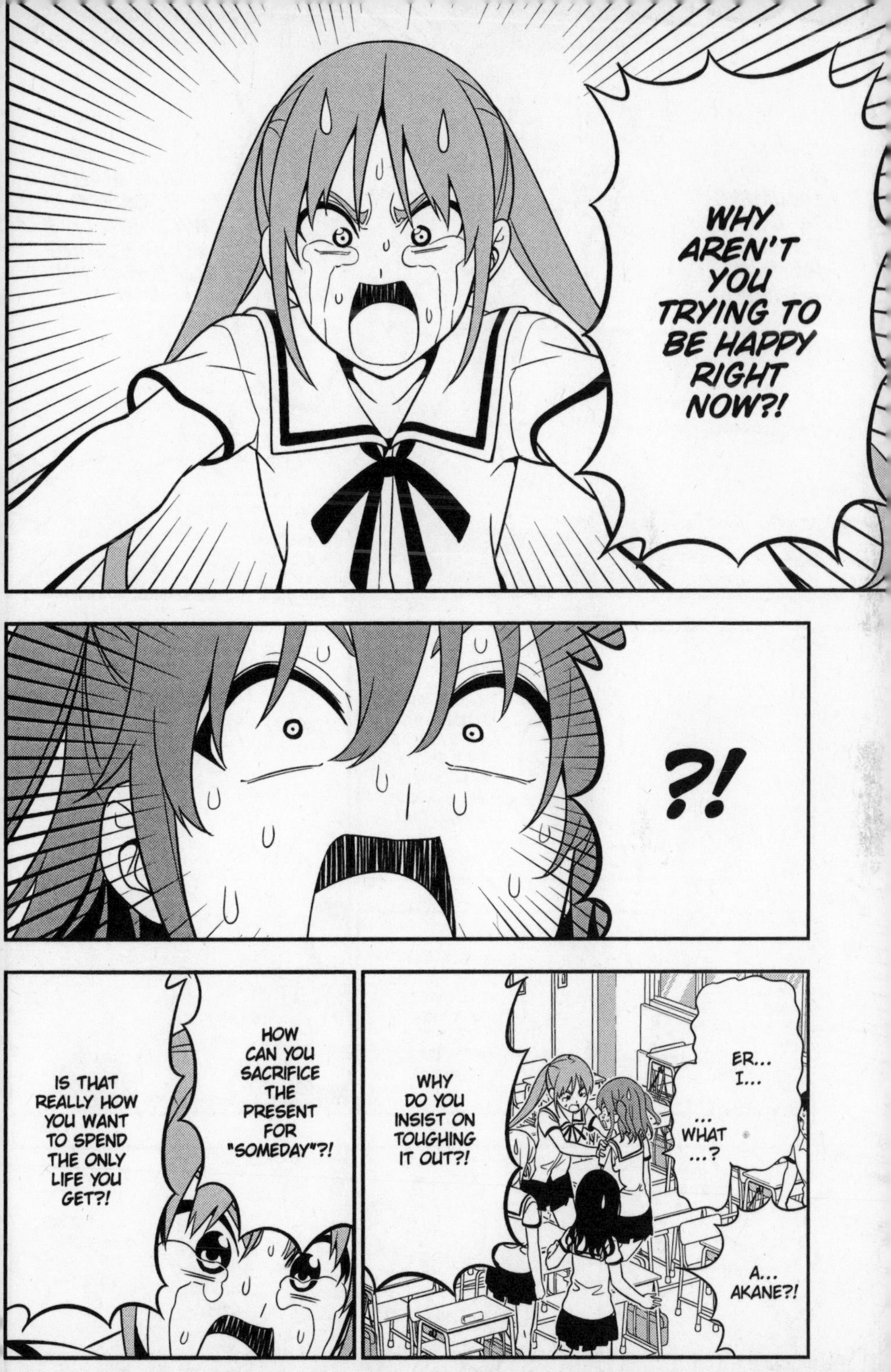
WHY AREN'T YOU TRYING TO BE HAPPY RIGHT NOW?!
?!
ER... I...
... WHAT ...?
WHY DO YOU INSIST ON TOUGHING IT OUT?!
A... AKANE?!
HOW CAN YOU SACRIFICE THE PRESENT FOR "SOMEDAY"?!
IS THAT REALLY HOW YOU WANT TO SPEND THE ONLY LIFE YOU GET?!

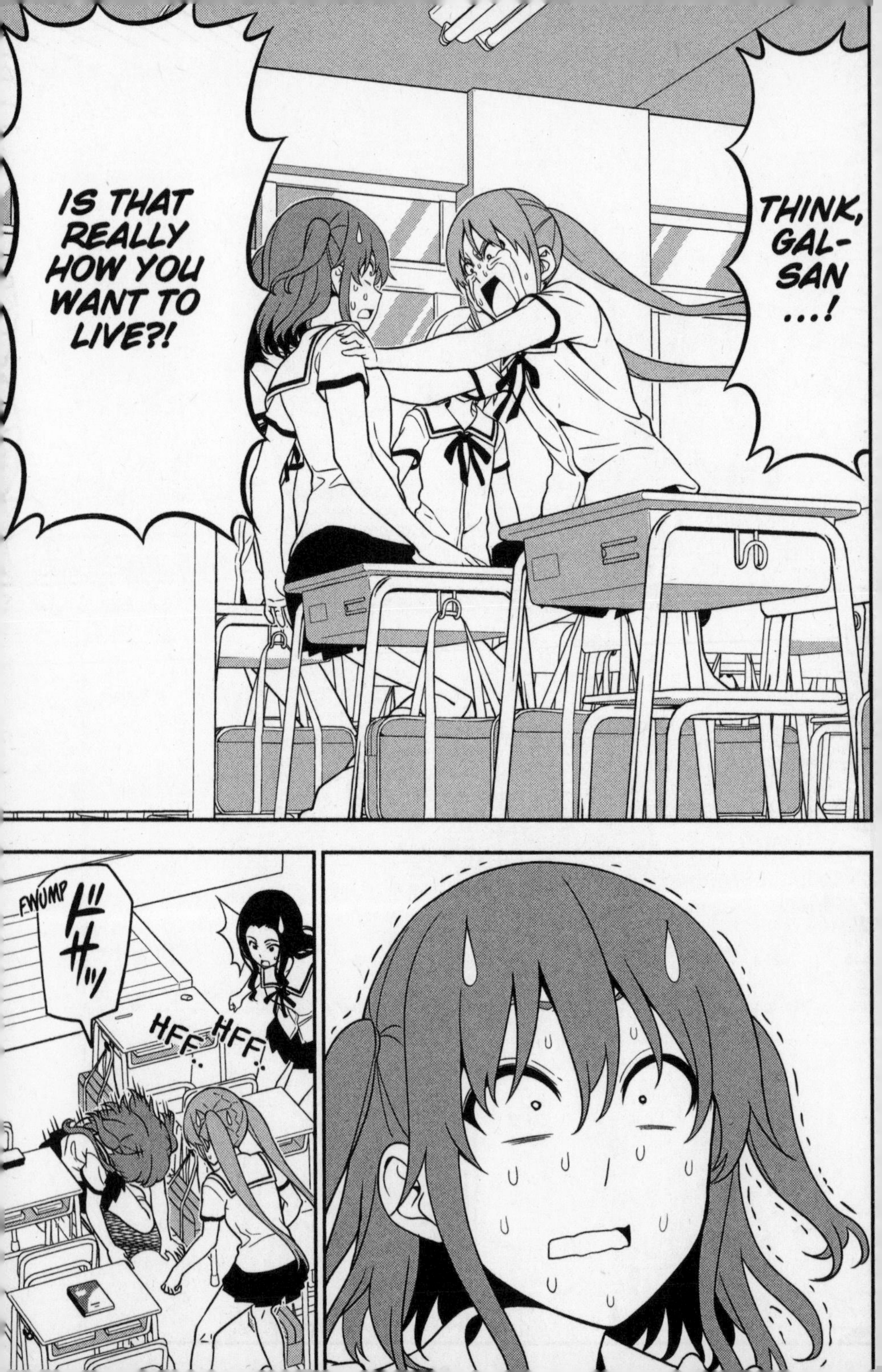
THINK, GAL-SAN ...!
IS THAT REALLY HOW YOU WANT TO LIVE?!
FWUMP
ドサッ
HFF HFF

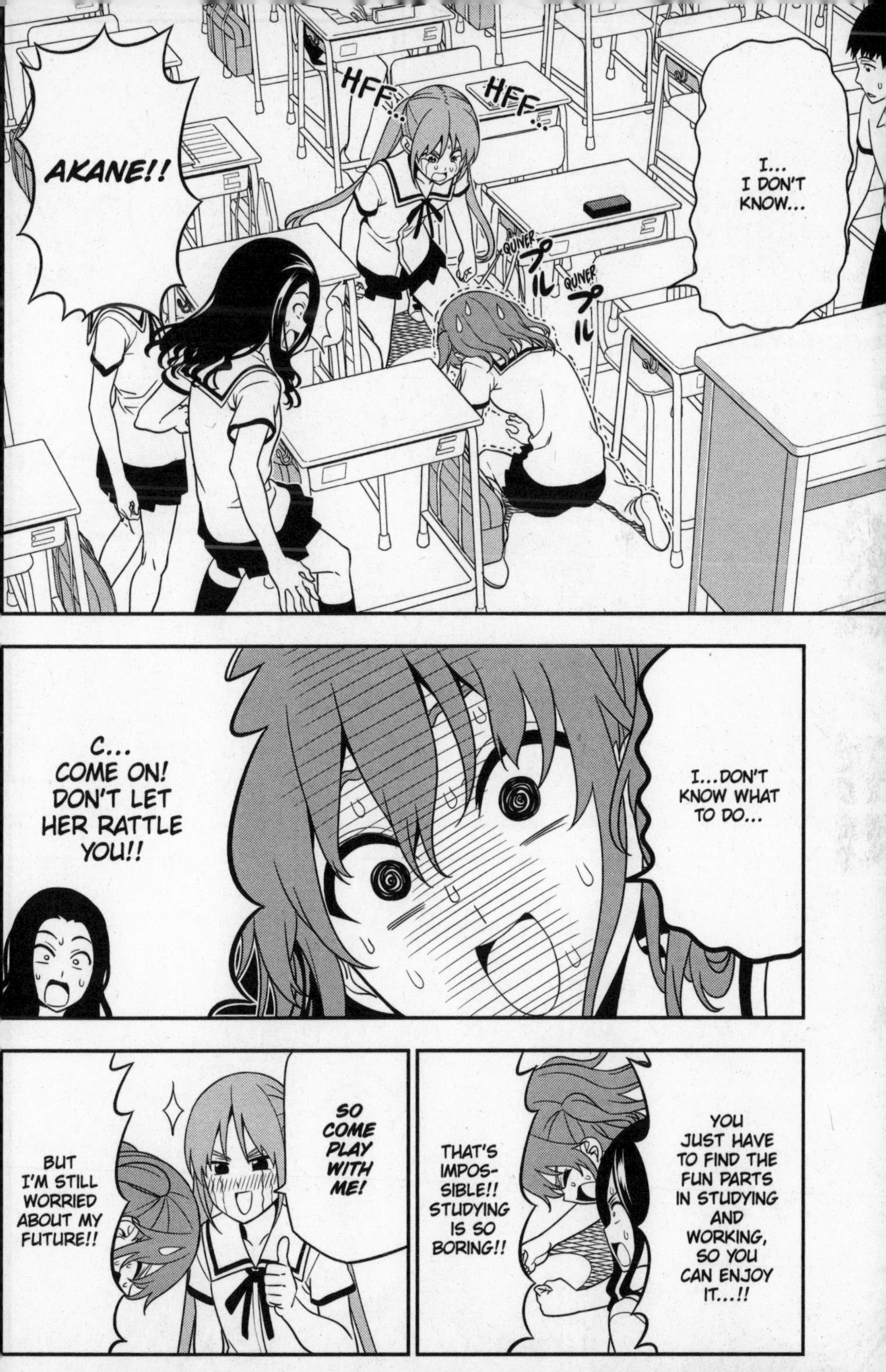
I... I DON'T KNOW...
HFF HFF
QUIVER
QUIVER
AKANE!!
I...DON'T KNOW WHAT TO DO...
C... COME ON! DON'T LET HER RATTLE YOU!!
YOU JUST HAVE TO FIND THE FUN PARTS IN STUDYING AND WORKING, SO YOU CAN ENJOY IT...!!
THAT'S IMPOSSIBLE!! STUDYING IS SO BORING!!
SO COME PLAY WITH ME!
BUT I'M STILL WORRIED ABOUT MY FUTURE!!

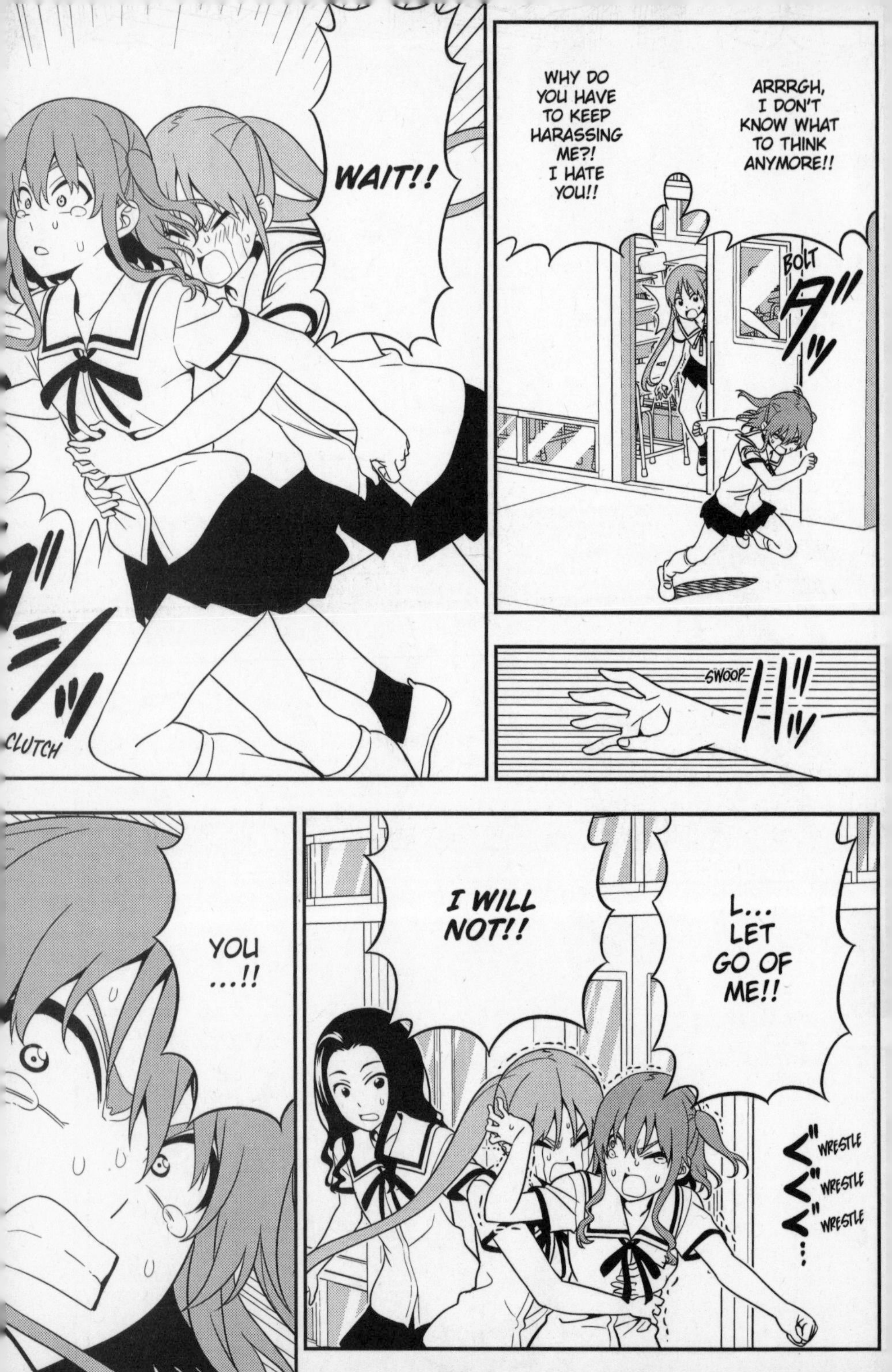
ARRRGH, I DON'T KNOW WHAT TO THINK ANYMORE!!
WHY DO YOU HAVE TO KEEP HARASSING ME?! I HATE YOU!!
BOLT
ダッ
SWOOP
WAIT!!
CLUTCH
L... LET GO OF ME!!
I WILL NOT!!
WRESTLE
WRESTLE
WRESTLE
YOU ...!!

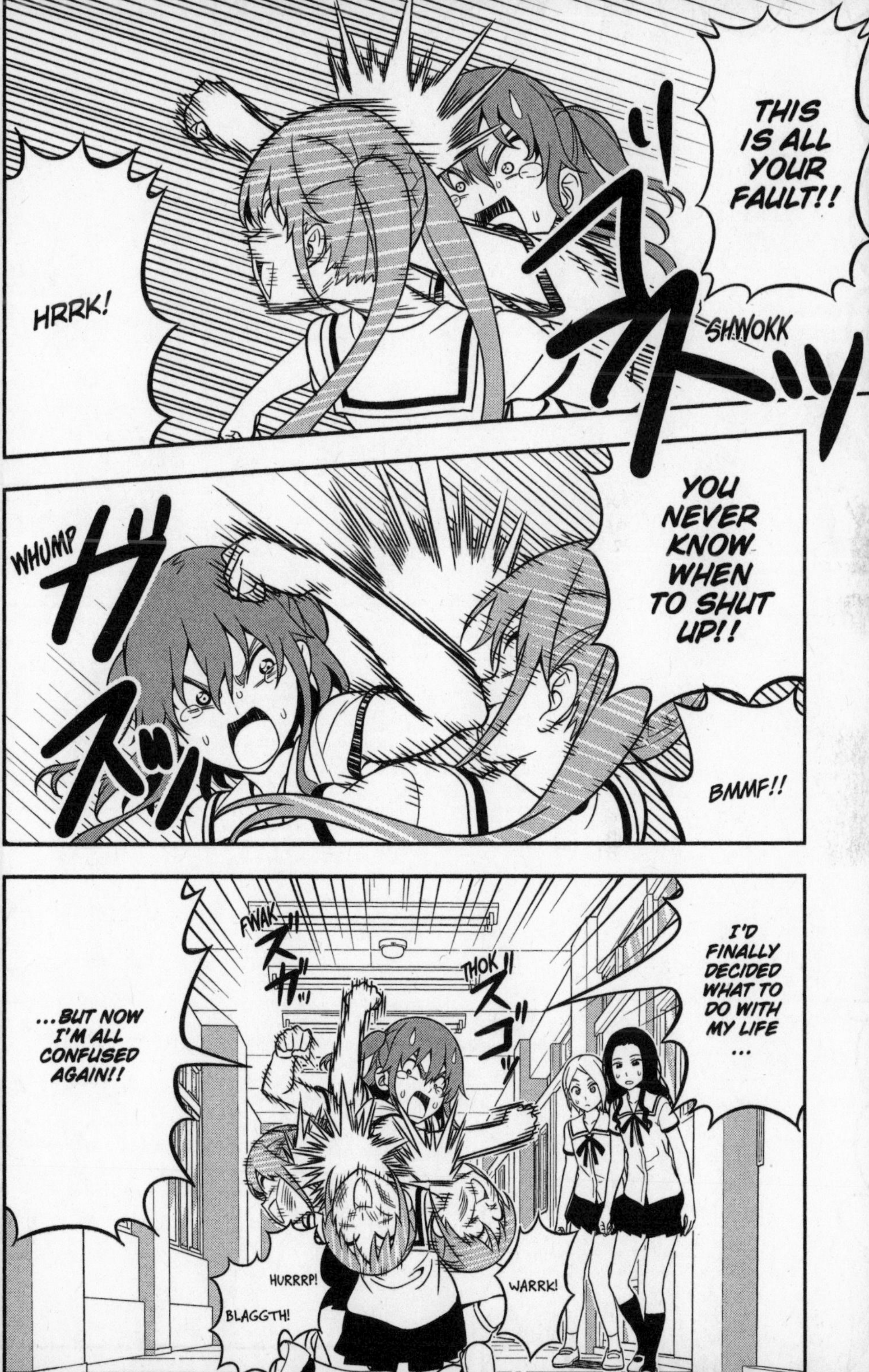
THIS IS ALL YOUR FAULT!!
SHWOKK
ズドッ
HRRK!
YOU NEVER KNOW WHEN TO SHUT UP!!
BMMF!!
WHUMP
ガスッ
I'D FINALLY DECIDED WHAT TO DO WITH MY LIFE ...
THOK
ズゴッ
FWAK
ズガッ
...BUT NOW I'M ALL CONFUSED AGAIN!!
WARRK!
HURRRP!
BLAGGTH!

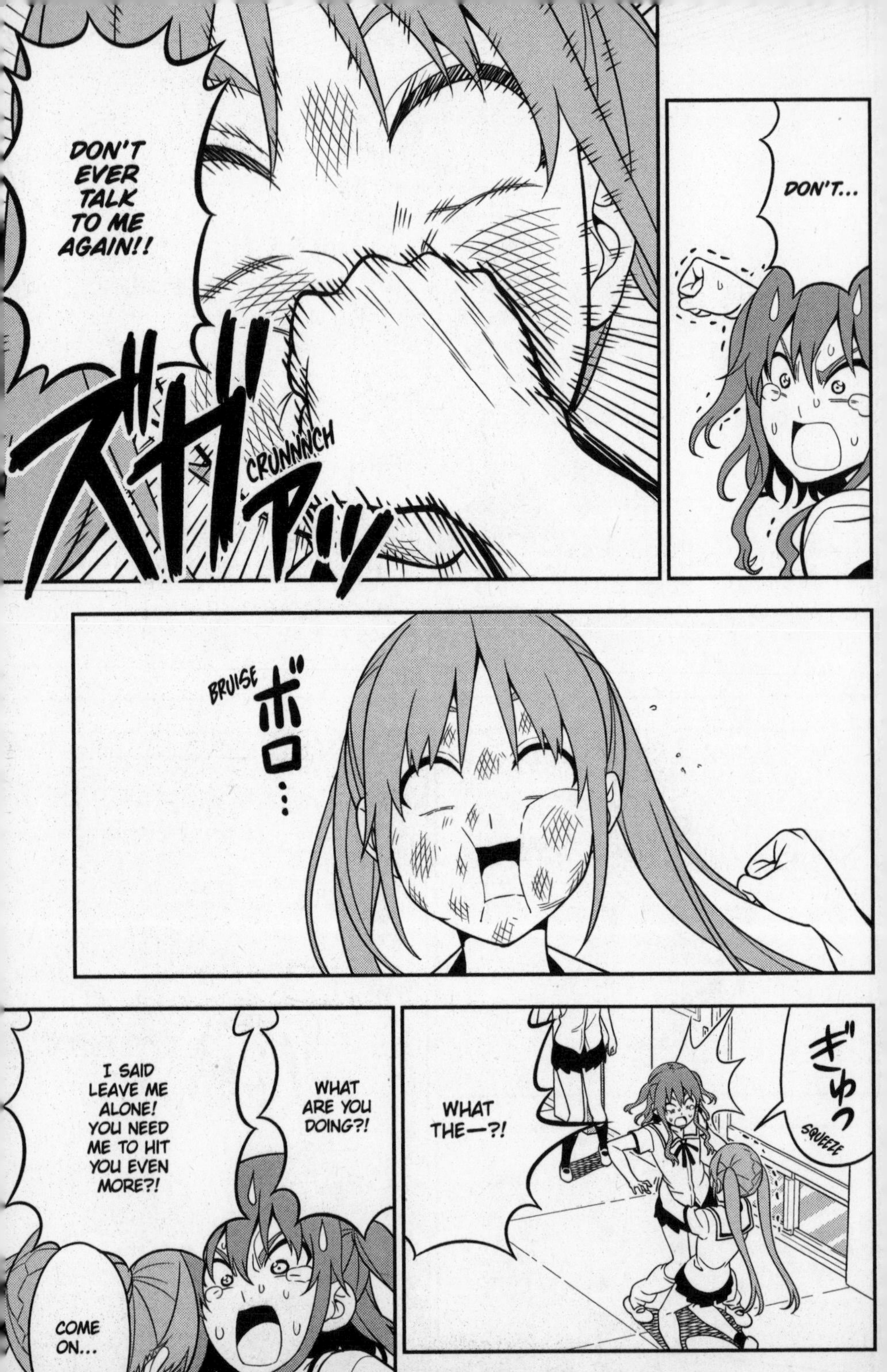
DON'T...
DON'T EVER TALK TO ME AGAIN!!
ズガァッ
CRUNNNCH
BRUISE
ボロ…
ぎゅっ
SQUEEZE
WHAT THE—?!
WHAT ARE YOU DOING?!
I SAID LEAVE ME ALONE! YOU NEED ME TO HIT YOU EVEN MORE?!
COME ON...

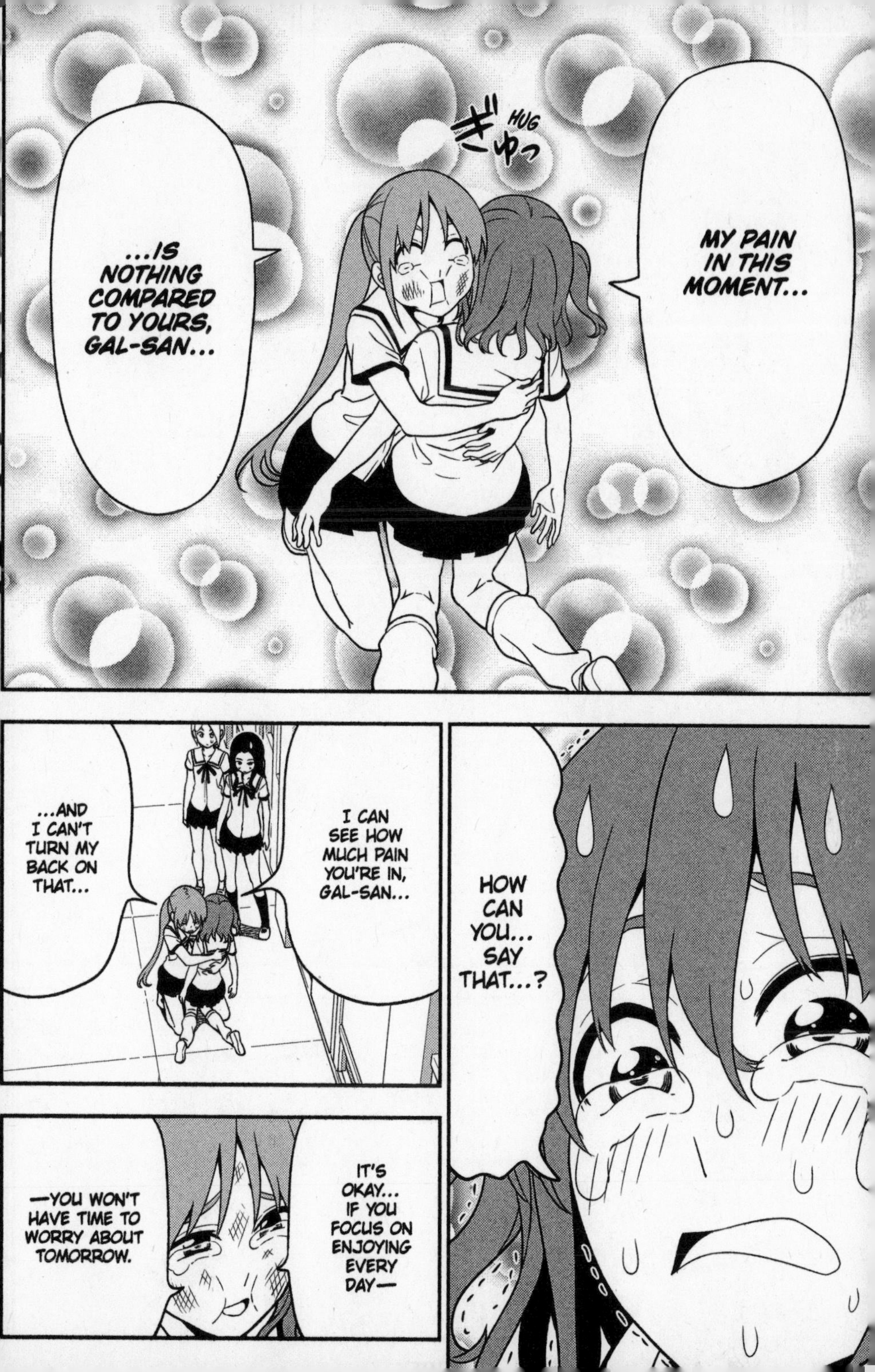
MY PAIN IN THIS MOMENT...
ぎゅっ HUG
...IS NOTHING COMPARED TO YOURS, GAL-SAN...
HOW CAN YOU... SAY THAT...?
I CAN SEE HOW MUCH PAIN YOU'RE IN, GAL-SAN...
...AND I CAN'T TURN MY BACK ON THAT...
IT'S OKAY... IF YOU FOCUS ON ENJOYING EVERY DAY—
—YOU WON'T HAVE TIME TO WORRY ABOUT TOMORROW.

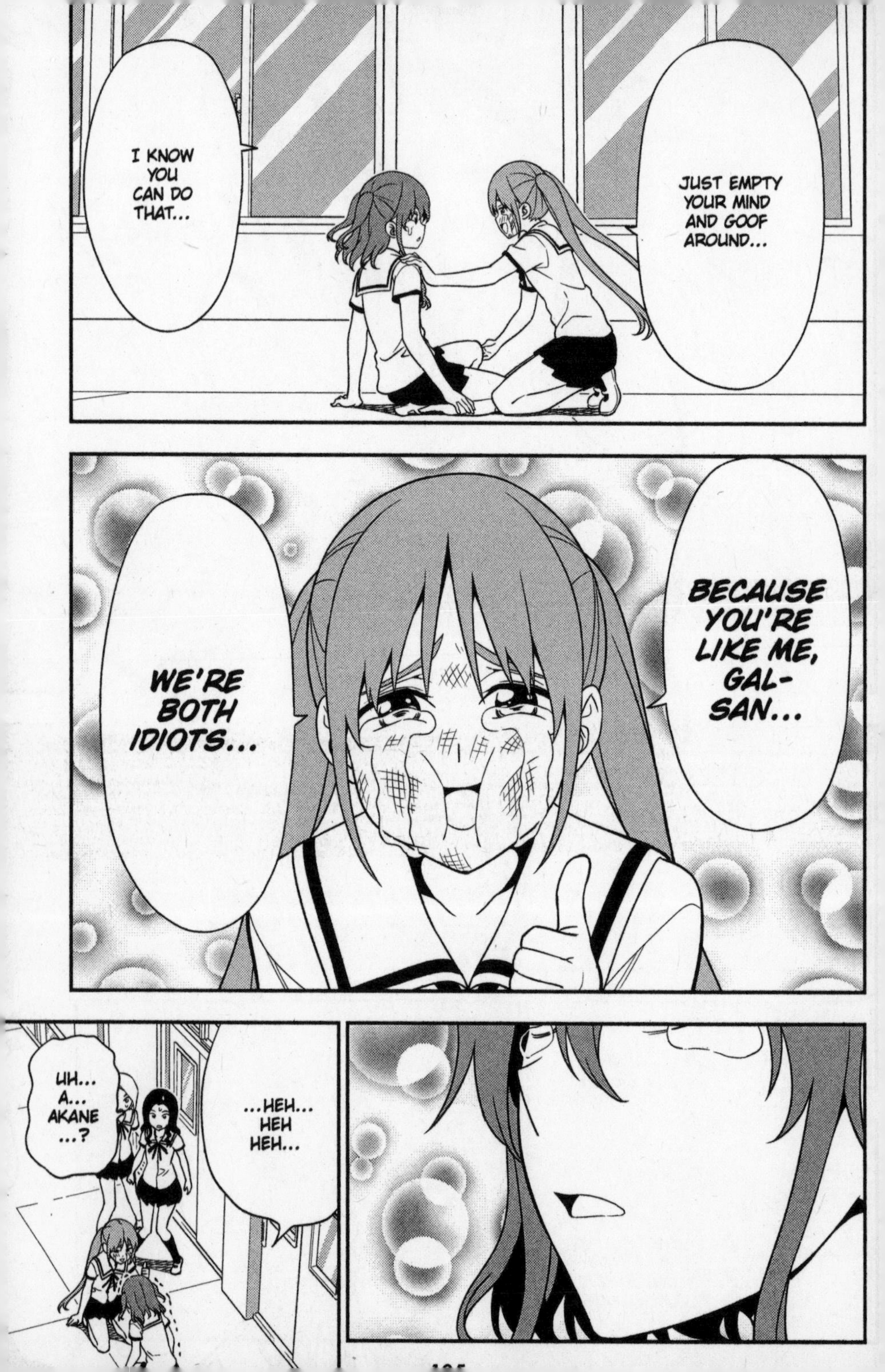
JUST EMPTY YOUR MIND AND GOOF AROUND...
I KNOW YOU CAN DO THAT...
BECAUSE YOU'RE LIKE ME, GAL-SAN...
WE'RE BOTH IDIOTS...
...HEH... HEH HEH...
UH... A... AKANE ...?

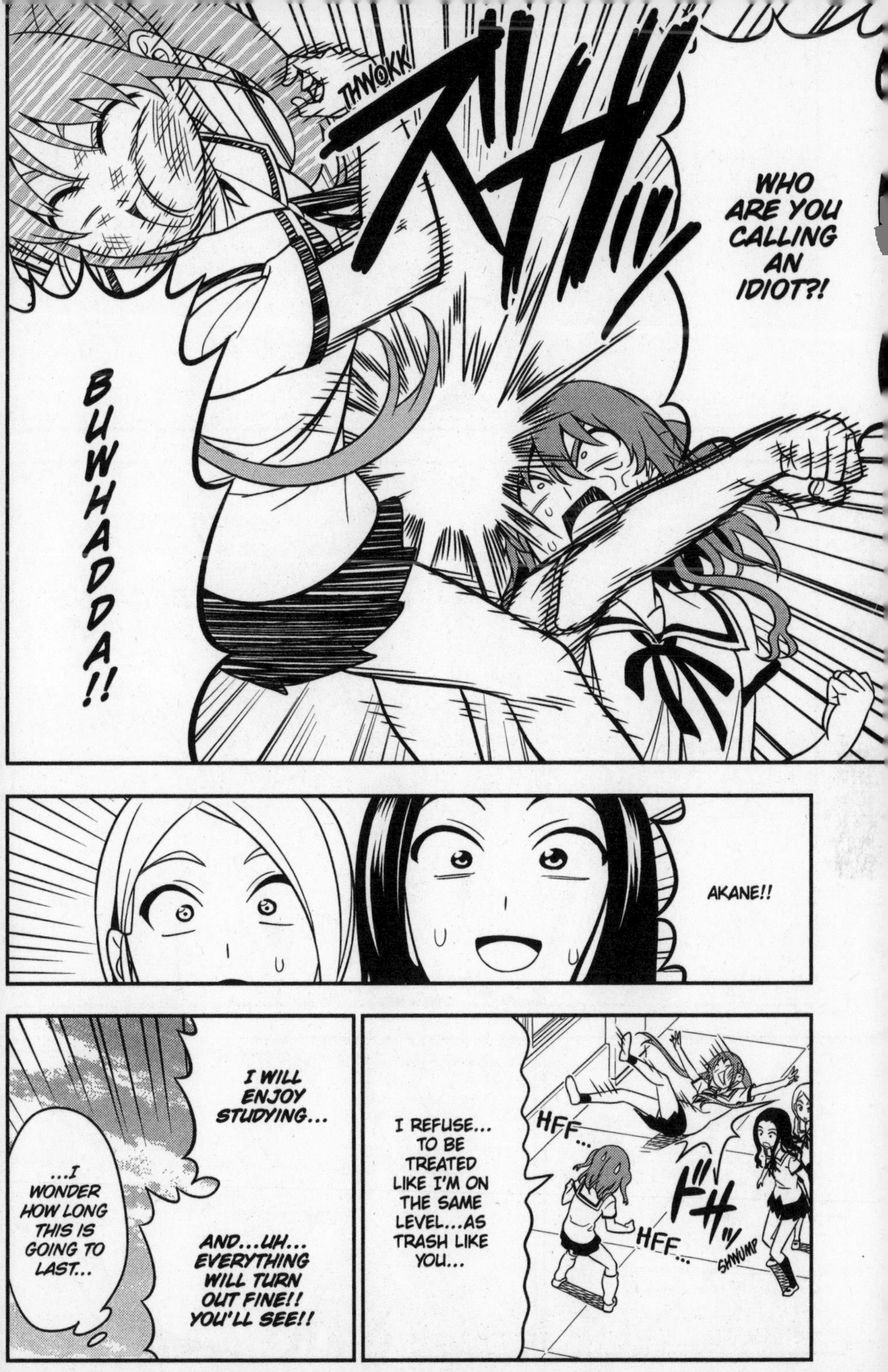
WHO ARE YOU CALLING AN IDIOT?!
THWOKK
BUWHADDADA!!
AKANE!!
I REFUSE... TO BE TREATED LIKE I'M ON THE SAME LEVEL...AS TRASH LIKE YOU...
HFF...
HFF...
SHWUMP
I WILL ENJOY STUDYING...
AND...UH... EVERYTHING WILL TURN OUT FINE!! YOU'LL SEE!!
...I WONDER HOW LONG THIS IS GOING TO LAST...

Got the Units Wrong

カリカリカリカリ
SCRIBBLE SCRIBBLE SCRIBBLE SCRIBBLE
I'M GONNA DO IT!! WATCH THIS!!
FIF-TEEN MIN-UTES LATER
... THIS SUCKS ...
THAT WAS QUICK ...

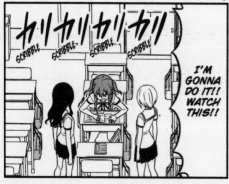

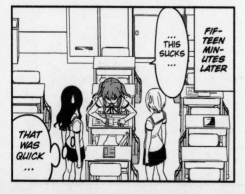

(When you go to college, will you be able to use that)

Aho-Girl

\\'ahô͵gərl\ *Japanese, noun*.
A clueless girl.

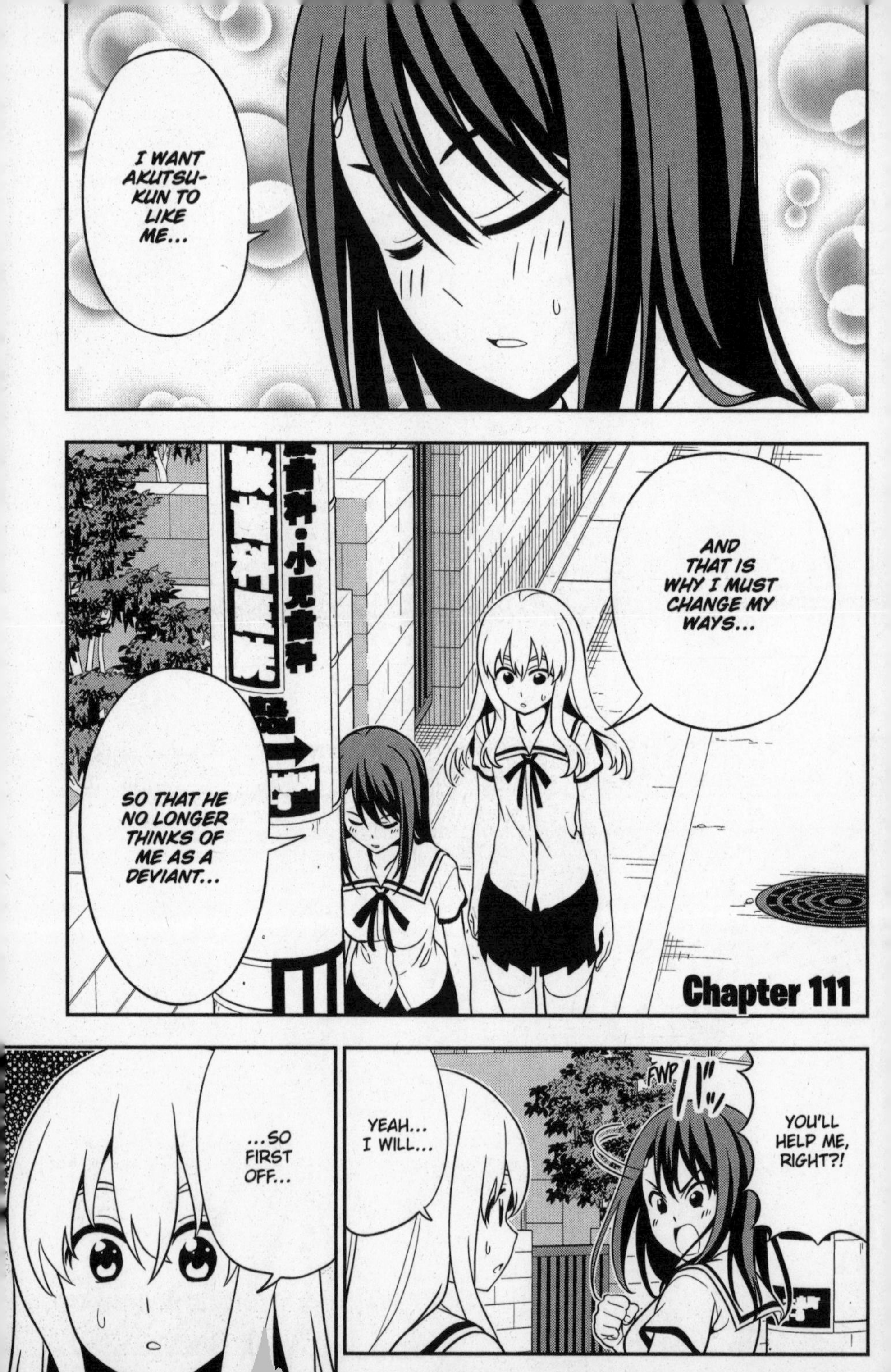
I WANT AKUTSU-KUN TO LIKE ME...
AND THAT IS WHY I MUST CHANGE MY WAYS...
SO THAT HE NO LONGER THINKS OF ME AS A DEVIANT...
Chapter 111
FWP
YOU'LL HELP ME, RIGHT?!
YEAH... I WILL...
...SO FIRST OFF...

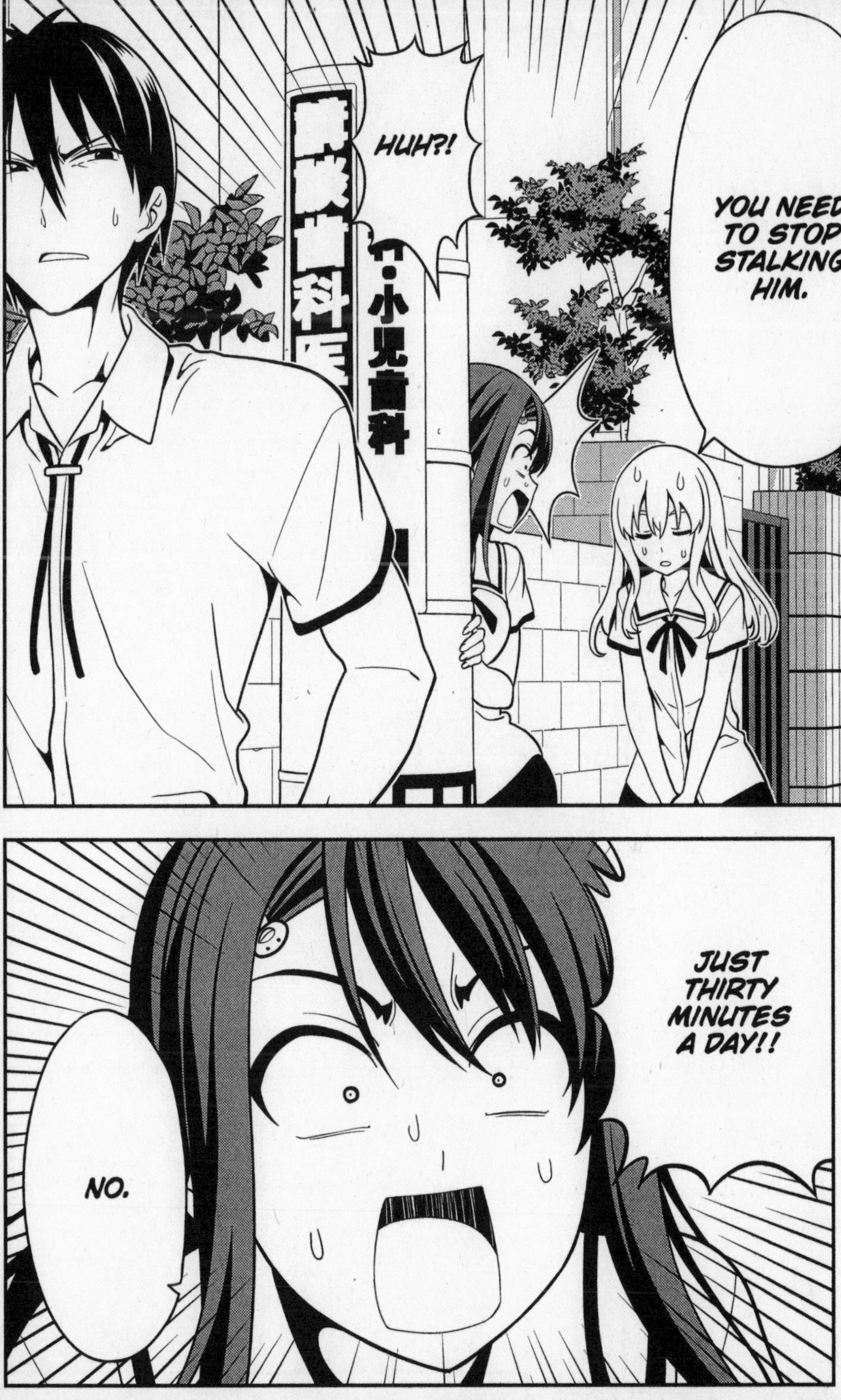
YOU NEED TO STOP STALKING HIM.
HUH?!
JUST THIRTY MINUTES A DAY!!
NO.

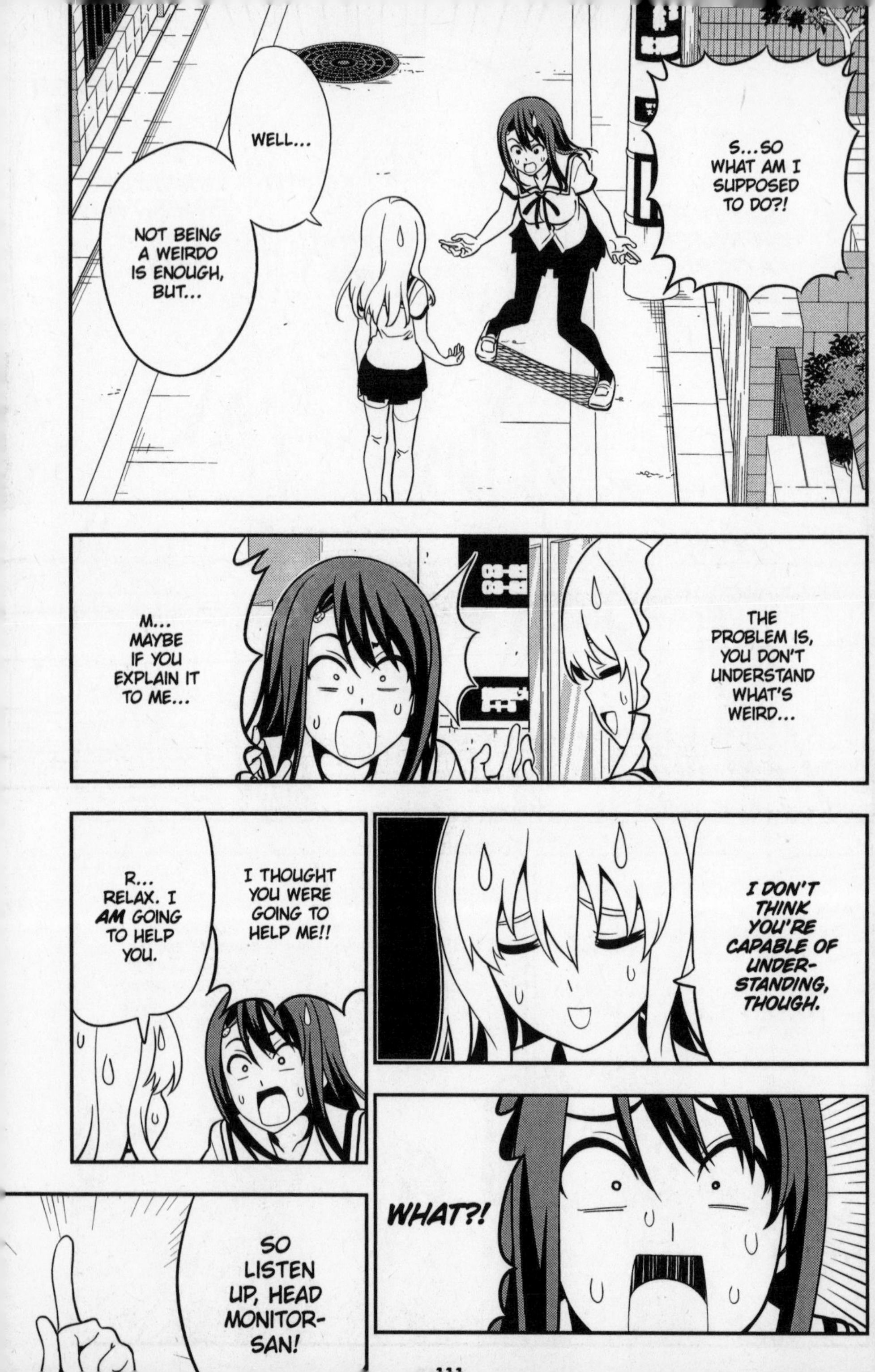
S...SO WHAT AM I SUPPOSED TO DO?!
WELL...
NOT BEING A WEIRDO IS ENOUGH, BUT...
THE PROBLEM IS, YOU DON'T UNDERSTAND WHAT'S WEIRD...
M... MAYBE IF YOU EXPLAIN IT TO ME...
I DON'T THINK YOU'RE CAPABLE OF UNDER-STANDING, THOUGH.
WHAT?!
I THOUGHT YOU WERE GOING TO HELP ME!!
R... RELAX. I ***AM*** GOING TO HELP YOU.
SO LISTEN UP, HEAD MONITOR-SAN!

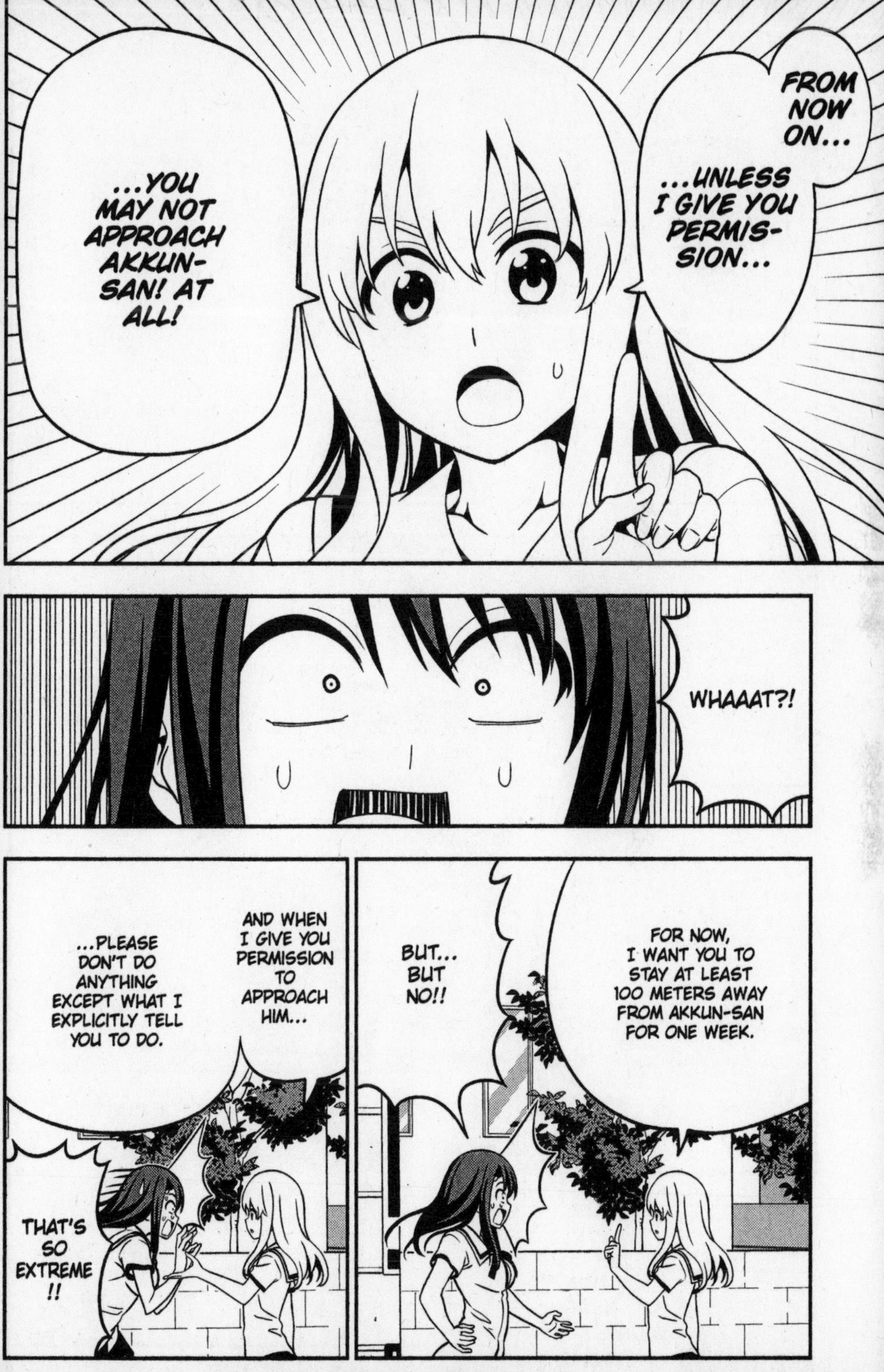
FROM NOW ON...
...UNLESS I GIVE YOU PERMISSION...
...YOU MAY NOT APPROACH AKKUN-SAN! AT ALL!
WHAAAT?!
FOR NOW, I WANT YOU TO STAY AT LEAST 100 METERS AWAY FROM AKKUN-SAN FOR ONE WEEK.
BUT... BUT NO!!
AND WHEN I GIVE YOU PERMISSION TO APPROACH HIM...
...PLEASE DON'T DO ANYTHING EXCEPT WHAT I EXPLICITLY TELL YOU TO DO.
THAT'S SO EXTREME!!

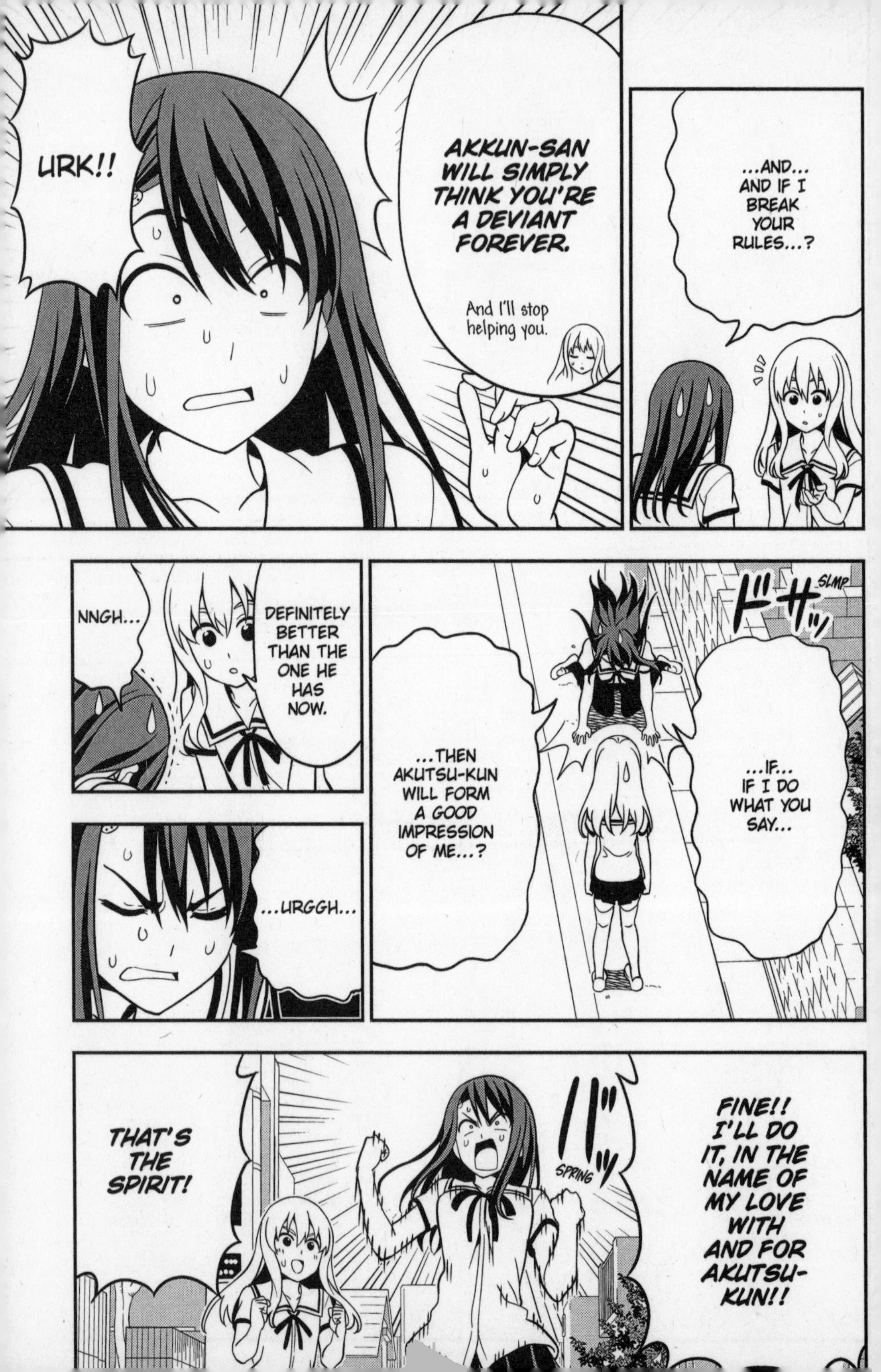
...AND... AND IF I BREAK YOUR RULES...?
AKKUN-SAN WILL SIMPLY THINK YOU'RE A DEVIANT FOREVER.
And I'll stop helping you.
URK!!
ドサッ
SLMP
...IF... IF I DO WHAT YOU SAY...
...THEN AKUTSU-KUN WILL FORM A GOOD IMPRESSION OF ME...?
DEFINITELY BETTER THAN THE ONE HE HAS NOW.
NNGH...
...URGGH...
FINE!! I'LL DO IT, IN THE NAME OF MY LOVE WITH AND FOR AKUTSU-KUN!!
バッ
SPRING
THAT'S THE SPIRIT!

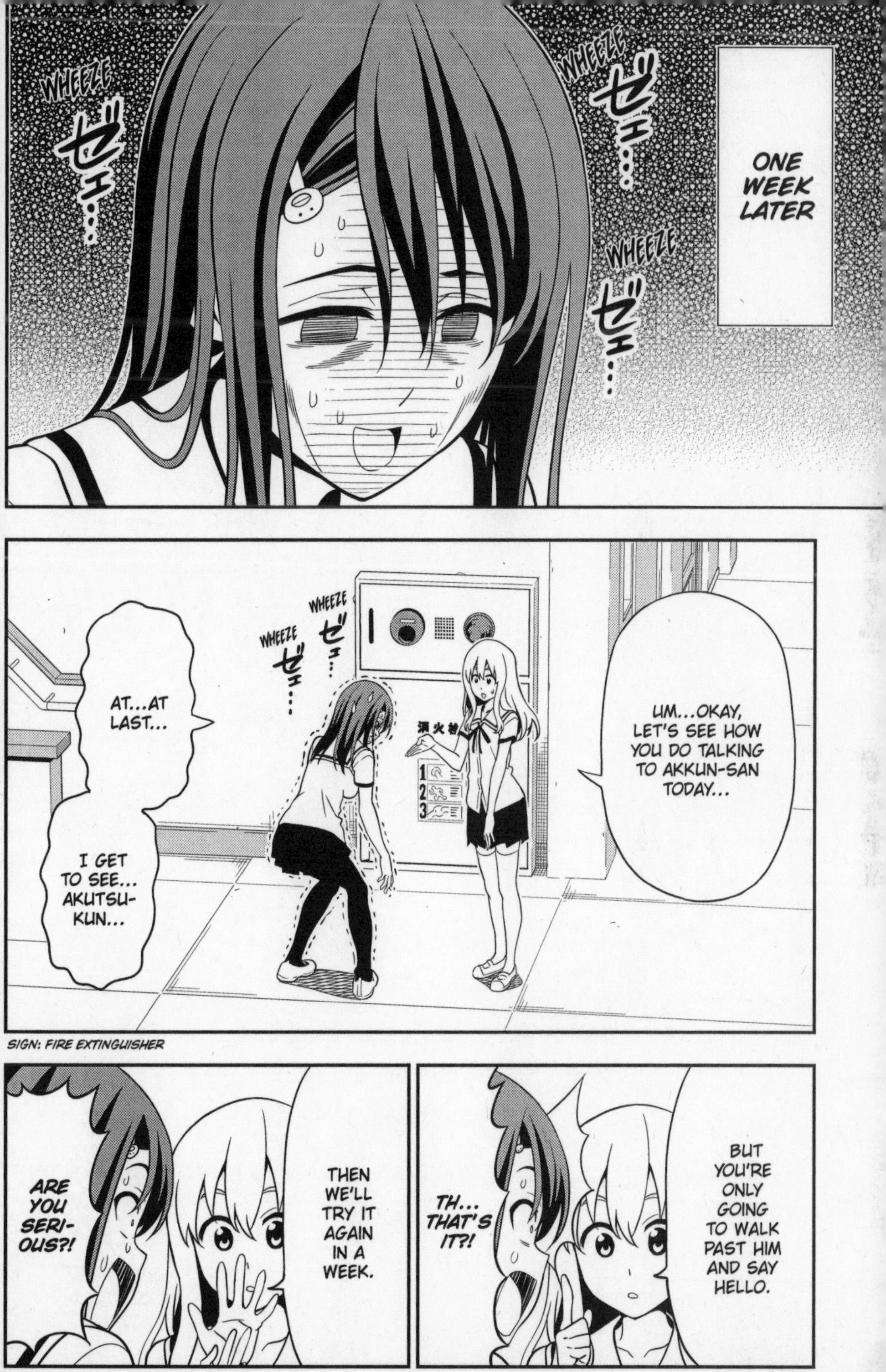
ONE WEEK LATER
WHEEZE ゼェ…
WHEEZE ゼェ…
WHEEZE ゼェ…
UM…OKAY, LET'S SEE HOW YOU DO TALKING TO AKKUN-SAN TODAY…
WHEEZE ゼェ…
WHEEZE ゼェ…
AT…AT LAST…
I GET TO SEE… AKUTSU-KUN…
SIGN: FIRE EXTINGUISHER
BUT YOU'RE ONLY GOING TO WALK PAST HIM AND SAY HELLO.
TH… THAT'S IT?!
THEN WE'LL TRY IT AGAIN IN A WEEK.
ARE YOU SERI-OUS?!

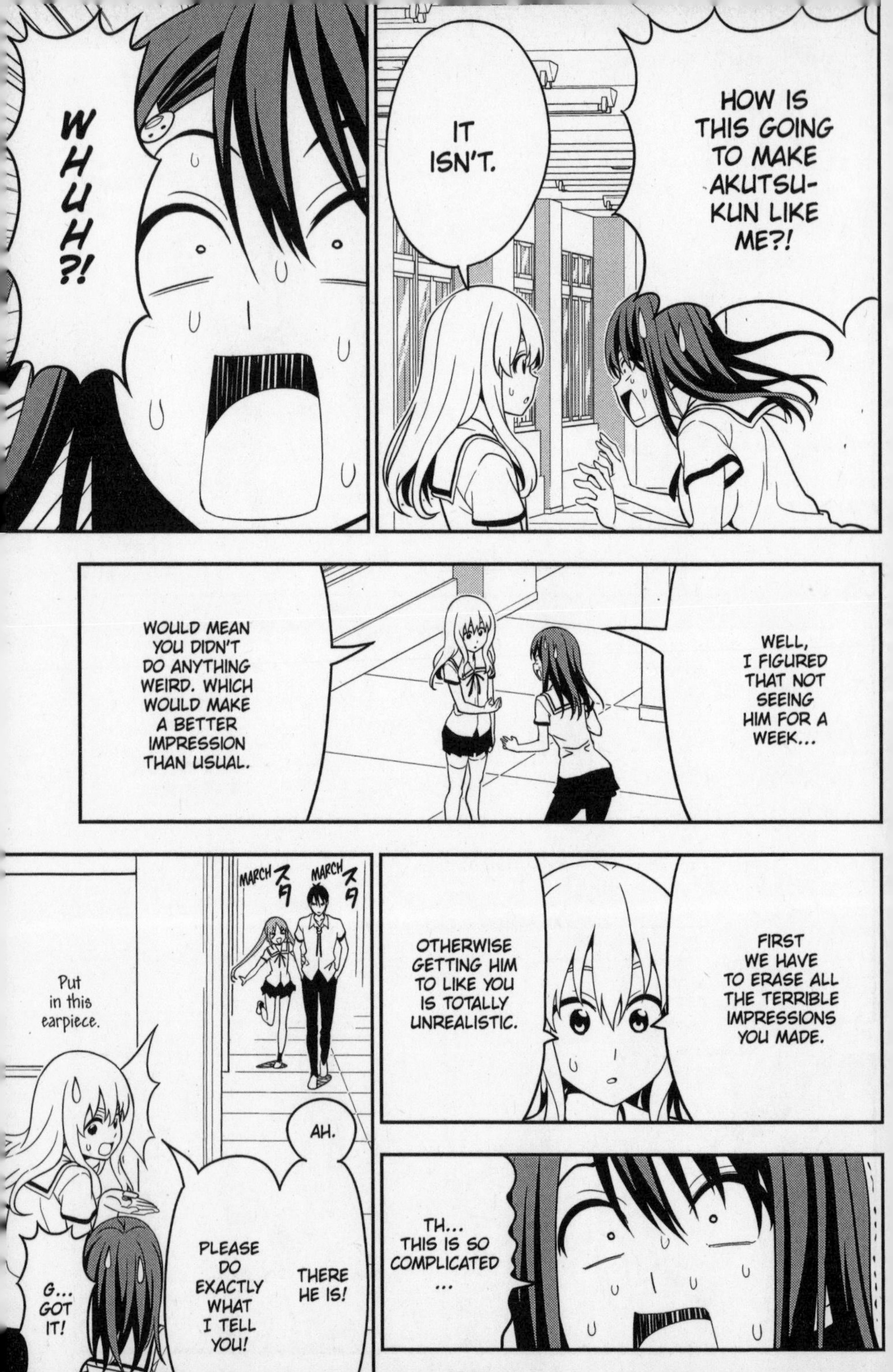

HOW IS THIS GOING TO MAKE AKUTSU-KUN LIKE ME?!
IT ISN'T.
WHUH?!
WELL, I FIGURED THAT NOT SEEING HIM FOR A WEEK...
WOULD MEAN YOU DIDN'T DO ANYTHING WEIRD. WHICH WOULD MAKE A BETTER IMPRESSION THAN USUAL.
FIRST WE HAVE TO ERASE ALL THE TERRIBLE IMPRESSIONS YOU MADE.
OTHERWISE GETTING HIM TO LIKE YOU IS TOTALLY UNREALISTIC.
TH... THIS IS SO COMPLICATED ...
MARCH スタ
MARCH スタ
AH.
THERE HE IS!
PLEASE DO EXACTLY WHAT I TELL YOU!
Put in this earpiece.
G... GOT IT!

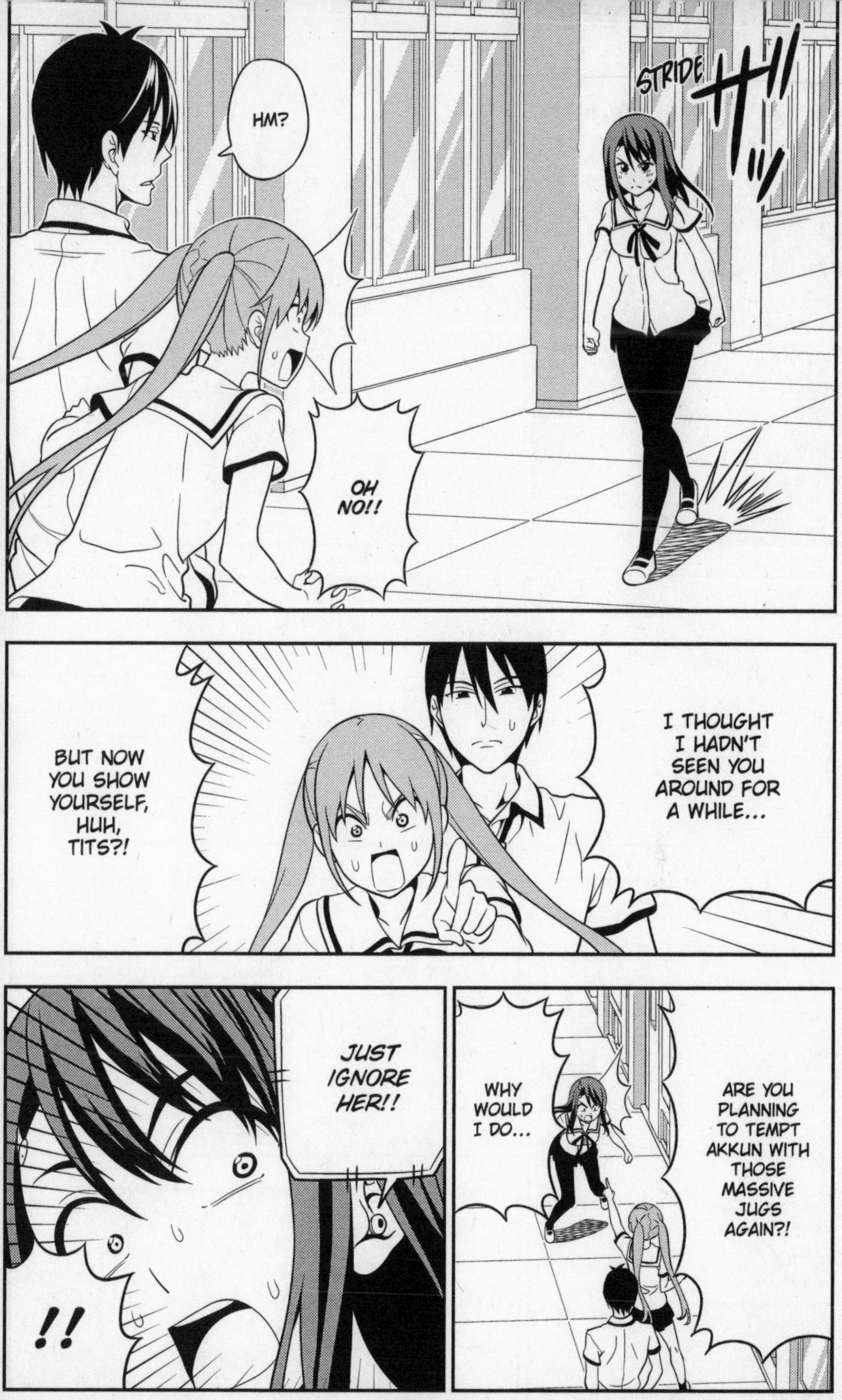
STRIDE
HM?
OH NO!!
I THOUGHT I HADN'T SEEN YOU AROUND FOR A WHILE...
BUT NOW YOU SHOW YOURSELF, HUH, TITS?!
ARE YOU PLANNING TO TEMPT AKKUN WITH THOSE MASSIVE JUGS AGAIN?!
WHY WOULD I DO...
JUST IGNORE HER!!
!!

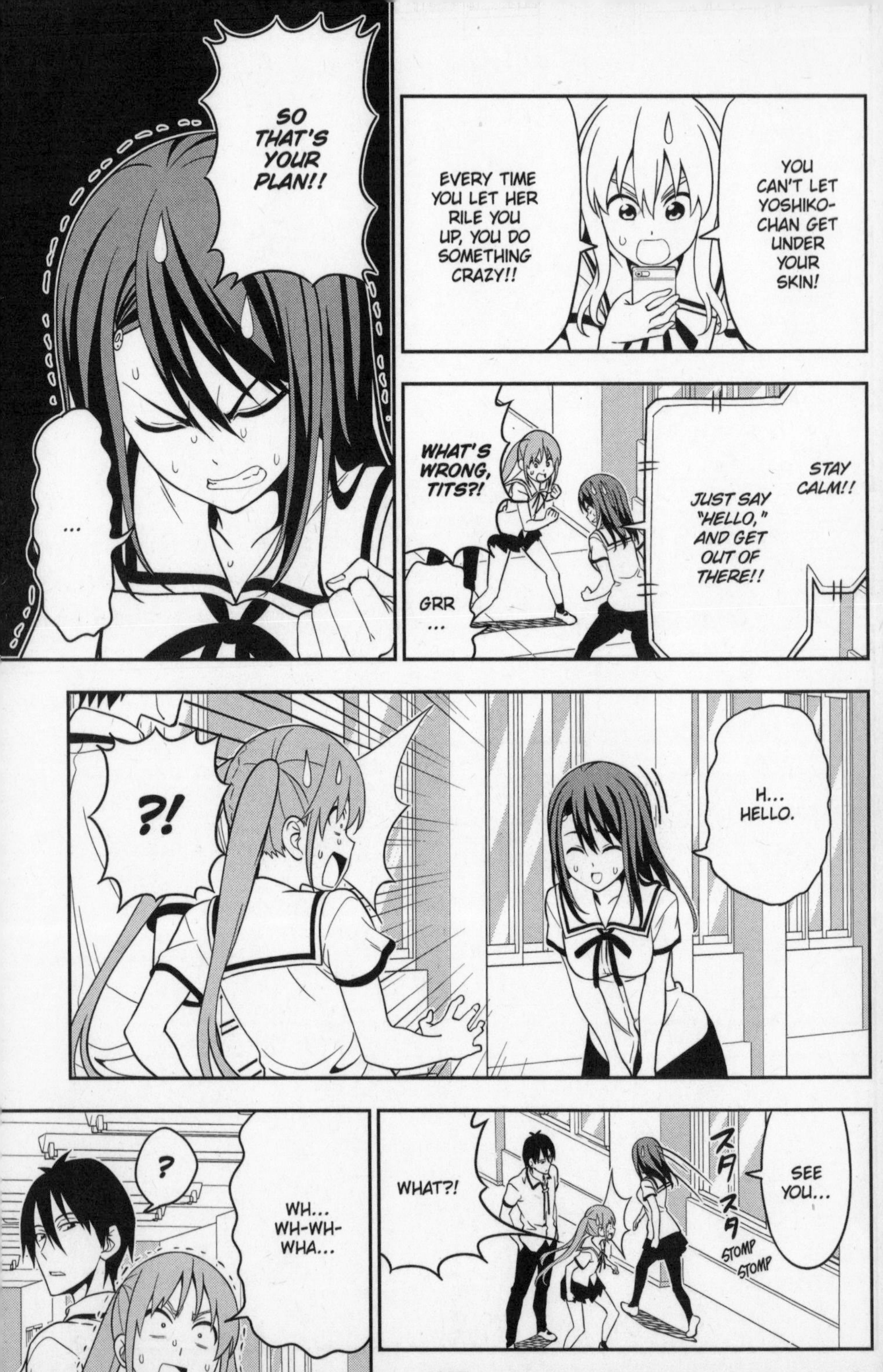
YOU CAN'T LET YOSHIKO-CHAN GET UNDER YOUR SKIN!
EVERY TIME YOU LET HER RILE YOU UP, YOU DO SOMETHING CRAZY!!
STAY CALM!!
JUST SAY "HELLO," AND GET OUT OF THERE!!
WHAT'S WRONG, TITS?!
GRR...
SO THAT'S YOUR PLAN!!
...
H... HELLO.
?!
SEE YOU...
スタスタ
STOMP STOMP
WHAT?!
WH... WH-WH-WHA...
?

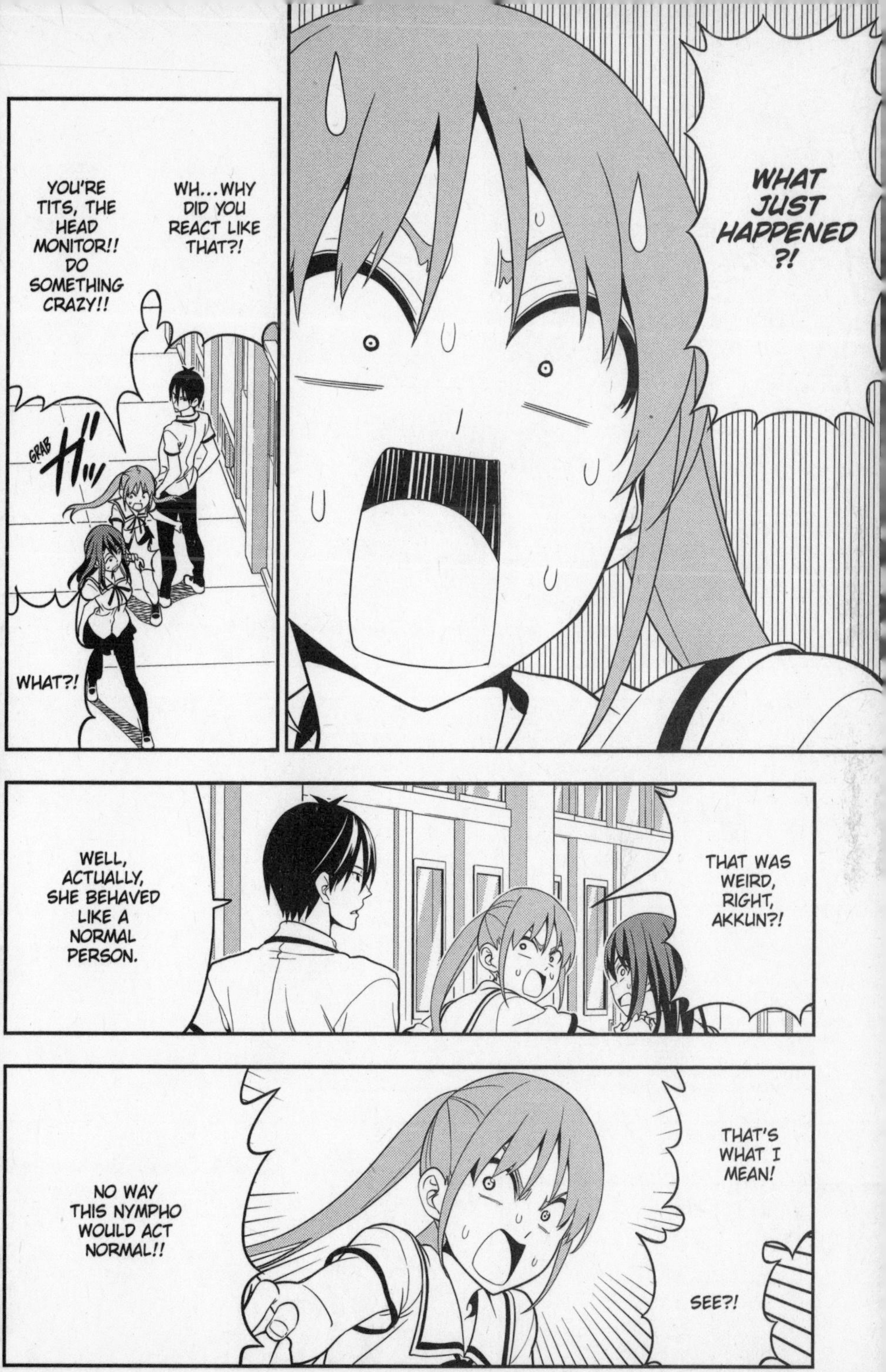
WHAT JUST HAPPENED?!
WH...WHY DID YOU REACT LIKE THAT?!
YOU'RE TITS, THE HEAD MONITOR!! DO SOMETHING CRAZY!!
GRAB
WHAT?!
THAT WAS WEIRD, RIGHT, AKKUN?!
WELL, ACTUALLY, SHE BEHAVED LIKE A NORMAL PERSON.
THAT'S WHAT I MEAN!
NO WAY THIS NYMPHO WOULD ACT NORMAL!!
SEE?!

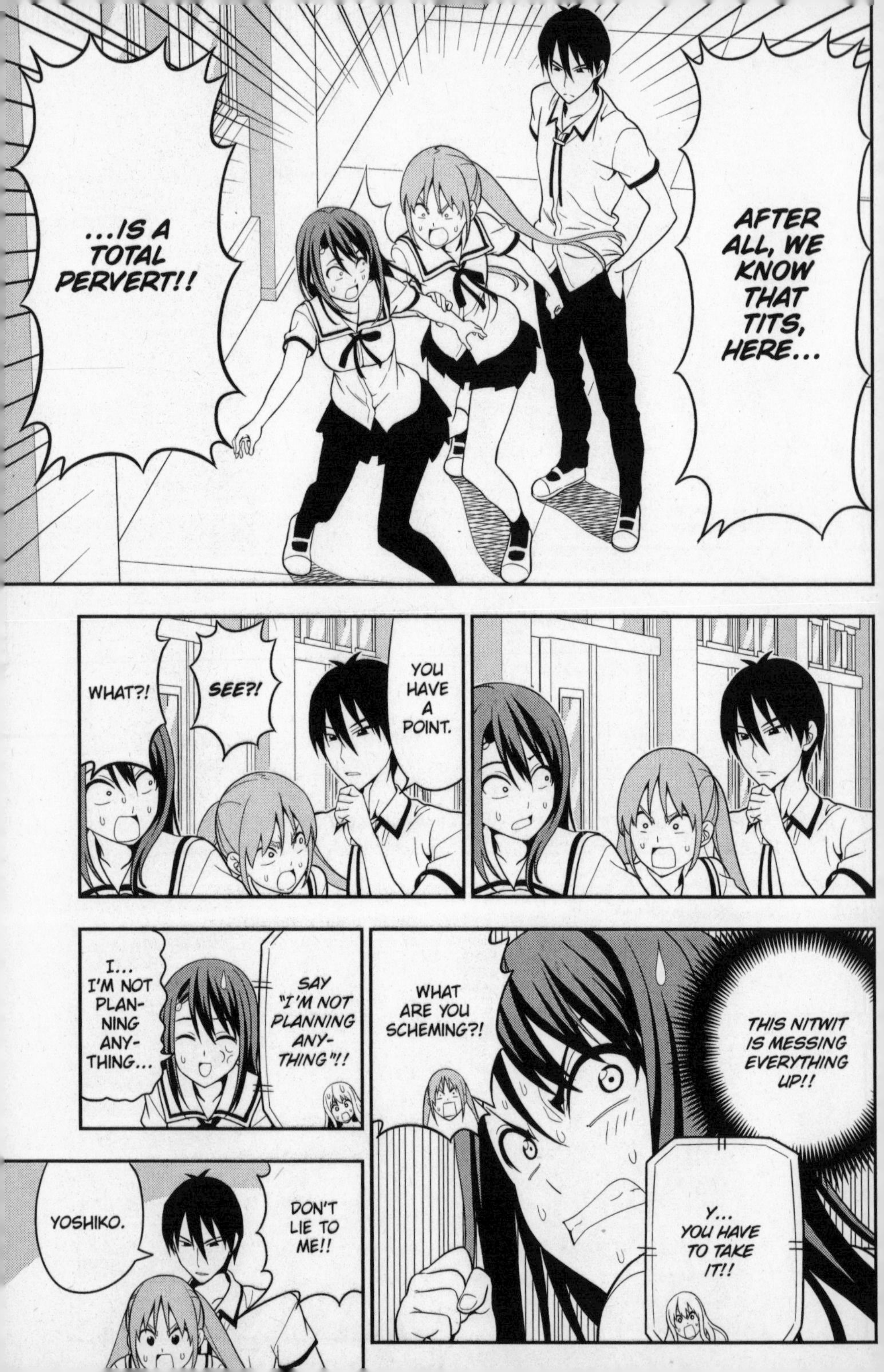
AFTER ALL, WE KNOW THAT TITS, HERE...
...IS A TOTAL PERVERT!!
YOU HAVE A POINT.
SEE?!
WHAT?!
THIS NITWIT IS MESSING EVERYTHING UP!!
WHAT ARE YOU SCHEMING?!
Y... YOU HAVE TO TAKE IT!!
SAY "I'M NOT PLANNING ANYTHING"!!
I... I'M NOT PLANNING ANYTHING...
DON'T LIE TO ME!!
YOSHIKO.

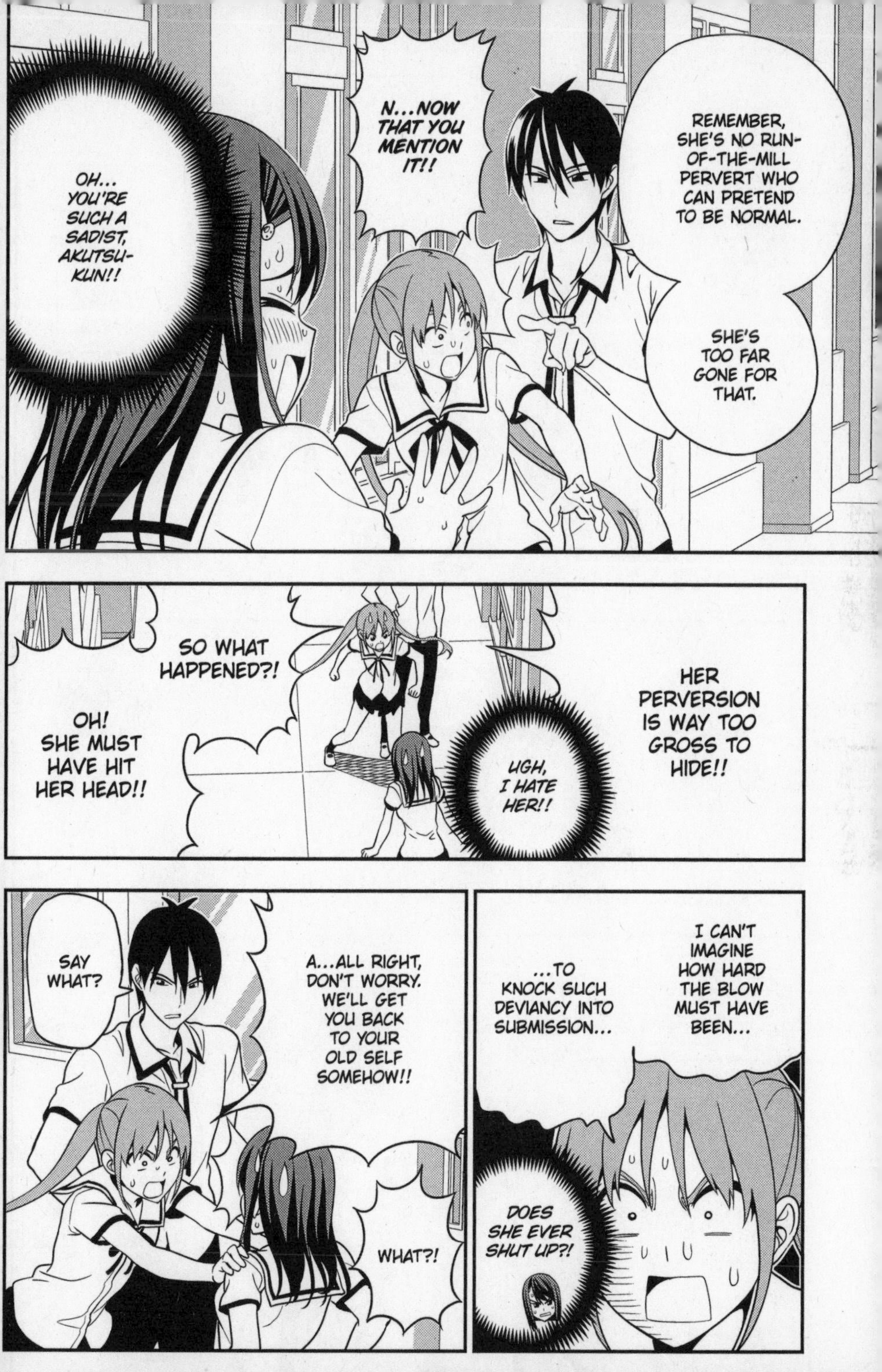
REMEMBER, SHE'S NO RUN-OF-THE-MILL PERVERT WHO CAN PRETEND TO BE NORMAL.
SHE'S TOO FAR GONE FOR THAT.
N...NOW THAT YOU MENTION IT!!
OH... YOU'RE SUCH A SADIST, AKUTSU-KUN!!
HER PERVERSION IS WAY TOO GROSS TO HIDE!!
UGH, I HATE HER!!
SO WHAT HAPPENED?!
OH! SHE MUST HAVE HIT HER HEAD!!
I CAN'T IMAGINE HOW HARD THE BLOW MUST HAVE BEEN...
...TO KNOCK SUCH DEVIANCY INTO SUBMISSION...
DOES SHE EVER SHUT UP?!
A...ALL RIGHT, DON'T WORRY. WE'LL GET YOU BACK TO YOUR OLD SELF SOMEHOW!!
SAY WHAT?
WHAT?!

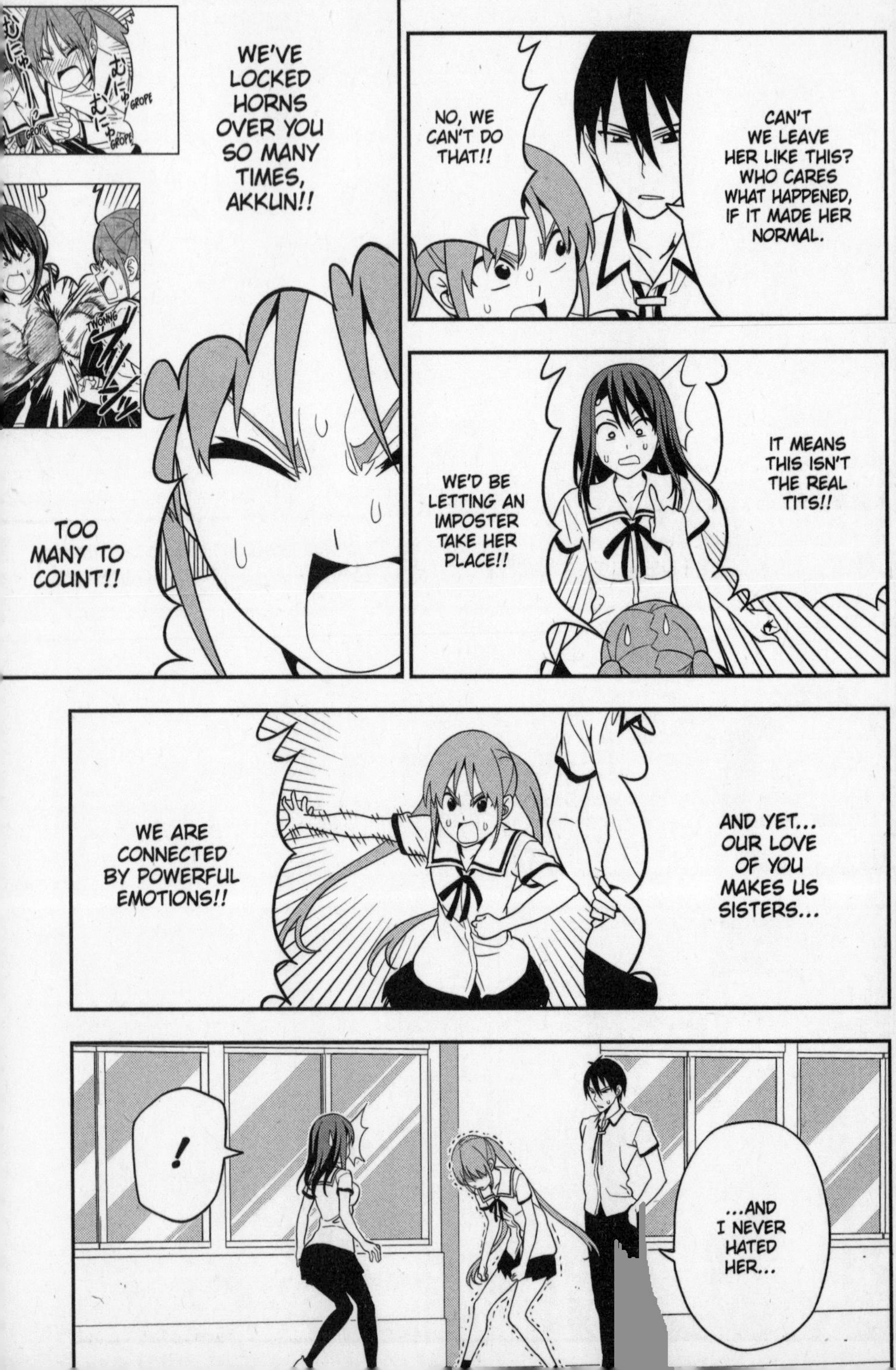
CAN'T WE LEAVE HER LIKE THIS? WHO CARES WHAT HAPPENED, IF IT MADE HER NORMAL.
NO, WE CAN'T DO THAT!!
IT MEANS THIS ISN'T THE REAL TITS!!
WE'D BE LETTING AN IMPOSTER TAKE HER PLACE!!
WE'VE LOCKED HORNS OVER YOU SO MANY TIMES, AKKUN!!
GROPE
GROPE
GROPE
TWONNG
TOO MANY TO COUNT!!
AND YET... OUR LOVE OF YOU MAKES US SISTERS...
WE ARE CONNECTED BY POWERFUL EMOTIONS!!
...AND I NEVER HATED HER...
!

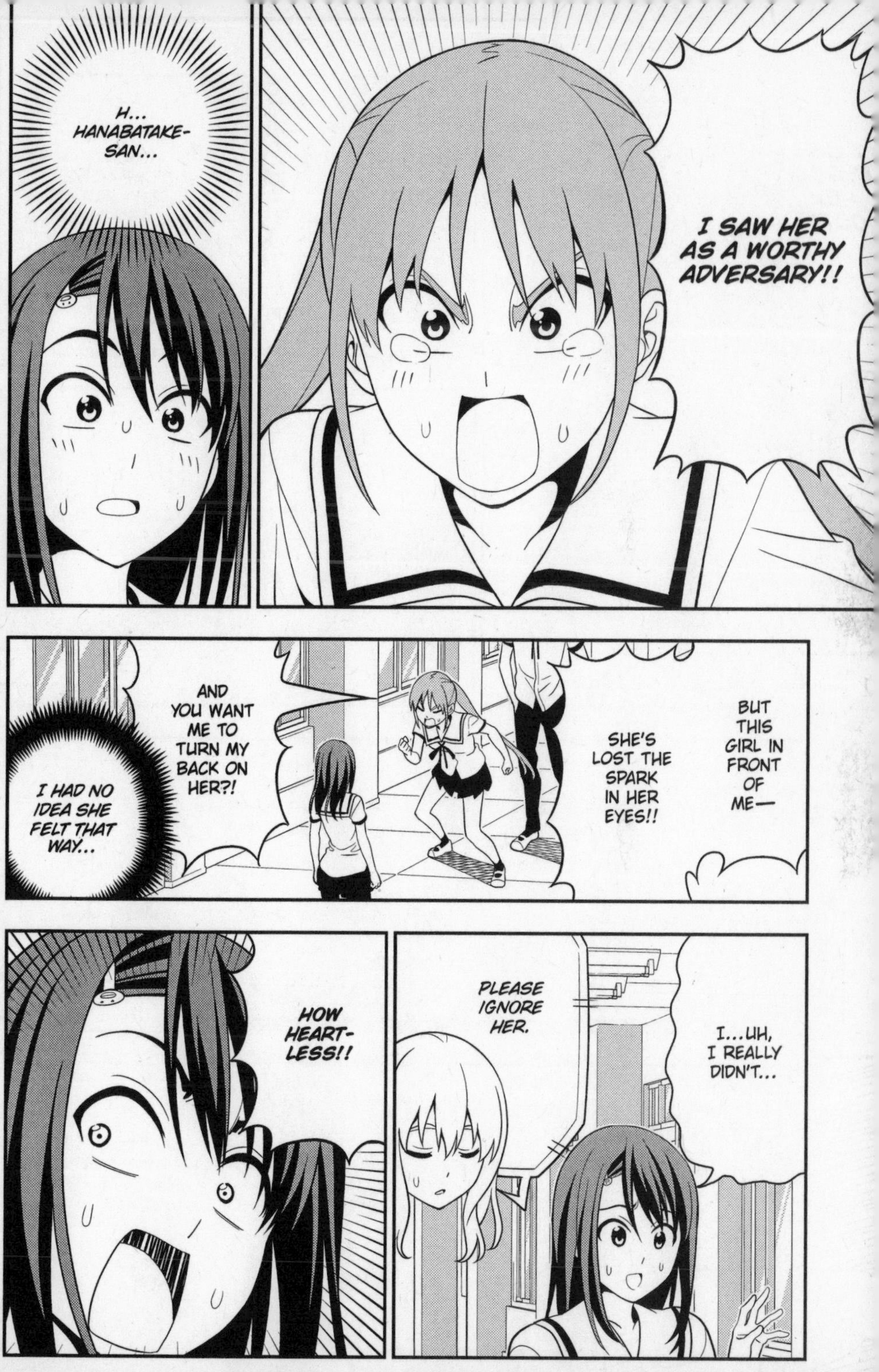
I SAW HER AS A WORTHY ADVERSARY!!
H... HANABATAKE-SAN...
BUT THIS GIRL IN FRONT OF ME—
SHE'S LOST THE SPARK IN HER EYES!!
AND YOU WANT ME TO TURN MY BACK ON HER?!
I HAD NO IDEA SHE FELT THAT WAY...
I...UH, I REALLY DIDN'T...
PLEASE IGNORE HER.
HOW HEARTLESS!!

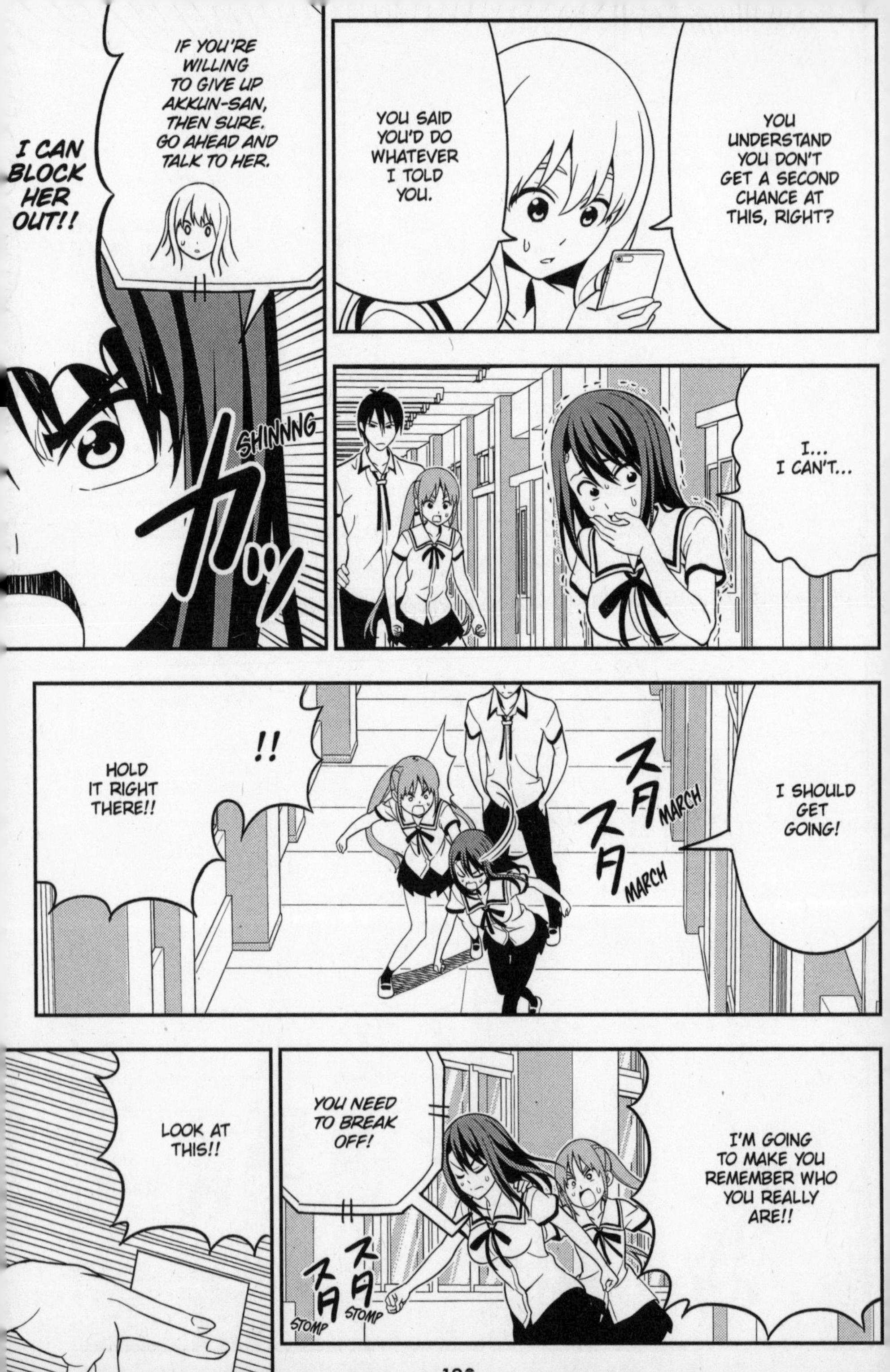
YOU UNDERSTAND YOU DON'T GET A SECOND CHANCE AT THIS, RIGHT?
YOU SAID YOU'D DO WHATEVER I TOLD YOU.
I... I CAN'T...
IF YOU'RE WILLING TO GIVE UP AKKUN-SAN, THEN SURE. GO AHEAD AND TALK TO HER.
I CAN BLOCK HER OUT!!
SHINNNG
I SHOULD GET GOING!
MARCH
MARCH
!!
HOLD IT RIGHT THERE!!
I'M GOING TO MAKE YOU REMEMBER WHO YOU REALLY ARE!!
YOU NEED TO BREAK OFF!
STOMP
STOMP
LOOK AT THIS!!

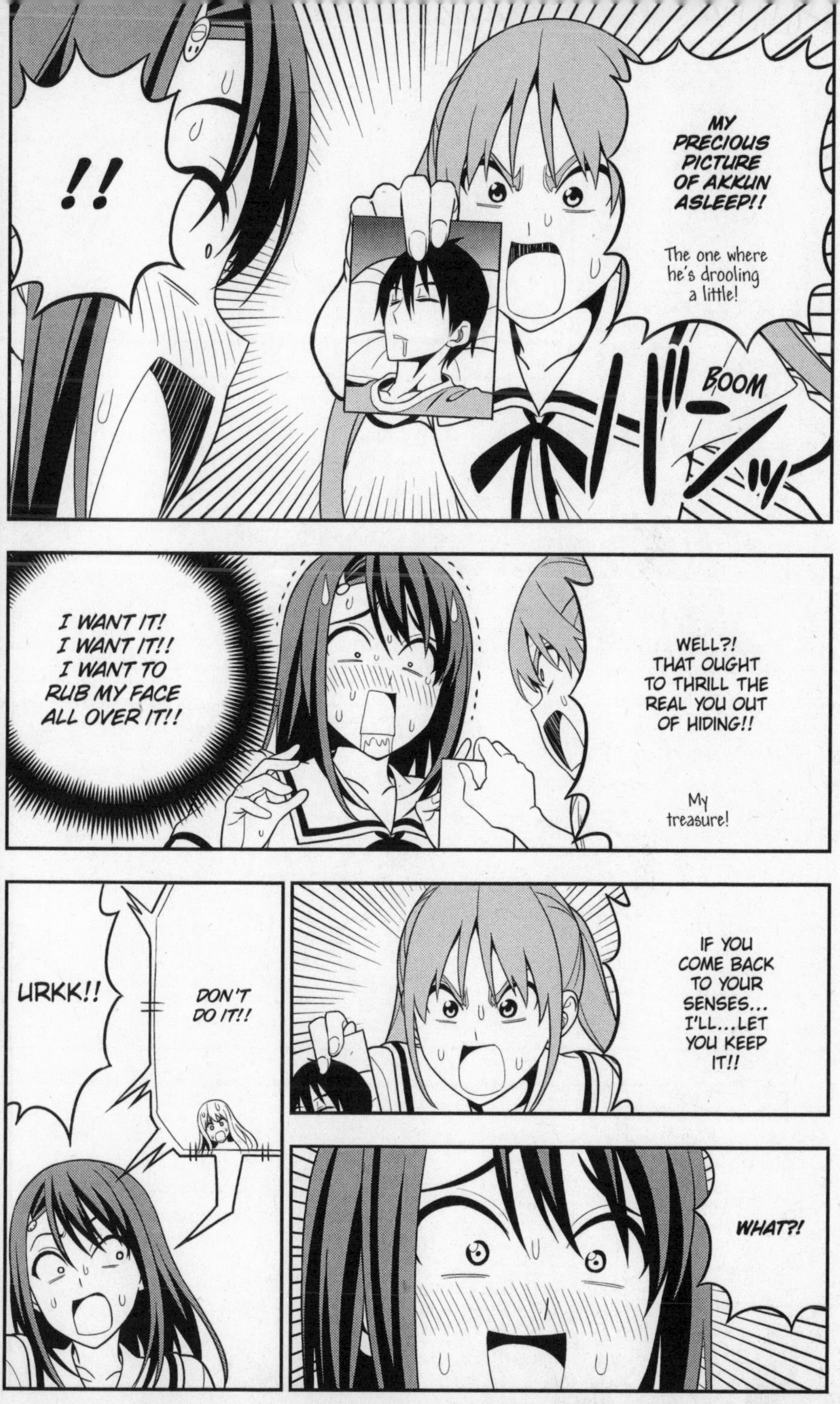
MY PRECIOUS PICTURE OF AKKUN ASLEEP!!
The one where he's drooling a little!
BOOM
!!
WELL?! THAT OUGHT TO THRILL THE REAL YOU OUT OF HIDING!!
My treasure!
I WANT IT! I WANT IT!! I WANT TO RUB MY FACE ALL OVER IT!!
IF YOU COME BACK TO YOUR SENSES... I'LL...LET YOU KEEP IT!!
WHAT?!
DON'T DO IT!!
URKK!!

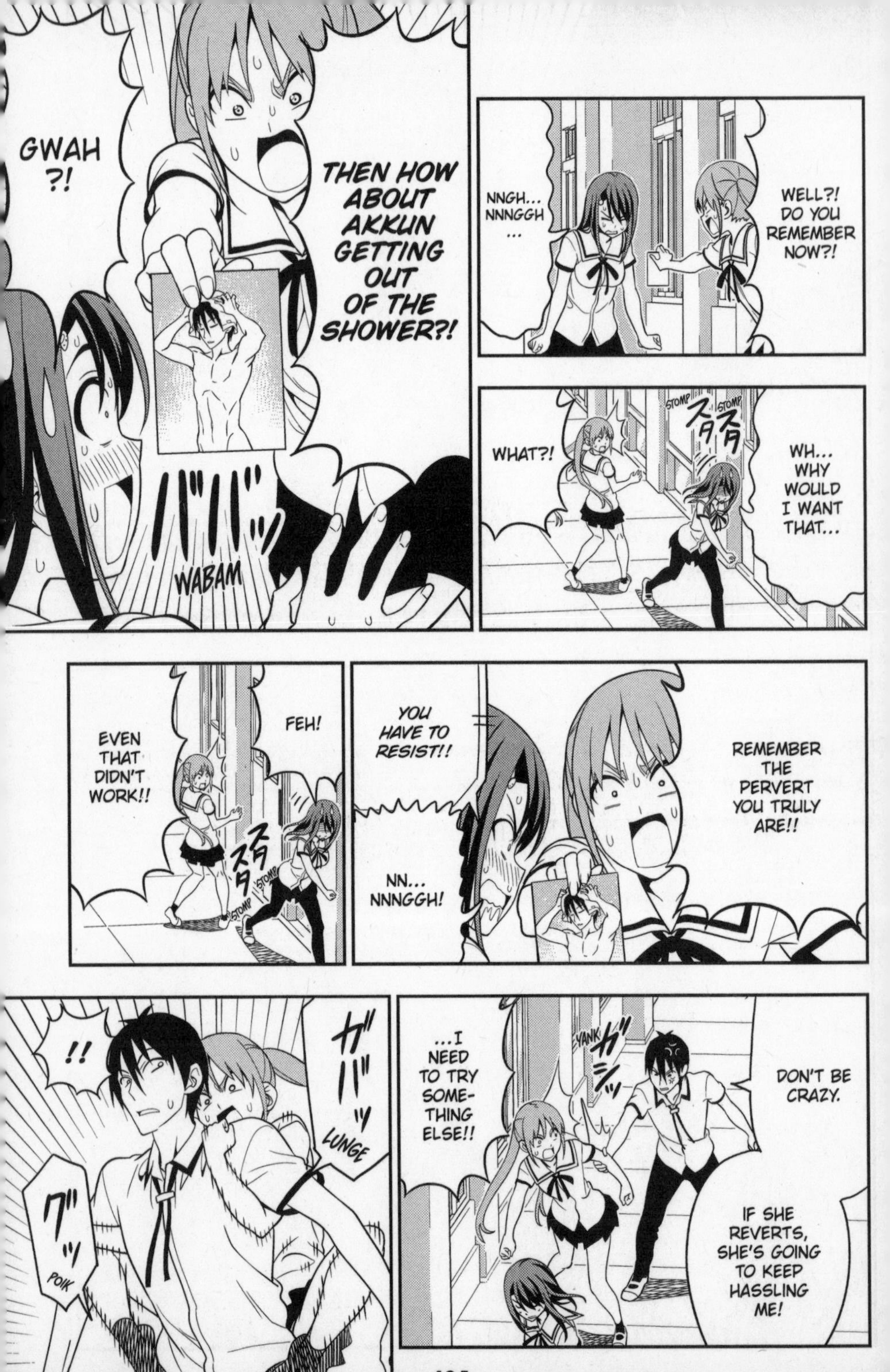
WELL?! DO YOU REMEMBER NOW?!
NNGH... NNNGGH ...
STOMP STOMP
WH... WHY WOULD I WANT THAT...
WHAT?!
THEN HOW ABOUT AKKUN GETTING OUT OF THE SHOWER?!
GWAH ?!
WABAM
REMEMBER THE PERVERT YOU TRULY ARE!!
YOU HAVE TO RESIST!!
NN... NNNGGH!
FEH!
EVEN THAT DIDN'T WORK!!
STOMP STOMP
DON'T BE CRAZY.
IF SHE REVERTS, SHE'S GOING TO KEEP HASSLING ME!
YANK
...I NEED TO TRY SOME-THING ELSE!!
LUNGE
!!
POIK

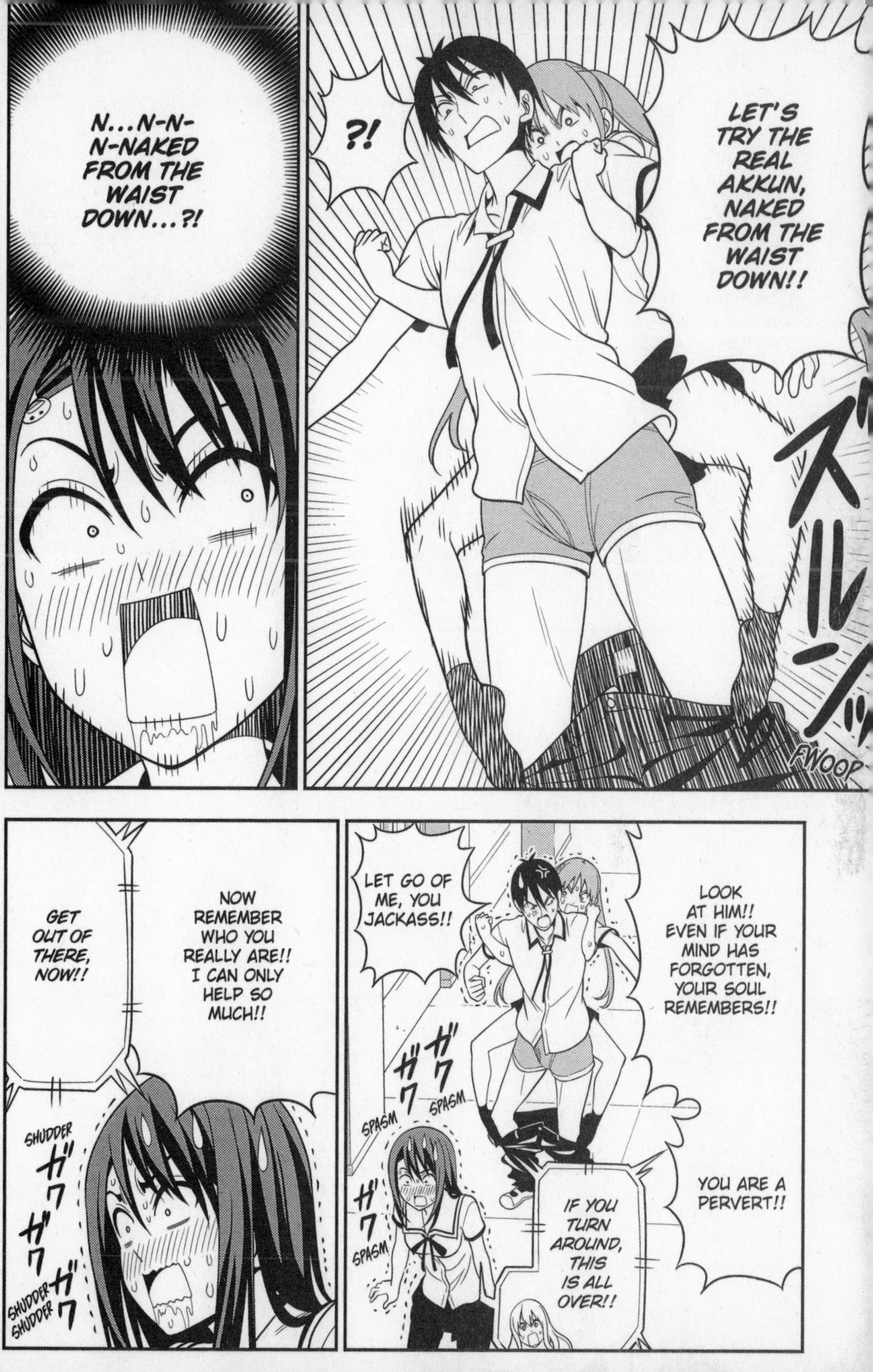
LET'S TRY THE REAL AKKUN, NAKED FROM THE WAIST DOWN!!
?!
FWOOP
N...N-N-N-NAKED FROM THE WAIST DOWN...?!
LOOK AT HIM!! EVEN IF YOUR MIND HAS FORGOTTEN, YOUR SOUL REMEMBERS!!
LET GO OF ME, YOU JACKASS!!
YOU ARE A PERVERT!!
IF YOU TURN AROUND, THIS IS ALL OVER!!
SPASM
SPASM
SPASM
NOW REMEMBER WHO YOU REALLY ARE!! I CAN ONLY HELP SO MUCH!!
GET OUT OF THERE, NOW!!
SHUDDER
SHUDDER
SHUDDER

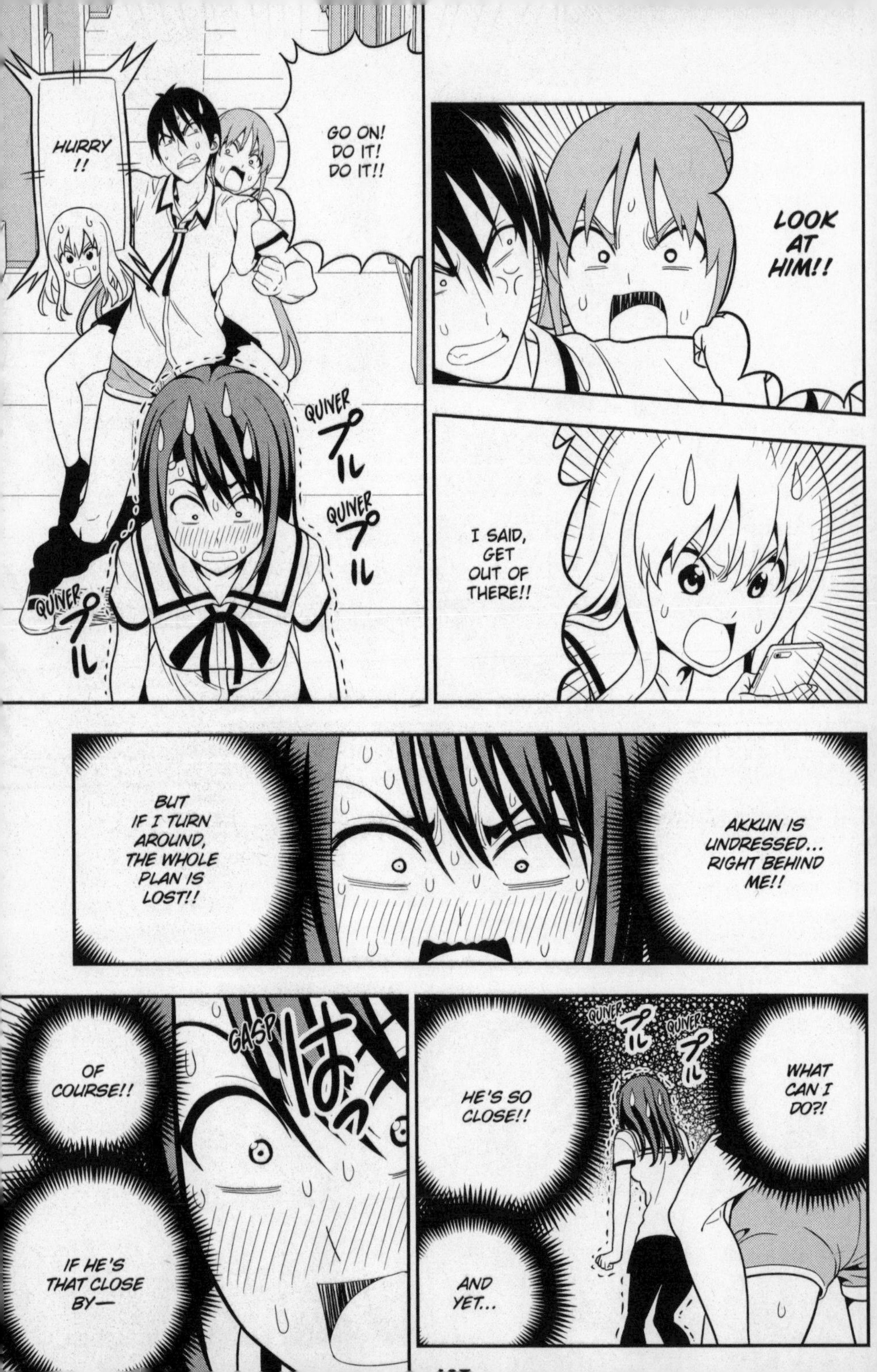
LOOK AT HIM!!
I SAID, GET OUT OF THERE!!
GO ON! DO IT! DO IT!!
HURRY !!
QUIVER プル
QUIVER プル
QUIVER プル
AKKUN IS UNDRESSED... RIGHT BEHIND ME!!
BUT IF I TURN AROUND, THE WHOLE PLAN IS LOST!!
QUIVER プル
QUIVER プル
WHAT CAN I DO?!
HE'S SO CLOSE!!
AND YET...
GASP はっ
OF COURSE!!
IF HE'S THAT CLOSE BY—

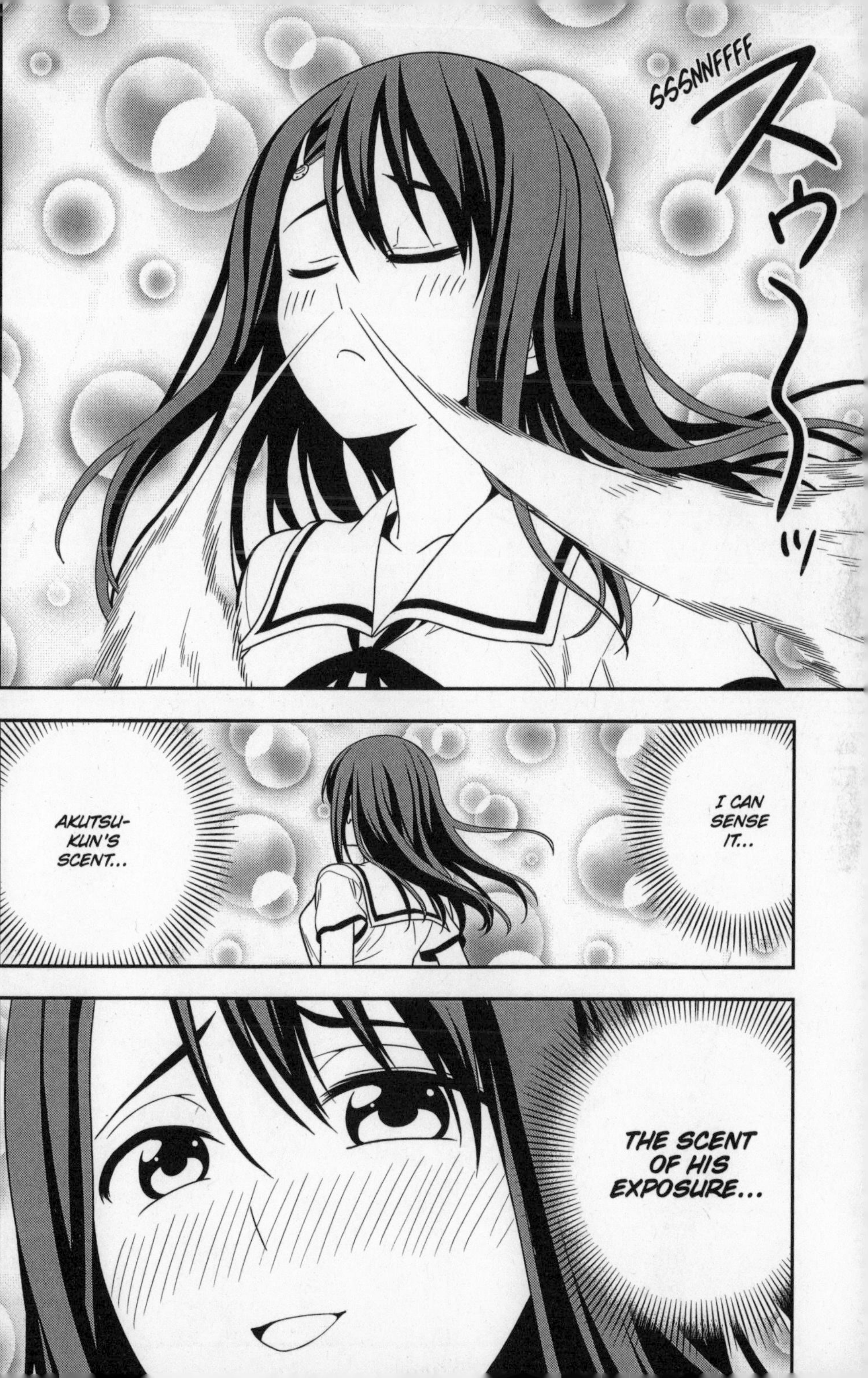
SSSNNFFFF
スゥ〜〜ッ
I CAN SENSE IT...
AKUTSU-KUN'S SCENT...
THE SCENT OF HIS EXPOSURE...

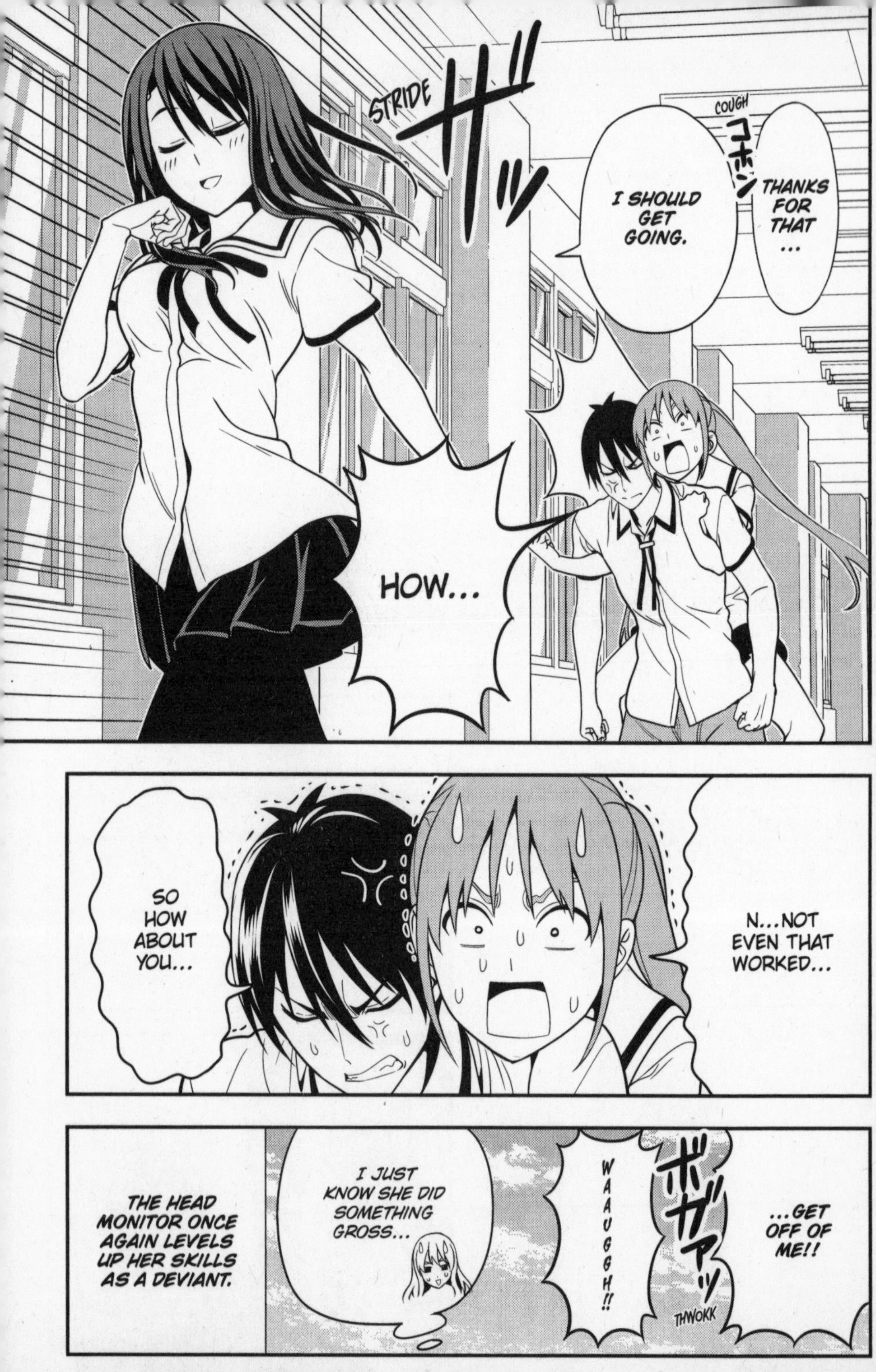
COUGH
コホン
THANKS FOR THAT ...
I SHOULD GET GOING.
STRIDE
ザッ
HOW...
N...NOT EVEN THAT WORKED...
SO HOW ABOUT YOU...
...GET OFF OF ME!!
ボガァッ
THWOKK
WAAAUGH!!
I JUST KNOW SHE DID SOMETHING GROSS...
THE HEAD MONITOR ONCE AGAIN LEVELS UP HER SKILLS AS A DEVIANT.

Sayaka-chan! The Misgivings Mount!!

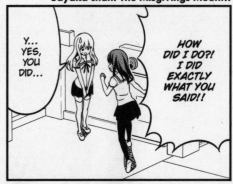

Y... YES, YOU DID...

HOW DID I DO?! I DID EXACTLY WHAT YOU SAID!!

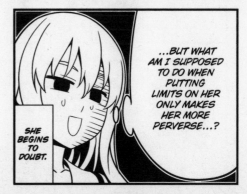

...BUT WHAT AM I SUPPOSED TO DO WHEN PUTTING LIMITS ON HER ONLY MAKES HER MORE PERVERSE...?

SHE BEGINS TO DOUBT.

Chapter 112

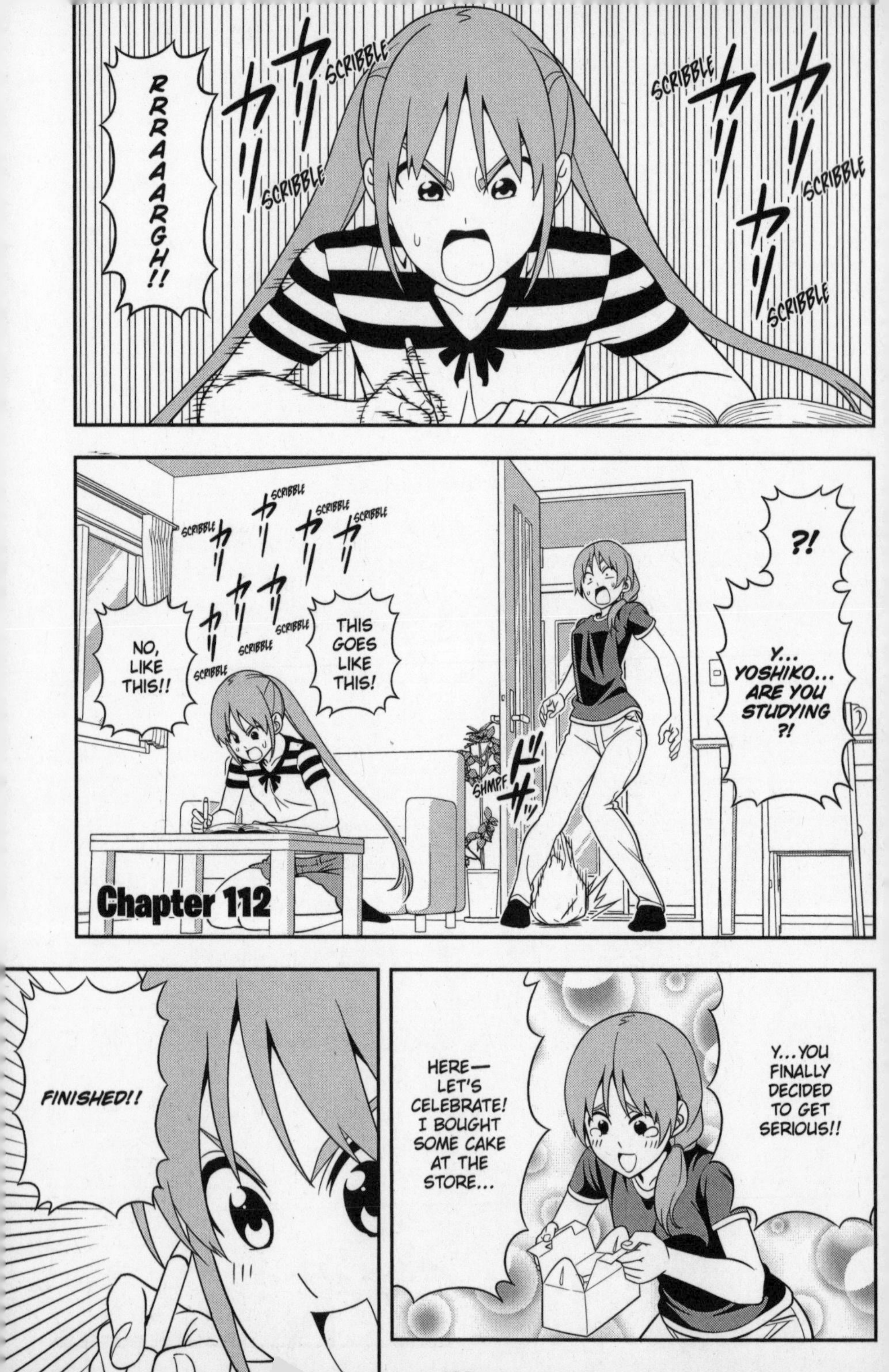
RRRAAAARGH!!
SCRIBBLE
SCRIBBLE
SCRIBBLE
SCRIBBLE
SCRIBBLE
?!
Y... YOSHIKO... ARE YOU STUDYING ?!
SHMPF
THIS GOES LIKE THIS!
NO, LIKE THIS!!
SCRIBBLE
SCRIBBLE
SCRIBBLE
SCRIBBLE
SCRIBBLE
SCRIBBLE
Y...YOU FINALLY DECIDED TO GET SERIOUS!!
HERE—LET'S CELEBRATE! I BOUGHT SOME CAKE AT THE STORE...
FINISHED!!

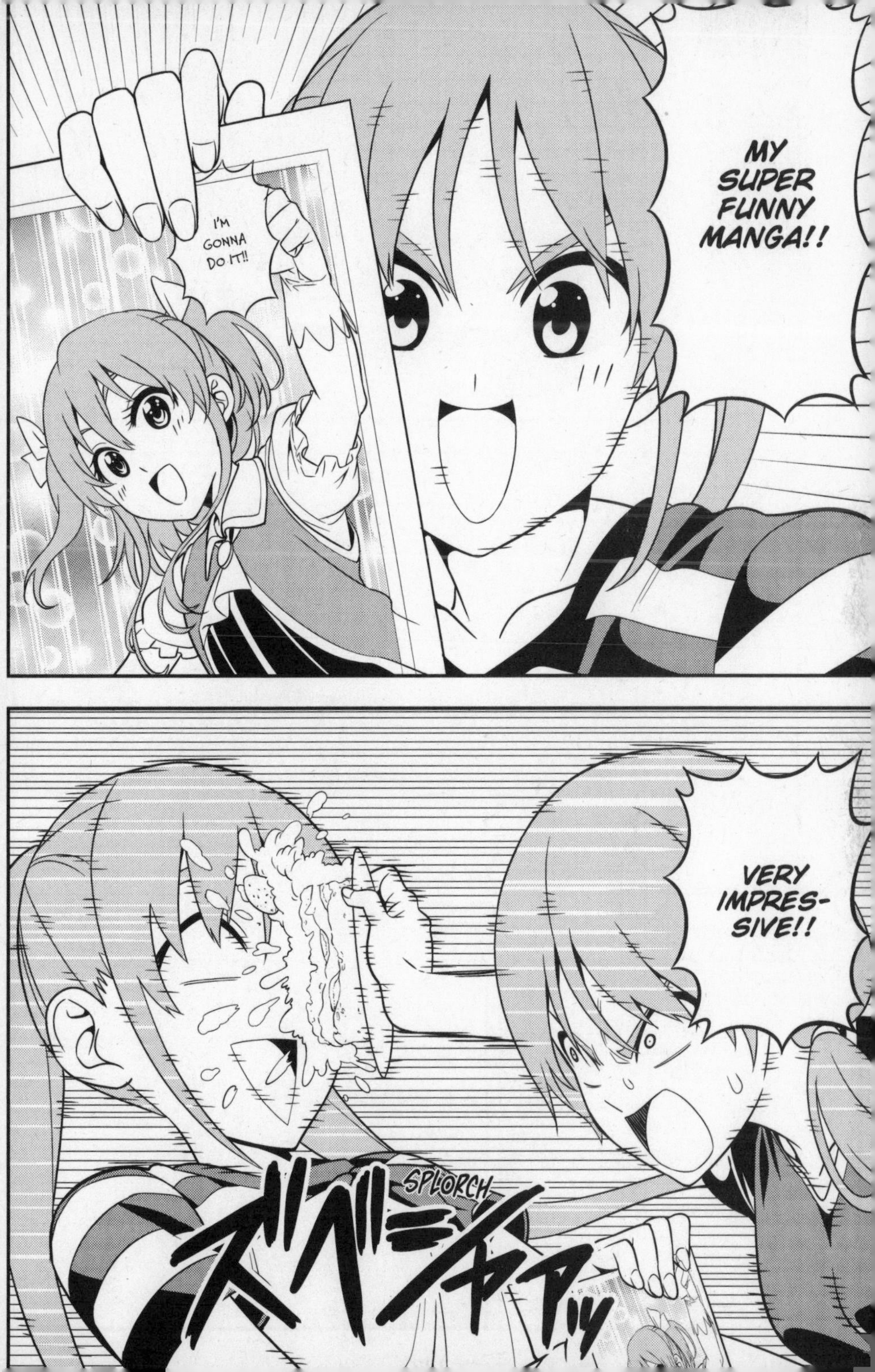
MY SUPER FUNNY MANGA!!
I'M GONNA DO IT!!
VERY IMPRES-SIVE!!
SPLORCH

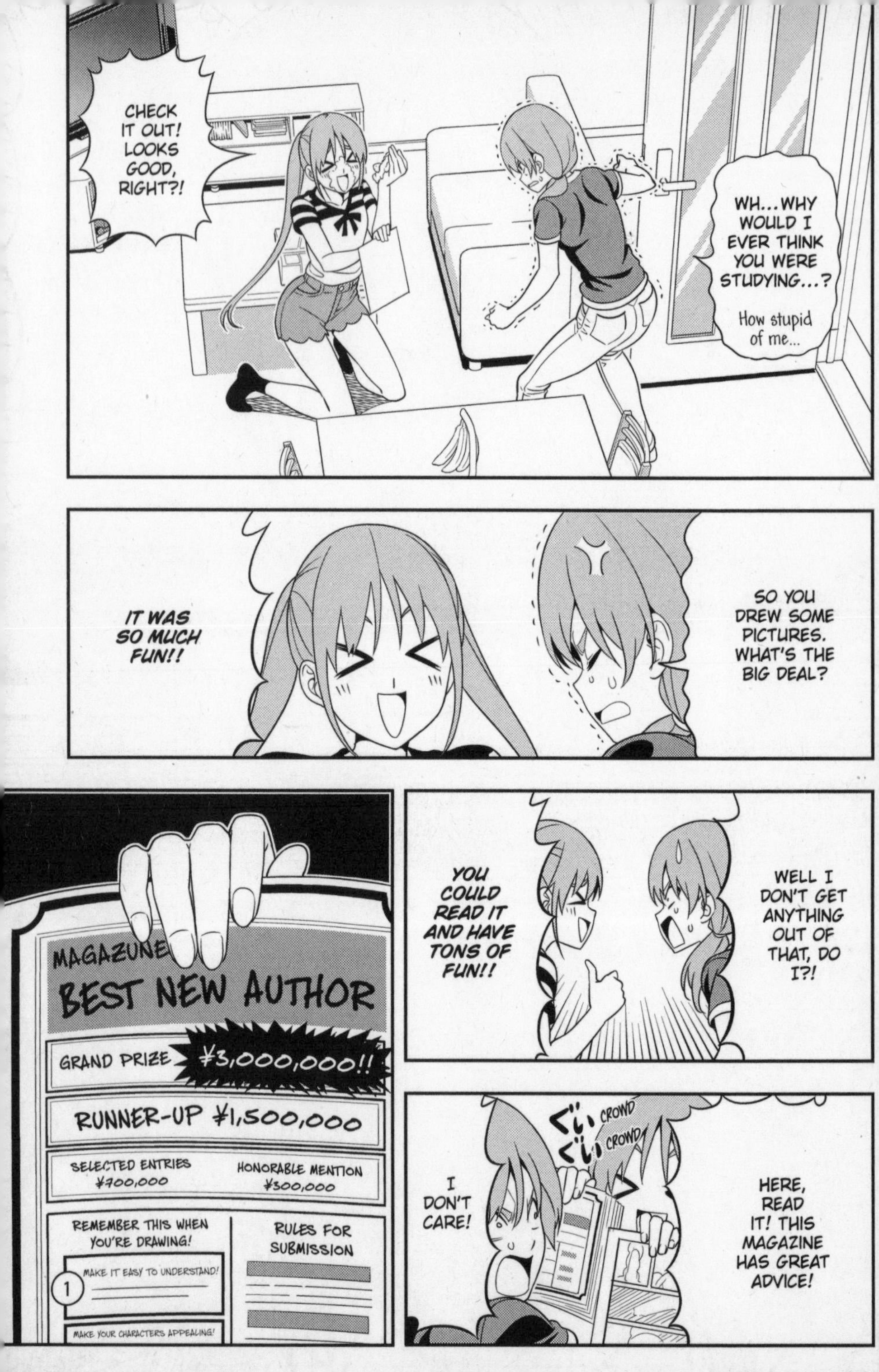
WH...WHY WOULD I EVER THINK YOU WERE STUDYING...?
How stupid of me...
CHECK IT OUT! LOOKS GOOD, RIGHT?!
SO YOU DREW SOME PICTURES. WHAT'S THE BIG DEAL?
IT WAS SO MUCH FUN!!
WELL I DON'T GET ANYTHING OUT OF THAT, DO I?!
YOU COULD READ IT AND HAVE TONS OF FUN!!
HERE, READ IT! THIS MAGAZINE HAS GREAT ADVICE!
CROWD
CROWD
I DON'T CARE!
MAGAZUNE
BEST NEW AUTHOR
GRAND PRIZE ¥3,000,000!!
RUNNER-UP ¥1,500,000
SELECTED ENTRIES ¥700,000
HONORABLE MENTION ¥300,000
REMEMBER THIS WHEN YOU'RE DRAWING!
1 MAKE IT EASY TO UNDERSTAND!
MAKE YOUR CHARACTERS APPEALING!
RULES FOR SUBMISSION

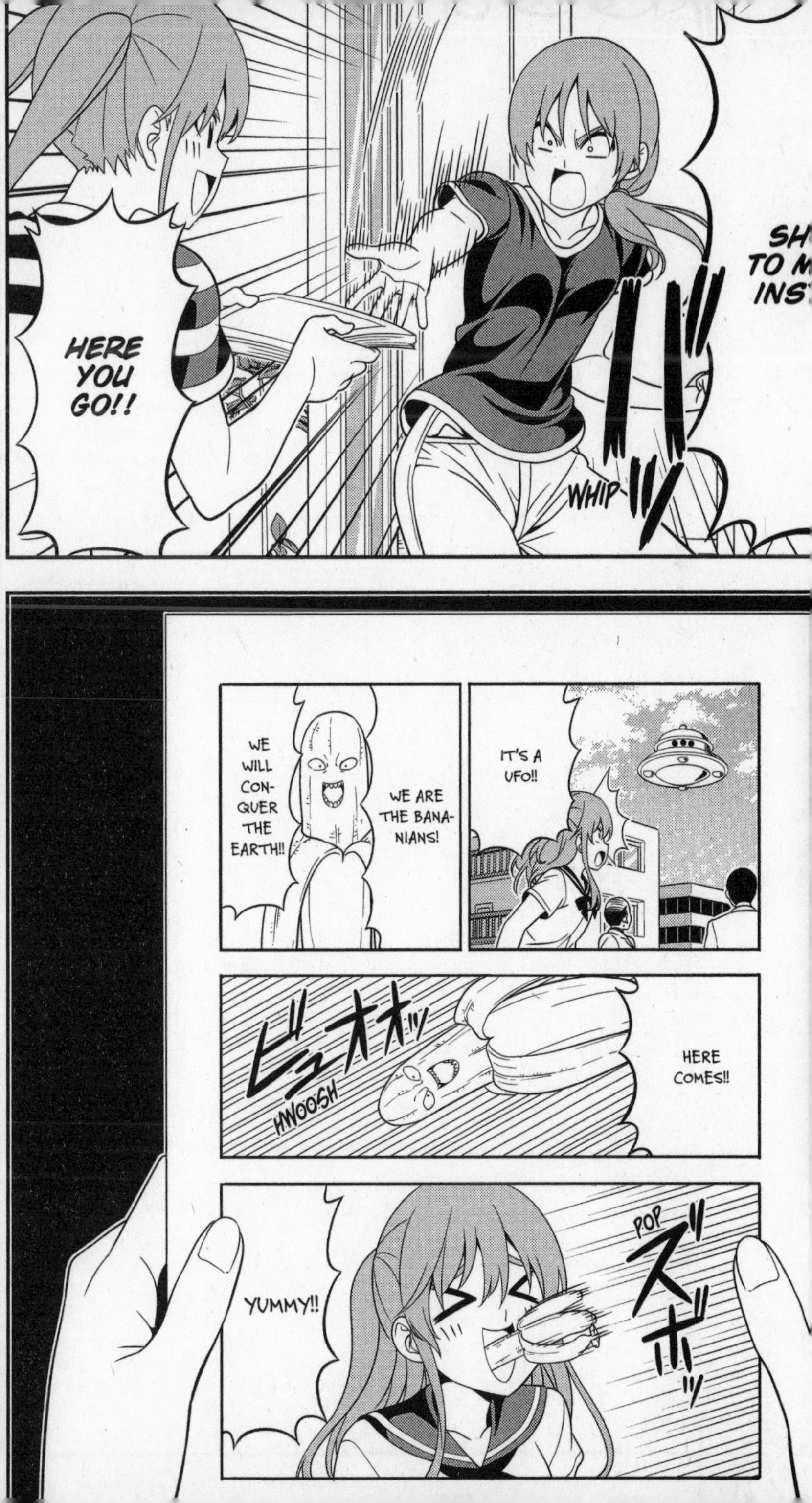
WHIP
HERE YOU GO!!
IT'S A UFO!!
WE ARE THE BANA-NIANS!
WE WILL CON-QUER THE EARTH!!
HERE COMES!!
ビュオオッ
HWOOSH
ズボッ
POP
YUMMY!!

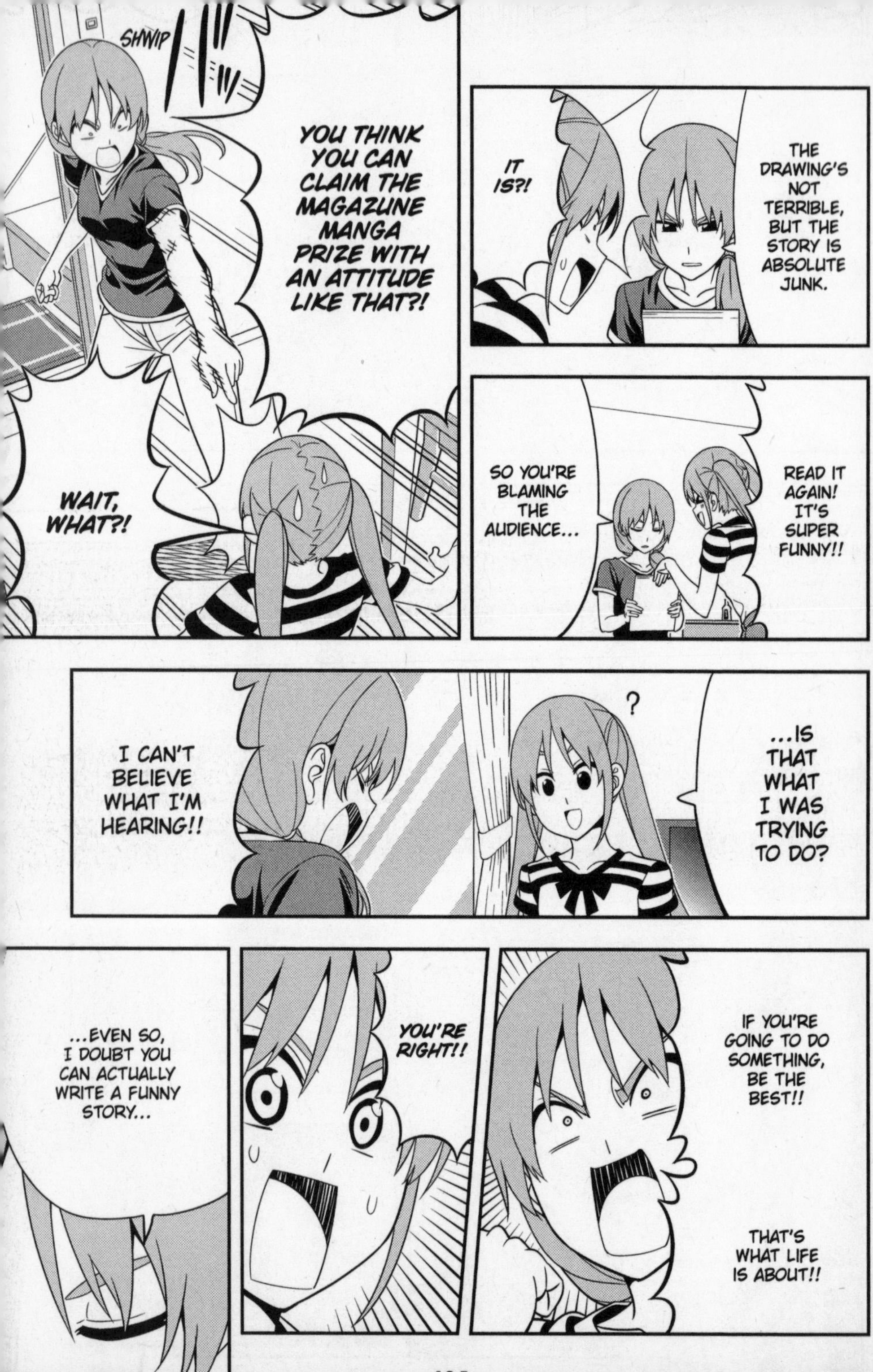
THE DRAWING'S NOT TERRIBLE, BUT THE STORY IS ABSOLUTE JUNK.
IT IS?!
READ IT AGAIN! IT'S SUPER FUNNY!!
SO YOU'RE BLAMING THE AUDIENCE...
SHWIP
YOU THINK YOU CAN CLAIM THE MAGAZUNE MANGA PRIZE WITH AN ATTITUDE LIKE THAT?!
WAIT, WHAT?!
...IS THAT WHAT I WAS TRYING TO DO?
?
I CAN'T BELIEVE WHAT I'M HEARING!!
IF YOU'RE GOING TO DO SOMETHING, BE THE BEST!!
THAT'S WHAT LIFE IS ABOUT!!
YOU'RE RIGHT!!
...EVEN SO, I DOUBT YOU CAN ACTUALLY WRITE A FUNNY STORY...

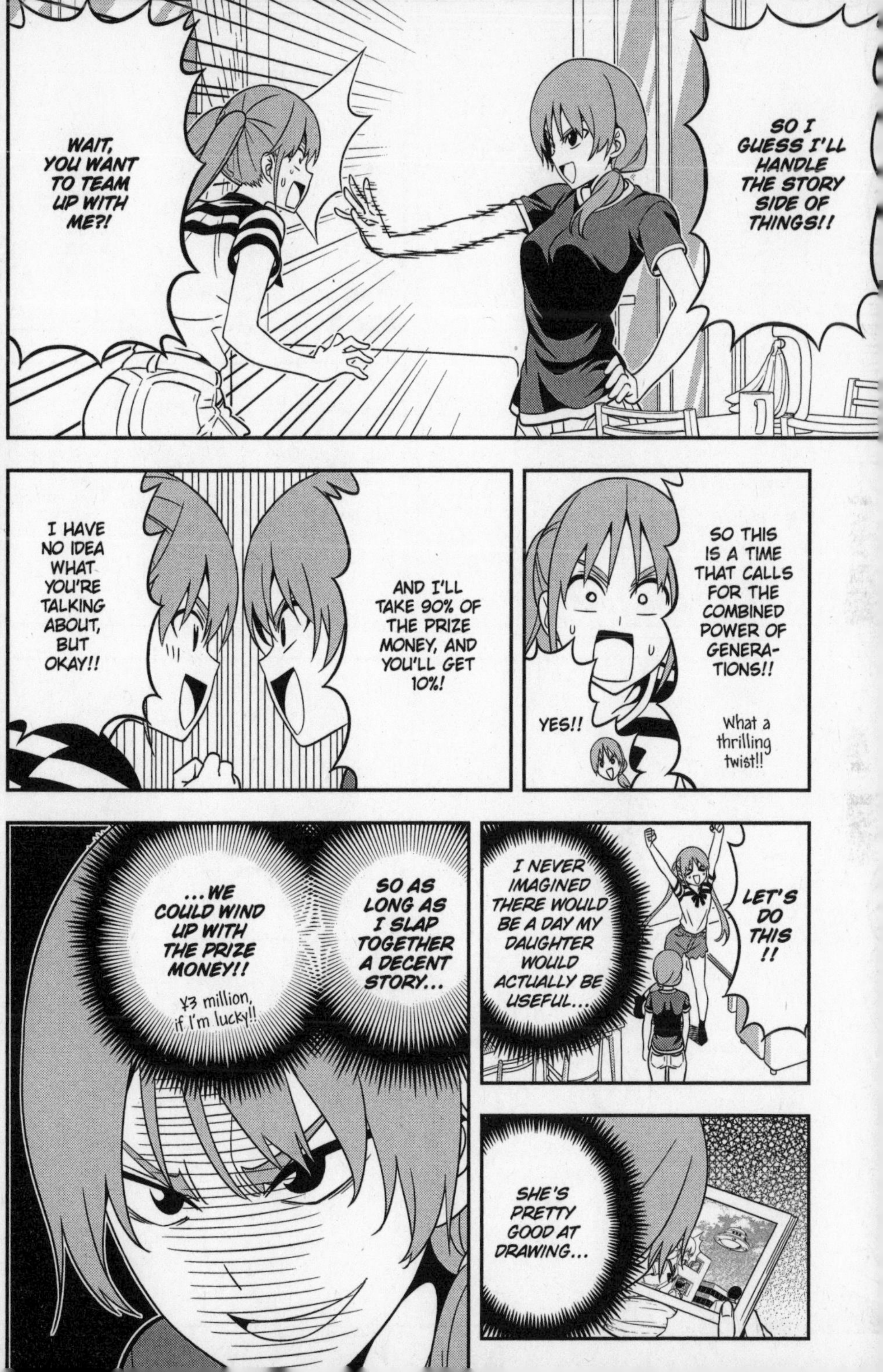
SO I GUESS I'LL HANDLE THE STORY SIDE OF THINGS!!
WAIT, YOU WANT TO TEAM UP WITH ME?!
SO THIS IS A TIME THAT CALLS FOR THE COMBINED POWER OF GENERA-TIONS!!
What a thrilling twist!!
YES!!
AND I'LL TAKE 90% OF THE PRIZE MONEY, AND YOU'LL GET 10%!
I HAVE NO IDEA WHAT YOU'RE TALKING ABOUT, BUT OKAY!!
LET'S DO THIS!!
I NEVER IMAGINED THERE WOULD BE A DAY MY DAUGHTER WOULD ACTUALLY BE USEFUL...
SHE'S PRETTY GOOD AT DRAWING...
SO AS LONG AS I SLAP TOGETHER A DECENT STORY...
...WE COULD WIND UP WITH THE PRIZE MONEY!!
¥3 million, if I'm lucky!!

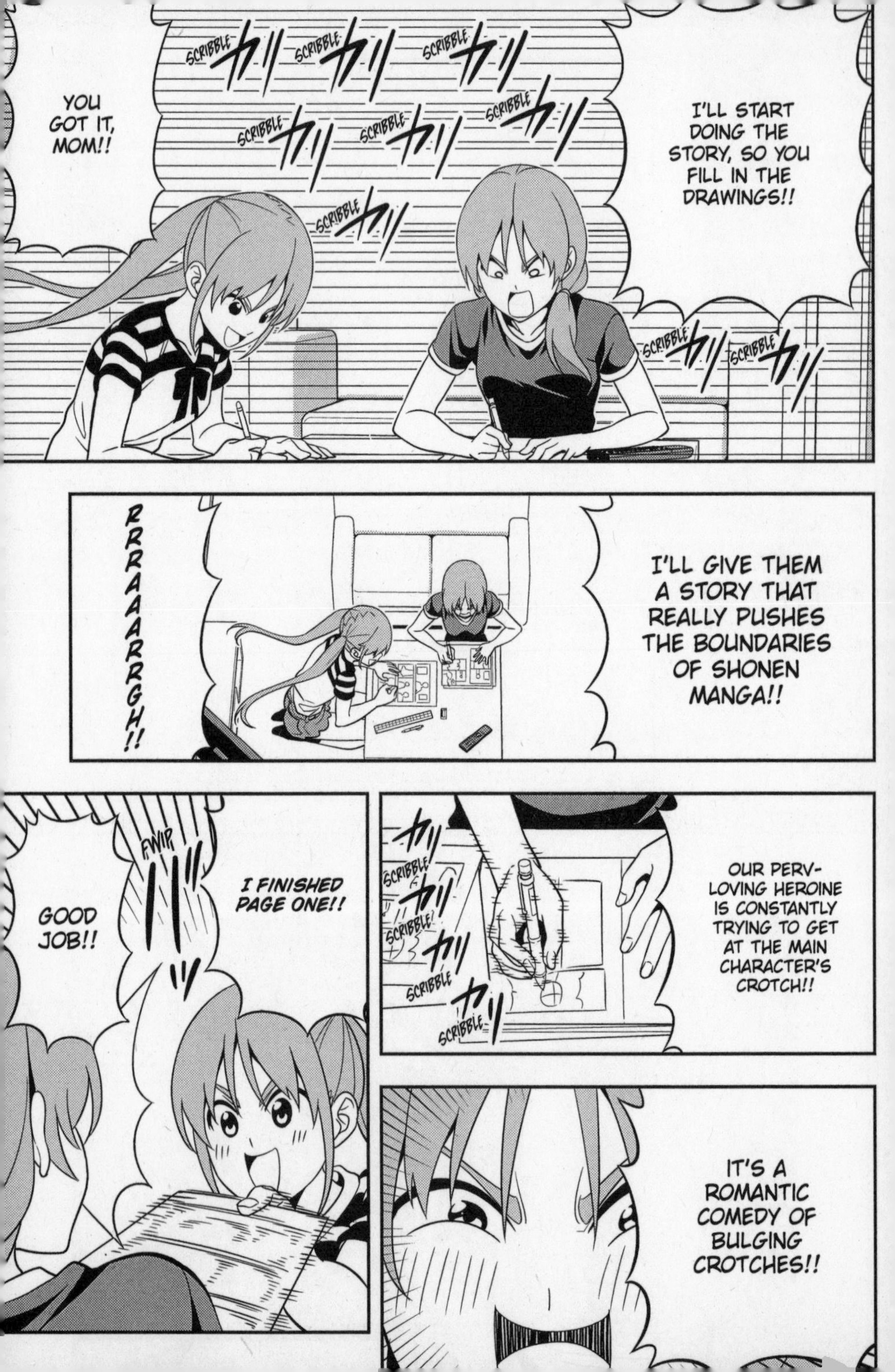
I'LL START DOING THE STORY, SO YOU FILL IN THE DRAWINGS!!
SCRIBBLE カリ
SCRIBBLE カリ
SCRIBBLE カリ
SCRIBBLE カリ
SCRIBBLE カリ
SCRIBBLE カリ
SCRIBBLE カリ
SCRIBBLE カリ
SCRIBBLE カリ
YOU GOT IT, MOM!!
I'LL GIVE THEM A STORY THAT REALLY PUSHES THE BOUNDARIES OF SHONEN MANGA!!
RRRAAAARRGH!!
OUR PERV-LOVING HEROINE IS CONSTANTLY TRYING TO GET AT THE MAIN CHARACTER'S CROTCH!!
カリ SCRIBBLE
カリ SCRIBBLE
カリ SCRIBBLE
カリ SCRIBBLE
IT'S A ROMANTIC COMEDY OF BULGING CROTCHES!!
I FINISHED PAGE ONE!!
FWIP
GOOD JOB!!

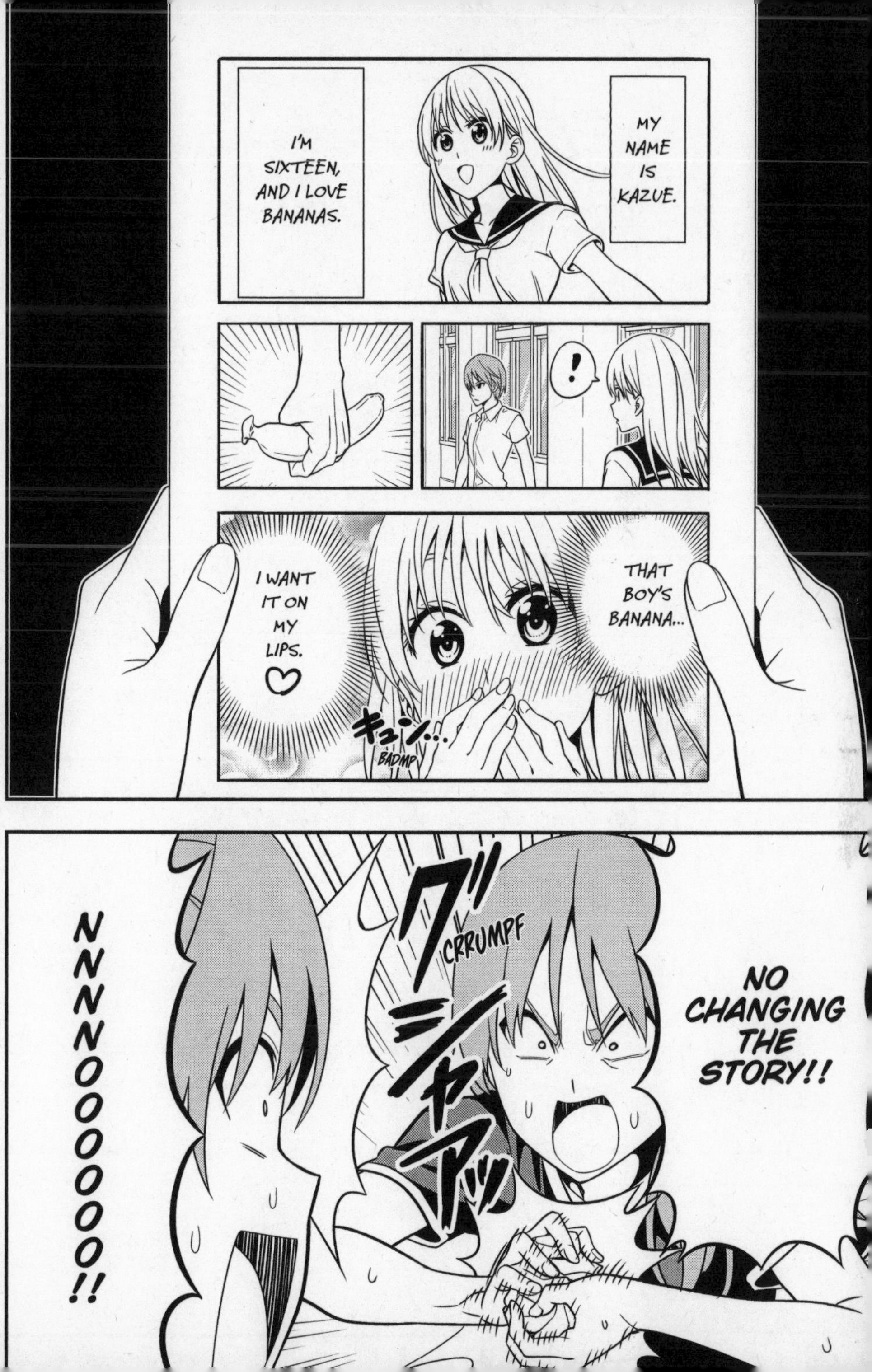
MY NAME IS KAZUE.
I'M SIXTEEN, AND I LOVE BANANAS.
!
THAT BOY'S BANANA...
I WANT IT ON MY LIPS. ♡
キュン… BADMP
NO CHANGING THE STORY!!
グシャアッ CRRUMPF
NNNNOOOOOOOO!!

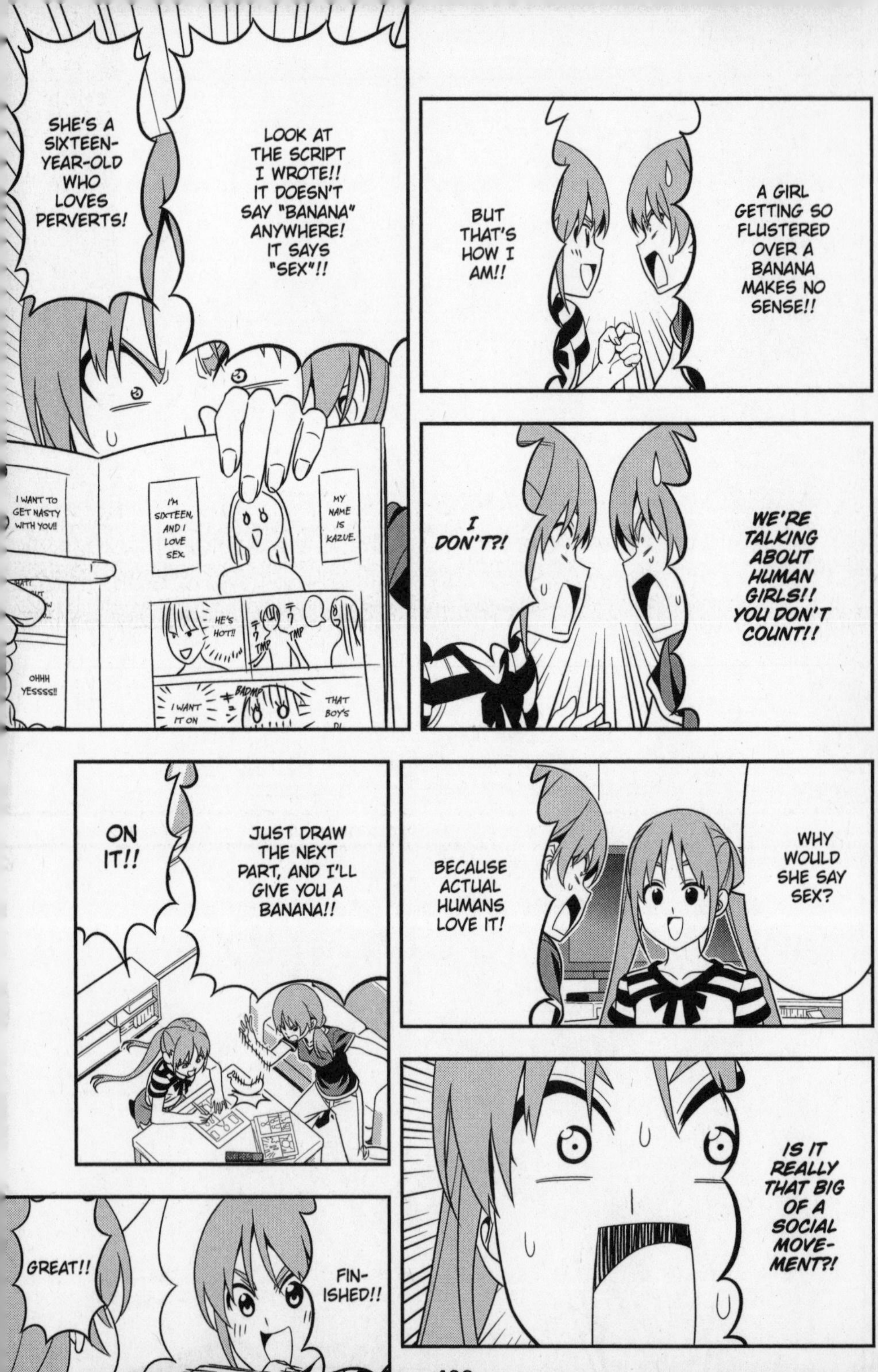

A GIRL GETTING SO FLUSTERED OVER A BANANA MAKES NO SENSE!!
BUT THAT'S HOW I AM!!
WE'RE TALKING ABOUT HUMAN GIRLS!! YOU DON'T COUNT!!
I DON'T?!
LOOK AT THE SCRIPT I WROTE!! IT DOESN'T SAY "BANANA" ANYWHERE! IT SAYS "SEX"!!
SHE'S A SIXTEEN-YEAR-OLD WHO LOVES PERVERTS!
MY NAME IS KAZUE.
I'M SIXTEEN, AND I LOVE SEX.
I WANT TO GET NASTY WITH YOU!!
TMP TMP
HE'S HOT!!
OHHH YESSSS!!
BADMP
WHY WOULD SHE SAY SEX?
BECAUSE ACTUAL HUMANS LOVE IT!
IS IT REALLY THAT BIG OF A SOCIAL MOVEMENT?!
JUST DRAW THE NEXT PART, AND I'LL GIVE YOU A BANANA!!
ON IT!!
FIN-ISHED!!
GREAT!!

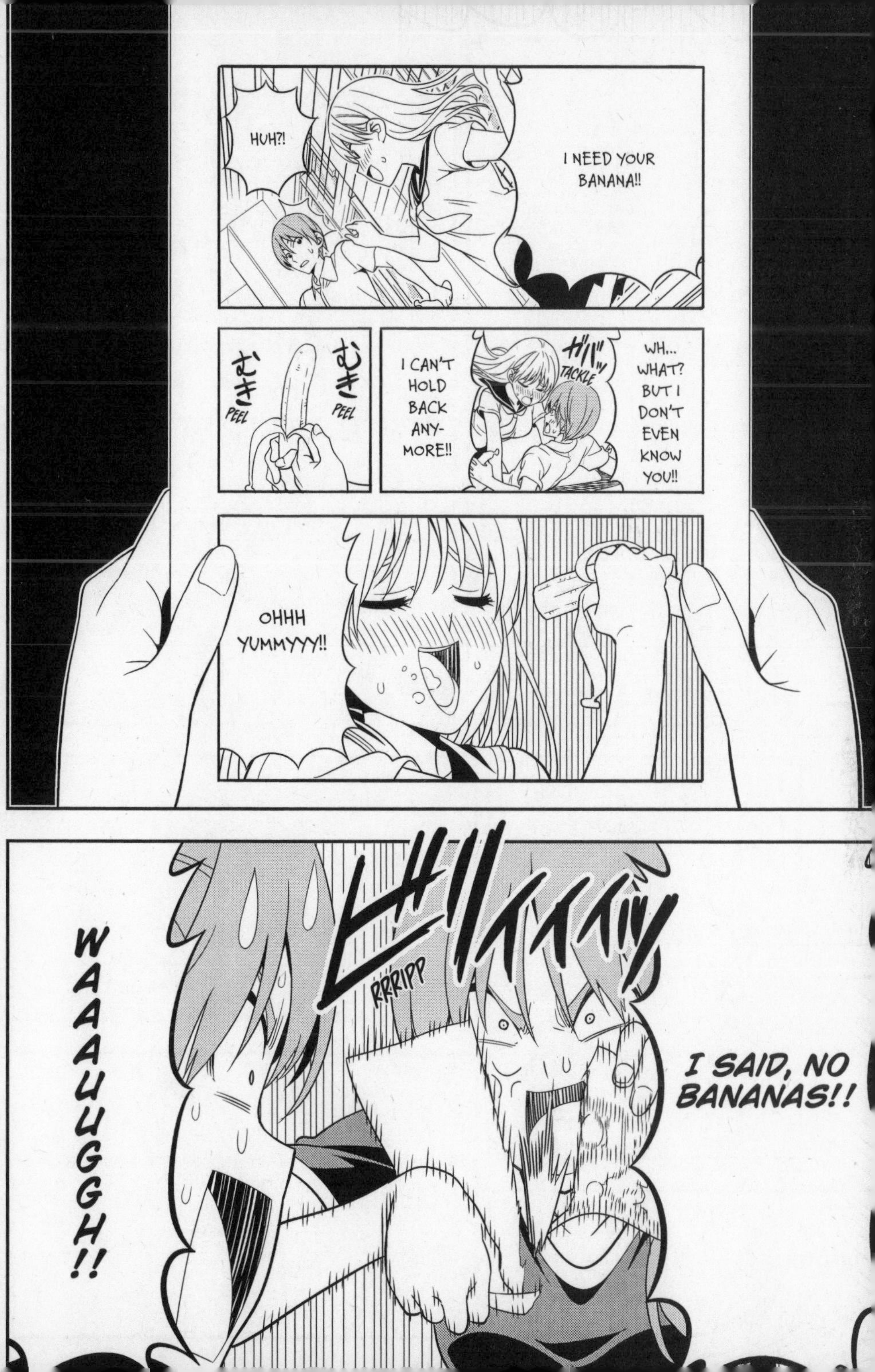
I NEED YOUR BANANA!!
HUH?!
WH... WHAT? BUT I DON'T EVEN KNOW YOU!!
ガバッ
TACKLE
I CAN'T HOLD BACK ANYMORE!!
むき
PEEL
むき
PEEL
OHHH YUMMYYY!!
I SAID, NO BANANAS!!
ビリイイイッ
RRRIPP
WAAAAUUGGH!!

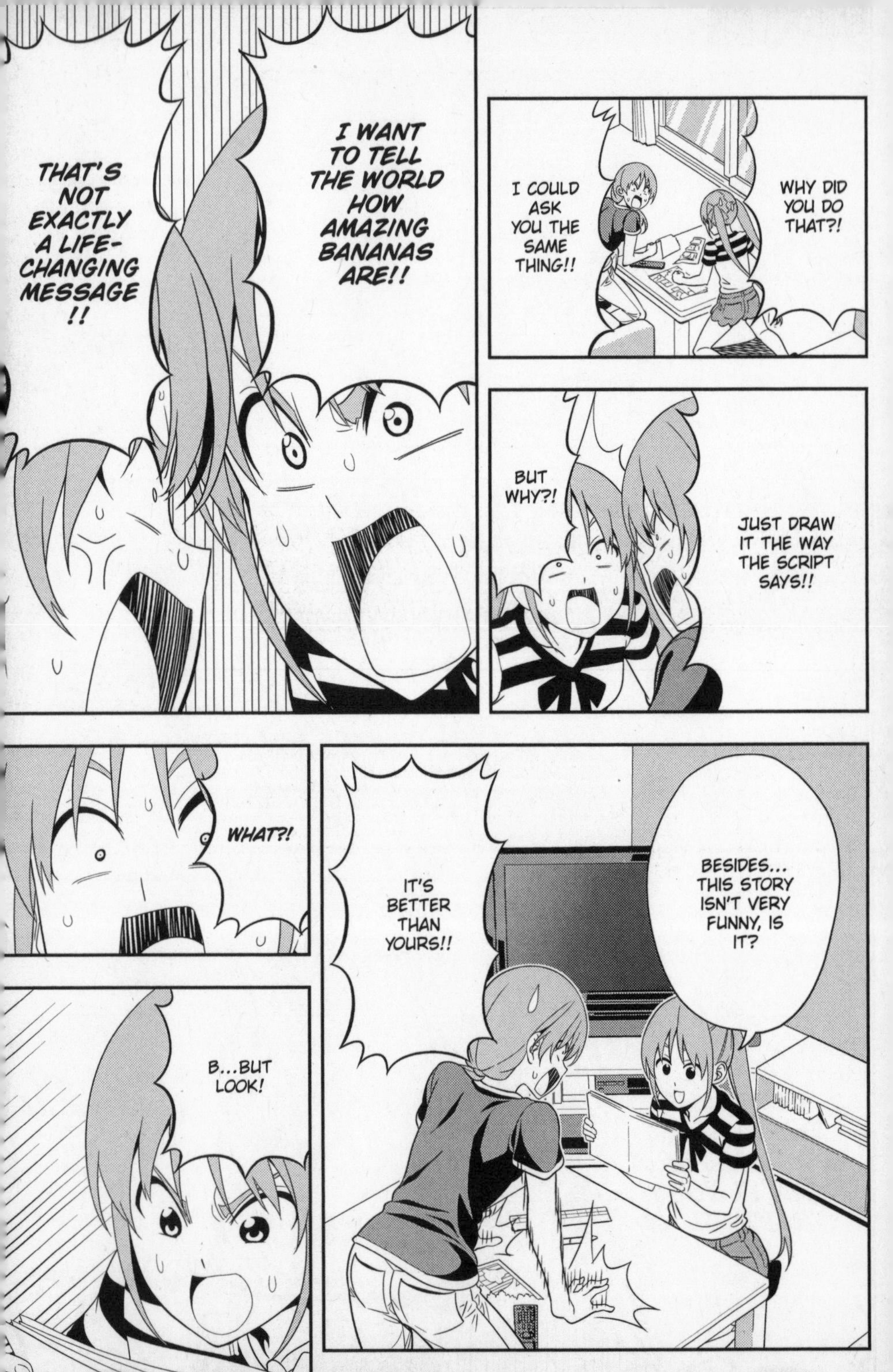
WHY DID YOU DO THAT?!
I COULD ASK YOU THE SAME THING!!
JUST DRAW IT THE WAY THE SCRIPT SAYS!!
BUT WHY?!
I WANT TO TELL THE WORLD HOW AMAZING BANANAS ARE!!
THAT'S NOT EXACTLY A LIFE-CHANGING MESSAGE!!
BESIDES... THIS STORY ISN'T VERY FUNNY, IS IT?
IT'S BETTER THAN YOURS!!
WHAT?!
B...BUT LOOK!

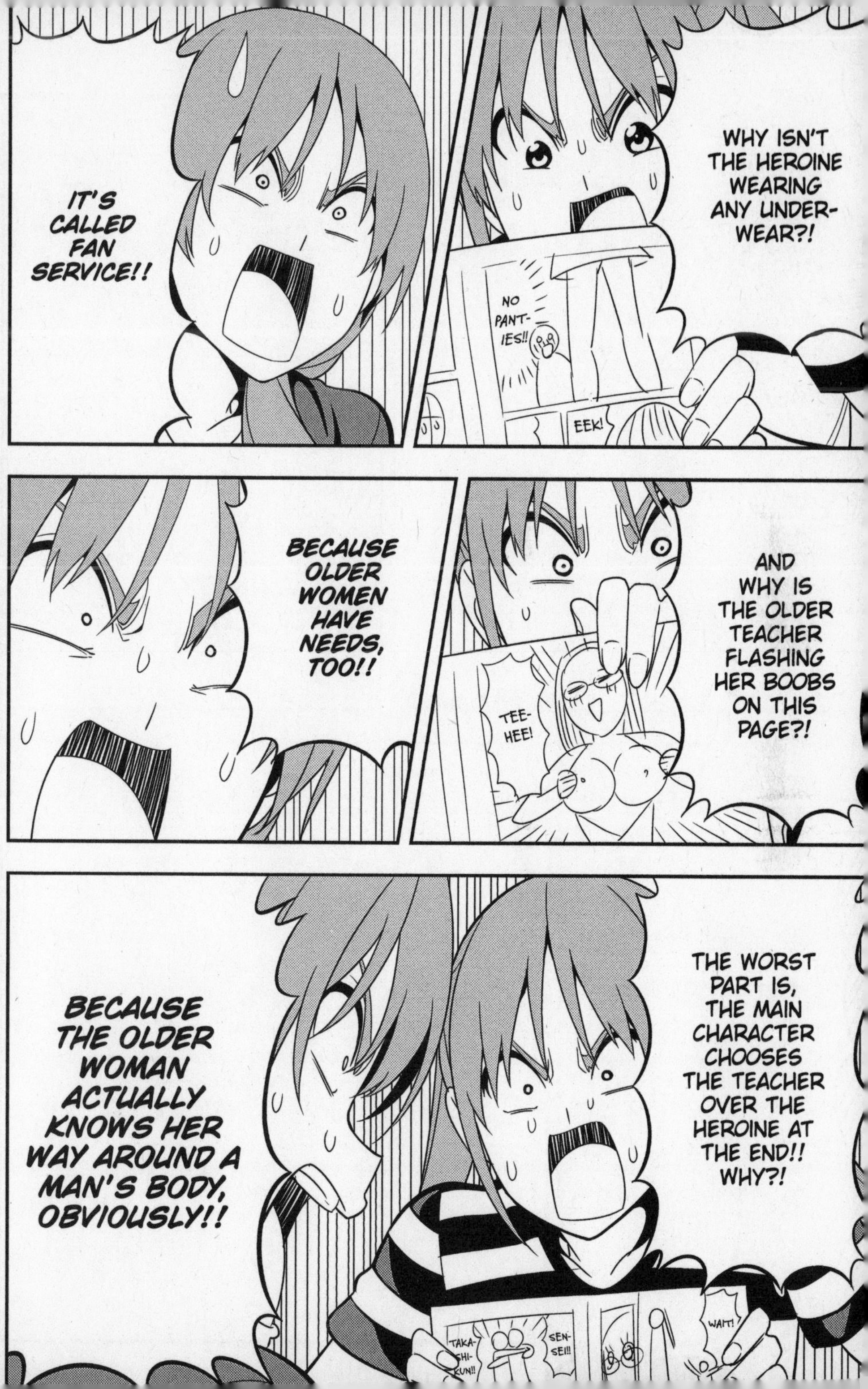
WHY ISN'T THE HEROINE WEARING ANY UNDER-WEAR?!
NO PANT-IES!!
EEK!
IT'S CALLED FAN SERVICE!!
AND WHY IS THE OLDER TEACHER FLASHING HER BOOBS ON THIS PAGE?!
TEE-HEE!
BECAUSE OLDER WOMEN HAVE NEEDS, TOO!!
THE WORST PART IS, THE MAIN CHARACTER CHOOSES THE TEACHER OVER THE HEROINE AT THE END!! WHY?!
WAIT!
BECAUSE THE OLDER WOMAN ACTUALLY KNOWS HER WAY AROUND A MAN'S BODY, OBVIOUSLY!!
SEN-SEI!!
TAKA-SHI-KUN!!

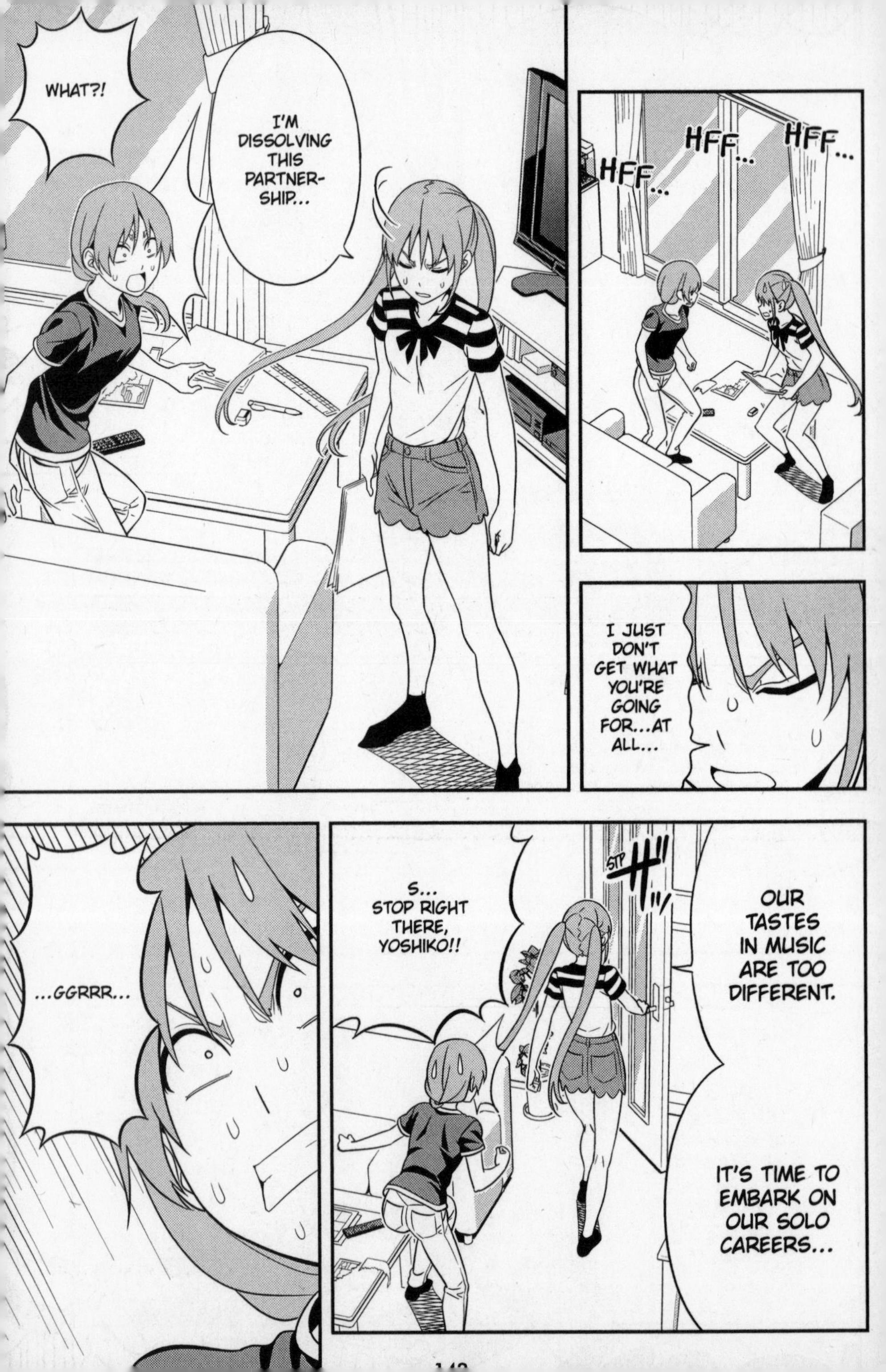
HFF...
HFF...
HFF...
I JUST DON'T GET WHAT YOU'RE GOING FOR...AT ALL...
I'M DISSOLVING THIS PARTNERSHIP...
WHAT?!
OUR TASTES IN MUSIC ARE TOO DIFFERENT.
IT'S TIME TO EMBARK ON OUR SOLO CAREERS...
STP
S... STOP RIGHT THERE, YOSHIKO!!
...GGRRR...

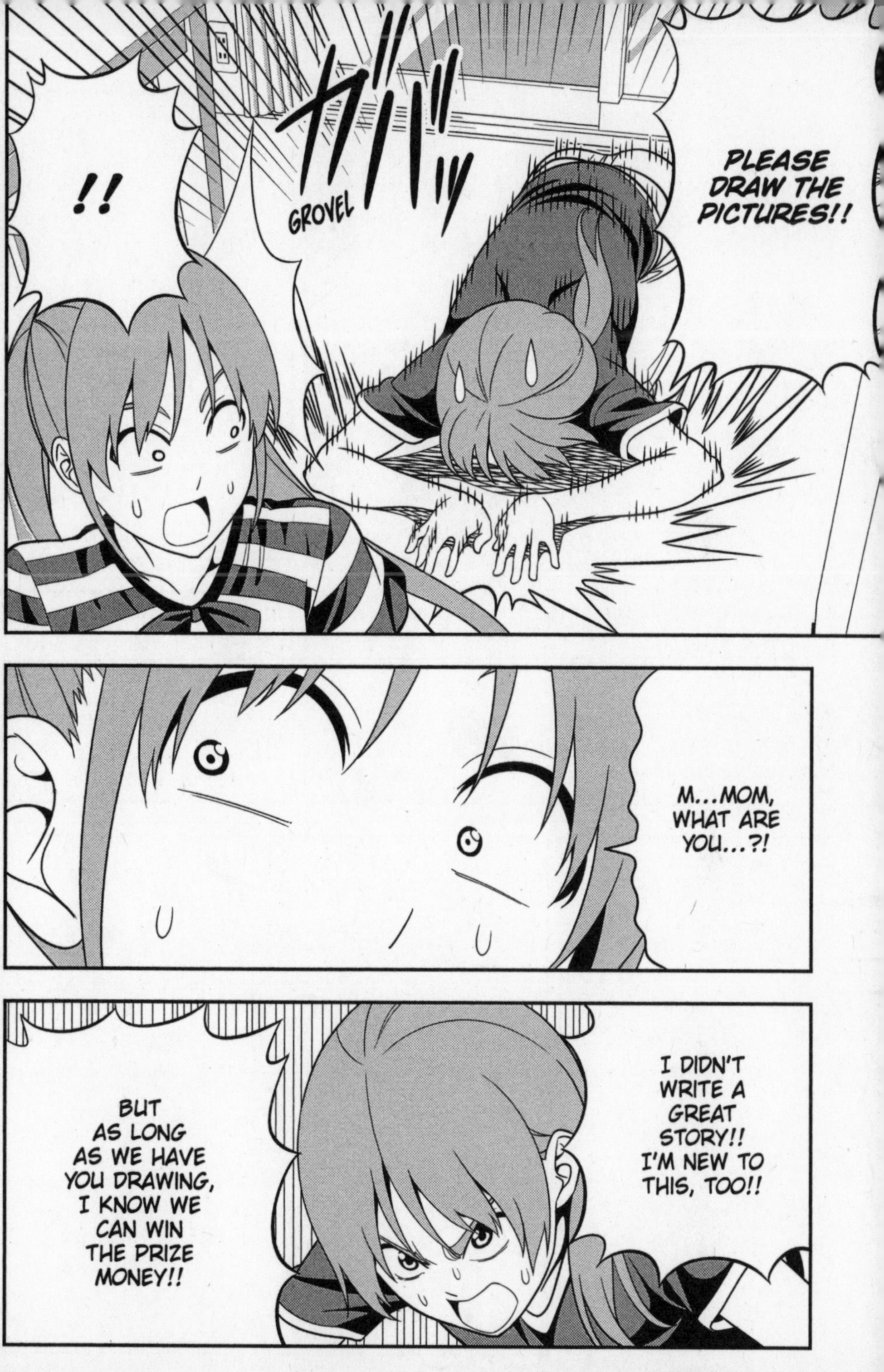
PLEASE DRAW THE PICTURES!!
GROVEL
!!
M...MOM, WHAT ARE YOU...?!
I DIDN'T WRITE A GREAT STORY!! I'M NEW TO THIS, TOO!!
BUT AS LONG AS WE HAVE YOU DRAWING, I KNOW WE CAN WIN THE PRIZE MONEY!!

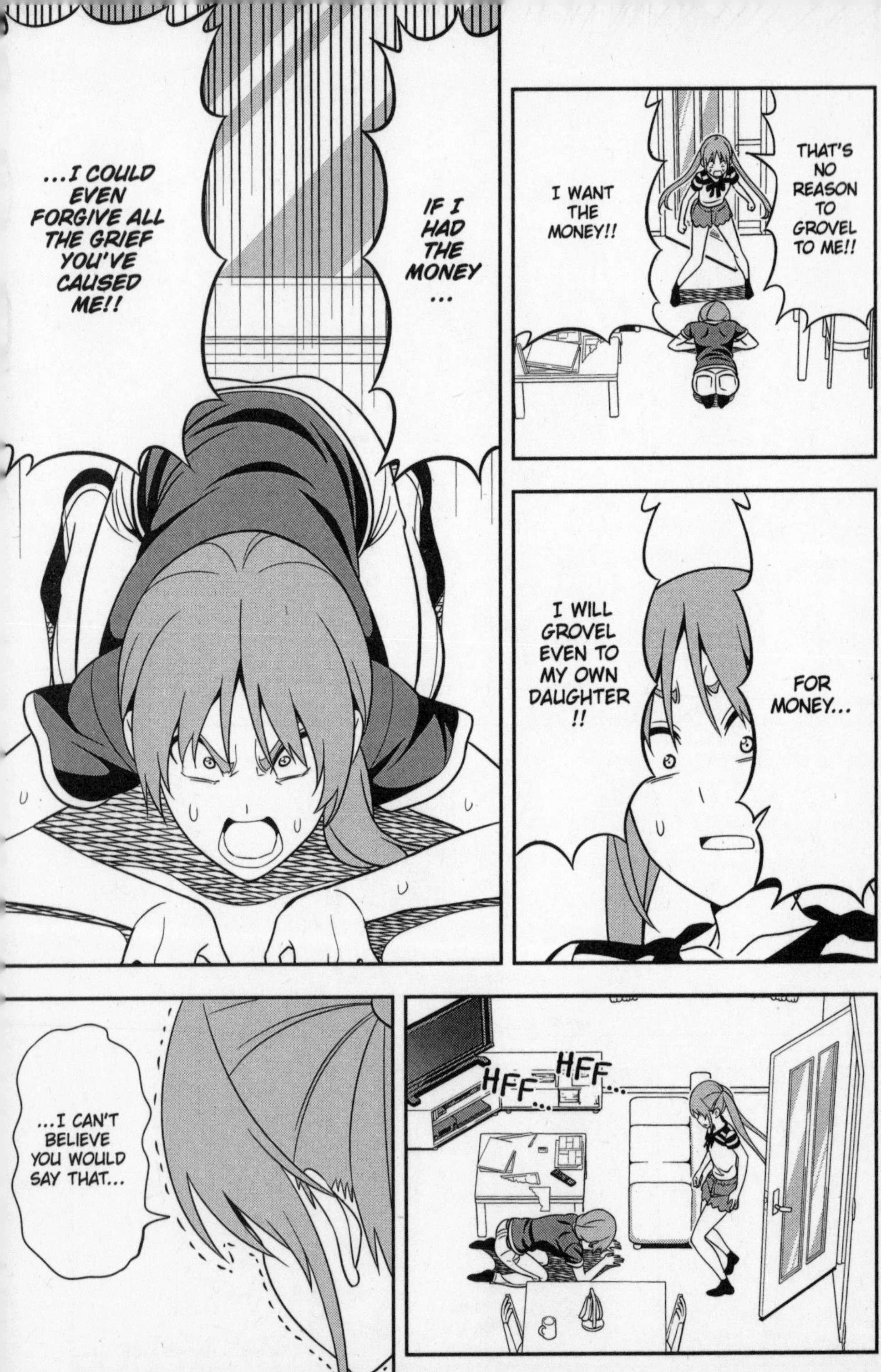
THAT'S NO REASON TO GROVEL TO ME!!
I WANT THE MONEY!!
FOR MONEY...
I WILL GROVEL EVEN TO MY OWN DAUGHTER!!
IF I HAD THE MONEY...
...I COULD EVEN FORGIVE ALL THE GRIEF YOU'VE CAUSED ME!!
HFF...
HFF...
...I CAN'T BELIEVE YOU WOULD SAY THAT...

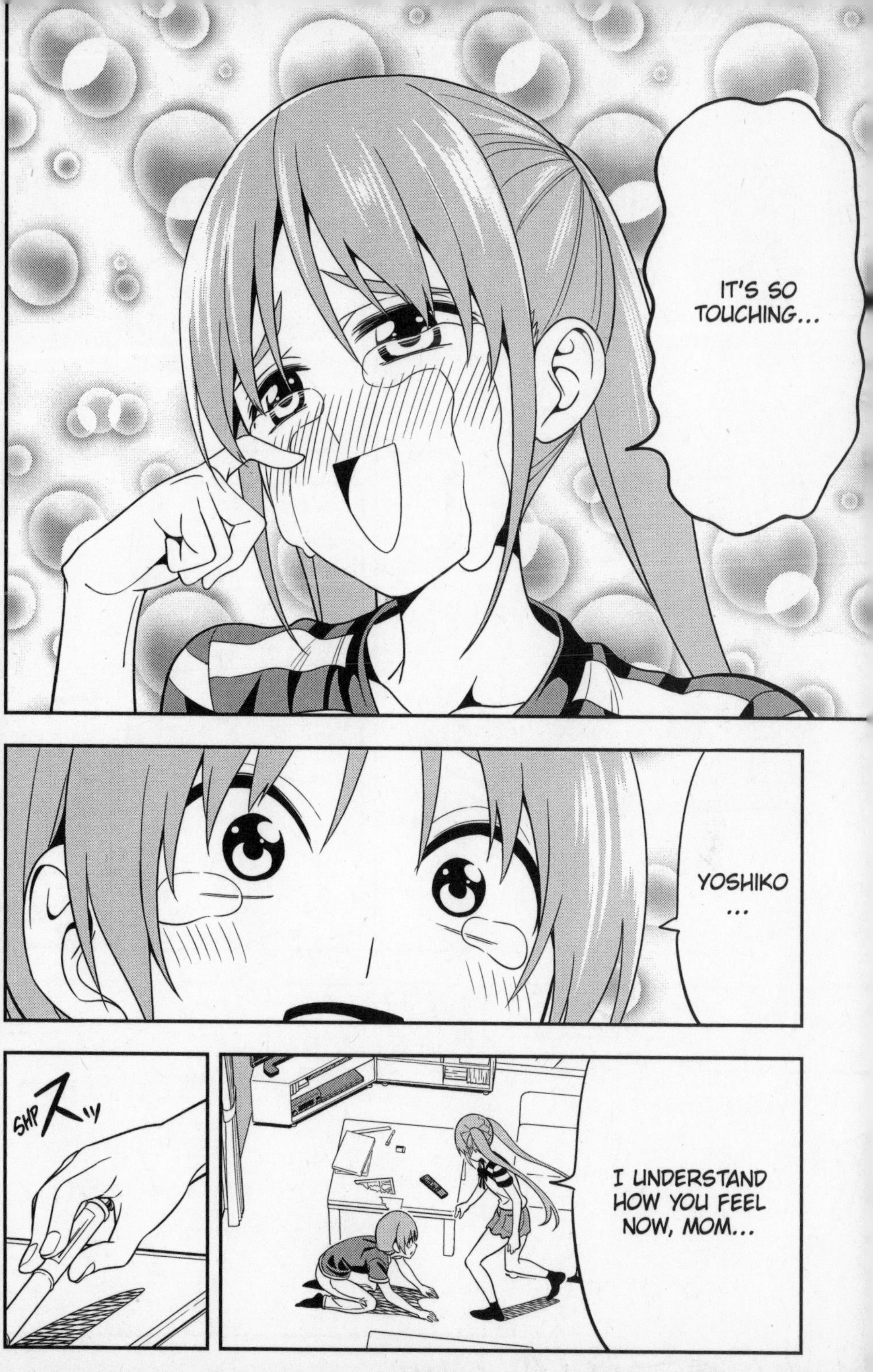
IT'S SO TOUCHING...
YOSHIKO ...
I UNDERSTAND HOW YOU FEEL NOW, MOM...
SHP スッ

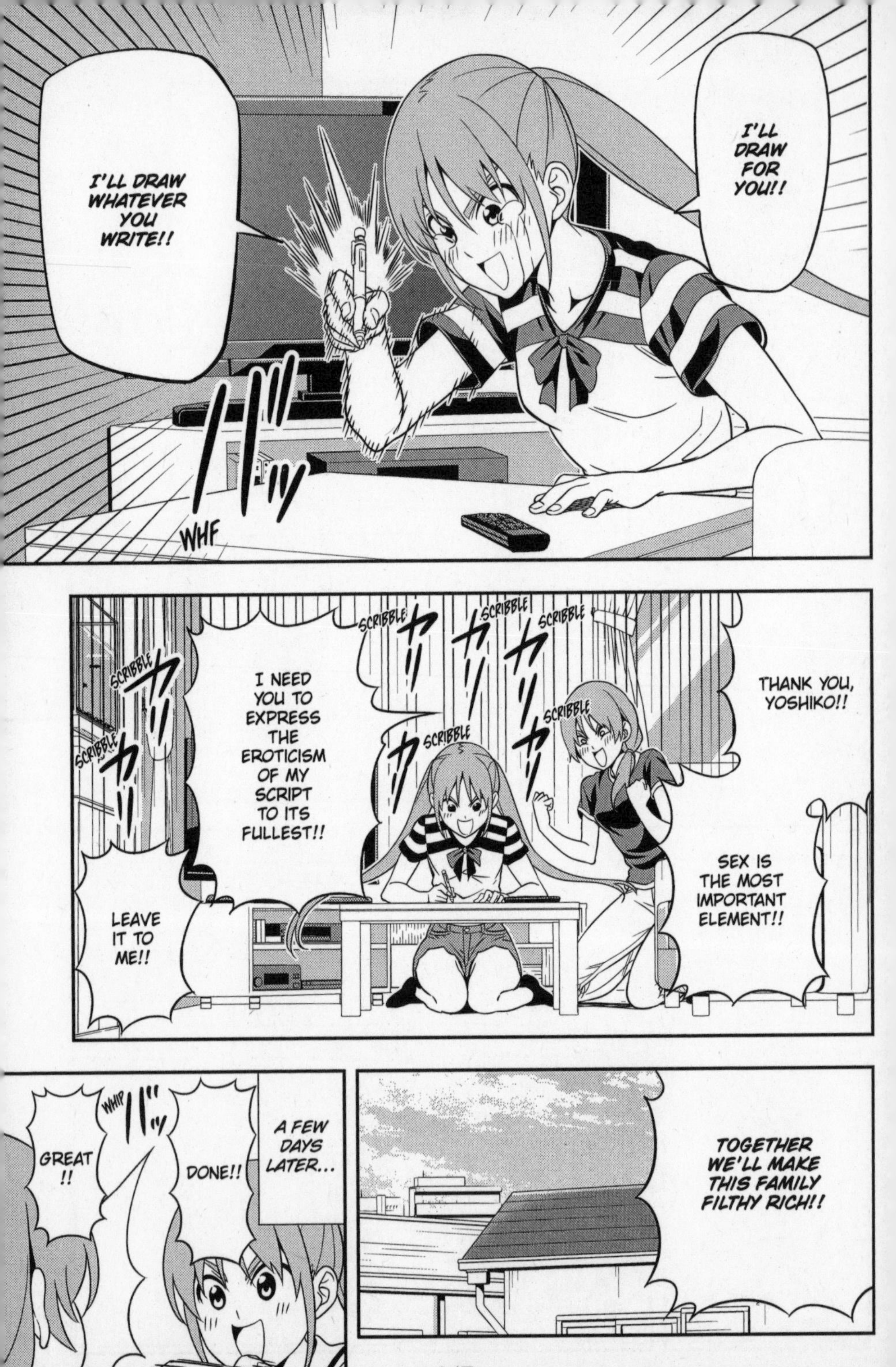
I'LL DRAW FOR YOU!!
I'LL DRAW WHATEVER YOU WRITE!!
WHF
THANK YOU, YOSHIKO!!
SEX IS THE MOST IMPORTANT ELEMENT!!
SCRIBBLE
SCRIBBLE
SCRIBBLE
SCRIBBLE
SCRIBBLE
I NEED YOU TO EXPRESS THE EROTICISM OF MY SCRIPT TO ITS FULLEST!!
SCRIBBLE
SCRIBBLE
LEAVE IT TO ME!!
TOGETHER WE'LL MAKE THIS FAMILY FILTHY RICH!!
A FEW DAYS LATER...
DONE!!
WHIP
GREAT!!

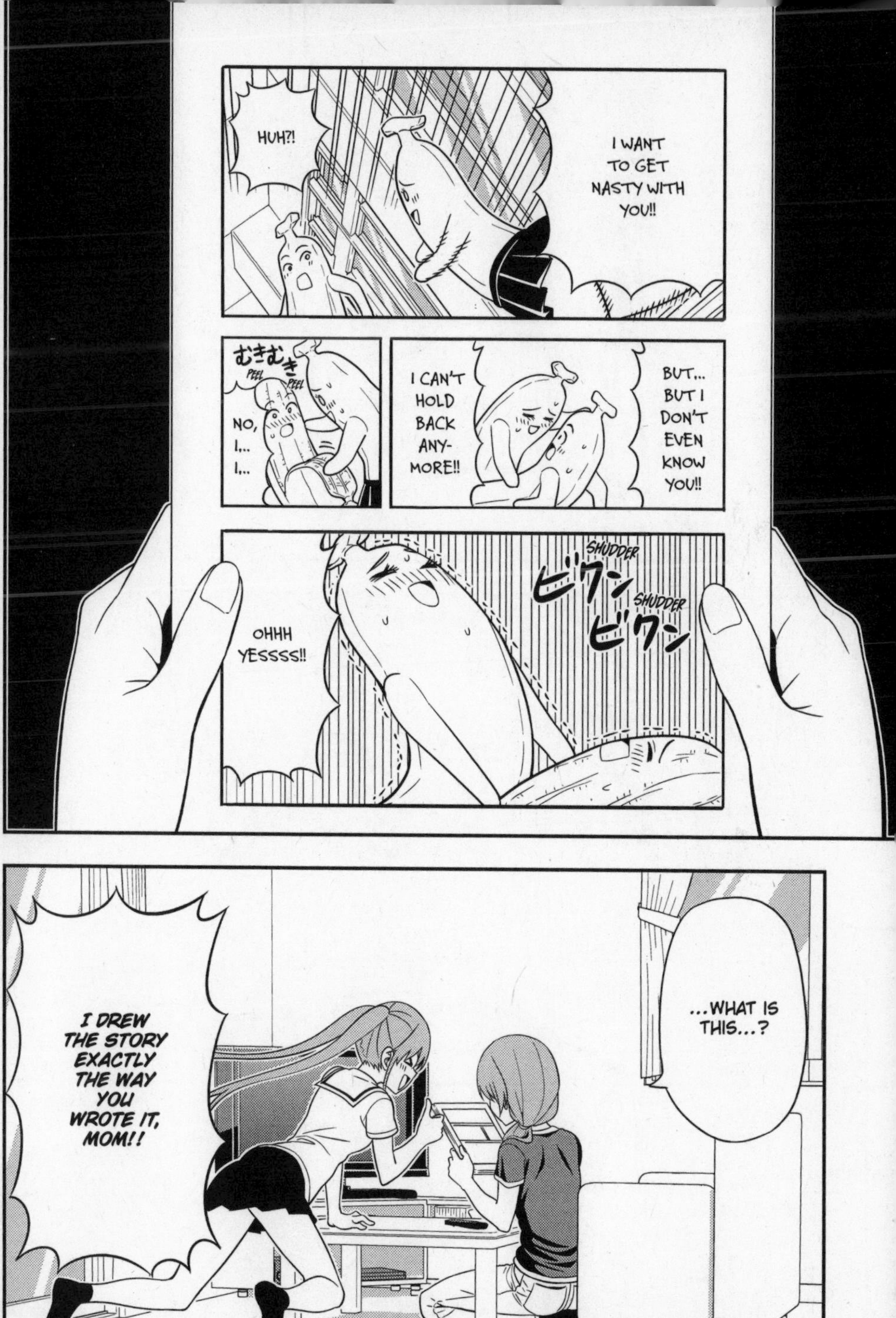
I WANT TO GET NASTY WITH YOU!!
HUH?!
BUT... BUT I DON'T EVEN KNOW YOU!!
I CAN'T HOLD BACK ANY-MORE!!
むきむき
PEEL PEEL
NO, I... I...
ビクン ビクン
SHUDDER SHUDDER
OHHH YESSSS!!
...WHAT IS THIS...?
I DREW THE STORY EXACTLY THE WAY YOU WROTE IT, MOM!!

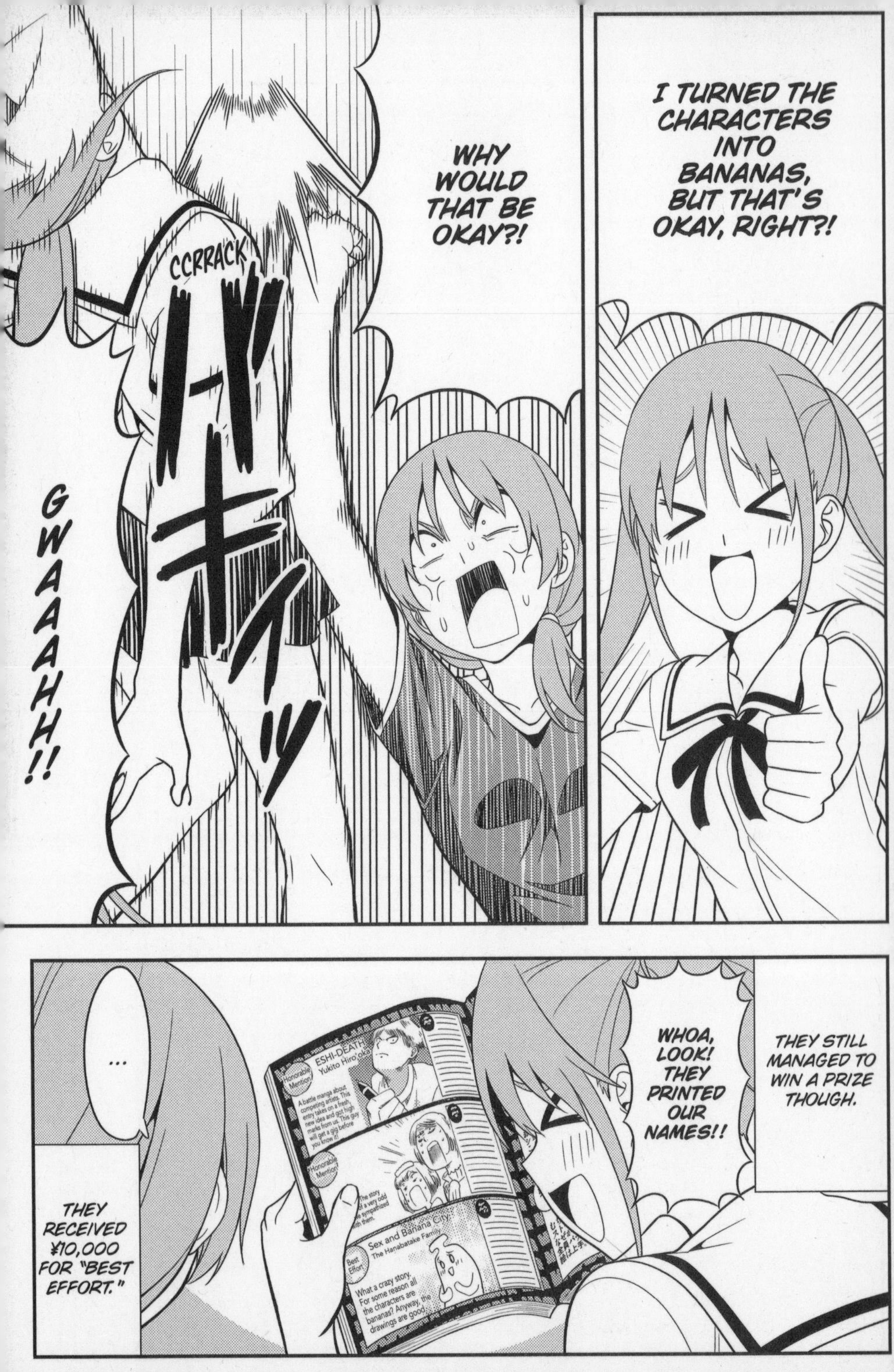
I TURNED THE CHARACTERS INTO BANANAS, BUT THAT'S OKAY, RIGHT?!
WHY WOULD THAT BE OKAY?!
CCRRACK
GWAAAAHH!!
THEY STILL MANAGED TO WIN A PRIZE THOUGH.
WHOA, LOOK! THEY PRINTED OUR NAMES!!
ESHI-DEATH
Yukito Hiro'oka
Honorable Mention
A battle manga about competing artists. This entry takes on a fresh, new idea and got high marks from us. This guy will get a gig before you know it!
Honorable Mention
Sex and Banana City
The Hanabatake Family
Best Effort
What a crazy story. For some reason all the characters are bananas? Anyway, the drawings are good.
...
THEY RECEIVED ¥10,000 FOR "BEST EFFORT."

We're Rich!!

...¥10,000, HUH...?
WHAT'S MY SHARE OF THAT?!
...ABOUT TEN BUNCHES OF BANANAS...
YYYYEEEEESSSSS!!

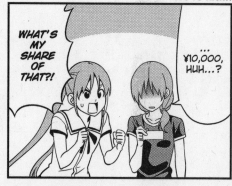

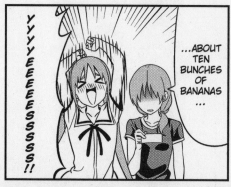

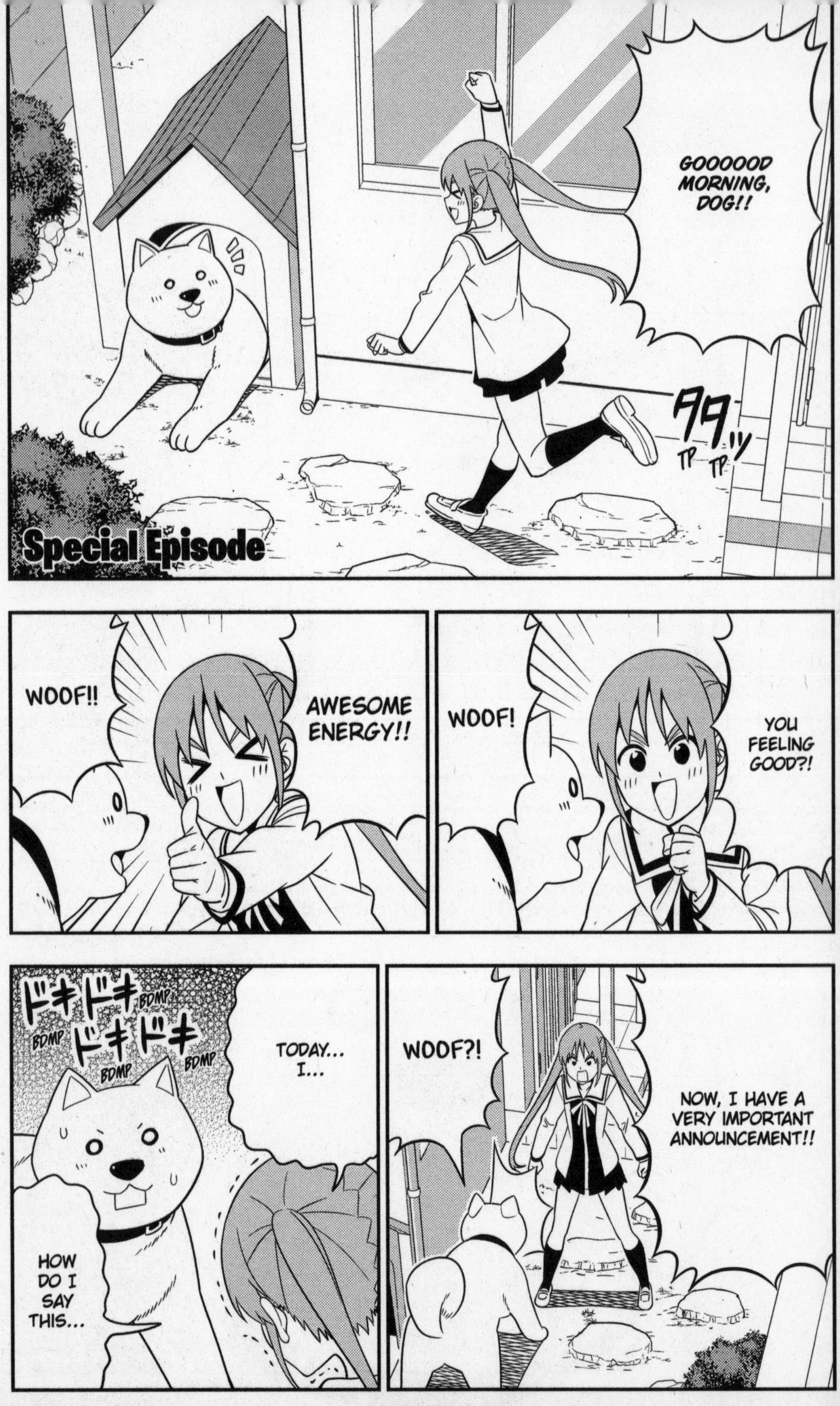
GOOOOOD MORNING, DOG!!
TP TP
Special Episode
YOU FEELING GOOD?!
WOOF!
AWESOME ENERGY!!
WOOF!!
NOW, I HAVE A VERY IMPORTANT ANNOUNCEMENT!!
WOOF?!
TODAY... I...
ドキドキ BDMP ドキドキ BDMP BDMP BDMP
HOW DO I SAY THIS...

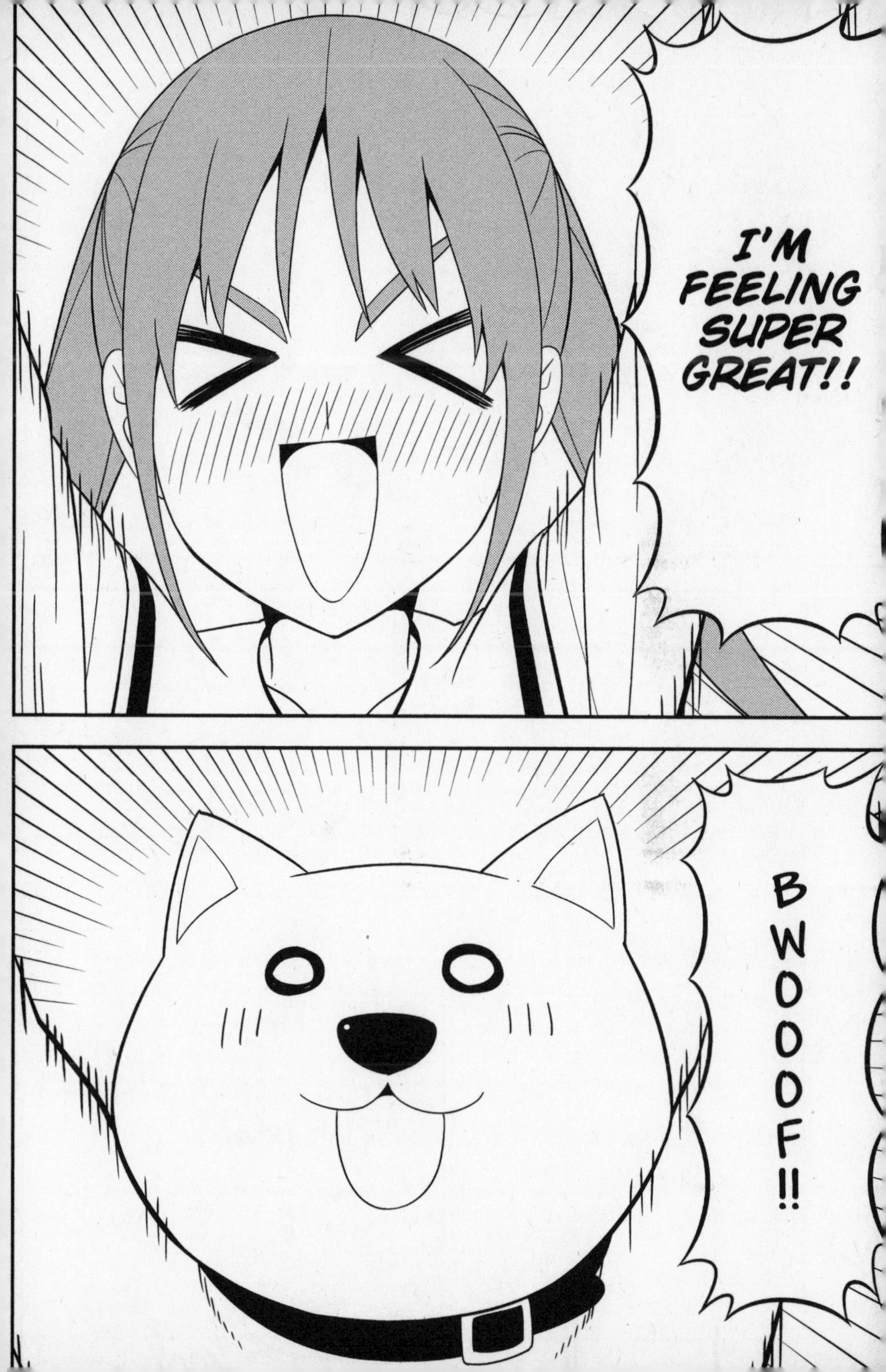
I'M FEELING SUPER GREAT!!
BWOOOOF!!

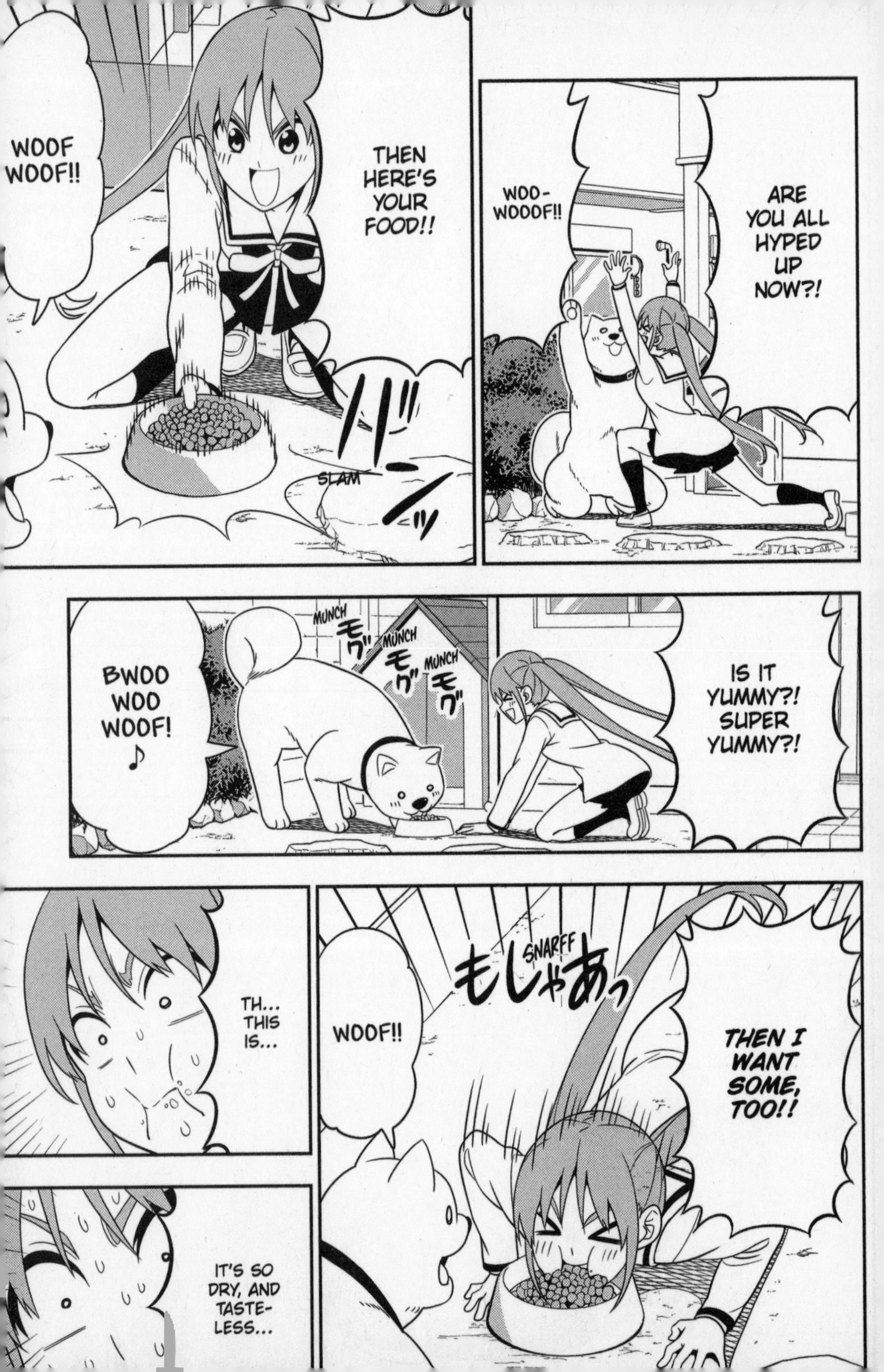
ARE YOU ALL HYPED UP NOW?!
WOO-WOOOF!!
THEN HERE'S YOUR FOOD!!
WOOF WOOF!!
SLAM
IS IT YUMMY?! SUPER YUMMY?!
MUNCH モグ
MUNCH モグ
MUNCH モグ
BWOO WOO WOOF! ♪
THEN I WANT SOME, TOO!!
SNARFF もしゃあっ
WOOF!!
TH... THIS IS...
IT'S SO DRY, AND TASTE-LESS...

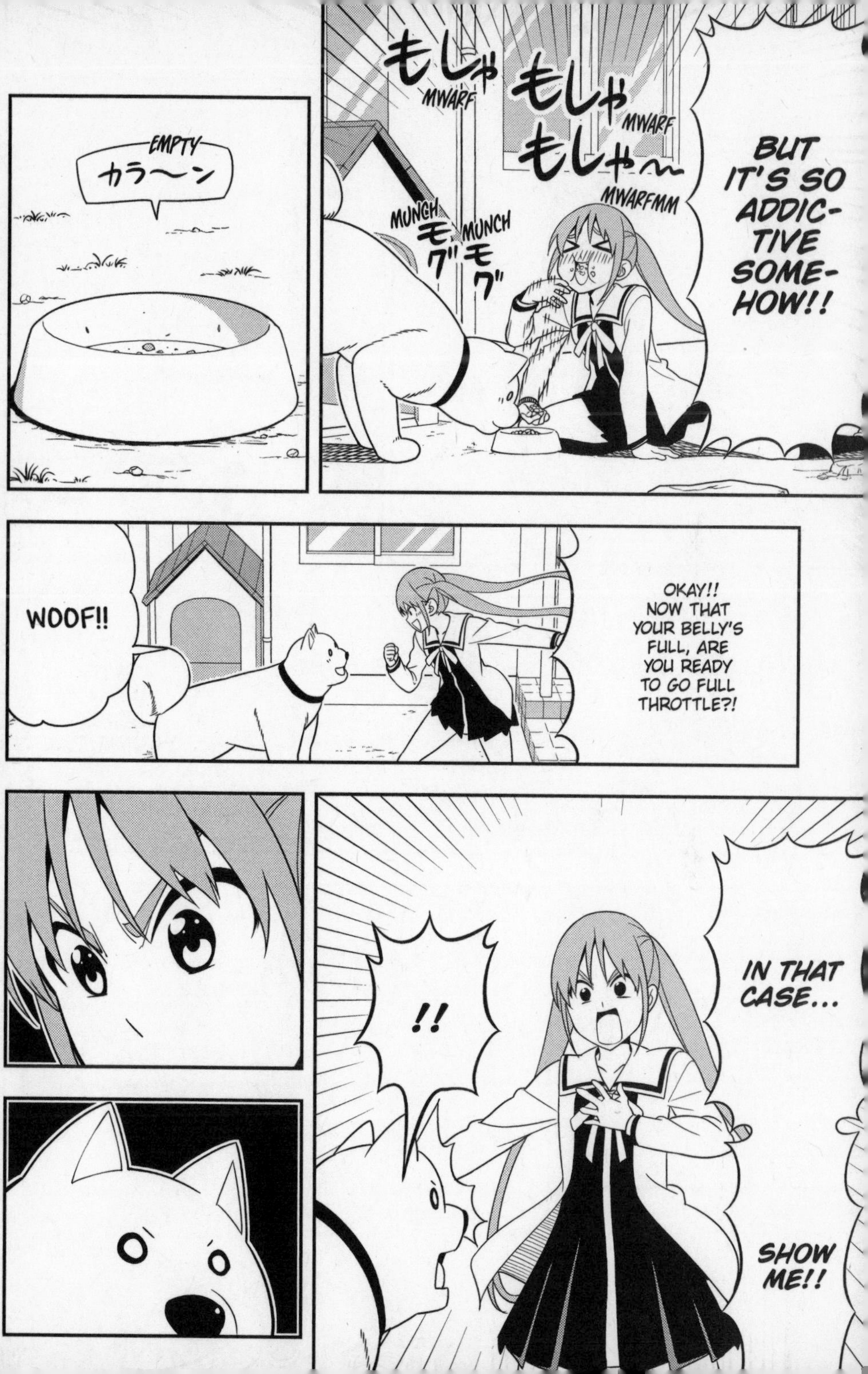
もしゃ
MWARF
もしゃ
MWARF
もしゃ〜
MWARFMM
BUT IT'S SO ADDICTIVE SOMEHOW!!
MUNCH
モグ
MUNCH
モグ
EMPTY
カラ〜ン
OKAY!! NOW THAT YOUR BELLY'S FULL, ARE YOU READY TO GO FULL THROTTLE?!
WOOF!!
IN THAT CASE...
SHOW ME!!
!!

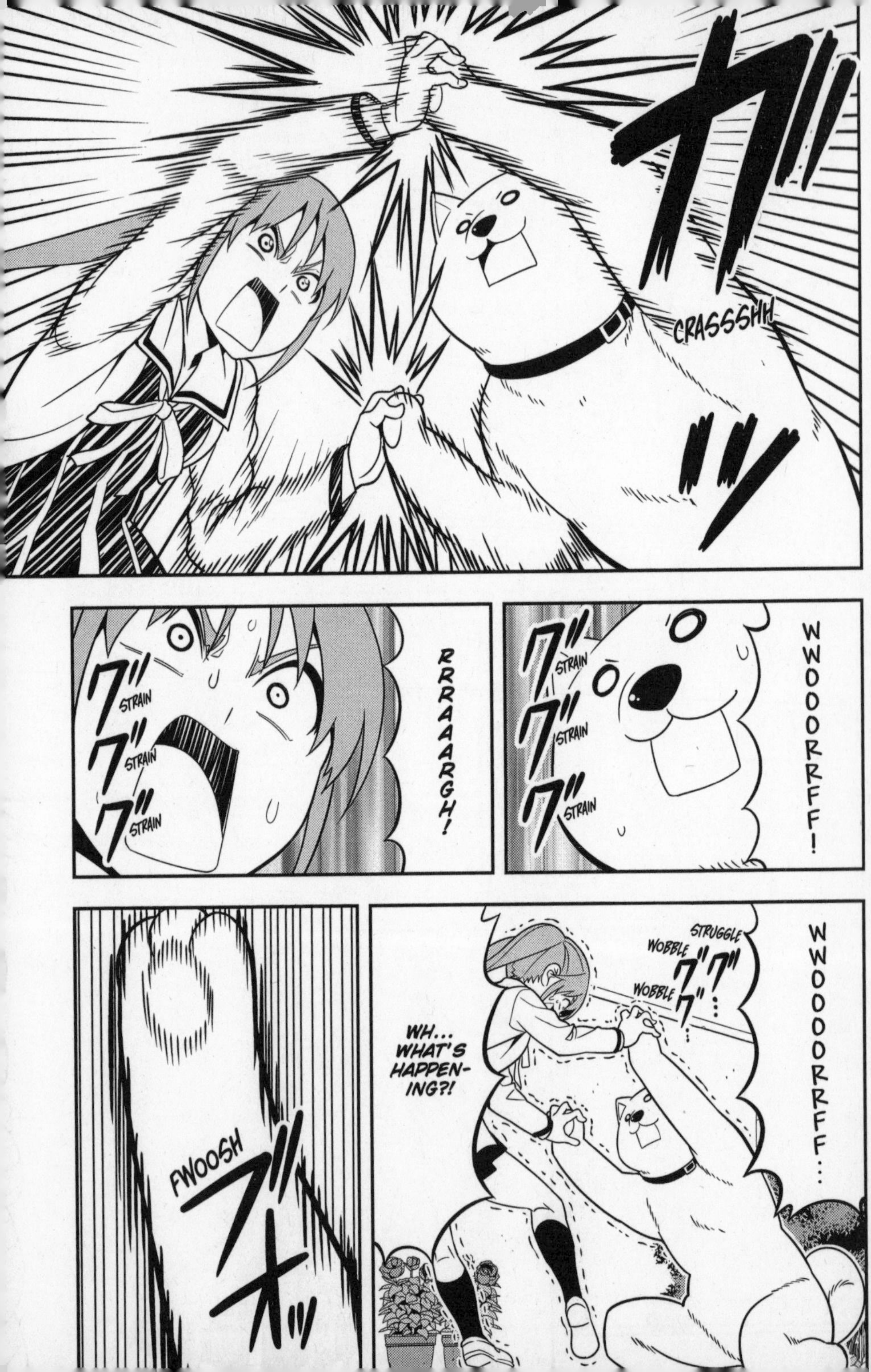
CRASSSHH
WWOOORRFF!
STRAIN
STRAIN
STRAIN
RRRAAARGH!
STRAIN
STRAIN
STRAIN
WWOOOORRFF...
STRUGGLE
WOBBLE
WOBBLE
WH... WHAT'S HAPPEN-ING?!
FWOOSH

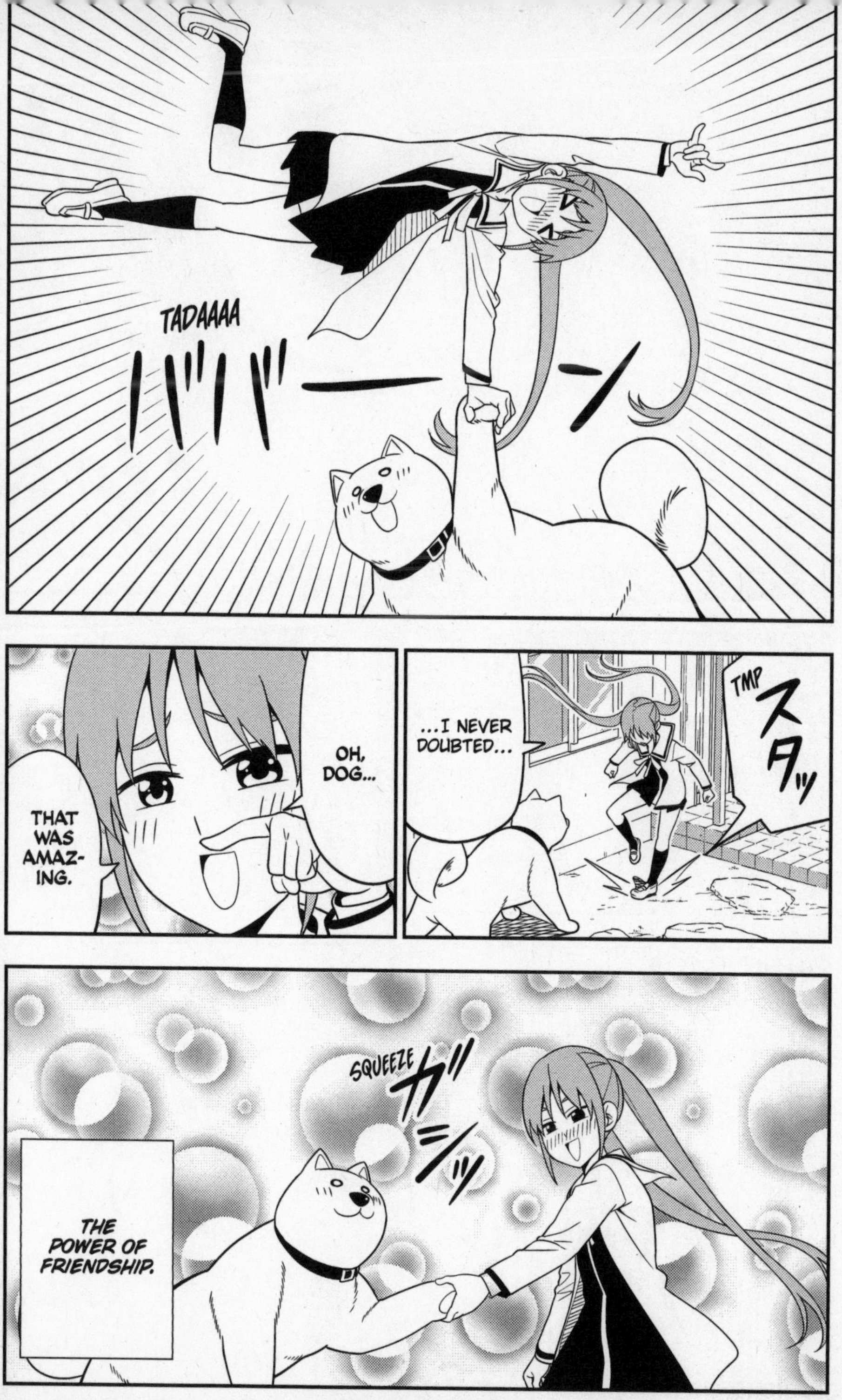
TADAAAA
ババーン
TMP
スタッ
...I NEVER DOUBTED...
OH, DOG...
THAT WAS AMAZING.
SQUEEZE
ガシッ
THE POWER OF FRIENDSHIP.

Continued in volume 9!

(For all you dog-lovers out there)

Aho-Girl

\ˈahô͵gərl\ *Japanese, noun.*
A clueless girl.

The Drama of How Hiroyuki Became a Manga-ka 7

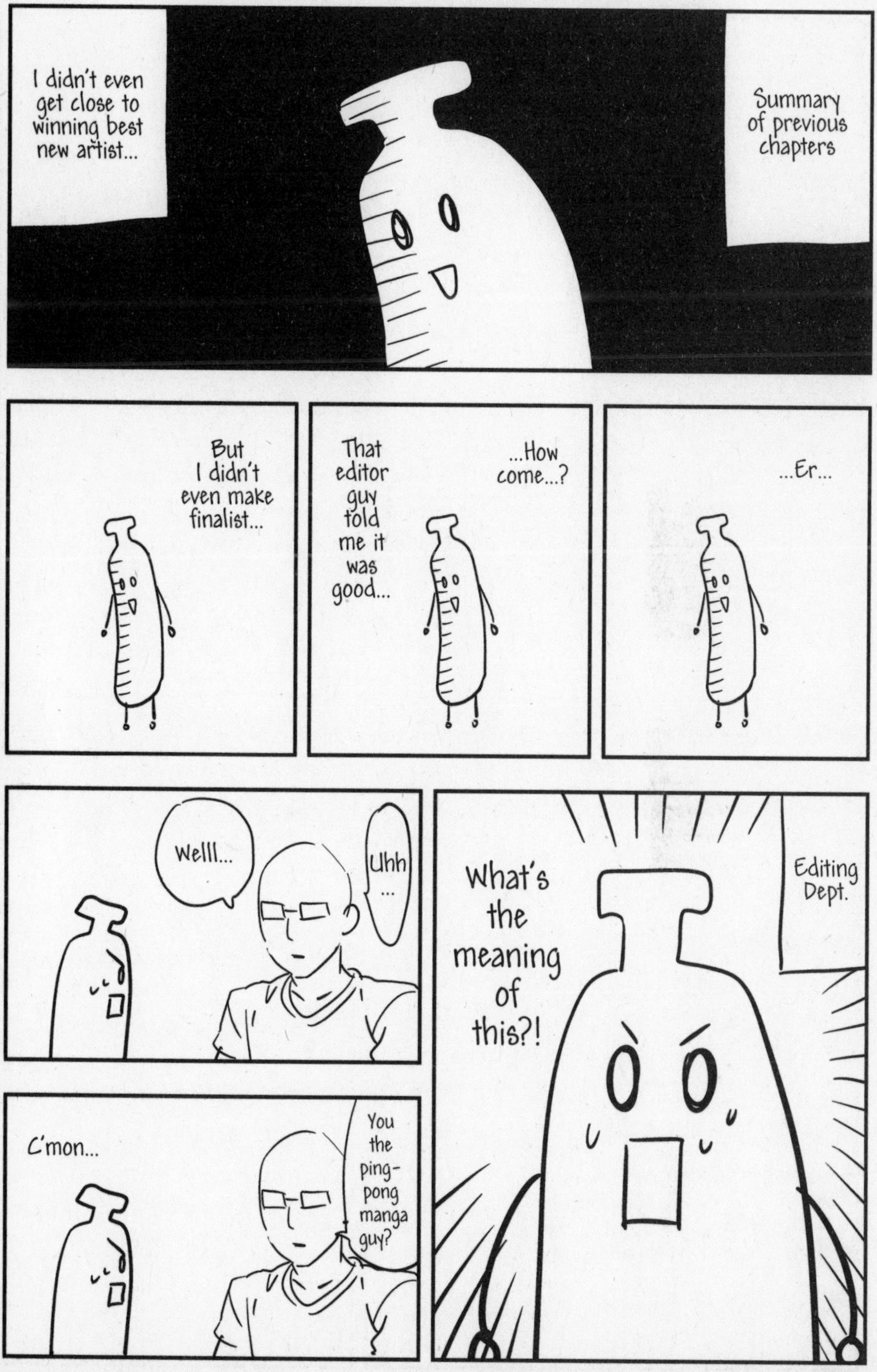
Summary of previous chapters
I didn't even get close to winning best new artist...
...Er...
...How come...?
That editor guy told me it was good...
But I didn't even make finalist...
Editing Dept.
What's the meaning of this?!
Uhh...
Welll...
You the ping-pong manga guy?
C'mon...

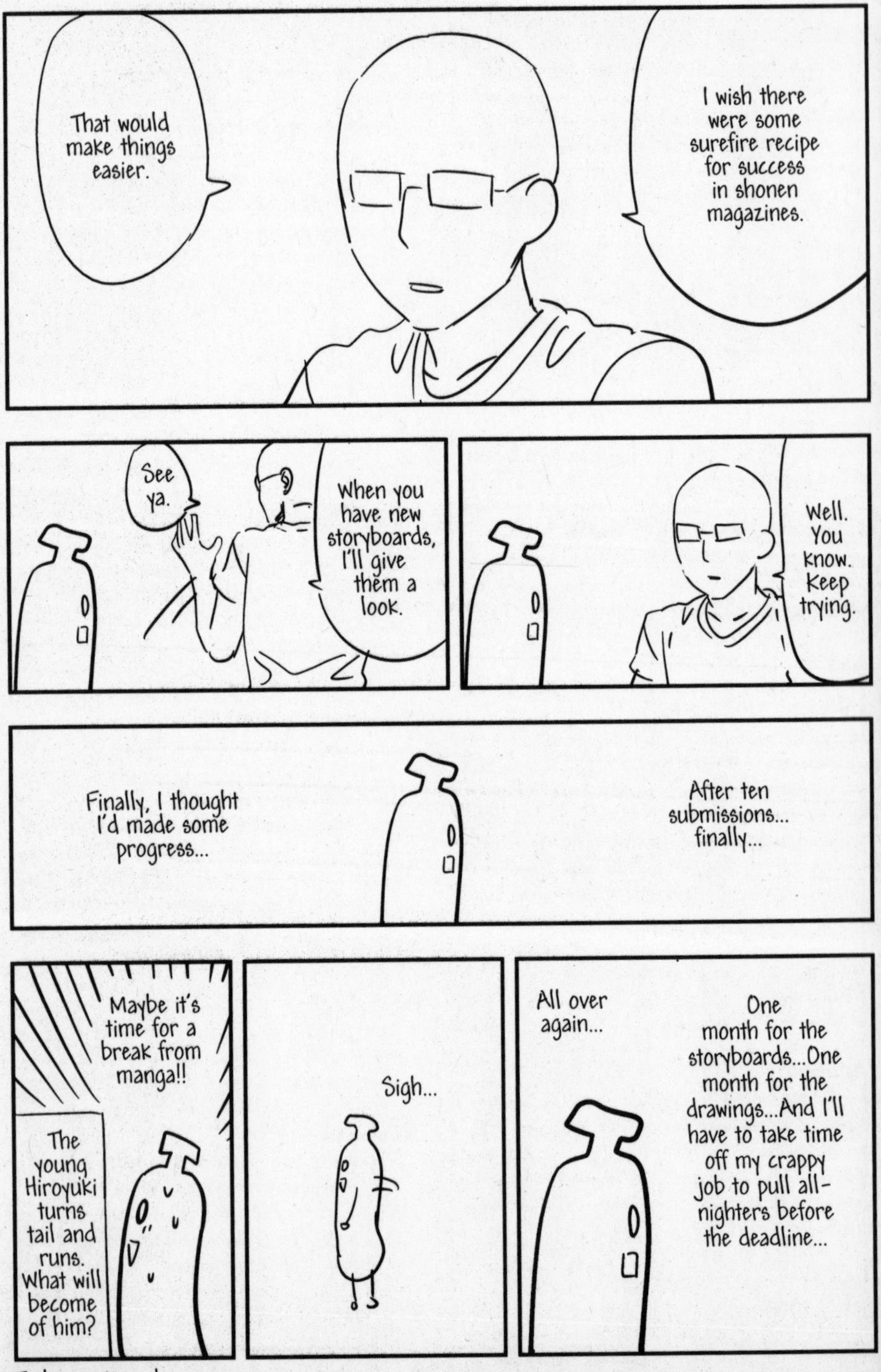
I wish there were some surefire recipe for success in shonen magazines.
That would make things easier.
Well. You know. Keep trying.
When you have new storyboards, I'll give them a look.
See ya.
After ten submissions... finally...
Finally, I thought I'd made some progress...
One month for the storyboards...One month for the drawings...And I'll have to take time off my crappy job to pull all-nighters before the deadline...
All over again...
Sigh...
Maybe it's time for a break from manga!!
The young Hiroyuki turns tail and runs. What will become of him?

To be continued

Translation Notes

Page 2
"Aggravated straight man"
This is an explanatory gloss of the Japanese term "*tsukkomi.*" The *tsukkomi* and *boke* duo are a common trope in *manzai*-style stand-up comedy routines. The *boke*, like Yoshiko, draws over-the-top and just plain stupid conclusions to the *tsukkomi*'s set-ups. The *tsukkomi* tries to remain calm and reasonable during the act, but is invariably pushed into extreme and sometimes violent reactions out of his frustration.

Page 3
"Gang of Gals"
The term "gal" (Japanese *gyaru*) refers to a broad segment of popular youth culture in Japan that began in the mid-1990s. The term encompasses many distinct subcultures with different stereotyped behaviors (such as extreme tanning, bleached-white hair, or casual dating in exchange for spending money) that are considered contrary to prevailing Japanese morality. In general, though, most people who are labeled by the term "gal" merely subscribe to a particular fashion aesthetic characterized by loose socks (the familiar slouchy socks that hang loose around the ankles), lightly bleached hair, extensive nail art or cell phone bangles, and school uniform skirts that are rolled up at the waist to be scandalously short.

"Head Monitor"
The head monitor's title in Japanese includes the word *fuuki*, which roughly translates to "moral order" or "discipline." She would not be merely checking for hall passes the way a hall monitor in a Western school might, and would be more broadly responsible for reporting anything in violation of the moral standards of the institution.

"G Cup"
Going by Japanese bra sizing conventions, the head monitor's "G cup" would be roughly equivalent to an American DDD.

Page 16
"You say you wanna live hard? Well"
This is a reference to the song "Are Yu Ready" by MINMI, an artist who mixes hip-hop with Caribbean music styles. The single was released in 2004 to lead off promotion of her album *Natural*. The line quoted here ends with a Japanese term that could be translated as "all right," "fine by me," or "let's do it."

Page 17
"Salted veggies"
The children are discussing a food called *shiomomi yasai*, literally "salt-kneaded vegetables." Typically, raw vegetables such as carrots, cucumbers, bell peppers, and cabbage are thinly sliced, then tossed with salt and a small amount of oil to coat the vegetables. The salt helps to remove the bitterness and just slightly soften the ingredients to create a minimalistic salad. Who knows what the teacher did to make this appeal to children.

Page 23
"Oneechan!"
Literally "older sister," the term is also used to address teenage to early 30s-aged women not related to the speaker. The parallel term for men is *oniichan*, "older brother."

Page 27
"I can't count how many times I've been to the lunchroom..."
The word translated here as "lunchroom" is more literally the "school meal supply center," which is an off-site location where school meals are cooked. The meals are then delivered to the school each day, and students eat in their classrooms.

Page 34
"If you really push yourself to your limits, you'll be surprised to find"
Featured in a commercial for a national chain of cram schools called Toshin High School, a teacher of classical Japanese literature named Keisuke Yoshino utters this encouragement to his students: "If you really push yourself to your limits, you'll be surprised to find those weren't your limits at all." This is the same chain of schools that Osamu Hayashi works for (see notes in *Aho-Girl* volumes 3 and 7).

Page 36
"Oniichan"
See "*oneechan*" note for page 23.

"Aitatsu!"
"Aitatsu! Master Idol" is a transparent reference to *Aikatsu! Idol Activity*, an arcade collectible card game launched by Bandai in 2012. The game has since been made into a TV anime series, two movies, manga series, and four Nintendo 3DS games. See *Aho-Girl* volume 6 (chapter 91) for details.

Page 42
Spoof songs
A common form of wordplay in Japanese is to assign numbers to replace homophone syllables in words

School-brand cram schools. Here, Hiroshi Imai, a teacher of English, asks his students "When you go to college, will you be able to use that English? And when you go out into the world?"

Page 112
"at least 100 meters away from Akkun-san"
Equivalent to well over 300 feet.

Page 133
"¥3,000,000"
The prize amounts and their rough equivalents in US dollars are:
Grand Prize ¥3,000,000 = $26,500
Runner-up ¥1,500,000 = $13,250
Selected Entries ¥700,00 = $6,200
Honorable Mention ¥300,000 = $2,650

Page 149
"¥10,000"
Equivalent to about $90 in US dollars.

Aho-Girl
\\'ahô͵gərl\\ *Japanese, noun.*
A clueless girl.

to create a kind of code, which can be either playful shorthand, or can be used in a mnemonic (as it is here). Because Japanese has many different pronunciations for each number, the system is quite flexible. Even so, the lyrics Akkun comes up with are woefully nonsensical. Here's one example of the original lyrics, taken from page 54:

"The moment I stepped out of the grass (9);
I faced my loneliness (3) head on;
and showed them the puffer fish (2);
all with tears (7) in my eyes."

Page 58
"If something looks off, take it back to"
This is another slogan featured in the Toshin High School cram school commercials referenced on page 34. In this commercial, Osamu Hayashi tells students that "If something looks off, take it back to basics" to figure the problem out.

Page 87
"But we're only second-years!!"
Akane's friends are right to be surprised that she hasn't started studying for college entrance exams yet. In Japan, nationally administered standardized tests are used to evaluate all students hoping to enter college in the coming year. These subject-specific tests are given once a year, over the course of two days in January. The school year in Japan begins in April, with the first term running from April to mid-July, the second term running from early September to late December, and the third term running from January to late March. Even though many students start preparing as soon as they enter high school, and some begin as early as elementary school, Akane seems to think that eight months will be enough time to study for the exams.

Page 92
"Make tea for everyone, and copy stuff...?"
Akane is referencing an increasingly antiquated view of low-to-mid-level female office workers as almost the stewardesses of a male-dominated office environment, taking care of small gender-appropriate tasks for the male workers. This theoretically allows the male workers to focus on the "real" work. While the practice of distributing refreshments to one's coworkers still exists, and is still viewed as a feminine task, it is nevertheless becoming more egalitarian in today's workplaces.

Page 108
"When you go to college, will you be able to use that"
Another entry from the commercials for Toshin High

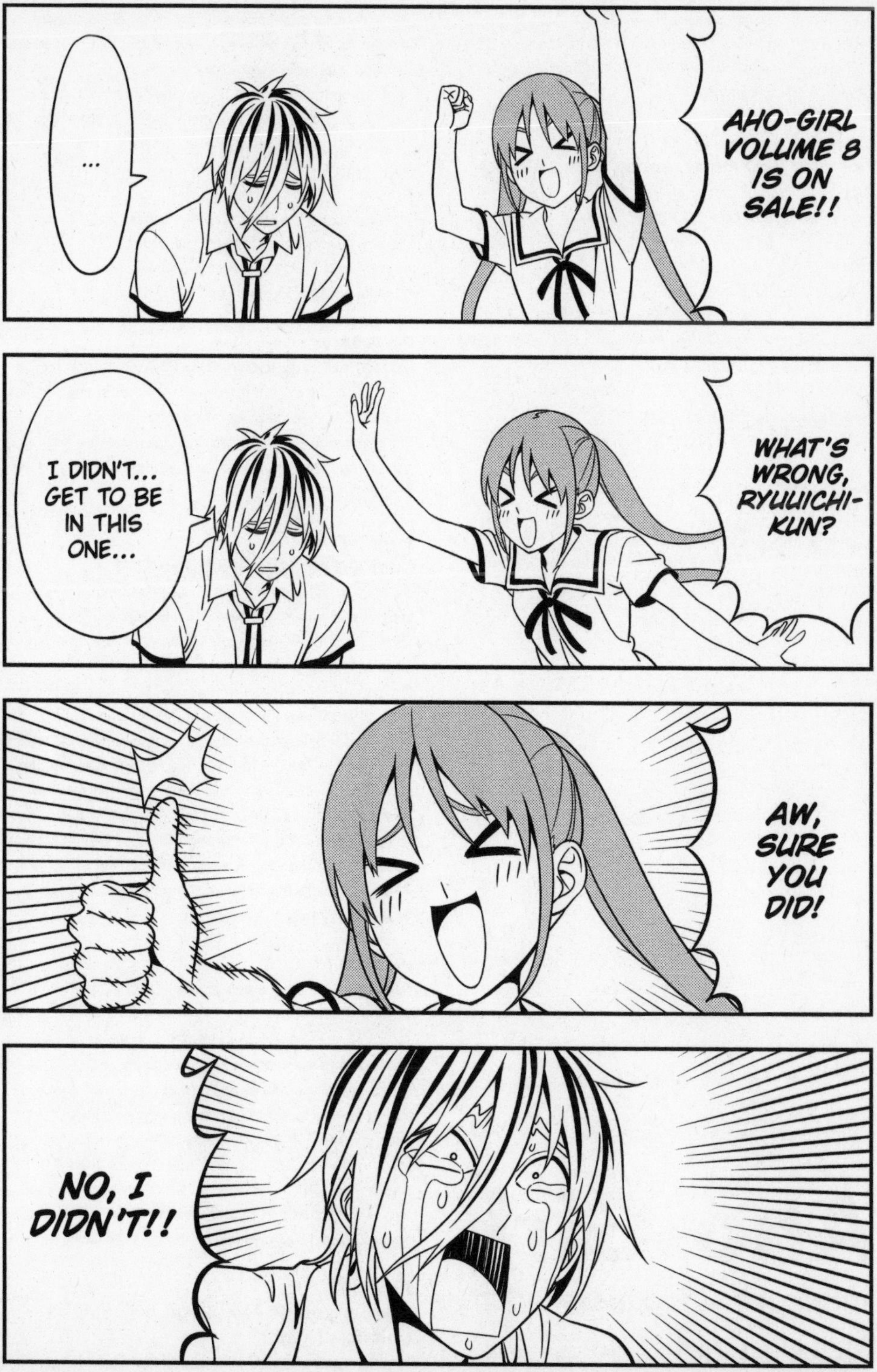
AHO-GIRL VOLUME 8 IS ON SALE!!
...
WHAT'S WRONG, RYUUICHI-KUN?
I DIDN'T... GET TO BE IN THIS ONE...
AW, SURE YOU DID!
NO, I DIDN'T!!

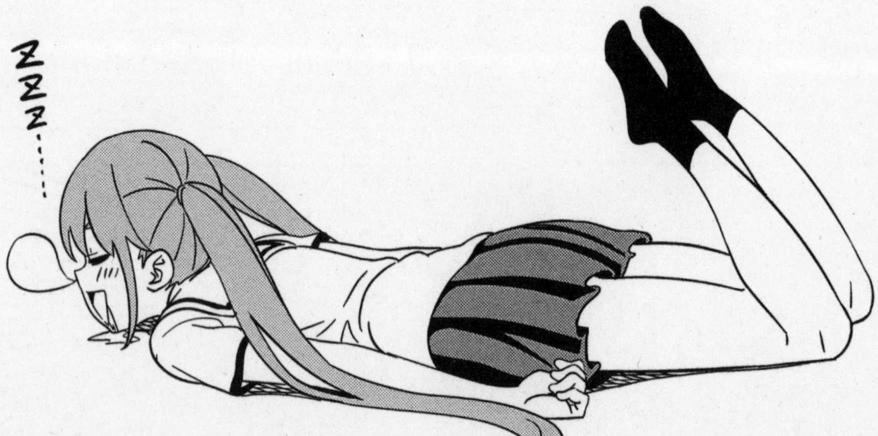
ZZZ......

Aho-Girl

\ˈahô͵gərl \ *Japanese, noun.*
A clueless girl.

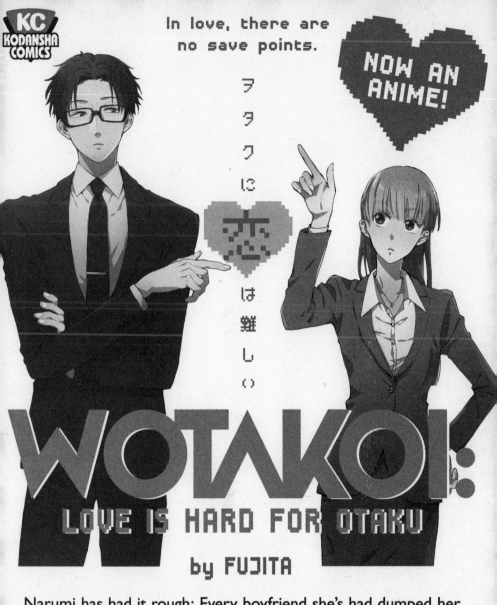

In love, there are
no save points.

ヲタクに恋は難しい

KC
KODANSHA
COMICS

WOTAKOI:
LOVE IS HARD FOR OTAKU

by FUJITA

Narumi has had it rough: Every boyfriend she's had dumped her
once they found out she was an otaku, so she's gone to great
lengths to hide it. At her new job, she bumps into Hirotaka, her
childhood friend and fellow otaku. When Hirotaka almost gets
her secret outed at work, she comes up with a plan to keep him
quiet. But he comes up with a counter-proposal:
Why doesn't she just date him instead?

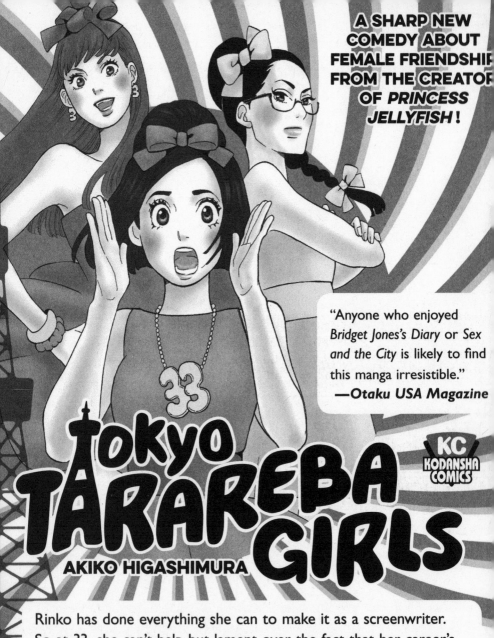

A SHARP NEW COMEDY ABOUT FEMALE FRIENDSHIP FROM THE CREATOR OF *PRINCESS JELLYFISH*!

"Anyone who enjoyed *Bridget Jones's Diary* or *Sex and the City* is likely to find this manga irresistible."
—Otaku USA Magazine

Tokyo TARAREBA GIRLS

AKIKO HIGASHIMURA

KC KODANSHA COMICS

Rinko has done everything she can to make it as a screenwriter. So at 33, she can't help but lament over the fact that her career's plateaued, she's still painfully single, and spends most of her nights drinking with her two best friends. One night, drunk and delusional, Rinko swears to get married by the time the Tokyo Olympics roll around in 2020. But finding a man—or love—may be a cutthroat, dirty job for a romantic at heart!

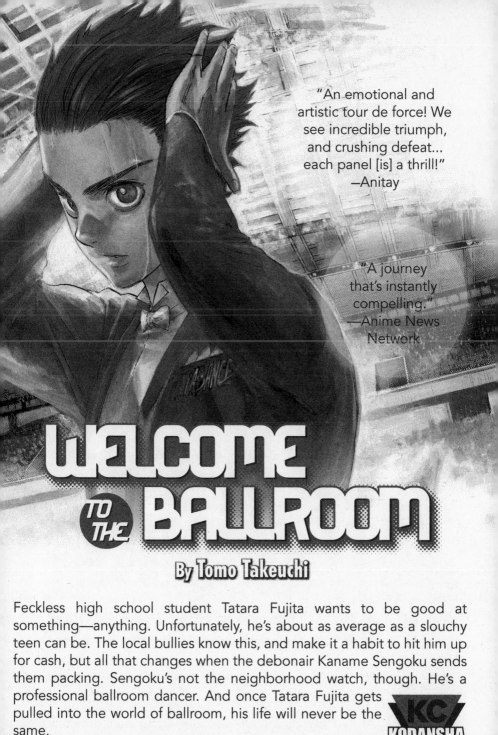

"An emotional and artistic tour de force! We see incredible triumph, and crushing defeat... each panel [is] a thrill!"
—Anitay

"A journey that's instantly compelling."
—Anime News Network

WELCOME TO THE BALLROOM

By Tomo Takeuchi

Feckless high school student Tatara Fujita wants to be good at something—anything. Unfortunately, he's about as average as a slouchy teen can be. The local bullies know this, and make it a habit to hit him up for cash, but all that changes when the debonair Kaname Sengoku sends them packing. Sengoku's not the neighborhood watch, though. He's a professional ballroom dancer. And once Tatara Fujita gets pulled into the world of ballroom, his life will never be the same.

KC
KODANSHA COMICS

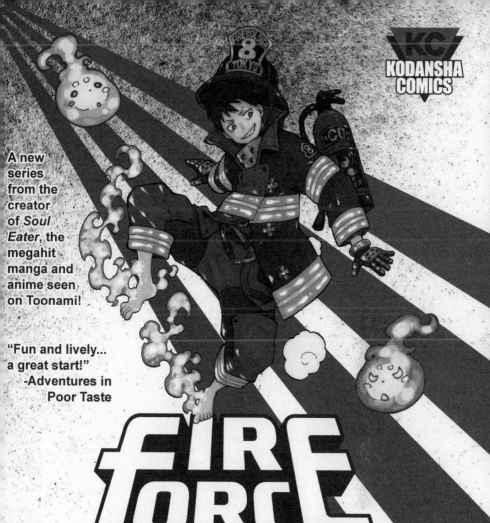

KC
KODANSHA
COMICS

A new series from the creator of *Soul Eater*, the megahit manga and anime seen on Toonami!

"Fun and lively... a great start!"
-Adventures in Poor Taste

FIRE FORCE

By Atsushi Ohkubo

The city of Tokyo is plagued by a deadly phenomenon: spontaneous human combustion! Luckily, a special team is there to quench the inferno: The Fire Force! The fire soldiers at Special Fire Cathedral 8 are about to get a unique addition. Enter Shinra, a boy who possesses the power to run at the speed of a rocket, leaving behind the famous "devil's footprints" (and destroying his shoes in the process). Can Shinra and his colleagues discover the source of this strange epidemic before the city burns to ashes?

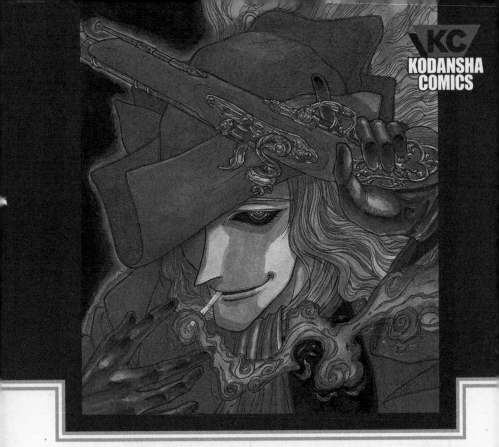

The Black Museum The Ghost and the Lady

By Kazuhiro Fujita

Deep in Scotland Yard in London sits an evidence room dedicated to the greatest mysteries of British history. In this "Black Museum" sits a misshapen hunk of lead—two bullets fused together—the key to a wartime encounter between Florence Nightingale, the mother of modern nursing, and a supernatural Man in Grey. This story is unknown to most scholars of history, but a special guest of the museum will tell the tale of The Ghost and the Lady...

Praise for Kazuhiro Fujita's *Ushio and Tora*

"A charming revival that combines a classic look with modern depth and pacing... **Essential viewing both for curmudgeons and new fans alike.**" — Anime News Network

"**GREAT!** The first episode of Ushio and Tora captures the essence of '90s anime." — IGN

KC
KODANSHA COMICS

Japan's most powerful spirit medium delves into the ghost world's greatest mysteries!

Story by Kyo Shirodaira, famed author of mystery fiction and creator of *Spiral*, *Blast of Tempest*, and *The Record of a Fallen Vampire*.

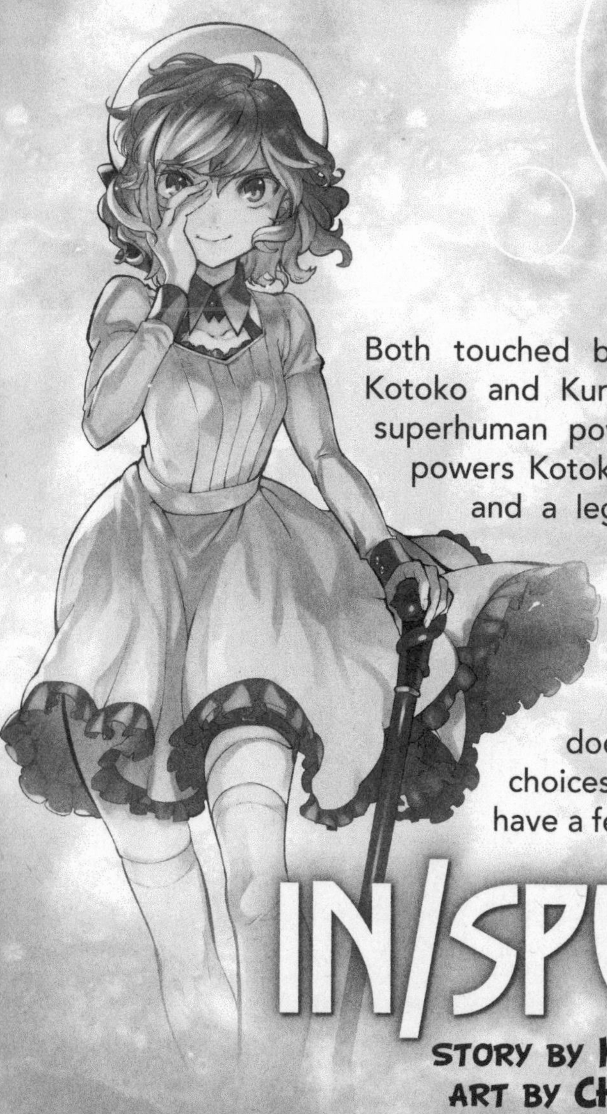

Both touched by spirits called yôkai, Kotoko and Kurô have gained unique superhuman powers. But to gain her powers Kotoko has given up an eye and a leg, and Kurô's personal life is in shambles. So when Kotoko suggests they team up to deal with renegades from the spirit world, Kurô doesn't have many other choices, but Kotoko might just have a few ulterior motives...

IN/SPECTRE

STORY BY KYO SHIRODAIRA
ART BY CHASHIBA KATASE

H·A·P·P·I·N·E·S·S

——ハピネス——

By **Shuzo Oshimi**

From the creator of *The Flowers of Evil*

Nothing interesting is happening in Makoto Ozaki's first year of high school. His life is a series of quiet humiliations: low-grade bullies, unreliable friends, and the constant frustration of his adolescent lust. But one night, a pale, thin girl knocks him to the ground in an alley and offers him a choice. Now everything is different. Daylight is searingly bright. Food tastes awful. And worse than anything is the terrible, consuming thirst...

Praise for Shuzo Oshimi's *The Flowers of Evil*

"A shockingly readable story that vividly—one might even say queasily—evokes the fear and confusion of discovering one's own sexuality. Recommended." —The Manga Critic

"A page-turning tale of sordid middle school blackmail." —Otaku USA Magazine

"A stunning new horror manga." —Third Eye Comics

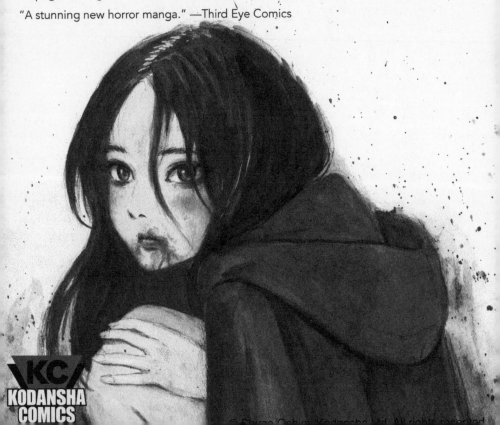

KC KODANSHA COMICS

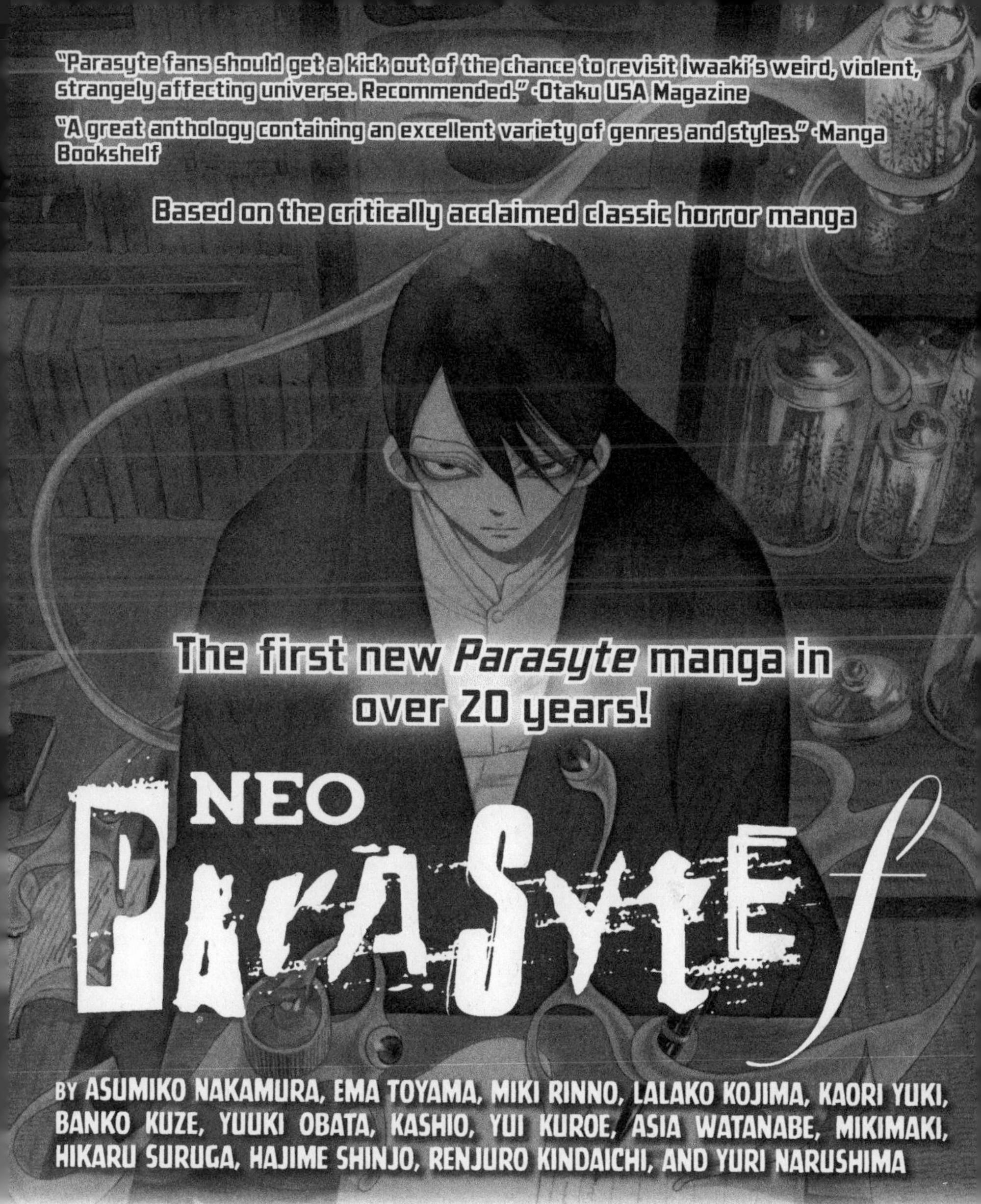

Based on the critically acclaimed classic horror manga

The first new *Parasyte* manga in over 20 years!

NEO Parasyte f

BY ASUMIKO NAKAMURA, EMA TOYAMA, MIKI RINNO, LALAKO KOJIMA, KAORI YUKI, BANKO KUZE, YUUKI OBATA, KASHIO, YUI KUROE, ASIA WATANABE, MIKIMAKI, HIKARU SURUGA, HAJIME SHINJO, RENJURO KINDAICHI, AND YURI NARUSHIMA

A collection of chilling new *Parasyte* stories from Japan's top shojo artists!

Parasites: shape-shifting aliens whose only purpose is to assimilate with and consume the human race... but do these monsters have a different side? A parasite becomes a prince to save his romance-obsessed female host from a dangerous stalker. Another hosts a cooking show, in which the real monsters are revealed. These and 13 more stories, from some of the greatest shojo manga artists alive today, together make up a chilling, funny, and entertaining tribute to one of manga's horror classics!

KC
KODANSHA
COMICS

New action series from Hiroyuki Takei, creator of the classic shonen franchise Shaman King!

In medieval Japan, a bell hanging on the collar is a sign that a c
has a master. Norachiyo's bell hangs from his katana sheath, but he
nonetheless a stray — a ronin. This one-eyed cat samurai travels across
dishonest world, cutting through pretense and deception with his blad

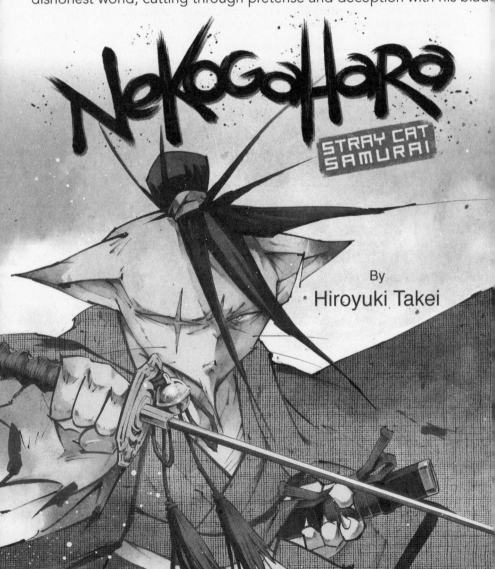

By
Hiroyuki Takei

A Kodansha Comics Trade Paperback Original.

Aho-Girl volume 8 copyright © 2016 Hiroyuki
English translation copyright © 2018 Hiroyuki

Published in the United States by Kodansha Comics, an imprint of Kodansha USA Publishing, LLC, New York.

Publication rights for this English edition arranged through Kodansha Ltd., Tokyo.

First published in Japan in 2016 by Kodansha Ltd., Tokyo, as *Aho Gaaru* volume 8.

ISBN 978-1-63236-612-2

Printed in the United States of America.

www.kodanshacomics.com

9 8 7 6 5 4 3 2 1

Translator: Karen McGillicuddy
Lettering: S. Lee
Editing: Paul Starr
Kodansha Comics edition cover design by Phil Balsman